CHRISTIAN THEISM

AND

A SPIRITUAL MONISM

CHRISTIAN THEISM

AND

A SPIRITUAL MONISM

*God, Freedom, and Immortality
in View of Monistic Evolution*

BY THE

REV. W. L WALKER

AUTHOR OF "THE SPIRIT AND THE INCARNATION"
"THE CROSS AND THE KINGDOM" ETC.

SECOND EDITION

WIPF & STOCK · Eugene, Oregon

Wipf and Stock Publishers
199 W 8th Ave, Suite 3
Eugene, OR 97401

Christian Theism and a Spiritual Monism, Second Edition
God, Freedom, and Immortality in View of Monistic Evolution
By Walker, W. L.
Softcover ISBN-13: 978-1-7252-9921-4
Hardcover ISBN-13: 978-1-7252-9922-1
eBook ISBN-13: 978-1-7252-9923-8
Publication date 2/1/2021
Previously published by T. & T. Clark, 1907

This edition is a scanned facsimile of the original edition published in 1907.

TO

THE DEAR MEMORY OF HER

WHOSE CONSTANT TRUST, SYMPATHY, AND ENCOURAGEMENT

SO GREATLY HELPED ME

PREFACE TO SECOND EDITION

I AM thankful for the very kind reception which this book has met with. While far from being indifferent to critical suggestions, I have only been able in this Second Edition to make some minor corrections I have added one sentence (at the close of the book) expressive of a truth which has deeply impressed me of late, namely, that since *God* in Himself is Spirit, the full and perfect life towards which we are moving must be that of *Spirit*. This may, however, manifest or express itself in some corresponding material form and activity, such as we see in the case of the Divine creative Life It is the purposive expression of the Divine life of Spirit that gives rise to the phenomenal world, and its goal must be the realisation of the idea that originates the movement—in which "matter" is simply instrumental.

There are many indications that a Spiritual Monism is being increasingly adopted.

W. L. W.

FERNIHIRST,
SHETTLESTON, GLASGOW, *August* 1907.

PREFACE TO FIRST EDITION

THE chief object of the pages that follow is to show how the great Christian pre-suppositions—God, Freedom, Immortality—in their specifically Christian character (including the reality of the Divine Incarnation in Christ and of Grace) can be established on the basis of such a Monistic conception of the world as the facts of Science demand and as Philosophy is feeling after. The subject, however, is not approached from the standpoint of Philosophy, but, rather, objectively—from that of the teaching of Science concerning ourselves and the Universe. The book is written for "the plain man," and seeks to follow an inductive method and to teach something that shall be, not vague merely, but distinctively Christian.

Monism has been brought very prominently forward of late by means of the writings of Professor Haeckel. Haeckel has perhaps been sufficiently replied to; but the element of truth in his Monism has not always been recognised. He will have rendered a real service to Religion if his writings serve to stimulate its defenders to seek to formulate such a *spiritual* Monism as shall be in harmony with both Science and Religion.

Science is certainly Monistic, and there are scientific Monists of a very different type from Haeckel in their relation to Religion. Monism must be in some form accepted—that is, for the explanation of the world that Science deals with and that we know in our experience; while, of course, the distinction between God in Himself and the world, and the reality of a spiritual world, remain unaffected. But there may be a spiritual as well as a materialistic Monism reached, not merely from the Idealistic point of view, but from the actual observation of Nature and ourselves. It is this which the present writer has endeavoured in his own way to work out. The subject has occupied his mind for a long period, the line of thought indicated is that which he has found most helpful to himself; it has grown steadily with him in clearness and force; and it is here set forth in the belief that it at least points to the direction in which we must move towards an assured faith at the present time.

He has sought to lead gradually up to this Spiritual Monism, and to set it forth as clearly as possible. If he has ventured to touch on some aspects of the current Idealistic Philosophy, it is because he believes that its conclusions need to be reached in a more objective and direct manner. To some extent what is attempted is pioneer work, but he has found much help and encouragement from the writings of Professor Lloyd Morgan, with which he only recently became acquainted. Sir Oliver Lodge —whose interest in the religious problem and contributions towards its solution in harmony with Science are to be warmly welcomed—speaks of any such attempt as is here set forth as a "most ambitious" one, not likely to be complete. But he adds the encouraging remark that "many may strive to make some contribution towards the great end, and those who think they have a contribution to make, or such a revelation entrusted to them, are bound to express it to the best of their ability, and leave it to their contemporaries and successors to assimilate such portions of it as are true, and to develop it further" (*Life and Matter*, p. 58). This is reassuring, and it indicates the spirit in which the present work is offered.

To those who have thought seriously on the subjects dealt with, and who have felt the difficulties with which faith seems to be confronted, apologies for imperfections will be unnecessary.

FERNIHIRST,
SHETTLESTON, GLASGOW, *May* 1906.

CONTENTS

PART I

CHRISTIAN THEISM AND MONISTIC EVOLUTION
SPIRITUAL MONISM

CHAP		PAGE
I.	INTRODUCTORY CHRISTIANITY AND CHRISTIAN BELIEFS, THEISM AND MONISM; METHODS OF ARGUMENT	3
II.	THE SOURCE OF OUR BEING	24
III	THE OPEN SECRET THE ALL-WORKING REASON	34
IV.	THE REVELATION OF SPIRIT WITHIN OURSELVES	66
V.	EVOLUTION. (I) GENERAL, (II) EVOLUTION IN THE PRESENT, (III) ORGANIC EVOLUTION, (IV.) INORGANIC EVOLUTION, (V.) THE MONISTIC POSITION	88
VI.	RECENTLY EMPHASISED FACTORS IN EVOLUTION	118
VII	SPENCER'S EVOLUTION DOCTRINE	138
VIII.	HAECKEL S MONISTIC EVOLUTION	153
IX	SPIRITUAL MONISM GENERAL, RELATION TO IDEALISM, ETC	179
X.	FURTHER ILLUSTRATIONS; WORLD-BUILDING, CONSCIOUSNESS, MORALITY AND RELIGION; NOT PANTHEISTIC IDENTITY	205
XI.	THE SAME CONTINUED CONSCIOUSNESS, FEELING, WILL-POWER, SUMMARY AND CONCLUSIONS	224
XII.	THE RELATION OF GOD TO THE WORLD	244
XIII.	THE ALL-WORKING POWER AS LOVE	267
XIV	THE DIVINE TRANSCENDENCE	276
XV.	THE INCARNATION OF GOD IN CHRIST	291
XVI	THE CHRISTIAN CONCEPTION OF GOD	306

PART II

FREEDOM AND MONISTIC SCIENCE

I.	THE QUESTION	325
II	"THE DETERMINISM OF PSYCHOLOGY"	331

CONTENTS

CHAP		PAGE
III. "THE DETERMINISM OF MATTER"		345
IV. THE RISE AND DEVELOPMENT OF WILL		363
V. IN RELATION TO GOD AS THE SOURCE OF THE WORLD AND OURSELVES, THE CHRISTIAN DOCTRINE OF FREEDOM		373

PART III

IMMORTALITY

I. ALTERNATIVE VIEWS.		385
II. REASONS FOR BELIEF		392
III. THE *POSSIBILITY* OF SURVIVAL		411
IV. THE CHRISTIAN DOCTRINE OF CONTINUED LIFE AND "RESURRECTION"		444
V. ETERNAL LIFE THE DIVINE PURPOSE CONCLUSION		461

INDEX 471

PART I

CHRISTIAN THEISM AND MONISTIC
EVOLUTION: SPIRITUAL MONISM

CHAPTER I

Introductory: Christianity and Christian Beliefs, Theism and Monism; Methods of Argument

CHRISTIANITY, practically regarded, is the Religion of LOVE. As such it does not require any argument to recommend it. It only needs to be exhibited in its truth. In every normal conscience Love makes itself known as the supreme Law of Life. Love, rationally directed, would not only make the individual life true to its highest law, but would, in time, transform the world into that which every man in his best moments desires to see it become The Christian Church may not have given such expression to this practical Christianity as she ought to have done, she has come far short of it; still, as far as she has been Christian at all, this has been her inspiration and her aim But if we turn from the Church to her standard in the New Testament, we can have no doubt at all about the character of Christianity. The God whom Christ proclaimed, and in His life as that of a perfect Son revealed, was the God of Love—the all-perfect Father, the complete ethical Being, to resemble Whom men were to strive. The sphere in which the Christian life was to manifest itself was the Kingdom of that God of Love, whose rule in the heart made men members of the Kingdom and children of that Heavenly Father, whose will should be done on the earth as it is done in heaven Christ's own life was from first to last the incarnate expression of the Divine Love, reaching its culminating utterance on that Cross of sacrifice on which He gave Himself up to death that men might be brought to God and be saved from sin, the root of which is selfishness. To be so delivered is the Christian salvation. When the Christian apostles went forth preaching the Gospel that was founded on the teaching and cross and continued life of Christ in the Spirit, it was the love of God for man that they proclaimed, and what they sought to see was the quickening of the life of Love in human hearts. The Holy Spirit, the Divine Power accompanying their preaching, was in its essential nature the Spirit of Holy Truth and Love. There were various "gifts of the Spirit", but in their ethical qualities they were all centred in Love. No mere outward gifts or powers could, Paul taught, be for a moment compared with Love. Though he had all other gifts, without Love he was nothing. Of the three abiding Graces—Faith, Hope, and Love—Love was the greatest and the sole abiding reality. And we reach at length the simple but sublime appeal that covers the whole of practical Christianity, "Dearly beloved, let us love one another, for love has its origin in God, and every one who loves has become a child of God and is beginning to know God. He who is destitute of love has never had any knowledge of God, because *God is Love*" (N T in modern English). If this is the character of Christianity, it should commend itself to every one who would be true to that which he knows to be highest, who wishes well towards his fellow-men, and who would fain see the evils of the world removed and men united in a real brotherhood of Love. It is just because Christianity is the religion of Love that it is so important, from a practical point of view, to uphold it.

Christian Beliefs

But Christianity is a RELIGION. By leading men to this life of Love it seeks to bring them into union with the living God who IS Love, and so to meet and satisfy the religious nature. And it is as a religion, bringing men thus into contact and union with God, that Christianity has its power. The Love that it quickens is the fruit of Faith, and only by means of faith can it be maintained. Take away faith in God, and the power of Christianity as a practical religion flows out and disappears Men have sometimes thought to have Christian practice without Christian faith, but experience has shown how impossible it is. That is, as respects the generality of men. There may be men who show that they have faith in the REALITY that God is, although they are unable to say that they believe in God, and, of course, on the part of such men we may witness what is a real *practical* Christianity, although they may stand outside the nominally Christian circle No doubt it should be natural for men to love one another, natural in the highest sense, but it is just this, his true nature, that man, necessarily rooted in a lower nature, is so slow to rise to. That "we love Him because He first loved us" is still true, and, "If God so loved us we ought to love one another," must still be the exhortation. If some men are able to live the highest life of love towards their brethren, we may well ask, What are these among so many? Not only so, but without faith in God our hearts cannot be upheld in the midst of the actual experience of the world. If some men can calmly contemplate an empty heaven above their heads and an eternal void beyond this life, and still persevere in the highest life and service, assuredly the generality of men and women cannot do so. God is necessary to them; as necessary to their spirits as the sunshine is to their bodies. History and observation prove that man has a religious nature and that he is impelled to seek its satisfaction. The human heart in its hidden depths thirsts for God, "yea, for the living God," as truly as the physical nature craves for that which will refresh and satisfy it. Man has ever felt that it is in the satisfaction of his religious nature alone that he can find the real fulness of his life. Somehow he has become conscious of a spiritual environment as truly as of a physical and a social one, and, until the life comes into harmonious adaptation to that spiritual environment, there is always something felt to be lacking. Amidst the perplexities of life, in the presence of its tragedies, under the burden of its sorrows and cares and disappointments, in the presence of death and before an unknown future, dimly felt to be real, the heart of man cries out for God, longs to find God and to be at peace. No substitutes can ever take the place of this faith in the living God. It is well that we should feel that, beyond all that Science can show us in the phenomenal world, there is "an unknown Reality", but we can never find rest or satisfaction, or the highest inspiration for our life, if we believe that that "Reality" is, and must ever be, "utterly inscrutable." Such a belief *may* be a real form of Religion, but it is by no means the highest form, or one that can bring mental rest and spiritual strength. That unknowable Reality may be, and doubtless is, *God*, but a Being dwelling in such impenetrable darkness can never be to us the God Whom we need, and Whom we seek to know. This belief in God implies also, of necessity, the conviction that man is a free personality, with a real *worth* or value attaching to him as such, and a possibility of entering into free, personal relations with the Eternal Source of his being, and into a life above Time and Sense; in other words, it implies belief in Freedom and Immortality.

There has been of late a tendency to belittle the importance of Reason and Belief in human life. But it is what a man *believes*, explicitly or implicitly, that inspires and guides his entire life. It is their different beliefs, more than anything else, that form the different types of men. Some words of Mr. Froude's, read long ago, come here into mind. "The generic type is formed by his creed. As is his belief so is his character. According to his views of what life is given him for, he becomes a warrior, a saint, a patriot, a rascal, a sensualist, or a comfortable man of business, who keeps his eye on the main chance, and does not go into dreams. And as you look along the ages you see a tendency in masses of men to drift into one or other of these forms. Carlyle, in Edinburgh, where some one was talking of the mischief beliefs had produced in the world, said, 'Yes, belief has done much evil, but it has done all the good.' . . . If we believe nobly about ourselves, we have a chance of living nobly. If we believe basely, base we certainly shall become."

Again, as Mr. Hobhouse has remarked in his *Democracy and Reaction*, some years ago much was hoped from the awakening of a better social or human feeling, even apart from Religion. But this hope has not been realised—" a good-natured scepticism having risen up, not only about the other world, but about the deepest problems and interests of this"; and he puts as the first of the causes of the present unsatisfactory state of things, "decay in vivid and professed religious beliefs." Mr. John Morley, in an interesting article founded on Mr. Hobhouse's book (in the *Nineteenth Century and After* for March 1905), after saying, with too great truth, that more might have been expected from the Gospel of Love—the Gospel that preaches Divine Fatherhood and Human Brotherhood amongst men as the sons of the one Heavenly Father— asks, "Why should decay in dogmatic beliefs about the supernatural lead to a decline in the influence of Christian ethics?" Mr. Morley is one of those men who have sought to stand in public life for the *Reality* that God is, one who has contended for those ethical principles which Christianity inculcates, in both the individual and the national life, with an earnestness which many professed Christians have failed to show. But why does he not see that that for which he so earnestly contends is truly *supernatural*? It is, admittedly, something above and beyond "Nature," and by his very contention it is equally above and beyond "men" as they are in general to be seen at this moment. It is an Ethical *Ideal* he is seeking to see realised. And, surely, to believe that this Ideal is *real* in the Source of the Universe, that it is centred in a just and loving God, Whose *will* it is that it should be realised "on the earth as it is in heaven," who brought the worlds into existence just in order that it might be realised in them all, who has shown the possibility of its realisation in, at least, *one* supreme human life, who has made the sacrifice that Christianity declares in order to manifest His love and to realise His purpose in the world, who calls us all to be co-workers with Himself in all that makes for the highest welfare of humanity, and "in Whom" we can be sure that our labour "is not in vain," but that the result shall be reached, "since God is God,"—in this we seem to see clearly the source of our highest inspiration, and to discern that the want of a *real* belief in these verities is just the deepest want of our time When men cut themselves off from the "supernatural," they sever themselves from the Fountain of Spiritual Power, and we need not wonder at the result. It is then only man, not the Power that makes us men, we are looking to. In the continuation of his article (*Nineteenth Century and After*, April 1905) Mr. Morley again touches on the religious question, although with characteristic reverence he abstains from discussing it. He thinks that the "share of the Christian religion, and its influence in this wide field of coming innovation, is obscure and doubtful " " The Sermon on the Mount has been reproved by bold critics as bad political economy, and it is unquestionably socialist " Now, the Sermon on the Mount may be socialistic in the best sense of the term, but it is first of all individualistic, and it may yet be found that it contains the secret of both individual and social salvation. Wherein does Mr. Morley believe that social salvation is to be found ? " Sacrifice," he says, " has been the law—sacrifice for creeds, for churches, for dynasties, for kings, for adored teachers, for native land." . " The salvation of democracy " depends upon men " instructed, able, diligent, disinterested, and bold," who will " tell both masses and directing classes the truth " But what is Christianity but just the Religion of Sacrifice? It both teaches and shows by a supreme example that only through the spirit and practice of self-sacrifice for the Ideal can salvation come to the world. If Christianity has lost the power to inspire men and women to such sacrifice, it can only be because they have lost faith in it and in its God. The restoration of faith will bring a renewal of the highest kind of power. The kind of man that Christianity seeks to produce is just that kind on which Mr. Morley says the salvation of democracy depends It has produced such men in the past ; we believe it can produce them still · if it cannot do so, we are again thrown back on the decay of living faith as the reason for the failure.

The Present Position

The felt need of God is, of course, in itself a testimony to the reality of God ; but it is not always seen to be so. At the present time, especially, it is very difficult for many a one really to believe in God. Science has so changed our point of view, that the supreme Object of the spiritual vision seems to have passed out of our visual range. Although the Materialism of a quarter of a century ago has largely passed away, a new and more subtle (if more silent) Agnosticism has taken its place The world no longer seems to bear witness to a good Creator. The darker aspects of Nature have, for some, ecclipsed its brighter aspects. To many Evolution has seemed to dispense with all creative agency. God is lost in Nature. The world by the action of "the persistence of Force" or "the law of Substance" seems to have made itself. there is no room for God. No point can be discerned at which He can come in; matter, with its accompanying energy and nascent spirit, seems to be able to do everything. Man in his highest qualities has developed from the lowliest animal forms through the potency of Protoplasm. The Universe thus seems to many to account for itself, and faith in God, it is feared by some, and loudly proclaimed by others, has been one of the dreams which man must leave behind him as he wakes up into a more rational life. And there are always with us those "evils in Nature" and unaccountable experiences in life which militate against belief in a God of Love. Of course, no lesser being can be God to us. For, not only would man be thus greater than his God; but, in Browning's well-known words,

> "The loving worm within its clod
> Were diviner than a loveless God
> Amid His worlds"

F. D. Maurice has somewhere said that it is often the hardest thing in the world really to believe in God. The present writer knows well how difficult it sometimes is. Very many of those who profess to believe in Him do not really so believe, they only believe that they believe, and sometimes not even that. A general real belief in God would wake the world into newness of life. Nothing is so greatly wanted But, at present, the honest mind that will not be satisfied with "make-believes," that must have "reasons relevant" to rely on, and firm ground whereon to stand, often finds itself in very great difficulty. Those difficulties have been felt to the full by the present writer, and it is out of sympathy with those who feel them that the following pages are written. These difficulties often arise from mistaken ideas as to what God really is, and as to where and how we are to look for Him. The writer believes that the line of thought here presented is that which is specially required at the present time, when an anti-Theistic Monism is so widely prevalent. What he has found most helpful to himself in times of the trial of faith, what in fact has upheld him and kept him true to Christian Theism amidst much that tended to test the things that could be shaken, he has here endeavoured to set forth in the light of the most recent knowledge of the Universe and of man.

Monism

That which we are confronted with at present is a "naturalistic" or "scientific" MONISM, in which one sole power works all things by a gradual evolution, and no distinction is made of man from Nature or of God from the world. It is this Monism which is at present the chief representative of anti-Theism, and it has been widely popularised by means of the writings of Professor Haeckel and his advocates. To the present writer this Monism is by no means new, and he has never regarded it as necessarily anti-Theistic. He has sought to set a spiritual and Theistic Monism over against naturalistic and agnostic Monism. Monism has had, of course, a long history, and there may be a spiritualistic as well as a materialistic Monism, in entire harmony with modern Science.

Any system that explains the phenomena of the Universe by referring them all to a single principle is

Monistic. Not to mention Indian Philosophy, there was a Monism in the early Greek Philosophy, and there is a sense in which it is true that, since the Christian Revelation, as Dr. Hutchison Stirling remarks, " Monism has remained the characteristic and the fundamental tendency of the whole of modern Philosophy." Any completely Idealistic system may be truly described as a spiritual Monism. This is specially true of the Hegelian system, the chief attraction of which is its deduction of everything from " the Idea,"—the world, culminating in man, being a growing manifestation of a spiritual principle—of the Divine Reason —in the course of a necessary (though not un-free) self-evolution. But deferring any criticism, the grounds of this Philosophy are difficult to grasp, and although the conclusion is a sound one, it needs to be reached in a simpler and more objective manner, as the result of the study of the whole of Nature, and so as to make it plain that we have in the beginning *God*, and a real distinction between God and the World. As the late Mr. T. H. Green, one of its ablest representatives, has said, " It still remains to be presented in a form which will command some general acceptance among serious and scientific men " (*Works*, iii. 146). There is also a strictly Psychological Monism.

But that which is now most distinctively known as " Monism " had its rise in the revolt from the extreme Dualism of Descartes, and had its chief representative in Spinoza. According to Descartes, soul and body were two quite separate and heterogeneous substances, with no action possible between them According to Spinoza, there was but *one* two-sided Substance—of which Body was the extended side, and Soul the thinking, mental, or spiritual side. So with respect to God and the World—God was the thought-side of the World.

The Monism with which we are confronted to-day,

INTRODUCTORY

while founding on Science, harks back to Spinoza, and claims also Goethe as its forerunner. But there were elements in the thought of both Spinoza and Goethe which are sadly awanting in the scientific Monism of to-day. Spinoza certainly believed that he wrote in the interests of Religion, and the same can be said of Goethe. Spinoza was "a God-intoxicated man." Although we speak of "scientific Monism," all Scientists by no means accept its conclusions. It goes beyond Science, strictly so called, and draws inferences as to what lies behind phenomena, or does not lie behind them. It is as much Philosophy as Science, and, while its statements of facts as observed in the physical sphere may be correct, the conclusions drawn from these facts may be quite mistaken. Some facts also may fail to receive due recognition. Of course, such Monism belongs only to the phenomenal world: it cannot deal with the Divine Being considered in Himself and as distinct from the world—a fact that needs to be constantly kept in view.

The chief representative of this scientific Monism in the more recent past was Ludwig Buchner of Tubingen in his *Force and Matter*, and other works, ending with his *Last Words on Materialism*; and in the present time it has its best known exponent in Professor Haeckel of Jena. This modern Monism earnestly disclaims Materialism; it acknowledges, in a way, Mind or Spirit, as well as Matter, and professes to regard it as equally fundamental. But, instead of the Dualism which is affirmed to be involved in speaking of "God and the World," it maintains that Force (including "spirit") and Matter are but the two sides of one reality or "Substance," which does everything and is everything. This Substance is in eternal motion, and the infinite Universe, with all that it contains, is the result of a perpetual and necessary process of evolution or development according to an invariable "Law of Substance" (or persistence), and evolution is invariably followed by dissolution—new worlds being born in never-ending cycles of life and death. God, Freedom, and Immortality are expressly denied. In such a system there is, of course, no place for them. Everything and every being in the world is the product of one sole Substance which operates continuously and irresistibly in the manner of an evolution. Its inner nature no one can tell. Each individual is but as a wheel, or a part of a wheel, in one great machine driven by this resistless power; everything is inexorably determined by that which has gone before, and, in time, each individual drops out of his place in the great machine, to be succeeded by others, who shall disappear in like manner.

A form of Monism, or perhaps we should say, various forms of it, not necessarily anti-Theistic, have been advocated in *The Monist* and other publications of "The Open Court Publishing Company" of Chicago — by Dr. Paul Carus in particular. The late Mr. G. J. Romanes was also in his scientific writings a Monist, although he became able to reconcile his views with Theism. Professor Lloyd Morgan also maintains a form of Monism, which is not by any means to be identified with the anti-Theistic Monism of Haeckel. Monism according to him "regards Nature and Experience as one and indivisible, and all apparent dualism as a dualism of aspect distinguishable in thought, but indissoluble in existence. It contends—that the individual on the one hand, and the Cosmos on the other hand, are alike products of an evolution which is one and continuous. " But it is," he says, "an assumption," "it leaves plenty of room for many divergencies and even differences of opinion."

Monism is not by any means necessarily anti-Theistic. Professor Lloyd Morgan is (as we shall see) an advocate of Theism. Dr. Carus also upholds Theism in his own sense of it. Even Buchner says there may be an underlying "Source of all things," of which Force and Matter represent "only two different sides or phenomenal aspects," which might be termed "God," if "stripped of its theological and anthropomorphic associations and not opposed to or set above the principle of the unity of Nature" (*Last Words on Materialism*, p. 116). There is more in such a statement than appears on the surface. And although Haeckel denies the existence of any Being that can be called God, he yet (as we shall see) leaves the Universe quite unexplained as respects its origin and spiritual constituents, placing us, after all, face to face with an unknown Reality which, for anything he can tell, may be the God in Whom we believe. The late Mr. Herbert Spencer, although his System of Philosophy is different in some respects, must also be included amongst Monistic writers. He works out everything by the one principle of the "persistence of Force," and, Mind and Matter are but the phenomenal manifestations of one unknown Reality. As we shall show, Spencer's position is not anti-Theistic, nor even necessarily Agnostic, but may afford a most valuable support to Theism.

It cannot be denied that Monism, professing to give us the *unity* which the mind craves for, building, as it does, on the facts of Science; and following out the course of a continuous evolution up to its issue in man with all his powers, possesses a strong fascination for the mind, and its anti-Theistic forms of presentation have exercised a widespread influence antagonistic to Religion. It is specially with this form of anti-Theism that we have to do to-day. That it points to a deep truth we have no doubt; any true theory of the Universe, as we know it, must be, ultimately, Monistic; but, in order to account for that Universe, it must be a genuinely SPIRITUAL Monism.

Methods of Argument

A very full statement and a strong advocacy of "scientific Monism" is to be found in the writings of Mr. W. H. Mallock, especially in his *Religion as a Credible Doctrine*, and his *Reconstruction of Belief*. He points out the inadequacy of the Theological and Philosophical methods of attack, and endeavours to establish religious beliefs, not as being in harmony with a Monistic view of the world, but purely on practical grounds, in spite of and even in contradiction to the scientific Monism, the truth of which he maintains. This method of dealing with the subject calls for special notice before going further; because we are convinced that it is a radically unsound one and extremely misleading If it were sound, indeed, it would be needless to go further, for, in attempting to base religious beliefs on rational principles in harmony with Science, we should be attempting the impossible.

Mr. Mallock maintains that the two systems are in absolute contradiction, as far as our powers are able to view them. But he urges that our powers are limited, that it is impossible for us to take in the totality of things in either system, and that we must seek relief in "a synthesis of contradictories." Although the scientific system is in direct contradiction to the beliefs on which the religious system rests, we must simply hold them both.

Now, of course, our intellectual powers are limited; but they are really more limited (in a different sense) than even Mr. Mallock makes them out to be : they are so limited that it is impossible for us to believe in contradictions. We may often have to believe in facts which we cannot at the time reconcile, but not in contradictions.

1. He maintains that we are *habitually* obliged to believe contradictories; all our knowledge runs up at length, not merely into the unknown, but into the contra-

dictory. This we cannot by any means admit. We believe that wherever there seem to be contradictories, it is the consequence either of error or of ignorance on the one side or the other. No one can believe in the really contradictory. "The law of contradiction" (or rather, of non-contradiction) is a primary law of thought underlying all logical reasoning. Contradictories cannot *both* be true. The same thing cannot both be and not be at the same time.[1] Science, for example, according to Mr. Mallock, says quite correctly and inexorably in its own sphere, that *Freedom* cannot be. To believe that it *is*, notwithstanding, as Mr. Mallock says we must do, is not to believe two contradictories, but to drop one of them. If Freedom is, then it *is*, whatever Science may say to the contrary. Closely examined, it would probably be found that in all the cases cited by Mr. Mallock as contradictories we do not have real contradictories at all, but only cases beyond our power at the time to reconcile as they are stated, but which may be wrongly stated on the one side or the other, and in themselves present no real contradiction. It is impossible here to examine all his illustrations But let us take one of the shortest in statement and simplest of them. "Infinity," says Mr. Mallock, "baffles our logic. . . . If we build a hall, and finding it to be too large for our purposes, run a partition across the middle of it, the cubic content of each of the two parts is necessarily half the cubic content of the whole, but if we imagine a partition, without top or bottom or ends, to be run across space in its totality, thus completely bisecting it, each of the halves, being on one side infinite still, will, in respect of its spacial content, be no less infinite than the two taken together.

[1] As Professor Ritchie remarks, "Contradiction proves falsehood somewhere. To profess to believe propositions which are strictly inconsistent with each other is a proof that there is a want of thoroughness somewhere, a want of clearness of thinking or a want of sincerity, or both" (*Philos. Studies*, p 142)

Each part equals the whole. The whole is no greater than the part" But surely it is evident that the cases compared here are by no means parallel. The hall was *bounded* before we began to divide it, and space is unbounded. We cannot halve the unlimited. By its very definition, it is impossible to divide the *Infinite*. It *is* Infinite, and it can never be anything less.

2 Mr. Mallock says that the grounds of our belief in the reality of the moral world (in spite of the demonstration by Science of its impossibility) are of the same nature as those on which we believe in the real existence of the cosmic world. We cannot prove to others or to ourselves the reality of an external world. We "get it neither from sense nor reason" "The belief in the external world is an inference" And "reason instead of supporting this inference . . entirely fails, as" (he says) "all thinkers now admit, to assure us of the existence of anything outside our individual selves" It is, as Hume said, "more properly an act of the sensitive than of the cognitive part of our natures" —"an act of faith or instinct." In the same way, he says, we must (as indeed all do) believe in the reality of the moral world, although Science shows that it can have no existence. But here again the cases are far from parallel. Without now discussing the grounds of our knowledge of an external world (which, it seems at least, we can no more get away from than we can jump out of our skin), all normally constituted men *do* believe in it, and they do so, according to Hume, in virtue of some quite natural faculty. Probably it is just because they begin to reason where no reasoning is necessary that difficulty arises for some. They make it for themselves. But certainly, none, save perhaps a few ultra-idealists, say that it is impossible that such a world can exist. Even those who say that we have no direct knowledge of it affirm its existence But in the case of the moral world (although here also all normally

constituted men believe in it), we are face to face with a system that says it is impossible that there should be such a world, and which (according to Mr. Mallock) proves its assertion. It professes to speak in the name of such carefully ascertained and sifted knowledge as ought to command assent. To give such assent and yet to believe in the existence of that moral world that is so *denied* is surely a very different thing from joining with the rest of humanity in believing in the reality of an external world—a world which, practically, no one denies.

3. Mr. Mallock shows that there are the strongest reasons for believing in the moral world It is necessary, not only for the highest and fullest life, but for anything that can be called *moral* life. So essential is it, indeed, that men like the late Professor Huxley and Mr. Spencer, who seemed by their scientific Philosophy to have banished this world, sought means by which they might bring it in again. "Men, indeed," says Mr. Mallock, "would not tolerate—or rather they are so constituted that they would not be able to tolerate—any surrender of that larger and deeper life of supposed spontaneity and freedom which has been theirs hitherto for one which has been narrower and shallower and is paralysed by necessity." But the natural inference from such statements surely is, not that those assertions in the name of Science which would, as Mr. Mallock says, make the existence of the moral world impossible, and so contradict and arrest human development, are true (although we must at the same time believe in the contrary), but that, in some way, those who make these statements, whether in the name of Science or in any other name, are mistaken That form of Monistic Science which Mr Mallock upholds is possibly not true Science, or it goes beyond the scope of Science, some inferences from its facts may be mistaken; some element of actual life may have been overlooked or forgotten. Recent discoveries show

that such things do happen; that our Science at any given moment is not absolutely final; that it is never omniscient nor infallible It may be possible that even Monistic Science may be so stated as to give room for belief in Freedom and Religion, if not, indeed, to give strong support to it.

We must go farther, and say that, if the reality of the moral world, with its implications of God, Freedom, and Immortality, be so essential for human life, which is surely the main thing in this world, that we *must* believe in it in spite of the contradictions of Science, we have the strongest grounds for holding that the contradictions cannot be real, but that the Science that denies the reality and the possibility of the moral and religious life *must* be in some way in error. That is, of course, if such be indeed the assertion of that which has a right to be called " Science." For it must be remembered that the term " Science " is used by Mr. Mallock with an extension which would certainly not be accepted by all who are entitled to be regarded as Representatives of Science.

The Method here followed

Our endeavour shall not be the unprofitable one of attempting to refute the well-established positions of Science, nor shall it be that which Mr. Mallock describes as characteristic of Theology, of seeking to find gaps or breaks or interferences through which a higher world may find entrance into the cosmic one. Such attempts, however much they may gratify a section of those who already believe, are of no value for the check of Scepticism or for the strengthening of a fearless, open-eyed faith. The only religious faith worth maintaining is one that cares supremely for truth, however hard it may seem at first sight to reconcile it with its beliefs. Nor shall we attempt to solve the problem by approaching it primarily from within, or by the methods of Idealistic Philosophy. We are at one with Monistic Science in a general acceptance of a unitary and continuous world-process, the working of a single Power. It will be our endeavour to show that all that is wanted in order to see, not only the harmony of the Scientific with the Religious view, but how truly Science supports Religion, is to give its due place to that *spiritual* element which is, in some form, at least verbally acknowledged by all the representatives of Monism; to observe and state the facts from their mental side instead of from their physical or material side merely, and to show that there is not some hypothetical third unknown element underlying both the bodily and the spiritual in the phenomenal world, but that Spirit itself (Reason, Love, Purpose, Power) is the one true and sole "Substance" of which all things are the manifestation. In other words, we shall seek to show that that to which we are led by the observation of Nature and of ourselves is not a materialistic or naturalistic Monism, but a genuinely *spiritual* Monism, such as gives grounds for our beliefs, not in a vague Theism merely, but in the Christian conception of God, and in Freedom and Immortality. We have avoided metaphysical modes of reasoning as far as possible, not because we do not believe in Metaphysics, but because we are convinced that simpler, more objective, and more truly inductive modes of argument are desirable. There is, indeed, nothing more to be desired than to be able to show that the highest conclusions of Idealistic Philosophy can be reached not merely on subjective, but on objective grounds, from the observation of Nature, after the methods followed by Science, on grounds open to the ordinary man, and not merely to those specially trained in Philosophy.

After showing the grounds of our certainty that there must be an adequate Source of our being, we have sought to show that the great question underlying all religion and all philosophy is one which, when it is properly asked, or correctly stated, really answers itself. It is, How to find a rational explanation of the world and its life? There can be but one answer to this question. Nothing but Reason itself can ever constitute a rationally explicable world or Universe. And we have shown that to this conclusion we are inevitably led by the evolutionary doctrine maintained by all Monistic writers.[1] Possibly, by itself, this might seem a too "short and easy method" with the Agnostic; but it is a perfectly sound one. We can never, with all our seeking, get really beyond it. Whenever we forsake our confidence in *Reason* and in a rational world, we are left to drift helplessly. If it seems too simple and easy, we would urge that, surely, an answer on which so much depends ought to be simple and within easy reach of all rational beings. If we can only be sure of God after we have mastered the intricacies of Science and Philosophy, we are in a bad case. We have not, however, left it to stand by itself; we have sought to show its truth objectively or empirically, to prove that the mode of the origin of Reason in man and the study of Nature lead to the same conclusion, to exhibit the support it receives from all our knowledge of Nature, and to show its harmony with Evolution. In this connection we have endeavoured to set forth that spiritual interpretation of the Universe on the basis of Mr. Spencer's System of Philosophy which he himself affirmed to be possible, and have criticised Haeckel's Monistic Doctrine, seeking at the same time to state such a true *spiritual* Monism as Science really gives support to, and to make it plain that it does not involve a Pantheistic Identity. We have also sought to meet the difficulties which are felt concerning God's relation to the World; to show that Love as well as Reason

[1] Throughout, our illustrations have been taken, as far as possible, from Monistic writers.

is at the foundation of our life—that Love, indeed, is one with Reason; to set forth the Divine Transcendence as well as a Divine Immanence, and to show, in the light of our modern knowledge of the World, the reality and supreme importance of the Incarnation of God in Christ—how we can conceive and hold that truth in harmony with all that Science teaches. We have endeavoured to state the principal elements contained in the specifically Christian conception of God, with their truth and lasting value. On account of the important place which the Freedom of the Will holds in relation to Religion, and the prominence of Determinism in a naturalistic Monism, a section is specially devoted to the discussion of that question. Finally, in order to complete our subject, we have sought to state the grounds of belief in Immortality and of the Christian faith in Eternal Life, and to suggest how, in the light of recent Science, Immortality may be realised.

It has not been deemed necessary to go back to the Agnosticism of Huxley, nor to discuss the conditions of knowledge in general. Science takes it for granted that in the world of experience we are dealing with something which, for the time being at least, is real, and that we can have knowledge to some extent. Of course, we can only know things in their relations. That we can only know them in relation to our own mind is no objection no other kind of knowledge is conceivably possible to us. The attempt after some other knowledge than that which is possible to *man* is futile and delusive

The chapter that immediately follows may be regarded as still introductory, but it could not be omitted.

CHAPTER II

THE SOURCE OF OUR BEING

THE grounds of our belief in God must be laid deep in each man's nature; belief in God cannot be dependent on reasons which are recondite or difficult of apprehension. If it be necessary for our highest life and well-being that we should believe in God, that belief must arise within us in the simplest and most natural way. If God may sometimes seem "a God who hides Himself," still, we are convinced that He is there

Perhaps the most general, original, and, we might say, at bottom, universal, ground of this belief, is the conviction that arises naturally in the mind that there must be a SOURCE OF OUR BEING, an adequate Source of the world and of ourselves, greater than we are, on Whom we, and all things, are dependent. This conviction is not reached at the end of a laboured argument from Causation, based on "Contingency" or proceeding along the lines of a "regress of finite causes." It arises spontaneously from our constant experience of our own personal action and of life in the world. We know ourselves to be, to some extent, CAUSES, and we are continually experiencing the effects of Causation. It is simply impossible for us to rest in the thought of anything in the world of our experience as wholly uncaused. Beyond mere sequence, we seek for a Cause. As Mr. Spencer has said, "When we inquire what is the meaning of the effects produced in our senses . . we are compelled to regard them as the effects of some Cause" (*First Principles*, p. 27). This is indeed, as Kant maintained, a primary intellectual principle; and we have now learned that it is such as the effect of the constant experience of the race—perhaps, as Mr. Romanes held, of even that of our animal ancestors. It is just for this reason that we are compelled to seek a causal explanation of the world and of ourselves, and that we naturally (we may say inevitably) believe in an adequate Source of our being

But while the principle of Causality is acknowledged on every hand—with Haeckel, it is the very ground of reasoning itself—what is termed "mechanical" or "scientific" causation has been placed by some as a substitute for God

"Mechanical causation," says Haeckel, "controls all the processes in the Universe." But this mechanical or scientific causation is not the single act or the simple thing that some seem to imagine. We never come upon anything that can be described as a single cause in itself, it is impossible to go back in any single, or direct, line of causation to eternity. A cause of anything in the phenomenal world may be described as the sum of the conditions which bring about the change which constitutes a new thing or event. There is a sense in which it is correct to say that the cause of anything is the reason (or reasons) why it happens or is what it is. This is at the root of all causation. We never know a cause as a single thing. For example, the sun melts wax, but bakes clay. These effects depend not only on the sun's heat, but also on the nature of the wax and the clay respectively. Besides, there was some agency that brought them into contact. The field always widens out indefinitely, In the world of experience there is always a concatenation of causes at work, and the effect itself in one aspect belongs to "the cause." As Mr. Whetham remarks (in

The Recent Developments of Physical Science), " When carefully examined, the difficulty of isolating the cause of any particular effect will be found to be insuperable. A long train of circumstances has preceded the phenomenon considered, and the phenomenon would not have appeared had any of these phenomena been absent. Each or all of them might equally well have been called the cause " (p. 30). We can never reach in experience any ultimate causation. " Only because we are so familiar with the great phenomenon of Causality do we take it for granted, and think that we reach an ultimate explanation of anything when we have succeeded in finding 'the cause' thereof, when, in point of fact, we have only succeeded in merging it in the mystery of mysteries " (G. J. Romanes, *Thoughts on Religion*, p. 116).

Scientific or mechanical causation, therefore, is one thing, and an ultimate explanation quite another. What we are impelled to seek is, not merely the explanation of this or that particular event or phenomenon, but of the unified working of that wide concatenation of causes which we know in experience—in a word, of the World as a whole. And it is this (although we do not put it to ourselves in a formal manner) that causes us to believe in a God who is the Source of the whole.

It is just this also that gives rise to Philosophy, as something beyond Science, and that keeps it alive. Science may give a proximate and more or less complete explanation of this or that particular change, and may point to a series of such changes, losing itself in eternity, but what we seek is not so much a " First Cause " that starts the series as a present Cause for the entire concatenation of causes now operating in an orderly manner, producing and upholding the world and ourselves. " The Universe," says Haeckel, " is an all-embracing unified whole " (*Wonders of Life*, p. 402). It is for this *unified whole* that we are impelled to seek a Cause—" a Cause of causes." After all that Science can show us, the need for this remains. In the words of Professor Lloyd Morgan, "Science asks what are the facts, the nature and order of the sequence of phenomena, the generalisations under which the facts and their observed sequences may be grouped. Beyond this Metaphysics asks, What is the source and origin of these facts, how comes it that the sequence is what we invariably find it to be; what conception, if any, can we frame of the cause of the events which we observe?" "The distinction between scientific causation in terms of antecedence and sequence within the field of experience, and metaphysical causation as the underlying reason for, or *raison d'être* of, the sequences is," he points out, an essential distinction, and the failure to realise it has been "the source of many misconceptions and of much confusion" (*Contemporary Review*, June 1904, see also Professor Upton, *Hibbert Lectures on Theism*, chap vi). It is the forgetting of this distinction and the formulation of what is known as the "argument from Causation" on principles only applicable to the phenomenal world, that has laid that argument open to criticism But the principle itself is fundamental to all our thinking

If we realise the above-mentioned distinction, we shall also see the error of the assertion sometimes made, that we must go beyond this ultimate Cause and seek a cause for the Cause of the Universe. That would be to extend the action of experiential Science far beyond its boundaries. In an adequate Cause of the Universe we have found all that we are impelled to seek; we have that which the mind can rest in, all that it craves for, all that it asks—the Cause of all the unified combinations of causes that are working in the phenomenal Universe. To seek a cause for that again would be to deny that we had found that which we are so impelled to seek. We cannot rest in any merely phenomenal causation. It may be said that the present system is the outcome of a previous system, just as the plant organism is the outcome of the seed of a pre-existing plant. But, in that case, we should still be impelled to seek the cause of the appearance of that previous system or succession of systems, and of their power to produce such results; we should still be in the region of the phenomenal only. If it be said that the Universe may have its cause in itself, it has none the less in it that which we must distinguish as "cause" from all its phenomenal manifestations. If the Universe be eternal, or one of an eternal series of Universes, this only leads us to affirm an eternal and constantly operative Source or Cause. Beyond this it is impossible to go.

This principle that the phenomenal world must have an adequate Source or Cause is either implicitly or explicitly accepted and acted on by all serious thinkers, whatever conclusions they may reach concerning the nature of that cause. Has not Mr. Spencer said, in words of wide-reaching and wholesome influence. "Amid the mysteries which become the more mysterious the more they are thought about, there will remain (to the thinker) the one absolute certainty that he is ever in the presence of an Infinite and Eternal Energy from which all things proceed"; and that the fact that there is a permanent Source of phenomena is "the certainty of certainties." The object of his whole System was to show how the Universe had proceeded from this Ultimate Source, although he held that it was in itself "unknowable."

What again is the motive of Haeckel's book, *The Riddle of the Universe*, which has made such a stir in recent times, but an attempt, on the principle of causation, to explain the Universe—so far at least? He seeks to show a sufficient cause for all that is manifested in the Universe in what he terms "the law of Substance" "The general law of Causality," he says, "taken in conjunction with the law of Substance, teaches us that every phenomenon has a mechanical Cause"; and in each so-called "chance" event he sees, as he does in the evolution of the entire Cosmos, "the universal sovereignty of Nature's Supreme law, the law of Substance." However inadequate the explanation may be, it is founded on the principle of Causality.

The most "crass Materialism" that ever was advanced has rested on the same ground, there was no reason for its appearance save as an attempt to explain the World by "matter" and its powers, on the principle of causation

The same is true of Spiritualistic arguments. As already said, the principle of causation is the chief source of the "consensus Gentium" or general belief in God; and almost all, if not the whole, of the arguments usually adduced for the Divine Existence are resolvable into this argument from Causation This is manifestly true of the "Cosmological Argument"; it is professedly based on Causation. The "teleological argument" also, whether in its narrower or in its wider sense, rests upon it. A Designer is inferred to account for what we interpret as design and adaptation in the world as its Cause So with the "ontological argument" in its best forms: God is affirmed as the Cause or Source of the idea of a perfect Being that arises within us. The "moral argument" rests on the conviction that there must be a Source above ourselves of the moral convictions which become law to us. And if we reason from the Ideals that arise within us and the spiritual experiences that come to us, it must be on the ground that these must have a Source or Cause above and beyond ourselves. Neither Mysticism nor Religion has any direct knowledge of God; men can only postulate His existence as the cause of their experience. The "Psychological" argument, based on man's deep *want* of God and *need* for Him, implies that *God* is the Source of the nature so constituted.

This ground may not be so obvious with respect to what may be termed "the modern Hegelian argument," and the reasoning of modern Idealism. Yet, closely looked at, it will be found to be equally true for both The first affirms that "all our conscious life rests on and implies a Consciousness that is universal. We cannot think, save on the presupposition of a thought or consciousness which is the unity of thought and being, or on which all individual thought and existence rest" (Principal Caird, *Intro. to Philos of Religion*, pp. 131, 132). It is an inference—a presupposition based on the nature of thought in ourselves. The argument is really,—since such is the nature of thought in man, there must be that which so constitutes our thought. Modern Idealism affirms that there must be a Universal Consciousness in order to give meaning to the Universe beyond ourselves. This argument, too, whether valid or not, really rests ultimately on the principle of Causation. It is assumed that the Universe before and beyond ourselves *has* a meaning, and a Universal Consciousness is postulated in order to account for or explain that meaning. Whatever validity any of these arguments have, rests ultimately on the common principle of Causation, so widely and deeply implanted in our nature. This is the ground that is patent to all.

We thus see that the necessity for believing that there must be an adequate Cause for, or Source of, the Universe and all our experience therein, is on every hand acknowledged. We simply cannot help believing it. We are so constituted by Nature itself that we *must* believe it. The real Theistic Question therefore is, not whether there is an adequate Source of our being, but, *what is the nature* of that Source or Cause?

It is, of course, contained in this assertion that the Source of our being is at least adequate to the production of the Universe and ourselves, distinguished, as we are, by

THE SOURCE OF OUR BEING 31

the possession of a spiritual nature An effect cannot transcend what there is in the power of its Cause to produce. A developing Universe can never at any point express the fulness that resides in the Cause that is producing it. All this follows from the ancient and universal axiom, *ex nihilo nihil fit* We cannot by any possibility get something from nothing, nor, what is the same thing, the greater from the less. In the words of Cudworth, "Nothing can give what it hath not, and therefore so much of the perfection or entity of the effect as is greater than that of the supposed cause, so much thereof must needs come from nothing or be made without a cause" (*Intellectual System*, ii. 162). As we have said, it is never the action of a single cause that we behold in the world of phenomena, but—because we fix our attention exclusively on one prominent factor only— it sometimes appears as if the less produced the greater But, as we shall see when we come to speak of Evolution, this is a great fallacy, for it is a fundamental principle of all thought that we can never by any possibility get something from nothing[1]

Finally, the nature of a cause is, so far at least, known from its effects, and can only be so known. This does not mean that the cause may not be very much greater than is manifested in any single thing or in any number of things that it effects Nor does it imply that it must *resemble* the effect, as has been sometimes foolishly said in reply to arguments for the Divine Existence. That which is produced may be very much less in any particular case, and

---

[1] Mr G. J Romanes remarks, in his Introduction to his projected reply to his own previous work, *A Candid Examination of Theism*, by *Physicus*, that he erred in not considering whether higher causes are not necessary to account for spiritual facts—*i e* , " whether the ultimate Being must not be at least as high as the intellectual and spiritual nature of man, *i e* higher than anything merely physical or mechanical. The supposition that it must, does not violate the law of Parsimony" (*Thoughts on Religion*, p. 102)

very different in form, from that which produces it, as, *e g.*, when a man makes a wheelbarrow. The wheelbarrow, if it could think, would have no right to suppose that it had been made by a greater wheelbarrow. But it would assuredly be right in concluding that its cause possessed the knowledge and the power that could produce that useful article. The very essence of a cause, it has been said, "lies in its power to produce something else." " The difference in form," says Dr Paul Carus, " constitutes the new state of things called the effect, and if the effect were not different from its cause there would be no change, and we should not be entitled to speak of causation at all" (*Primer of Philosophy*, p. 152). So, although the Source of the Universe can in no way be said to be *like* the Universe or like any particular constituent of it, we are certain that it must contain the knowledge and the power competent to produce the Universe; and we see that Cause most fully revealed in its *highest manifestation*—in that which the nature that has been produced in us recognises as the highest. While the making of a wheelbarrow could not reveal anything concerning the moral *character* of its maker, who nevertheless *had* a moral character of some kind,—if a king were to constitute a State governed by moral laws, this would certainly indicate something of the character of that king So, if the Universe to which we belong culminates in a moral and spiritual Kingdom (or in a moral and spiritual nature), we shall see something of the real character of its Source, or of the causative Power which originates and carries onward the Universe towards this end, revealed in the laws of that moral and spiritual Kingdom or nature, and in the highest expression of that nature. While the merely *mechanical* Universe may indicate nothing more than Wisdom and Power, such a culmination in a moral and spiritual Kingdom or nature would reveal in the Source of our being those very qualities which we recognise in ourselves as the highest.

The Source of the Universe must contain in itself the fulness of that which is increasingly revealed in its highest phenomenal forms in themselves, and in their highest relations to each other.

Let us now proceed by way of interrogation of the Universe itself, to inquire what it reveals concerning the nature of that Cause which it is universally acknowledged must in some form exist.

CHAPTER III

THE OPEN SECRET. THE ALL-WORKING REASON

As we have seen, the Mind is impelled to seek an explanation of the Universe—of our entire experience—beyond that which Science gives us. As it has been well stated, "The Mind cannot be satisfied with a statement of facts and of laws which are only more general facts. It longs to understand, to pursue facts to the end, and reach the intelligible. Philosophy is just this striving after the intelligible, this desire to discover the meaning of things" (Janet and Séailles, *A Hist. of the Problems of Philos.*, i. 25, 26).

Now, the very fact that the Mind is impelled to seek a rational explanation of the Universe and to reach that truly intelligible in which alone it can rest, implies both that there is such an understanding or explanation of the Universe to be reached, and that only one kind of satisfactory explanation can possibly be found. It is Reason in man that seeks this rational explanation of the Universe, but clearly such an explanation is only possible if the Universe be rationally constituted. Viewed in this light, the secret of the Universe may be said to be an open one.

The advocates of the current Monism, whether in its Materialistic, Agnostic, or other forms, never weary of assuring us that REASON is supreme over man and over all things. Their great aim, they tell us, is to lead men to

THE OPEN SECRET: THE ALL-WORKING REASON 35

a rational way of thinking and acting, through the destruction of the ignorance and superstition that hold us back and keep us down. They constantly inveigh against "the irrational" as that which is false and injurious to man. "Reason," says Haeckel, "is man's highest gift, the only prerogative that essentially distinguishes him from the lower animals." "Pure Reason" is to rule in every sphere; only by the use of Reason can we reach any measure of truth; only by following Reason can good come to the individual or to Society.

With all this, of course, we heartily agree, if only by "Reason" is meant, not my individual Reason merely, i.e. Reason as it is presently organised in and perceived by me, but Reason itself as that which becomes more or less organised in us all, but which is always higher or greater than that which is at any given moment present in, or to, me, or any number of men. Reason is something above and beyond us all, and it is ever becoming more and more completely organised in men as they follow its teaching as it is expressed in Nature and as it shines within themselves. How great is the difference in this respect between, say, an African Bushman and an English Scientist or a German Philosopher. The writers to whom we have referred must have *this* conception of Reason in view, for they are constantly appealing to men, already in some measure rational, in order to make them more rational; and surely they cannot believe that, even in themselves, Reason exists in its full or absolute perfection. There is, therefore, a Reason above and beyond us all, to which we constantly appeal. What is this Reason above and beyond ourselves in its fulness—this Reason the supremacy of which every man must maintain, and to which in all that he says he must ever make appeal? Is it not just another name for GOD in one aspect of His Being—an aspect which is manifested in the Universe around us, finding its culmination in ourselves? Is it not just *the presence and working of this prior Reason* that makes us rational beings?

Not at all, we are told, we simply deceive ourselves. We are only projecting our own Reason into the Universe. Professor Karl Pearson ridicules the Stoics and Hooker for inferring Reason behind the concatenation of phenomena. " Reason," he tells us, " is known to us only with accompaniment of a certain type of nervous organism. Thus to infer Reason in what has been previously postulated as outside and independent of this type of nervous organism is unjustifiable ; it may be dogma, it is not logic. . . . As soon as man begins to form conceptions from his sense-impressions, to generalise, then he begins to project his own reason into phenomena" (*Grammar of Science*, first edition, pp. 108, 109). There is nothing more common or more popularly effective than the affirmation that Reason is only known to us in association with a certain type of nervous organism "Universal Law is not a product of a Universal Mind," says Dr. G. Gore in his *Scientific Basis of Morality*, " because there exists no known Mind without a Brain" (pp. 22, 27). On this ground Haeckel even audaciously asserts that the God of the Theist must be " a gaseous Vertebrate." The effectual answer to all this, as given by several of these writers themselves, will appear immediately, and other objections will be dealt with in due course.

There are *three ways* in which the existence and supremacy of Reason in ourselves leads us to a conviction of the reality of God, in virtue of which the Universe should be to us " an open secret."

1. *From the Origin of Reason in Ourselves*

Whence did the Reason that is organised in ourselves and which we regard as the highest thing in us come?

THE OPEN SECRET: THE ALL-WORKING REASON 37

We shall find a very clear answer to this all-important question if we ask HOW Reason comes to be organised in us In common with the most recent Science, Monistic writers with one voice assure us that this result has been achieved solely through the relation of organisms to the Universe around them and their constant interactions therewith, the results of which we inherit. In this way they exhibit the gradual development of Mind from its lowliest commencements to its supremacy in man. "The mind of man," says Dr. Gore, "must to a large extent agree with universal law and order, simply because the Universe has to a certain extent educated and trained the human brain to be its mirror and representative" (p. 22), and he quotes Buchner in his *Force and Matter* to the same effect.

Now it is just this that proves the priority of Reason in the Universe, and that gives the most effective answer to the anti-Theistic and the Agnostic argument.

This is a matter of so great importance in its bearing on an ultimate interpretation of the World, that it is desirable to support our assertion by some quotations from Agnostic and Monistic writers, especially as the real significance of this great truth is not so generally apprehended as it ought to be. Spinoza said long ago that the order and connection of ideas is the same as the order and connection of things In Mr. Spencer's teaching it is a distinctive element —one now widely acknowledged—that all that constitutes human faculty consists of accumulated modifications caused by the interaction of the organism with its environment, registered organically, and inherited by us. From his writings we might quote many passages in support of this, but the following from the *Principles of Psychology* is sufficient · " Regarded under every variety of aspect, intelligence is found to consist in the establishment of correspondences between relations in the organism and relations in the environment, and the entire development of intelligence may be formulated as the progress of such correspondences in Time, in Space, in Specialty, in Generality, in Complexity." "From first to last its growth (that of Intelligence) is due to the repetition of experiences the effects of which are accumulated, organised, and inherited" (i. 385, 507). What are called "innate ideas" are, he maintains, wholly the results of the experience of the race which have become organised in us. We remark, in passing, that it is not, of course, the *ideas* that are inherited, but the organic structure which subserves them, and which has had *all along* a mental side. From many passages in Buchner we select the following from his Essay on "*A Priorism and Evolution*": "The human reason or intelligence is but a mirror that reflects the whole; it is the last outcome of the constant intercourse which has been maintained with the outer world for ages innumerable" (*Last Words on Materialism*, pp 64, 65); and he quotes Nageli that "the apparent *a priori* character of general ideas arises from the circumstance that the same order and the same logic hold sway in the subject, as part of the whole, as in the Universe at large" (p. 297). Haeckel's famous theory of mental development is based, of course, on the same principle "The higher vertebrates," he says ("especially those mammals which are most nearly related to man), have just as good a title to "reason" as man himself, and, within the limits of the animal world, there is the same long chain of gradual development of reason as in the case of humanity." (Of course, he means "reason within the limits of the animal organism.") (*The Riddle of the Universe*, pp. 44, etc.) In *The Wonders of Life*, he remarks that Kant's error was failing to recognise that "the Mind, with its innate quality of Reason, had a history—a development." "The curious predisposition to *a priori* knowledge is really the effect of the inheritance of certain

THE OPEN SECRET: THE ALL-WORKING REASON 39

structures of the Brain which have been formed in man's vertebrate ancestors slowly and gradually by adaptation to an association of experiences, and therefore of *a posteriori* knowledge" (p. 11). Therefore Dr. Paul Carus can say " The laws of the world are the prototypes of rationality itself. Human wisdom, and all wisdom of any possible rational being, develops from those conditions and remains in accordance with the formal laws of the cosmos. Human reason is conformity to, it is an expression of, the order of the All. The order of the All contains the possibility of developing reason" (*The Soul of Man*, p. 15).

What is thus stated is not only perfectly true, but it is a truth of the greatest importance, and it is in it that we find the effectual refutation of Materialistic and Agnostic doctrines. It is a necessary conclusion from any real doctrine of Evolution. If all that is in man be the result of a process of gradual development, there is nothing more certain than that the Reason that is in us has been derived solely from the Universe around us.

This follows of necessity even from Spencer's definition of *Life* as " the continuous adjustment of inner relations to outer relations." In the words of Mr. Fiske· " Step by step in the upward advances towards humanity, the environment has enlarged. . . . Every stage of enlargement has had reference to actual existences outside The eye was developed in response to the outward existence of radiant light, the ear in response to the outward existence of acoustic vibrations, the mother's love came in response to the infant's needs, fidelity and honour were slowly developed as the nascent social life required them; everywhere the internal adjustment has been brought about so as to harmonise with some actually existing external fact. Such has been Nature's method, such is the deepest law of life that Science has been able to detect " (*Through Nature to God*, pp 186, 187).

From outside of ourselves, therefore,—from the relations of a long line of ancestral organisms to the Universe as the environment of their life,—the Reason that rises in us has been derived. We are made rational only because phylogenetically we have stood in constant vital relation to a rationally constituted Universe—one that was such both in itself and in its relation to our life. Reason is active and formative in Nature before ever it can become organised in man. We are made rational solely because Nature is throughout rationally constituted. We have here, of course, the answer to Professor Pearson's argument. We do not merely project "our own reason" into Nature, any reason that we possess is derived solely from the relations in which our ancestors have stood to a rationally constituted Universe. REASON was there before ever there was a human or an animal Brain, and only because of its presence could such Brains be formed. It was there, operative and dominant, before ever it could be organised in us. If human reason is but, as we are assured it is, "the reflection in us of the Universe outside of us," then, clearly, the Reason was there, expressed in the Universe, before it possibly could be so reflected in us. It is our relation to the Universe that makes us rational.

If any further confirmation of this truth be necessary, we find it when we ask what the process which we call "reasoning" really is on its physical side, and how it leads to correct conclusions or to truth. The newer Psychology enables us to answer these questions very clearly. It shows us that, while reasoning has a mental side of which we are, to a large degree at least, conscious, it also has a physical side the operation of which proceeds quite unconsciously to ourselves, the results only appearing in Consciousness. Every perception we have and every concept that we form leaves traces in the marvellous substance of the Brain, and the process proceeds (on the physical side) by means of the coming of these into agreement. It is only when this agreement is reached that we have that feeling of mental rest or satisfaction which accompanies the reaching a sound conclusion or the finding of a truth And further, it is obvious that the soundness of our reasoning and the truth of our conclusions consist in their agreement with external reality, if we are dealing with objects outside ourselves ; in other words, it is reason in us at one with the Reason in Nature. Here again we may quote Mr. Spencer. " Life, whether physical or psychical," he assures us, " in its most abstract definition, is the continuous adjustment of internal relations to external relations Every advance in intelligence essentially consists in the establishment of more varied, more complete, and more involved, adjustments Even the highest generalisations of Science consist of mental relations of co-existence and sequence that occur externally. . . . What we call truth, guiding us to successful action, and the consequent maintenance of life, is simply the accurate correspondence of subjective to objective relations , while error, leading to failure, and therefore towards death, is the absence of such accurate correspondence " (*First Principles*, pp 61–63) The whole subject is fully illustrated in *The Principles of Psychology*.

We have already, to some extent, seen how the universal working of Reason throws light upon, and is itself supported by, those facts of pre-conscious intelligence which the newer Psychology brings to light Our conscious intelligence is now generally acknowledged to be the outcome of a long series of steps of a truly mental, though pre-conscious, nature, and our whole conscious life is but a wave on the surface of a deep sea of mentality of which we are not conscious (while we may be partially conscious of its presence within us). This unconscious foundation of our intelligence, this intelligence beneath consciousness, on which our consciousness rests, is the most wonderful thing about our mental life. All our conscious intelligence arises out of this unconscious, but intelligent, action. How great it is and how essential to our mental life in this world, will appear if we think of our constant unconscious interpretation of the often extremely delicate physical stimuli which come to us into mental terms; the numerous very minute and complex co-ordinations of muscles, etc., in seeing, hearing, speaking, singing, and in the various kinds of dexterous, often automatic, action; the extremely delicate, yet distinct, perception of colours in scenes, and of sounds in music But if it be indeed *Reason* that forms all things and that works all in all, up to the point of our free voluntary action (where, as it were, it lends itself to us in conscious form), we find the explanation of what is otherwise so inexplicable. On the one hand, all the elements that enter our life are rationally ordered elements, and, on the other hand, the Power that is working at the basis of our life is the same rational Power that has wrought all in the external world. We need not wonder, therefore, to see that Power working as Reason in ourselves, or to behold it showing itself as Consciousness.

It thus clearly appears that all that man speaks of as "reasoning" and the very highest achievements of human reason are possible only because Reason is first expressed in the Universe around us, working in all things; and that our reasoning is true only when it truly reflects the expression of the Reason that is outside ourselves. *Apart from the Reason expressed in the Universe around him, man could never have become the rational being that he is.*

We would place special emphasis on this fact, because its importance (or even the fact itself) is not always perceived, and because we have in it, by the showing of those same writers who seem to many to make the reality of a Divine Reason uncertain, if they do not always, as in some instances, flatly deny its existence, an unanswerable proof of the reality and working of that Reason. Were there no prior Reason working in Nature, there could never, by any possibility, be in man that Reason which is his chief boast, to which anti-Theistic writers make their appeal, and which they say they desire to see made supreme in every sphere of life. But, indeed, to the open mind it must seem an utter impossibility to derive the rational from the non-rational.

2. *Any Real Solution must be a Rational one*

We are sure beforehand that any real solution of the problem of the Universe, or any sound philosophical explanation of it, MUST BE A RATIONAL ONE.

It is reason in us that enables us to see that there is a problem to be solved; it is for the satisfaction of our rational nature that we desire a solution; it is reason alone that can attempt to find it; and the only solution that we can rest in must, we are sure, be one in accordance with reason, one in which reason will find satisfaction. The irrational must be rejected just because it *is* irrational any offered explanation will gain acceptance just according to the measure in which it is rational.

Now, what does all this imply? It implies the supremacy of that Reason which is only another name for God, and it makes it certain that, if any satisfactory explanation be possible at all, the Universe must be rationally constituted, for only from such a Universe can a rational explanation be derived. Reason asks for a solution, and yet knows, *in the very asking*, that only in an explanation which shows Reason in all things can the solution be found. No possible answer is there save that which is implied in the very asking of the question. We demand a rational explanation of the Universe; but by the very terms of our requirement, such an explanation can only be given if the Universe be constituted *by Reason*. It is the reason in us that asks, and only in the recognition of the same Reason outside of ourselves can the reason that is in us be satisfied. Why this is so we have already seen: it is because the Reason that works outside has come to be organised in us; and this is really so much of God in us, so that there is a sense in which we may say with Emerson,

> "Thou askest in fountains and in fires
> He is the Essence that inquires"

It is something of God in us—Reason—that leads us to seek after God. Strange, surely, that in name of the same reason—derived as it must have been—we should deny His existence!

3. *The Intelligibility of Nature*

THE STUDY OF NATURE IMPLIES THAT NATURE IS INTELLIGIBLE

We seek our explanation of the World by means of the study of Nature · we come to Nature to interrogate her and to try to understand her. We seek to interpret Nature in the light of the reason that shines within us. But, surely, this implies that Nature *is* interpretable by reason, that Nature is intelligible, that if we interrogate Nature we shall get rational answers. This is the assumption that underlies all Science, and it is abundantly justified by the results of our study of Nature. What is any Science but the formulated statement of the rational answers which men have received to their interrogation of Nature—the discoveries they have made of the Reason in the "things" or "laws" of Nature?

It is true that our mental construction of Nature may not always be correct, although it may *seem* quite rational to us. Scientific theories which have been left behind for truer ones, show this quite clearly. But still, all that

THE OPEN SECRET: THE ALL-WORKING REASON 45

this proves is that we make mistakes; the principle that leads to rectification is always the conviction that rationality dominates Nature. Science finds, to use a phrase of Romanes', that Nature is "instinct" with Reason; "tap her where you will, reason oozes out at every pore."

The Uniformity of Nature

On every hand we are assured that the guiding principle of Science is that of the UNIFORMITY OF NATURE. But this uniformity is there solely because of the rationality of Nature. It implies an order, a unity, an undeviating principle and mode of action in Nature. "The belief underlying all Science is that an orderly sequence is invariably present, could it only be traced" (Whetham, *The Recent Development of Physical Science*, p. 30) Why is there such a unity and such a uniform order in every particle, in every movement, and in all the interactions of Nature, so that the Mathematician can go far beyond the Physicist, and, following the conceptions of "pure reason," reach conclusions which may be long afterwards experimentally established? Solely because Nature represents Reason in every part and movement, whether in the infinitely great or the infinitesimally minute. This may sometimes be hidden from us by phrases, as when "the uniformity of Nature" is said to mean simply that "like causes everywhere in like circumstances produce the same effects." There may seem to be only the fact that it is so, with no explanation of it necessary or possible. But that like causes always produce like effects, is only another form of affirming that Reason rules in Nature. Strictly speaking, there is no such thing as this apparently simple causation known to physical Science; the whole exists in one great concatenation, and the principle of the uniformity of Nature is at bottom the statement that there is order, even rational order, in the whole. As Mr. J. T. Merz remarks in his *History of European Thought in the Nineteenth Century*, "The subject which remains for discussion is not any special form of order, but the fact that any kind of order exists at all and that it is accessible to the human intellect. Clearly this is a question which affects Nature the object, as much as the human intellect, the subject."[1]

The Rationality of Nature

It is this rational constitution of Nature alone that makes Science possible. What can we find more rational, within its limits, than an accurate, well-grounded work on any Scientific subject? But where does it all come from, if not from the rational Universe? If the Universe were not rational at every point, there could be no Science and no knowledge of Nature. All this has been often said before, but it will bear repetition in view of recent attempts to deny it—made so strangely, too, in the very name of Reason.[2] The phrase "the Book of Nature" is more than

[1] This, it may be noted, was one of the discoveries which led the late Mr. Romanes from Agnosticism to Theism In his *Candid Examination of Theism* he had replied to the Rev. Baden Powell's powerful statement of the existence of reason "in the immutably connected order of objects examined, independently of the mind of the investigator," by asserting that all was explained by Spencer's principle of the "persistence of Force" He came to see that "physical causation cannot be made to supply its own explanation," and that "the mere persistence of Force, even if it were conceded to account for particular cases of physical sequence, can give no account of the ubiquitous and eternal direction of Force in the constitution and maintenance of universal order." "It is enough," he says, "to take our stand upon the (broadest) general fact that Nature is a System and that the order observable in this system is absolutely universal, eternally enduring, and infinitely exact , while only on the supposition of its being such is our experience conceived as possible, or our knowledge conceived as attainable" (*Thoughts on Religion*, pp. 69–72)

[2] See especially Dr. Samuel Harris's *The Philos Basis of Theism* and *The Self-Revelation of God*, and quotations from Idealistic authors given in Note III , at end of chapter.

THE OPEN SECRET: THE ALL-WORKING REASON

a convenient expression We do not indeed read Nature as we read a book in which the symbols that express thoughts or reasons are already understood. We come rather to Nature as to some Script which we believe has an ordered connection and meaning, and this we strive to understand and express in rational terms. The one thing we are sure of is that there *is* an orderly connection there, capable of being found and of being expressed in terms of Reason. It is only the fact that there *is* an order represented there—the fact that all things stand, not in a haphazard relation, but in a rational connection—that makes it possible for us to read the Book of Nature. Nature is, in this sense, the Book from which all that is written in our books of Science is derived As Sir John Lubbock in his Presidential Address to the British Association in 1881—referring to the progress which had been made in Biology—said: "Fifty years ago ... the Book of Nature was like some richly-illuminated Missal, written in an unknown tongue ... of the true meaning little was known to us; indeed, we scarcely realised that there was a meaning to decipher Now, glimpses of the truth are gradually revealing themselves, we perceive that there is a reason—and in many cases we know what that reason is—for every difference in form, in size, and in colour, for every bone and every feather, almost for every hair." To this we add one of the most recent statements of "the intellectual Ideal" from the standpoint of Biology, which is equally true for the other Sciences· "Like any other Science, Biology has, for one of its ideals, to gain a clear, orderly, correlated, and interpretable view of Nature. It analyses and pulls to pieces, but only as a means to an end, in order, sooner or later, to put them together again, unified in intelligence. Many a chaotic corner is acquiring a semblance of rational order," etc (Professors Thomson and Geddes in *Ideals of Faith and Science*, pp. 74, 75).

If we go down to those atoms, which are the "building stones" of the physical Universe—"the alphabet of God"—we see the same evidence of law and order, "each molecule (atom) bears," Professor Clerk Maxwell said, "the stamp of a metric system as distinctly as does the metre of the Archives at Paris, or the double royal cubit of the Temple of Karnac . . . the exact equality of each molecule to all others of the same kind gives it, as Sir John Herschel has well said, the essential character of a manufactured article, and precludes the idea of its being eternal and self-existent." This is strikingly manifest in that "periodic law" of Mendeléef which has been called "the fundamental law of the mystery of matter," which states that "the properties of an element are a periodic function of its atomic weight"; so that, to quote Professor Duncan, "if you know the weight of the atom of the element, you may know, if you like, its properties, for they are fixed." This indicates a great fundamental scheme of, or rather, *expressed in*, the very elements, which is never departed from, and in its working out really gives us the entire physical Universe, for the law prevails in the farthest star as truly as on the earth.

So sure and unchangeable is this law of the elements, that, "when Mendeléef enunciated his law and made his table (of the elements) originally, he found it necessary, in order to make the table true, to leave . . . three spaces vacant for *undiscovered elements*, and, not content with this, he proceeded in 1871, on the basis of the law, to predict the properties which these elements should possess when discovered." He did this "with extreme minuteness." And, wonderful as it may well appear, "out of the night of the unknown, one after another"—of these very elements, with their identical properties as predicted—"came to meet him. One from the hills of Scandinavia, another from the Pyrenees of France, and a third from the mines of Germany" (*The New Knowledge*, pp 22–34).

THE OPEN SECRET: THE ALL-WORKING REASON

No doubt it may be said that the concepts of Science are only a kind of "mental shorthand" in which we express what we have reason to believe to lie beyond our "sense impresses" and our interpretation of them. But we gain thus a wonderful statement in terms of Reason of that which we believe to exist as the order of the Universe, so far as we can reach it. We find that these concepts and our formulæ of rational order *work* when applied to facts, and give us a measure of command over the things of the material Universe, so that they serve our advancing life, where they do not so work, we know that we have erred, and we correct them accordingly. It may be true, also, that "we can only study Nature through our senses—that is, we can only study the model of Nature that our senses enable us to construct; we cannot decide whether the model, consistent though it may be, represents truly the real structure of Nature; whether indeed there be any Nature as an ultimate reality behind its phenomena" (Whetham, *op. cit* p. 14). But one thing we *do* know, of one thing we can be sure. we always find order, rational order; the rational order which our interrogation of the Universe reports is real, for it is its presence alone that makes Science possible, and it is the source of all that we know as "reason" or "rationality," of the only light in which we can see at all, or can ever hope to see in. It is itself the only light that can be seen; we have in *it*, not in "things," that which belongs to real knowledge.

To say, as the new Philosophical School of Pragmatism or Humanism seems to do, that our rational interpretation of Nature is one which is made to serve our human purposes, does not throw any doubt on the validity of that interpretation. It is simply to say that we make it in the only way in which we could conceivably make it, viz, in the effort to live our life. This is precisely the way in which, as Science shows us, we have become rational beings.

When it is said that if our senses were different, the world would be different to us, it is forgotten that the senses of man, as well as those of all animals, have been formed by actual contact with the world. They *could not be different* from what they are And, as Buchner remarks, " Were our senses *increased*, as conceivably they might be, we should not find the world different from what we do now, but perhaps be able to perceive directly movements in Nature which we only now learn by observation and experiment. In other words, our direct world-picture would probably be richer and more comprehensive, but not substantially *different* from what it is. It would be, not a subversion, but an expansion, or, more properly, a relief of our knowledge." Even if the movements in the outer world acquire in our sense organs a number of properties which we ascribe to them, they are none the less real and the foundation of all our knowledge (*op cit.* pp 294, 295).

Anything that can be rightly called knowledge is possible only because our minds are in relation to a rationally constituted, that is, a spiritual, world. This the late Mr. T. H. Green made very clear. Our perceptions are not of isolated elements, whether of matter or of force, but of things in their relations—of the relations between them. Our knowledge consists solely of relations apprehended and held together by the mind: " A perceived object is an apprehended fact, it is a synthesis of relations in consciousness." If then our knowledge consists of thought-relations, it is an inevitable conclusion that the world that we gradually come to know must consist of thought-relations also— it must be " a single all-inclusive system of relations ; intelligible to my reason, though not yet all understood." It involves in its very nature as a related whole, "some principle which renders all relations possible, and is itself determined by none of them " (*Prolegomena to Ethics*, Fairbrother, *The Philosophy of T. H. Green*).

And although all our knowledge comes to us through the senses, and even if we were, as certain Subjective Idealists affirm, wholly shut up within our Material Organism, sitting, as it were, cooped up within the narrow walls of our prison house—at " the termination of our nerves of sensation," so that we had nothing to go by but the sense impressions that find their way in to us, the fact that that which they convey is ever the *intelligible* and the only source of anything that can be called intelligence, proves that there is no reason to doubt that Intelligence is at the other end, before and outside ourselves. There is no reason to doubt this save, as Miss E. M. Caillard remarks, " the fear of being involved in Metaphysics or Theology " (*Contemporary Review*, March 1905). But, surely, such a fear is unworthy of those who profess to follow Reason and to seek the Truth.

Finding Truth

There is yet another way in which we may put it The possibility of finding TRUTH implies a rationally constituted Universe. We seek Truth, we say, but, what is Truth ? Truth is the agreement of our thought with reality. But if reality be not apprehensible in thought, there can be no such thing as *truth* for us If reality be not presented in the phenomenal world, how can it ever be represented in Thought by our minds ? It is always Thought that is the reality. It is in the forms of reason or of Thought that all manifestations of being whatever reveal themselves to us. They are only known in Consciousness in intellectual or spiritual forms. What comes to us as physical, we translate into spiritual forms or terms, and unless the spiritual were that which underlies and is expressed in and by all material forms and forces, any real knowledge or Truth would be for ever impossible to us. There is no mysterious, impenetrable " thing in itself " behind the objects of the external world, such as Kant left as an unknowable quantity; but there is a " thing in itself" beneath each *material* object in the sense that each material object is so far an expression of rational thought, in the same way as the *Meaning* underlies the words and each letter of the words, which in their connection make up a rational sentence. It is just this rational connection and meaning that we get at in things and their relations, in so far as we get at truth, meaning, reality, at all.

The Reality of Thought in its various forms of expression

Thought, every one knows, can be expressed in an endless variety of ways. It can be written in a thousand different languages, it can be expressed in shorthand by an infinite diversity of symbols, spoken on the fingers, or by lip movements, and indicated by glances and gestures. It can be expressed in hieroglyphics or ciphers, which it is impossible to read until we discover the key to them ; yet it is the same thought, the same REALITY in all these forms Thought can be embodied in sculpture, made to shine forth in painting, or to swell out in music so as to stir the deepest emotions of our souls. We see it working in all our machinery,—some of our automatic machines seem almost living, thinking things,—standing forth in our buildings, embodied in institutions,—in short, in the world in which we live, almost everything is the expression of Thought or Feeling ; and the thoughts and feelings are so truly prior to, and often so much greater than, that which gives them expression, that the artist or the thinker never feels that he has given adequate expression to that which was in him. Nothing is commoner, indeed, than to hear people say that they are unable to put their thoughts into words.

However expressed, it is ever the THOUGHT that is the

THE OPEN SECRET: THE ALL-WORKING REASON

reality: "ideas move the world." John Wickliffe, for example, reaches certain weighty thoughts on religion, and he expresses them, let us say, in the English tongue—the *words*, whether spoken or written, being simply the symbols of his thoughts. Those who understand English can share his thoughts, feel their inspiration, become his followers John Hus in Bohemia hears of these new doctrines, and he wishes to know them. But to him the English words convey no meaning; not because they are not the expression of thoughts or that the thoughts they express are not realities, but because they are symbols which he cannot interpret. But let him find them translated into Latin (in which language, of course, Wickliffe's principal works were actually written), and he at once takes in their meaning and receives the thought of Wickliffe; they so influence him that he goes at length to the stake in his devotion to them. He, in turn, translates these thoughts into the common language of Bohemia, and men arise as if created anew. Gradually these thoughts are extended by means of various other symbols, and the whole face of Christendom becomes changed. The reality all through has, clearly, been, not the material forms or symbols, but the thoughts that could be thus variously expressed, while they remained identical in all their forms.

Thought is thus a reality prior to and independent of its expression, it is the one Reality in the world; and there is no reason why it may not find expression in the forms and laws of Nature as truly as in words spoken or written by men, or in human machines and institutions. It is a higher and prior Thought to ours that is expressing itself in Nature, and it is this fact alone, we repeat, that makes Truth or Science possible to us. We go to Nature and get the meaning and connection of things in some particular department, and the result is what we term Science or knowledge of Nature. We express by certain symbols our interpretation of certain other symbols which we find in Nature. We put together what our interpretation of these Nature-symbols gives us, and the outcome is the intelligible and charming story of the Sciences. Let it not be said that we put a meaning into what we see that is not there. The prime necessity for a scientific interpreter of Nature is that he should be a careful observer and a truthful recorder, setting down nothing but what he actually finds there. He notes his facts and sets them down; he brings them into relation amongst themselves and into relation with other facts, and what we find as the result is the very ideal of that which we all agree to regard as rational.

Nature is *mechanism*, we are told. But who ever heard of a machine that was not a construction of *Mind*? It is always Mind that constitutes the various separate parts a mechanism, and makes them all work together to some definite end. As a recent writer says, " What do we mean by saying that the Universe is intelligible? As regards our own human workmanship, intelligence is exhibited in all work in which there are parts which bear an ordered relation to each other, and in which the whole is something more than the mere sum of the individual parts" (Dr. J. A. Fleming in *The Evidence of Things not Seen*, which gives in succinct form the proofs of order in the Universe).

Causation and Reason

Indeed, we must ask, Is not this principle of REASON identical with that of CAUSATION? Mr. Romanes has written impressively concerning the marvel of this universal fact of Causation. " That every thing that happens should have a cause, that this should invariably be proportioned to its effect, so that no matter how complex the interaction of causes, the same interaction should always produce the

THE OPEN SECRET: THE ALL-WORKING REASON

same result; that this rigidly exact system of energising should be found to present all the appearances of universality and of eternity, so that the motion of the solar system in space is being determined by some causes beyond human ken, and that we are indebted to billions of cellular unions each involving billions of separate causes, for our hereditary passage from an invertebrate ancestry,—that such things should be, would surely strike us as the most wonderful fact in this wonderful Universe." Yet, beyond the fact that "our knowledge of it is derived from our own activity when we ourselves are causes," it has never been explained (*op. cit.* pp. 116, 117). Is not the only explanation that is possible of the rational connection manifest in all natural causation, the constant operation of *Reason* everywhere? Causation is really the fact that one thing follows another because of the rational connection of things. "Cause and Effect" is only a form of stating that constant Divine action which we ascribe to "Reason."

Nothing is more rational than Science; but a rational Science of an irrational Universe would be an impossibility, we can only have a statement of the facts of Nature in terms of Reason if the Nature which we read and record is first of all rational—that is, constituted by Reason. It is only by our ability in the light of the Reason that has come from Nature itself to shine within us, to read so much of the great Book of Nature, that our books of Science can be written. It is possible only because we are thus enabled in some measure, as Kepler said, "to think God's thoughts after Him." If Nature were not the expression of Reason, it would no more be possible to get Science or knowledge from a study of the Universe than it would be to derive rational meaning from a book which no rational Mind had ever written.

Monistic Criticism of the Argument

Mr. McCabe, in his able defence of Haeckel, ventures to characterise a similar argument to that which we have advanced under this head, as being "simply an audacious assertion," if there be a real world, although it would be correct, he says, if there were only an ideal world. But it is precisely of the real world that we make the assertion, and because of what we find therein. He ridicules the statement of Dr. Iverach, that "a system which at this end needs an intelligence to understand it must have something to do with intelligence at the other." "To show the inanity of the assertion," he says, "one has only to ask . . . whether even a chaotic and disorderly Universe would not need an intelligence to understand it." We fear that not even the intelligence of a Haeckel would be able to understand such a Universe. He might *describe* it in a way; but the statement of it would be that of "a chaotic and disorderly Universe," not that statement of order and rational connection which Science brings us from the Universe that we actually know, and from which the intelligence in ourselves is derived. In Wilkie Collins' story of *The Evil Genius*, a difficult cipher, supposed to contain the secret of the whereabouts of a large sum of money, is brought to an expert to read. He rejoices in it just because of its difficulty, believing that, after due study, he will discover the key to it, and he ultimately succeeds in deciphering the markings. But if these markings, strange as they were, had been "chaotic" merely, and not the expression of thought or of rational meaning—in other words, had there been no *rational order* at all in them, he could never have translated them into rational terms. No more could Nature ever be so interpreted, unless it were the expression of Reason. In our first attempts our rendering may be wrong, but there is always something that gives us to see this, and we are impelled again and again to try just because of our confidence that a rational order *is* everywhere expressed, if only we can read it aright.

Summary

We say, therefore, that the secret is an open one. The rational Universe declares its origin in Reason to the rational nature in ourselves. The reason that inquires has itself come from the Universe it inquires about, and it can only have so come because that Universe was, first of all, rationally constituted. In every answer that we bring, and in all that we say, we must make our appeal to a Reason greater than the Reason that is, as yet, organised in ourselves. The answer, we know beforehand, must be a rational one, and that is only possible if the Universe is the expression of Reason. Again, only Reason can satisfy Reason, Reason can only be at rest when she finds herself in the Universe, and only in a rationally constituted Universe can she so find herself; for only such a Universe is susceptible of a rational explanation. Finally, in any attempt to study the Universe, we must assume that it is so constituted that it will answer to our reason; and going to it thus, we are not disappointed. In other words, underlying our own rationality, and at the foundation of all our Science and of all our knowledge of Nature, there is implicitly the assumption of an all-organising Reason, and this assumption is borne out, not only by the results of such study of Nature, but also by what Science now shows us regarding the way in which we have ourselves become rational beings. In its establishment of this last-mentioned point, Science has rendered (however unconsciously) the greatest service to Religion. In every way we are carried to a prior Reason that manifests itself in the Universe, to the working of which therein we owe our own rationality. On every hand, therefore, the reality of GOD is witnessed to us. For, what is this prior, this universal, this all-organising Reason, but God as the Universe reveals Him to the reason which has come to shine in us as the highest outcome of the working of Reason in the Universe?

How far does this carry us?

But, it may be asked, How far does this carry us? Does it lead to the Christian conception of God? Does it give us a personal God? Is this Reason conscious of itself? Is it anything different from "necessity"? At this stage we will only very briefly indicate the answers to these questions.

1. The contemplation of the Universe apart from the supreme manifestation of the moral and spiritual life in its Source as it found expression in Jesus Christ, cannot, of course, reveal God to us in the full Christian sense. This is only to say that we cannot know the truth of that which is the deepest formative principle till we behold its highest manifestation. But it prepares the way and enables us to recognise the manifestation when it is given. There is more at the foundation of the Universe than "Reason" abstractly considered: there is Power, Purpose, Will, Love But what is implied in the thought of a perfect Reason will appear as we proceed with our argument.

2. The idea of a rational world leads us certainly to that of a Divine Mind as its Source and producing Power. Reason in us is founded in the experience of Law and Order in our life in its relation to the world It implies an ordered connection of things, our "reasoning" is just the seeking and finding and practical following out of those connections in things or in subjects of thought. It implies, therefore, that the Universe, as it has revealed itself to us and within us, is embraced in *one Ideal system*. The connection in

which all its parts stand manifests this, and we can only conceive of such a system as existing in a Mind or Purpose.

3. We cannot think of the all-containing Reason save as being self-conscious. The very idea of *Reason* as distinguished from blind unreason, of rational as opposed to irrational action, implies knowledge of what is being done—conscious, purposive action. Apart from this it would not be "Reason" at all. At the same time, as will be yet shown, we must distinguish between the Divine Reason *as it is in itself* and as it becomes *conditioned* for the purpose of creation

4. Whether we are led to a personal God or not, depends on whether we make the above-mentioned distinction, or, in other words, whether we rise above "Nature" or not. As we shall see more fully at a later stage, the Reason that is actually conditioned and working in the evolving world, or in "Nature," is rather, *as we see it there*, a *principle* comparable to that of an organism, than a personal Being But when we rise from this conditioned manifestation of God to the Divine Reason that is its Source and from which it is never to be severed, we cannot, as already said, think of that Reason in itself as other than self-conscious. This contains in it, we believe, all that is required for personality When we try to go beyond this we are in danger of forgetting the Christian definition of God as *Spirit* (not *a* Spirit), and of making Him a finite person amongst other persons merely, which, of course, He cannot be. As the all-containing Reason of the Universe, He is certainly not impersonal, or lower than "personal," but has in Himself all the elements that constitute personality in us, without their limitations.

5. Moreover, we cannot think of this Reason save as being in constant expression. We cannot imagine the Divine Reason as at some moment of Time *beginning*

to express itself. To give expression to itself belongs to the very idea of Reason.

6. As regards the equivalence of Reason with Necessity, it is certainly in this form that, in the physical world, it appears to us. But the necessity that rules there is such, just because it is all the expression of Reason. It is a *rational necessity*—a rational, necessary *connection* that reigns everywhere, forming the intelligible world and constituting us rational beings. Of course, when once we are constituted rational beings, with freedom of choice and capacity of action from a rational centre in ourselves, Reason is differently conditioned.

The relation of the Divine Reason to the World and ourselves, as well as some of the other questions here noticed, will come up again for fuller consideration. Meanwhile, it is something to have seen that the Universe around us and the presence of Reason in ourselves, bear indisputable witness to the reality of a Reason prior to our own, from the workings of which reason in ourselves has been derived. We have thus one aspect of God so clearly revealed to us that the question of the nature of the Source of our being may be truly said to be "an open secret" to all who care to read it.

We will conclude this portion of our subject by a brief statement of the light that is thus thrown on the relation of Science to Religion.

Science and Religion

It is the proud boast of Science as represented by many savants, that in it "a new factor has been introduced into all problems whatsoever," and that it "will end by destroying all pretensions to mysterious beliefs and every form of superstition" So says M. Berthelot, and Haeckel speaks in much the same strain Now, Science has, without doubt, rendered much real service to Religion. So far as it is the Truth, it can only serve the Truth, although the harmony of old and new Truths may not at once appear. On the other hand, Religion has rendered far more help to Science than is commonly acknowledged, notwithstanding the opposition in which it has sometimes stood towards Science. It was, deepest of all, a religious impulse that led to the earnest study of Nature.

No one would wish for a moment to detract from the glory of Science, to doubt the possibilities of progress in every direction that its faithful study contains, to be without admiration for the devotion of its followers, or to regret its destruction of every form of superstition. But, under this last function, the destruction of Religion itself is too often included, as witness the proceedings at the Free-thought Congress, in 1904, in Rome, presided over by M. Berthelot. Of course, there are many who are justly entitled to be regarded as the representatives of Science who would repudiate any hostility to Religion, and who seek rather by means of Science to serve Religion. We must also discount certain conditions peculiar to the Continent in relation to Religion. But if the position which we have maintained be a sound one, this opposition to Religion on the part of certain Scientists implies a strange and lamentable misunderstanding. Whence does Science derive its insight and power? From no other source but the relation in which the human organism has stood to the world around it. And whence is the knowledge which Science applies derived? Unquestionably from the same source In both ways we see that the Reason in man, of which he is so proud, and which is to do such mighty things, has been derived from the working of Reason in Nature, and is but the continued working of the same Reason as it has become consciously organised in the human Brain—as it has committed itself to us, in fact. The greatest achievements of Science also—of Reason in man—are but repetitions of what Reason in Nature has wrought before him. When, for example, we see M. Berthelot "creating" organic substances, he is but accomplishing what has been done in Nature for countless centuries. The conscious Reason in him is only taking up and carrying on the work which Reason, otherwise conditioned, has been doing in Nature. So that, instead of there being any cause for a breach between Science and Religion, we behold in Science the truest witness to the presence and working of a prior Reason in Nature. That which Science accomplishes can only be done because so much of the Divine Reason has, through man's relation to Nature, become organised in man in a finite, conscious form. The true man of Science, therefore, with that loyalty to fact that distinguishes him, and with that view to the progress of humanity in every direction that ought to animate him in all his work, is really, if he only knew it, the Agent of that Divine Reason which has from the first been working in the world—the Agent through whom that Reason seeks to continue and to complete its work—giving to man in his freedom a personal share therein, and thus, so far, constituting him, not merely a servant, but a son of God. "My Father worketh hitherto, and I work," said Christ, the perfect Son.

Note I. The doctrine of the gradual development of man's mental faculties, up to Reason itself, from the relation of his organism to his environment, aided by natural selection, etc, is simply that of Evolution in general. To the quotations already given from Monistic writers, we add some others from recent writers whom we do not attempt to classify. (1) Although Dr. Wallace differs from most other Evolutionists with respect to the origin of man's higher intellectual and moral nature, he accepts the *principle* which, carried out, gives the results affirmed by most Evolutionists. In his *Darwinism* he says: "We may admit, at all events provisionally, that the laws of variation and natural selection, acting through the struggle for existence and the continual need of more perfect adaptation to the physical and biological environments, may have brought about, first that perfection of bodily structure in which he (man) is so far above all other animals, *and in co-ordination with it the larger and more developed brain* (italics ours) by means of which he has been able to utilise that structure in the more and more complete subjection of the whole animal and vegetable kingdom to his service" (p. 461).

(2) Mr Hobhouse, in his *Mind in Evolution*, summarises thus "We start from a condition in which ancestral experience, acting indirectly through heredity and the elimination of the less adapted, fits responses to stimuli into an order suited to maintain the racial type in the environment in which it finds itself. Passing out of this condition, we enter on a process in which life is more and more dominated by intelligence" (p. 372).

(3) Dr. Archdall Reid, in his *Present Evolution of Man*, says: "The entire passage, from reflex action in its lowest manifestation to Reason in its highest manifestation, is a process of increasing adaptation to enviroment, increasing in complexity." He holds that it is only the "*tendency to vary*" that is inherited.

Note II. In an article in the *Contemporary Review* for May 1905, Professor Lloyd Morgan thus expresses his belief in Reason in Nature· "The ideal construction of naturalism is admittedly rational and connected. But when this scheme (which is the product of our rational thought) is applied to the data of sensory experience (which are independent of our rational thought, and over which our reason has no control) it is found to fit the given changes of configuration. Hence, just in so far as the connections of the ideal scheme coincide with the sequences of sensory experience, may we assume that these sequences have some underlying connection—something which makes them of such a kind that they can be rationally treated. Science, however, does not attempt to discuss the question why the antecedences and sequences which it studies are of such a kind as we find them them to be. Some of us, nevertheless, as Professor Lamb indicates" (in his Presidential address before Section A. at the meeting of the British Association in 1904, from which the writer had already quoted), "are impelled by the very nature of our rational thought to seek an answer to this question. We, too, have our ideal constructions. We, too, have our beliefs which perchance include more than we can definitely prove. I for one believe that the connected and rational character of our ideal schemes of naturalism have their source and origin in the rational and connected character which underlies objective existence" (p. 622).

Note III. What has been affirmed concerning Reason in Nature is, of course, fundamental in modern *Idealism*. As Dr. Edward Caird says of Hegel, the principle that "the intelligible world is relative to the Intelligence"—"which was expressed by Kant, but of which Kant, by his distinctions of phenomenon and noumenon, reason and faith, evaded the full meaning, is taken in earnest by Hegel" (*Hegel*, p. 140). In further illustration we quote a passage from a recent article by Professor Henry Jones in criticism of Mr Balfour: "Hence, according to the idealistic view, natural science, when it is engaged upon its natural problems, is endeavouring to interpret an aspect, element, or province of a world which is intelligible, and therefore a manifestation of reason. When it seeks to represent such a world as evolving the senses and the reason of man, it does not find itself confronted with the impossible task of showing how the natural can become spiritual, the non-rational rational, or the non-moral moral. Evolution, for it, is not a breach of identity, or the achievement by means of Divine preferential action of something at the end of the process which did not in some potential way exist there at the beginning. It is a process by which a rational world—that is, a world which is the object of reason—gradually reveals and realises itself as a manifestation of reason" (*The Hibbert Journal* for April 1905, p. 474).

So Professor Ritchie also. "All thinking, all effort to know and understand the Universe, in however partial a way, makes the assumption that, in so far at least as we can understand it, it is intelligible, *i.e.* it is a coherent, intelligible system. Philosophy, which aspires to know the Universe as a whole, is one coherent, intelligible system, though there may be much that to minds such as ours must always remain unintelligible" (*Philos. Studies*, p. 73).

But by no one has the principle been stated more clearly or emphatically than by the late Principal Caird "All Science starts," he says, "with the tacit presupposition that Nature is intelligible, that there is reason or thought in things, and its progress is only the ever-advancing discovery of laws, of rational relations, of a coherent, self-consistent system, in the objects and events of the material world. The history of Science is the history of Mind or Intelligence finding itself in Nature." "If Nature were a mere chaos, without law or order or intelligible constitution, knowledge would be impossible, thought could find in the outward world nothing to grasp. But it is because law, rational order and sequence, in one word, because reason exists in Nature that Nature yields itself up to thought or intelligence,"—"throughout the whole realm of Nature there is nothing irrational or unintelligible" (*Introd. to the Philos. of Religion*, pp, 25, 238, 240).

CHAPTER IV

THE REVELATION OF SPIRIT WITHIN OURSELVES

IN another way the secret of the nature of the Supreme Power in the Universe is revealed within ourselves; the Power that works all things in the Universe shows itself as SPIRIT within our own consciousness. Since the doctrine of the "transformation of Energy" (although, as we shall see, this phrase may mislead) has been established and the marvellous unity of Nature been thus more fully brought into view, it is an accepted principle that there is only one sole Power manifested in all the phenomena of the physical Universe On every hand we behold the manifestation of *Power*, and we know its reality from our own experience. If there are those who think they see reasons for stopping short at Life or at Mind in the direct line of the working of that Power, still it cannot be doubted that Life and Mind are but different forms in which the one all-working Power is manifested. But if so, we have the Power that works all in all distinctly revealed within ourselves as Mind or Spirit It has other forms of manifestation in the external world, but it cannot be denied that Mind is one form of its manifestation. And surely it is the highest. It is only through Mind that we know anything about the Universe at all, that we know there is such a thing as the Universe, and it is admittedly in Mind or Spirit that all the working of the one Power in the Universe culminates.

REVELATION OF SPIRIT WITHIN OURSELVES 67

We are therefore bound to look upon Mind or Spirit as the highest revelation of the nature of that Power.

What the Universe contains and reveals

If we take the Universe which we seek to understand as it is actually before us, we find its constituents to be (if we are to regard them separately) Matter, Ether and Energy, Motion, Life and Mind; and if we follow out the conception of these, as far as they are known, we shall find ourselves always carried back to the working of a single *Power*.

Matter and Ether

If we ask what "Matter" is, we know that *practically*, in our everyday experience, it is but the instrument, or material, that serves our purposes; in our everyday life we find Matter ready to our hand, to be used as the servant of our spirits—that through which, in countless ways, we give expression to our ideas and realise our purposes. If we inquire more particularly into its nature, we find that Science is as yet unable to give a complete answer to our questions, although recent developments carry us a long way beyond our former knowledge. For a certain stage of the history of Matter, the Atomic theory still holds good, and it is seen to possess those definite qualities which led Sir John Herschell and Professor Clerk Maxwell to speak of it as "a manufactured article." This character of Matter certainly appears at a certain point, and holds good without a flaw, throughout the Universe, as Spectrum Analysis proves. And if we go back as far as the most recent Science can carry us, we still see the atom appearing as something "made"—the product of a prior Power. Science now goes behind the chemical elements of Dalton, and the old atomic structure of the physicists, to a more primitive element from which the elements as we know them, have been evolved. The original "hard" atoms that were once believed in are now given up, and an approach is being made to a *dynamic* conception of Matter in its constitution. But indeed, as Mr. Spencer remarked long ago, even the old atom was, not only something utterly invisible, and hypothetical, but "a triply ideal conception."

Boscovich's conception of the atom as a centre of force has not yet proved sufficient to meet all the facts, although there is a school of Chemistry which recognises only energy at the foundation of everything. Years ago Lord Kelvin advanced the theory that Matter had its origin in vortex motions in the Ether. We were thus thrown back on the Ether; Matter arose through motion in the Ether, which, of course, implied a Power setting up, and manifested in, that motion. More recently, largely as the result of the experiments of Professor J J. Thomson on the conduction of Electricity through Gases, and of the phenomena manifested by Radio-activity, an *Electric* origin of Matter has been advanced, which still, however, throws us back on the Ether, and on motion in the Ether. What the Ether itself is we are still to a great degree ignorant. It is the medium which conveys to us Light and radiant Heat; it is concerned with the phenomena of Magnetism and Electricity, with life itself, and with nearly every function in the Universe, living and non-living. It is believed to fill all space, carrying Light to us from the farthest stars, and filling the interspaces of what seems to outward appearance the most solid Matter. Its million-fold, yet distinct, undulations, such as are involved in our perceptions of colour, show it to be possessed of the most wonderful powers. If there are those who do not admit the existence of this Ether as something different from Matter, they postulate finer particles of Matter which practically play the same rôle. *Matter is*

REVELATION OF SPIRIT WITHIN OURSELVES 69

now held to be the result of electric movement in the Ether.

Much has been recently written on the subject, but we may most conveniently state this new conception of Matter in the words of Mr. Whetham of Cambridge, whose work on *The Recent Developments of Physical Science* gives in a clear form the latest information on the subject: "To explain all the properties with which we know the chemical atoms to be endowed, and, more especially, their power of complex radiation, it is necessary to represent the atom as a structure containing a large number of electrons in steady orbital motion round each other, somewhat as the planets move within the solar system" (p. 284).[1] Instead of the atom as ultimate, we are now asked to think of extremely minute corpuscles, or electrons, each one of which is negatively electrified, moving in orbits as indicated in the above quotation. It seems that we may best picture to ourselves an atom of Matter as being like a miniature solar system in which some hundreds, or it may be thousands, of electrons are moving round a central *ion*.[2] The property of "mass" or "inertia," which seems to be the outstanding quality of Matter as we see it, is explained as an effect of electricity in motion, so that, in the words of Mr. Whetham, "the physicist may well ask the meta-

[1] Professor Duncan's recent work, entitled *The New Knowledge*, may also be referred to as containing a clear and interesting account of "the new physics and the new chemistry in their relation to the new theory of Matter"

[2] Similarly Professor Duncan states that facts show "that Matter is made up of Electricity and nothing but Electricity" The atom is a sphere of positive Electrification enclosing a number of negatively electrified corpuscles exactly balancing the positive Electricity of the enclosing sphere "*Mass*," or the quantity of matter, is "due to the bound Ether carried along by the charge in its motion" The Electrical charge itself possesses no mass "All mass is the mass of the Ether, all momentum, whether electrical or mechanical, (is) the momentum of the Ether, all Kinetic energy the Kinetic energy of the Ether" (*op. cit* pp. 171, 179, 185).

physical question: Has matter an objective reality; may not its very essence be but a form of disembodied Energy?" (p. 186). This question cannot be answered, of course, till we know better the nature of electricity, which is now regarded as consisting of certain indivisible units arising in some way in the Ether (in current electricity the corpuscles are "handed along" from one atom to another through the wire (Duncan)); but the tendency to a *dynamical* explanation of matter is manifest, and the phenomena of Radio-activity has proved that Matter is not something eternal, but is itself the result of Evolution and is probably undergoing disintegration and transmutation. It is a manifestation of *Power* acting in the Ether.

As for the Ether which underlies ordinary matter, we are told that the tendency now is to give up the old conception of it as an elastic solid, so difficult to comprehend, and to secure the necessary rigidity by thinking of something like a "spin" in it (such as is seen in a top maintaining its vertical position against its weight). It is conceived as "a gyrostatic Æther in which the rigidity is secured by the motion of some still more primal material. Perhaps the Æther is composed of a number of interlacing vortex filaments; its structure may be fibrous like a bundle of hay" (Whetham, p. 279).[1] Matter is thus still thought of as "an Ætherial manifestation," as resulting from a strain in the Ether, although the Ether itself is differently conceived. Electrons, which are "unit charges of Electricity," form the bases of all kinds of Matter. "Matter," says Mr. Whetham, "at any rate in its relation to other matter at a distance, is an electrical manifestation; and Electricity is a state of intrinsic strain in a universal medium. That

[1] Professor Duncan points out that *Mendaléef*, "the doyen of chemical Science, has originated the conception that the Ether, instead of being some mysterious form of non-matter, as generally believed, is actually the lightest and the simplest of the elements, and a definite form of matter" (*op. cit.* p 250)

medium is prior to matter, and, therefore, not necessarily expressible in terms of matter, it is sub-natural, if not super-natural" (p. 282). Matter is thus revealed to us as the result of the operation of Power, and the Ether as the seat or medium of that Power.

Even in atoms, of course, Matter is something extremely minute. We are told that in a cubic centimetre of water—that is, about as much as would go inside the shell of a small filbert—there are about as many as ninety thousand million billion atoms (Shenstone). There is also constant movement, translatory, vibratory, or rotatory. The corpuscles or electrons which make up the atom are small almost beyond expression. One of them, within the (to us) invisible atom, has been compared to a fly buzzing about in a cathedral.

It is held by some that all the phenomena of the Universe depend simply upon different MOTIONS of Matter, so that, since Matter itself is the result of Motion in the Ether, everything may be said to result from different modes of Motion. But wherever there is Motion there must be some moving Power, so that, in any view of it, Matter is essentially a form of manifestation of the One all-working Power.

Energy

The same is clearly true of ENERGY. The old conception of the Forces of Nature and of "Force" itself is now abandoned, *one* ever-changing Energy taking their place As Professor Dolbear remarks: "Analysis has shown that these Forces, Heat, Light, Electricity, etc., differ 'chiefly in the character of the *motion* involved in the phenomena.' So that 'forces' as such have been banished from physical Science, leaving not even a single primal force, for as each one can be changed at will into any of the others, there is simply a closed chain of phenomena, no one of which can be called an elementary one more than any other" (*Matter, Motion, and Ether*, p. 240, etc.). Energy manifestly implies power, its scientific definition is "the power of doing work." Professor Duncan defines it as "the power to change the state of motion in a body." As such it can be measured, and in all its transformations the equivalents can be made manifest. Disappearing in one form it appears in another, and in yet another, going through the whole round of "the various forces of Nature." It is only one single Power that works in them all. Energy is always the manifestation of motion, whether in a sensible form among masses, or in an insensible form amongst molecules or atoms, or sub-atoms. So that, here again, we are brought up to a manifestation of *Power*. The most recent Science leads us to regard the energy in the primitive elements which form the atom of ordinary matter (and which becomes stored up in them), as something "enormously transcending the energy that is involved in ordinary physical and chemical changes in which the atom suffers no alteration." "The energy available for radiation in one ounce of radium is sufficient to raise a weight of something like ten thousand tons a mile high" (Whetham, pp. 239, 241).

What is this marvellous Energy that can be thus stored up in such a very small compass? Is it anything material? It cannot be rightly described as such, although it is associated with that which we call "matter." It is the "force" which holds together the corpuscles which make up atoms, and it represents the *Power* which brought these corpuscles together and which set them a-spinning in their orbits in such a wonderful way. All "the correlated forces" are manifestations of this Power. Every form of actual energy is ultimately reducible to *movement*, of masses, or of molecules, or of atoms, or of the Ether. But movement is impossible apart from something that causes it, or sets it up: it is always the manifestation of *Power*. But Power is not anything material, although constantly manifested through, or by means of matter. Power itself is immaterial or spiritual. The only knowledge or conception we have of Power is due to our own experience in exertion or resistance. The only Source of movement that we know is our own will. Energy thus declares itself to be, in all its forms, but the manifestation of Spiritual Power. "Matter" is thus *seen to be* only something formed by some *Power*, and acting as the medium of some primal Energy.

Life

If we take LIFE next, we shall see that the same thing is true of it. The real, inner nature of Life is still *sub judice*; but whatever it may be in itself, and however it may arise, it depends for its manifestation on certain forms of energy. In the course of its working through matter, the one sole Power becomes manifested in the peculiar substance termed Protoplasm, which is, so far as it is known, a chemical compound of extreme complexity and instability. It is possessed of the remarkable powers of assimilating "dead" matter into matter like itself, and consequently, of growing; of contractility, or movement in a visible way; of sensitivity, or irritability, or the "feeling" of stimuli, and of responding to external conditions, also of reproduction of its kind in new living forms (Dolbear). So far as has gone, living matter has only been derived from previous living matter, and its *irritability* "may possibly be the manifestation of something beyond anything due to its chemical and physical qualities" (McDougall, *Text Book of Botany*). In living matter we certainly have something quite unique in its powers as compared with all other substances. While it is not necessary to contend for an exceptional origin of living matter, it has never yet been shown to be the result of the action of merely physical and chemical forces. When it is said that "vital forces are transmutable into, and derivable from, physical and chemical forces, that sunlight falling on the green leaves of plants is absorbed and converted into vital force, disappears as light to reappear as life,"—statements which we often see made in various forms,— it is forgotten that these transformations can only be made in the presence of living protoplasm, and through its influence. The protoplasm seems to use the sunbeams to do its own specific work. No doubt, protoplasm is being manufactured continually by plants and by the lowest forms of life,—by all living beings, indeed,—but, as a popular Agnostic writer remarks: "In all these instances there was the living principle to start with, existing in the primitive speck of protoplasm from which the rest were developed" (Samuel Laing, in *A Modern Zoroastrian*, p 84) The real question is, as this writer says, "Can this primitive speck be artificially manufactured by chemical processes?" To this we add the recent statement of two accomplished Biologists—Professors Thomson and Geddes After quoting other testimonies, they say, "We see then that, while modern Biology no longer postulates a 'vital force,' that is a hyper-mechanical factor, a mystical power, a non-material agent presiding over the activities of the body, it admits, through, probably, the majority of its experts, that the phenomena distinctive of life cannot at present be re-stated in the language of Chemistry and Physics." They further say truly that if it should yet become possible so to state them, "if we could show that inorganic processes contain implicitly the potentiality of life, then our conception of what is often brutally called 'dead matter' will have to be altered, that is all" (*Ideals of Science and Faith*, pp. 55, 56; see also the writings of Sir Oliver Lodge).

But whatever may be thought of the nature of *Life* (a question which will be more fully considered in a subsequent chapter), Protoplasm, we repeat, has been produced in the course of the working of the one only Power, and it becomes to us a higher revelation of that Power. In those very actions which distinguish it, protoplasm shows itself to be the seat of a form of *power*, and in whatever way it has come to exist, we must see in it a manifestation of the one sole Power that works all in Nature. It is not a question of the derivation of the living from the non-living, but of the manifestation of *the one Power* in a new and higher form.

Mind

When we come to MIND, we admittedly have something quite different from anything that we witness in physical forms of energy, or even in life in the vegetable world. It may well seem impossible that Mind can be brought into the direct line of the transformations of energy, at least as these tranformations are commonly stated In Consciousness, even in its lowliest manifestation, we have something *sui generis* There is not only irritability and a response to stimuli, but an *awareness* of their presence; there is at least some dawning sense of it; there is given, not merely a reflex, but at least a nascent, volitional response. The humblest conscious Being can look out on the world to which all previous forms were confined as passive links in an unconscious chain; it begins to stand, in some degree, over against the external Universe, a new order of *Subjective* Life here makes its appearance, a new kind of Being has entered the world. Starting with Consciousness in its lowest form, it is no doubt possible to trace the development of conscious life from those lowly forms right up to its highest manifestations in man. But Mind *in its humblest form* is just as impossible to be accounted for on a merely physical basis as it is in its highest forms. While modern Psychology acknowledges a mechanical side to Mind, while it is certain that every psychical fact has its physical concomitant, the tendency is to look upon the psychical as an order in itself, to regard it as first and deepest. As Professor J. H. Muirhead says, "The general result of the analysis now generally accepted in psychology, is the vindication for the Mind of a reality of its own independent of the physical order" (*Ideals of Faith and Science*).

Yet it cannot be said to exist *for us*, or in its manifestation, in entire independence of that order; or as something separate from it, whether we think of mere concomitance, or of parallelism, or of any other form of the relation of Body and Mind. While Tyndall's dictum that "the passage from the physics of the Brain to the corresponding facts of Consciousness is unthinkable," points to a great truth, for the *manifestation* of Mind or Consciousness there is still dependence on the operation of energy in a certain form. It is found only (in this world) in association with a certain form of living protoplasm. This is true for the manifestation of finite Mind. This new form of Being must therefore be regarded as the outcome of the working of the same single Power to the working of which all the other phenomena of the Universe is due; and if we have in these any manifestation of that Power at all, we assuredly have in Mind its highest, its culminating manifestation, its *self-revelation* given within ourselves. While Mind, certainly, cannot be reached by a "transformation" of any physical force into mentality—the error underlying such a conception we shall see immediately—Mind comes into manifestation in the line of the continuous working of the one all-working Power. It reaches here the last stage of its previous working and the beginning of a new order; and Mind is best regarded as the self-revelation of that Power in its real spiritual nature, given within our own selves [1] This will appear perhaps still more plainly in the criticism of the current Monism that follows.

Scientific Monism

MONISM, of course, as its name indicates, maintains, either one only Power, or a single two-sided " Substance," deriving everything in both the physical and the mental world from the operation of that one Substance and its laws, including the operations of Mind when once it has been produced. Sometimes, as with Buchner and Haeckel, the stress seems to be laid on the material side—on matter and its powers. Of course, in any complete view of the Universe, matter must be taken into account. Wherever there is motion there must be something that is moved: matter is thus the instrument, agent, or nidus of motion and the vehicle of energy or Power. Whatever powers may be ascribed to matter, the question always remains, Whence have these powers been derived? The source of these powers is the real source of the Universe. No one in his senses could seriously attribute the existence of the World to a mere dead and blind something called " matter." The old " crass Materialism," if ever there was such a thing as pure Materialism, is dead and buried for ever. Monism formally disclaims Materialism, but it demands the full recognition of Matter as one side of that which is on the other side denominated, sometimes " Force " and sometimes " Energy," which is manifested in the Motions through which the Universe comes to be, and through which it is upheld and carried onward. The stress that is sometimes laid on Matter and the language employed, create the impression that what is affirmed is really Materialism. Thus, when Buchner says that " Matter and its movement " are

[1] For fuller treatment see the chapters on " Spiritual Monism."

"the ultimate factors to which all things can be traced" (*Last Words on Materialism*, p. 115), or that they "produce all things," we seem to have sheer Materialism. But it is to be noted that it is not to "matter" merely that everything is ascribed, but to "matter and its movement" —a very different thing. Matter, he is careful to point out, is not something "hard, inert, and devoid of intrinsic movement." It is this "intrinsic movement" that is the main concern. "We do not affirm," he says, "that consciousness and thought are themselves material. No one has ever asserted that size, colour, motion, extension, heat, hardness, softness, etc, are in themselves matter; nor do we affirm that of the mental processes. Just as the former phenomena are only produced by matter, so consciousness and thought are merely manifestations of it in a condition of extreme complexity and organisation. Life is not itself matter, but the outcome of a long series of processes which have led to the appearance of matter in its organised condition" (p. 5). It is evident, thus, that the outcome is due, not to matter, but to those *processes* which have been carried on by means of matter   "Everything," he says again, "is due to the motion of atoms or the ultimate particles of bodies, matter and energy are so united as that they can be separated in thought only; never in reality." This is not Materialism, but it is laying the stress on that which is merely the visible side, so to speak, the merely instrumental side of the process. It is manifest even from these statements that what Matter is and does is determined by the Power that constitutes it and acts through it.

Mr. Herbert Spencer, it is well known, derived everything in the phenomenal world from what he termed "the persistence of Force (or Energy)," which, as known to us, is but the phenomenal manifestation of an unknown and unknowable Power. Everything is ascribed to the working of this *Power*. Most earnestly does he repudiate Materialism, and while maintaining a thoroughgoing doctrine of " the transformation of Force," right on to the highest human attributes, he asserts that this gives a " spiritualistic rather than a materialistic aspect to the Universe." He even plainly affirms that we know the all-working Power as spiritual in ourselves · " the Power manifested throughout the Universe, distinguished as material, is the same power which in ourselves wells up in the form of consciousness ," they are but " different modes of the same Power " ; " the Power which manifests itself in Consciousness is but a differently conditioned form of the Power which manifests itself beyond Consciousness " Now, if we know this sole Power within ourselves as *spiritual*, surely this is all that we need to know in order to be certain of its nature. But special criticism of Spencer's position and arguments, and also of Haeckel's Monism, we reserve for separate chapters, as well as the fuller illustration of what we may term true spiritual Monism. We desire at this stage to avoid complicating the issue We are at present concerned only to show that, up to this point, even Scientific Monism does nothing against the conviction that the Power that works all in the Universe is revealed within ourselves as Spirit, but rather confirms it.

The Anti-Theistic Application

The supposed *anti-religious application* of the doctrine will appear from the following quotation from a recent writer, whose work is published by " The Rationalist Press Association " (London) Following Spencer and Haeckel, Mr. Dennis Hird, Principal of Ruskin College, Oxford, states the matter thus " Extension and motion may be the necessary properties of matter. At least we know that where there is motion there is matter, and whether we use the terms ' Matter and Force,' or ' Matter and Motion,' we recognise the accepted conclusions of Science that both are indestructible. This greatest of discoveries teaches us that neither can be destroyed, so that it is almost certain as they can have no end, that they had no beginning." The recent discoveries with reference to Radium throw doubt on this last assertion, but the chief point of interest is in what follows: "Add to this that heat, light, colour, magnetism and electricity, are all of them only modes of motion, and then we shall be prepared to admit that the same force may show itself in different forms at different times. This is called the transformation and equivalence of forces. That is, just as the same particles of matter may at one time form parts of a rose and at another time parts of a mushroom, so the same force may at one time strike a church as lightning and at another time may be the mother-love which rocks the cradle" (*An Easy Outline of Evolution*, pp. 184, 185).

Whatever the writer may have intended to convey, this is supposed by many to do away with the need for God and to overthrow Religion. At first sight, certainly, it seems a purely materialistic or even Atheistic statement; but, viewed more closely, it is seen not to be by any means necessarily such. Instead of its discrediting a religious view of the Universe, we can see in such a statement, rightly taken, one of the strongest confirmations of that view.

1. Supposing the doctrine of the "transformation of Energy" to be established all along the line, we are entitled to judge of the real nature of the Power that is working *at this end*, within ourselves, rather than at the other end, where we cannot come into touch with it at all. Nay, it is only, as Mr. Spencer has taught, from our own experience that we can conceive such a thing as "power." It is only in our own voluntary effort that we have any idea of its exertion. Power makes itself known

within as *spiritual*, its analogue is Will, and wherever it works in the Universe it cannot be confounded with the matter that serves it Power may have material effects, but in itself it is never material, but spiritual. It may not only pass into various forms of manifestation, but may be in abeyance in the form of "potential Energy." The power that is latent in a charge of gunpowder is something more than any actual motion amongst the molecules of the Matter. Power, or even "energy," is never a material, but always a spiritual reality

2. The phrase "the transformation of Force (or Energy)" is a misleading one, and may cover a very serious error. It is not the fact that physical vibrations or motions are themselves transformed into psychical sensations or other elements of Mind or Feeling Force itself, as we have seen, is simply *a mode of motion* in which some Power is manifested. Probed to the bottom, all the forces which are said to be "transformed," the one into the other, are simply various *modes of movement*, which are the manifestation of a single Power variously conditioned It is never *the Power* that is changed, but only the form of its manifestation, or mode of operation. The Power itself remains unchanged, but it may pass from a lower to a higher mode of manifestation, or expression

3. It is particularly to be observed that it is only in relation to those combinations of matter in which *living beings* are expressed that these higher, mental manifestations can take place—that Consciousness, or even the lowest form of actual sensation, can be awakened and maintained Apart therefrom, there would be but *physical* consequents, not mental. But as all these combinations of matter have been formed through the working of the one only Power, and as we have here, indeed, every form of force, and the result of all its previous working in all its varied forms represented, we have in our spiritual selves the highest

form in which the all-working Power reveals itself. It is not any *single* form of energy, force, or motion, or of the Power manifested in these, that appears as Mind or Consciousness: that which we know as Mind only shows itself as the result of the play of Force in all its varied forms from the beginning, and it shows us that these have been from the first, not material but spiritual in their nature. As already said, we never know any material or physical *thing* called Force or Energy or Power. This is always something *other than the matter* which it constitutes, through which it works, or with which it is associated. When we see it in its highest form in ourselves, we *know* it to be spiritual. It *reveals* itself within us.

With these explanations, it will be seen that we need have no hesitation in accepting the doctrine that it is one and the same Power that is revealed in the external and in the internal world. Instead of landing us in Materialism, the doctrine, rightly taken, carries us quite beyond it. Far from being hostile to Religion, we can find in it the strongest support for a religious conception of the world. It is just along the lines of this theory that we can see most clearly the revelation of the one sole Power as Spirit, *given by itself* in our own consciousness; and that we can find the explanation not of the higher through the lower, but of the lower through the higher, as surely it *must* be found. If Materialists have sought to explain the higher by the lower, why should any validity be supposed to belong to such an explanation? The rational course followed in all similar cases in practical life is to explain the lower by the higher.

And now, with these explanations before us, let us look again in the face the passage just quoted from Mr. Hird. There is a sense, of course, in which it would be obviously incorrect to say that "the same Force may at one time strike a church as lightning, and at another time may be the mother-love which rocks the cradle." It may be the same Force in the wider sense of the word, but certainly not in the narrower. The Force that strikes a church as lightning is a very different Force indeed from the gentle mother-love that rocks the cradle. The one is blind and unconscious, so far as we know, the other is clear of vision and full of feeling No one in his senses could say that the two, taken thus, were the same. What is meant is, evidently, that the same *Power* which at one time is manifested as electric force, at another time shows itself in the form of Mind and Feeling. This, we think, is undeniable, but instead of making against a Theistic conception of the Universe, it helps us greatly towards it. The power in the mother is spiritual, without doubt, but it is *Power*, capable of showing itself in ways equally manifest with the lightning flash, and far more impressive. What is there that a mother's love will not *move* her to do for her child? What a train of heroic conduct, expressed it may be in physical forms of action, of suffering, and of self-sacrifice, may it not fire? It is a spark of the Love which proves itself to be "the greatest thing in all the Universe."

As such it is surely *higher* than all physical manifestations of force. "The mother-love that rocks the cradle,"—we are thankful for the phrase, with all that it implies and has affiliated with it in the still higher manifestations of Love that are possible to us,—is surely, judged by all the rules that bear on such a case, something very much superior in value and in content, or character, than the lightning that strikes a church, or any other merely physical manifestation.

If then there is, as Scientific Monism affirms, only one Universal Power, of which all that we see is the manifestation, we surely know its nature best in its highest manifestation in ourselves Just as we know the true nature of a flower when it blooms, so we know that of the

Power that gradually rises in its manifestation in the world, when it blossoms in ourselves. We know it in this way to be *spiritual*, not through speculation or assumption, but by its own *direct revelation* within ourselves. We find here the bridge between the internal and the external, which, if we have only courage enough to trust it, will carry us to an assured Faith. To know this Power as spiritual is to know it as having (at least) its source and origin in God. In this revelation of the nature of the one all-formative Power as spiritual, we have found a Power truly competent to produce the Universe that culminates in ourselves—the only kind of Power that is competent to do so. Spirit can accomplish what neither matter nor energy alone, nor both of them together, can possibly effect. We have here the harmony of the Power manifested in the Universe with that rational character of the Universe on which we dwelt in the previous chapter. Reason is *Spirit*, and it is only *rational Spirit* that can account for the Universe that we know which culminates in our rational selves. Having this revelation within ourselves, what do we require further?

In the face of such a revelation, Agnosticism seems a strange, an unaccountable phenomenon. That we should actually *know* "the Omnipresent Power" as mental or spiritual in our own Consciousness, (since our Consciousness *can* be nothing else than a manifestation of that Power); knowing that we have in *Spirit* the revelation of such a real Cause as that which we seek for the world, and yet to continue to speak of it in terms of Matter, or to persist in saying that we do not know its nature at all, is surely a strange thing. That we should continue to think of, or to denominate this Universal Power, after its lower modes of manifestation, and not after its highest, can only be accounted for by what Mr. Spencer calls "an overwhelming bias."

Summary

Let us endeavour to sum up in a few words the position we have reached. We have seen in the previous chapter that every thing and being in the Universe is the manifestation of Reason; that this fact alone makes the Universe intelligible or constitutes us rational beings. We have now seen this Reason revealed as *Power*—as the Power that works all in all, and we have seen that Power—which works, first of all, outside of us—revealed within ourselves as *Spirit*. "Beginning with matter," says Mr. Mallock, "we have in a gradual and unbroken ascent; first, matter commonly called lifeless, but really consisting of atom-cells, full of inward activity, then matter which lives in the sense recognised by the biologist, but which is by the biologist not recognised as thinking; then matter which thinks, remembers, and even purposes—which performs the functions of mind—but without personal consciousness, and lastly, matter which is Mind, with a personal consciousness emerging from it" (*The Reconstruction of Belief*, p. 29). But it is manifest that the "matter" we thus begin with is not "matter" at all, in the ordinary sense of the word as distinguished from Spirit, it is matter which owes, not only all its possible functions, but its very existence, to the "inward activity" of its "atom-cells", it is matter which is really a manifestation of Power (which is not material but spiritual), and we have, at the end—at the highest stage of the manifestation—this so-called "Matter" distinctly revealed, it is said, as Mind—"Matter," Mr Mallock says, "which *is* Mind" (italics ours), "with a personal consciousness emerging from it." Now, what we have at this end is *not* Matter but *Spirit*. It is absurd to say that "Matter thinks," or that "Matter is Mind." If there is any meaning in words, Matter does *not* think; Matter is *not* Mind. It need not be, as is often said, its antithesis; it is rather the organ, or instrument, or expression, of Mind. We can only understand this emergence of Mind or Spirit in ourselves as being the revelation of that which was really deepest and formative all through, expressing itself and acting by means of Matter, formed for that purpose.

Could we have a clearer revelation of the nature of the Power that operates in all things than that which is thus given us? It is by universal consent *one* sole Power, and it declares itself within ourselves as Spirit. It is, of course, only as finite Spirit that we know it—as individuated and conditioned in us, yet not as severed from its Source, nor from other spiritual beings. As we shall yet see, there is no Pantheistic identity. But though it is *conditioned* in us, it is still *Spirit*, always in some measure accompanying, or expressed in that which we call "matter," but never to be confounded or identified with it. What is Spirit? Not a "thing" that can be touched or handled, but, as we know it in ourselves, real, personal being, though wholly invisible and intangible. "The essence of Spirit," as Hegel and Coleridge said, "is freedom." As spiritual, we know ourselves as relatively free personalities, arising out of Nature (as will be shown yet more fully), as centres of Thought (Reason), Love (Feeling), Volition (self-originated action). These elements have been generally accepted as the attributes of Spirit, and in their possession by ourselves we know, so far at least, what God, the Source of our being —of the Power that rises gradually in its manifestation in the world till it reaches this self-disclosure in ourselves— must be.

The Reference to Evolution

The naturalistic Monism of Haeckel and others, however, affirms that, as Mind or Spirit in us is itself a *result* of the pre-working of "Substance" (which, although

REVELATION OF SPIRIT WITHIN OURSELVES 87

it has from the first a spiritual as well as a material side, has it only in an undeveloped condition), Mind or Spirit in us is the outcome of an *evolution* with respect to which we have no right to affirm Mind or Spirit in a complete state at the beginning. "The whole evidence," says Mr. McCabe in his exposition and defence of Haeckel, "points to the conclusion that conscious mind is an outgrowth of unconscious, and that this is the generally diffused Cosmic force" (*Haeckel's Critics answered?* p 58) The Whole is the result of an *evolution* which was mindless (in the real sense of the word "Mind") in its origin.

We have already seen, so far, the reply to this in the evidence adduced of that presence and working of Reason in the world to which Reason in us is directly due, but let us now give our special attention to the whole subject of this "Evolution" which is said to accomplish such marvellous things in the world's history, and which plays so great a part in all anti-Theistic theories.

CHAPTER V

EVOLUTION

1. *General*

SINCE the work of Darwin, Wallace, Spencer, and others, " Evolution" (in itself a very old doctrine) has become almost universally accepted as being in some form "a modal theory" of the becoming of the Universe. There is still much discussion regarding the various factors of the process and the degree of influence to be attributed to each—on which matters only those who have qualified themselves by special study are competent to speak with any authority—into which, therefore, we do not propose to enter. The subject, in its details, seems to be, to use Darwin's words one of "infinite complexity." We intend to view it chiefly in a broad way, in its relation to that Theistic conception of the Universe already suggested.

We believe most earnestly in Evolution; but not as the fetish that some would make it. It is the great magic-worker of Monistic-Agnostic, and anti-Theistic Philosophy. By its means the most apparently incredible feats can be accomplished. Given only matter and energy to start with, by this potent agency we are led directly onwards till we reach mind in man with all its achievements. We seem to see our spiritual selves being born, or made, as it were, out of nothingness. If there are difficulties, Evolution is the universal solvent. If it seems to sober sense impossible to derive the rational from the non-rational, we are assured that Evolution can accomplish it. Let us therefore ask, in the first place, What *is* Evolution?

If we go to the Dictionary, we find that " Evolution " is "the act of unrolling or unfolding, gradual working out, or development, a series of things unfolded" (Chambers' *Twentieth Century Dictionary*; see also " Webster" to the same effect). So taken, it certainly implies something *pre-existing* or latent in some way which *is* unfolded. You cannot unfold or unroll *nothing*. The definition which follows (from the same source) gives the sense in which the word is commonly used in relation to the production of the world—"the doctrine according to which higher forms of life have gradually arisen out of lower." But this cannot mean that the lower in itself has *produced* the higher forms that have arisen out of it. Arising *out* of it they rose *above* it, and their appearance necessarily implies some adequate power which has produced *both* the lower and the higher. If we say that the higher was latent in the lower, or in some way potentially in it, that too implies a power behind, or in, both, operating, it may be, in varied forms, bringing about results in the higher beyond aught that had been expressed in the lower forms out of which the higher have come The higher forms are not there merely in virtue of something in the lower forms, but only through the continuous action of the same Power (or unfolding of the same Reality) that formed the lower as well. Evolution is, in this aspect, rightly defined when it is said that " new forms of life are evolved out of pre-existing forms by means of influences actually operative in Nature without man's or any other agent's interference" (De Varigny, *Experimental Evolution*). Evolution is thus, not a power in itself, but only a suitable word to express the action of the Power that is constantly working in such varied forms in all Nature. Strictly speaking, the " evolution " is always *the result* of the action, or self-unfolding of this Power.

Two things at least are always presupposed or implied: (1) a latent capacity or potentiality in the lower form to be raised to something higher, and (2), the action of Power conditioned in various forms of influence, operating on (or in) the evolving life-form, and so raising it from, or out of, the lower, into a higher form. Evolution in itself does nothing, it only stands as a term whereby the action or the results of the action of these two factors are expressed. Some Evolutionists (*e.g.* Nageli) add, perhaps rightly, a third essential element, viz., an innate tendency to progressive development in organisms.[1]

The process that we have set before us under the name of "Evolution" is one which proceeds by means of the continuous action of a single Power, whereby the supposed simpler arrangements of matter have become the extremely complex arrangements which now obtain, whereby the inorganic has been raised into the organic, the non-conscious into the conscious and rational. The whole is the result of one continuous process. All the existing forms of life have come by slow and gradual changes from simpler forms—the entire development proceeding without any real "break" up to man in his psychical as well as in his physical nature. And the same conception is extended backwards to the inorganic world. In the words of Professor Huxley, "The hypothesis of Evolution supposes that in all this vast progression there would be no breach of continuity, no point at which we could say, 'This is a natural process,' and 'This is not a natural process', but that the whole might be compared to that wonderful operation of development which may be seen going on every day under our eyes, in virtue of which there arises out of the semi-fluid, comparatively homogeneous substance which we call an egg, the complicated organism of one of the higher

[1] In a recently published work by the late Professor Young, entitled *Evolution and Design*, this element has been specially noted.

animals. That in a few words is what is meant by the hypothesis of Evolution" (*Lectures on Evolution*; New York, 1876).

It may be questioned whether organic Evolution has been actually *proved*. An able advocate of the doctrine asks: " Can we consider the doctrine of the transmutation of species as firmly established, as demonstrated by fact in an unmistakable manner?" He answers, "Certainly not." Evolutionists are convinced of the truth of their doctrine; they can point to a number of facts that fit in with it; but they cannot give the required demonstration " (De Varigny). There has been progress since this was said; but the question whether there is *evidence* of the transmutation of one species into another depends on the determination of certain results in experimental Evolution in both the plant and the animal worlds, for which it is claimed by some that they represent actual new species. In any case, there are so many facts in support of the theory that it is almost universally accepted, and the author just quoted believes that in time, by means of suitable experiment, *proof* may be given. It is possible that, as some maintain, it has already been given. In addition to the large amount of evidence that exists for it, the theory gives such unity to our thought in relation to the world, explains so much that is otherwise obscure, and is in such harmony with our experience, that we feel instinctively that, in some form, the Evolution doctrine must be true.

But when it is said, as it often is, that "the higher has evolved from the lower," that which is a sheer impossiblity is affirmed. The higher can never be evolved from the lower (or the greater from the less) in virtue of anything in the lower considered in itself, or regarded as a cause; the higher result can only be brought about by the continued action of the same Power which has produced the lower form. Otherwise we should have something from nothing, which is impossible. No kind of growth or becoming, or of such evolution as we *know*, suggests the possibility of such a thing. The evolution of the world as a whole is something we cannot directly see or know; we can only infer its probable nature from what we witness in the more limited evolutions that are open to our observation. But in these instances there are always the two things already mentioned—the potentiality in some way pre-existing in the seed or germ, and the powers that are for ever acting on the evolving organism. We never start with the absolutely "simple," or purely "homogeneous," matter we hear so much about. Professor Huxley in the passage we have quoted, comparing Evolution in general to that of an individual organism, is careful to speak only of the "comparatively" homogeneous substance we call an egg. Every one knows that an egg is very far from being a homogeneous substance. In the "matter of eggs there are such varieties of constitution as make all the differences between a dove and a hawk, between a sparrow and an eagle." In the words of a famous Biologist, "The species is contained in the egg of the hen as completely as in the hen, and the hen's egg differs from the frog's egg, just as widely as the hen from the frog" (Nageli, quoted by Professor Thomson in *The Science of Life*). As will be more fully shown at a subsequent stage, the egg, germ, or primitive cell, from which each living being is derived—truly *evolved*—is a most complex production. Recent research has made this fact increasingly manifest. "The little word, 'cell'—which once seemed to express a simple fact—has now to cover a perplexingly intricate microcosm" (Thomson, *The Science of Life*, p. 106). It is also the seat of a force or energy, a form in which Power has been conditioned, apart from which no evolution would be possible, and there are other forms of power operating in the environment which are equally essential for the result. We witness the evolution of a plant from a seed, and of an animal from the protoplasmic germ, but these can never occur apart from the conditions which we have mentioned. There is always the potentiality in the germ, with the power that is increasingly active in it, in harmony with an ever-increasing environment. Man's body and brain, like those of any other animal, are built up by means of Protoplasm, and at length he becomes the consciously rational being that he is, but it would be absurd to suppose that Protoplasm *makes* man, or can account for him. The more distinctly a purely chemical character is claimed for Protoplasm, the more clearly does the impossibility of such a thing appear. Man, like every other creature, is the product of his *entire environment* and of the Power that is actively conditioned in his protoplasmic substance. His environment is not merely physical, but mental, moral, and spiritual as well, and only through the action and interaction of the whole can man be accounted for

So of the Universe itself as a whole. There must have been from the first that *potency* which, under the influence of the Power that works in and through matter, could at length become the world that we know, culminating in rational and spiritual beings. Only from Spirit can the world that culminates in Spirit have proceeded, and only by the working of Reason can a rational world be produced The whole process must be regarded as the working out, unfolding, or *evolution* of a rational thought and purpose which lay behind the first visible beginnings, and which has never ceased to work. If we take, as all Evolutionists do, the analogy 'of the evolution of an individual living form from the germ, such a conception is forced upon us. It is not *Evolution* otherwise; we have left out the most essential feature of every kind of evolution that we know, there is *nothing* to be evolved.

2. *Evolution in the Present*—(1) *In the human sphere*

We have already seen that we have the Power that is adequate to produce the world and man revealed in our own consciousness as rational and spiritual—that the *Reality* underlying everything and manifested in everything is fundamentally *Reason* or *Thought* Let us now ask, whether in Evolution we do not see everything, not only in harmony with that conception, but also affording further confirmation of it. Evolution is something which we can look at for ourselves to-day. It is not something absolutely finished and done with, belonging to the past only; it is still proceeding in its higher phases. Let us then, in the first place, view it as it is at present going on before our eyes; let us ask, *What is the dominant factor in its present course?*

1. There are four stages in the evolution of the world Instead of looking to the far end, so to speak, to the distant beginning, concerning which we can only form guesses, let us look at that which is nearest ourselves, and therefore best known to us. The present course of evolution is carried on largely through the agency of man himself, in it we behold the action of a Power, partly beyond ourselves, and partly within ourselves, consciously and purposively exercised by us. Ever since the dawn of Intelligence in the evolving world, Intelligence and ultimately, Reason in its self-conscious form, have been the chief factors in Evolution (see Mr. Hobhouse's *Mind in Evolution*; also Professor Lloyd Morgan's *Habit and Instinct*). If we confine ourselves, for the present, to the historical human period, we find that, as Mr. Spencer remarks, " Whatever takes place in a Society, is due either to natural or free agencies, from the undirected physical forces

EVOLUTION

around, from the physical forces directed by men, or from the forces of the men themselves." Human Society, with its laws and morals and institutions, is evolved by man, partly under the influence of powers in his environment which operate on him, it may be quite unconsciously to him, and which carry him onward in spite of himself; but partly also, under the influence of his own consciously directed reason. That which proceeds beyond himself, unconsciously to him, he can take up into himself and carry forward consciously. There is much in man deeper than "reason" in the narrower sense, just as there is in Nature; there is emotion, feeling, sentiment, sympathy, love answering to the Love that is deepest in the Universe; his action, also, may not be always, by any means, truly rational: still, it is by a rational or reasoning being that it is conceived and carried out. We take "Reason" here in its widest sense, including also the ever-growing "rational" environment.

In the invention of tools, culminating in our modern machinery, and instruments of discovery, in the reclamation and improvement of lands; in the building of cities, and ordering of Society within them; in the occupation and civilisation of the world; in the Christianisation of savages,—in short, in all that we embrace under the terms "progress" and "civilisation," we see Evolution carried onward under the dominant influences of Reason, emotion and will in man. We repeat that, although the action may not always be rational in the highest sense, it is under the influence of man's power of Reason (or of his rational nature) that it proceeds Reason, with its accompanying elements, in our nature, is manifestly the chief influence in this, the latest, and presently-proceeding, phase of Evolution. So far as man can take up and carry onward the process, he does it by means of the exercise of Reason. It is only the true application of Reason that is needed to complete the process. Matter and Energy are, to a large degree, placed as servants or instruments in man's hand.

This is largely true even with reference to man's relation to and dealing with living matter and actually organised living beings. Man can, through the exercise of his Reason, so modify breeds of animals as to bring out quite distinct varieties In Mr. Darwin's words, " Nature gives successive variations, man adds them up in certain directions useful to him In this sense he may be said to have made for himself useful breeds. . . . Breeders habitually speak of an animal's organisation as something plastic, which they can model almost as they please," and he gives many interesting examples with respect to both plants and animals (*Origin of Species*, pp 22, 23). Here we witness the action of Reason in man taking up and carrying on the work of Evolution, which, it would almost seem, has been committed to him, since Reason has become organised in him Of this kind of action and of the necessity for it, many illustrations might be given. We see it in that domestication of wild animals so that they become the tame and useful servants or companions of man, or contributories to his sustenance, and in that cultivation of wild plants and flowers to which we owe our wheat and several of our most useful vegetables and fruits, and most beautiful and fragrant flowers. It is to be seen to a remarkable degree in the present work of Mr. Burbank of California, in relation to plants and flowers. By a careful, and generally, long continued process of culture and selection, he has brought into existence several new varieties of form, flower, and fruit, if not, indeed, as some think, new species. The Burbank experiments, it is said, prove that the plant world is "plastic to human touch; that we may shape it at our will", that "we hold a master-hand in the game of Evolution"—that "man can produce species, and do it in a dozen summers" (G. P Serviss in *The Cosmopolitan* for November 1905).

In fact, the evolution of the world is manifestly incomplete till it is taken up and perfected by Reason in man. This is evidently the design of the all-working Divine Reason itself. It is the one rational Power which seeks to work thus through our consciousness of its presence in ourselves, and in obedience to its dictates; but which as *rational* beings we are of necessity *free* to obey or to disobey.

Does not all this suggest that up to the point where the action of human reason begins, a creatively conditioned Reason outside of man has been the organising and evolving Power; that what Reason, beyond our consciousness, has been doing, it seeks to continue and perfect through the conscious reason in ourselves? This also, as we shall see later on, throws light on the nature of the relation of the Reason that works outside ourselves to the world in which it operates.

Moreover, in human History we witness the overruling of a higher Reason than our own, whether, as individuals, we choose to work along with it or not "The Power Eternal, not ourselves," ever shows itself as a Power that "makes for Righteousness" Civilisations or Dominions founded on injustice and oppression ultimately perish, and, however many backsets there may be, there is, on the whole, an onward march of progress In the words of Dr. Flint, "All particular causes are so arranged, co-ordinated, and controlled, that they subserve a rational end. They may seem forces of the same rank as Reason, and able to oppose it with success, but are forced to be in the long run its instruments. They so operate as ultimately to profit Reason. Nature and History may appear to exhibit merely the play of blind forces, but, in fact, each is a drama of which the law and issue is the glory of rationality and morality" (*Agnosticism*, p. 450).

There is also in man himself a presently-proceeding evolution, not only of a spiritual kind, but of a mental and physical nature. In his *Present Evolution of Man*, Dr. Archdall Reid points out that, side by side with the evolution of Brain and Body along ancestral lines, there has gone on a more intangible evolution, chiefly against disease, especially zymotic disease — that is, disease due to, or produced by, living micro-organisms. The chief agency in this, he holds, is Natural Selection, leading to greater powers of resistance in the surviving members of the races affected. This, of course, is organic, but we refer to it in order to point out that the value of this knowledge manifestly consists in the measure of possibility there is for the free reason in man to adapt itself to the operation of this natural process and to work with it and through it There is also, he maintains, a *mental* evolution in relation to the power of resistance to the craving for alcohol, opium, and other narcotics and stimulants. And here it is said, with reference to alcohol especially, that the chief hope lies "in the future, when the reign of prejudice has grown weaker and our legislation more rational, when only those with an innate power of resistance will be allowed to perpetuate the race" (p. 347). Just in the same way, he says, we may hope to banish zymotic diseases. We need not now discuss these opinions; but we cannot fail to see that the ultimate appeal here is to *reason* in man, and that on the showing of one who regards Natural Selection as the sole agency in Evolution, reason in man, working in line with, and in continuance of, the Power that works in Nature, has a dominant part to play in the Evolution of the present and of the future. Indeed, as this writer remarks, "In man the power of developing mentally, in response to stimulation from the environment, has grown to be so great and is of such importance in his struggle for existence, that his survival is determined mainly by virtue of it " (p. 181).

Organic Evolution. Animal Life

(2) In the next lower stage—that of animal life, where (beyond ourselves) we can best see and follow the working of "Evolution"—we witness again the same two factors operating. There is the living animal substance with its nascent feeling, rising into consciousness,—into rational self-consciousness in man,—and there is the constant action of the environment upon it. Within the living being itself (after a certain stage at least), we behold the entire process carried on under what are, strictly speaking, *spiritual* influences. This can be seen very clearly, in its higher phases especially, if we follow the course of nerve and brain development as it is exhibited by Dr. Bastian, Dr. Carus, or any competent writer. The organisation of nerve tissue is always made in obedience to a *sensation* felt by the creature, or, in other words, in obedience to a *want* that is experienced, or *felt* in some way. Now these feelings are—as all feeling is—*spiritual*, something of which the creature is conscious more or less clearly. Or, if at an earlier stage, those sensations are, as some Monists affirm, beneath feeling in the full sense of the term, they are acknowledged to belong to the *subjective* side of Reality. They belong to the realm of *Mind*, and we see here clearly, that in organic life, even at this low stage, it is *the mental element* that dominates and carries onwards the evolution. In his Appendix to his work, *The Soul of Man*, Dr. Carus, dealing with the great progress which has been recently made in depicting the structures of living organisms, gives the following description of the nature of organised life, entirely in harmony with what we have just stated it to be · " The nature of organised life consists in the maintenance of a constantly repeated action which is called *function*. The structure whose commotion

conditions the progress is called an organ. And the law according to which life develops may be stated in the formula, 'Function precedes the organ.' This at first sight seems puzzling, but it is natural and necessary. There is no mystery about it. There is first a need, and the need in sentient things is felt as a want. Thus a desire to supply the demand originates, producing an activity of a certain kind. Such is the origin of function. Repeated functioning leaves traces in the living substance, that is to say, memory renders easier the repetition of reactions upon a constantly repeated stimulus, and the result is the formation of organs."[1] Now, as the formation of organs has been the chief means by which animal evolution, culminating in man, has been carried forward, we see that Evolution in the sphere of animal life proceeds mainly under those spiritual elements which declare themselves in their fuller truth in ourselves.

The other main factor is *the environment*, which, in fact, gives rise to the "feelings" or "wants" which the organism experiences. It is from the environment, and from the environment alone (whether physical or spiritual), that those influences and stimuli can come which affect the organism and lead it onward and upward, and this entire environment, we have already seen to be, beyond all question, rationally constituted. Whether, therefore, we have regard to the one main factor, or to the other, *spiritual* elements show themselves to be the dominant powers in organic Evolution.

Doubtless there are other factors that have to be taken into account as contributories to the result. At the foundation of the Darwinian theory of Evolution there is (1) the tendency to *variation*, along with the effects of habit, use and disuse, etc.; (2) the *heredity* by means of which, in *some way or other*, the new developments are handed on, (3) the process of "Natural Selection" and

[1] See further illustration in Part III. chap. III.

kindred agencies by means of which the work is expedited and perfected.

(1) The source or cause of *Variations* has long been seen to lie at the root of Darwinian Evolution, and the question concerning their origin has seemed difficult to answer. Mr. Darwin said in *The Origin of Species* that "deviations of structure are in some way due to the conditions of life to which the parents and their remote ancestors have been exposed during successive generations," "to which changes the reproductive system is eminently susceptible" (chap. v.). Biologists are now coming more and more into agreement with this statement, and to see that the source of variation must be found, in some form, in the environment. This becomes increasingly complex, and affects the innermost structure of the organism as well as its more external parts. As Mr. Spencer has said, "Were it not that individuals are ever being made unlike each other by their unlike conditions, there would not arise among them those contrasts of molecular constitution which are needful for producing the fertilised germs of new individuals. There does not seem to be any other cause required for the variations than plasticity in the organism and dissimilar conditions in the environment" (*Principles of Biology*, sect 96). Haeckel also lays great stress on the environment.[1] But this environment as a whole—to the relation of organisms to which variation is due—is, we have seen, so rational in its constitution and relations, that it is through the interaction of the organism with it that animals grow in intelligence, and that man has been made a rational being. It is the *one Reason* that constitutes the environment and the beings that are developed by means of their relation to it. The one cannot be separated from the other. The whole is *one rational working*

[1] The same is true of Weismann, as will appear from the quotations given in the next chapter

(2) As for *Heredity* (which, whatever the mode of its operation may be, is an undeniable fact), the various elements that are handed down through the organism must be in some way expressed in the matter of the germ, and Science is now able to recognise fully the possibility of this; but these various elements so expressed often represent *spiritual* facts or elements in the living creature, and, indeed, may *all* be regarded as definite "ideas" that become so expressed and that reappear in the new being that is produced. In order to be convinced of this, it is not necessary to suppose that all "acquired characters" are inherited, but only such as affect the germ-plasm. We see here again *the spiritual* finding expression in the material and, as a most real power, dominating the evolution of both individuals and species.

(3) *Natural Selection*, through the struggle for existence and relation to the conditions of life in general, leading to the elimination of the unfit and the "survival of the fittest," was the agency specially emphasised by Darwin, and it is still regarded by many of his followers as the chief, if not almost the sole, factor in organic Evolution. There can be no doubt that it is a most important agency—perhaps, after a certain stage is reached, by far the most important perfecting agency in natural or organic evolution. But the whole of the essential elements in the process must be there and operative before Natural Selection (in its usually accepted sense) can begin to act; so that it and its kindred agencies are rather super-added, preservative, and perfecting agencies, than the primary powers in Evolution.[1] The primary influence is that which is derived from the creature's

[1] "Selection," says Weismann, with whom it is the chief agency in Evolution, "can only give rise to what is suited to its end, *beyond that it can call forth nothing*" (italics his) (*The Evolution Theory*, ii. p 393).

Again, "Selection does not create primary variations, but it determines the paths of Evolution which these are to follow," and thus controls "the whole course of organic Evolution on the earth" (Preface).

relation to its environment, leading to those feelings of want which are met by the development of suitable organs. Natural Selection, as Mr. Henslow remarks, has had for its chief work " the weeding out of that which was unfit." It becomes a real *perfecting* agency, and it is probable that its action begins (as Weismann and others contend) at a much earlier period than is visible. But what is Natural Selection but *the most consummate action of Reason* itself? [1] The very idea of it seems to have been suggested to Darwin by man's selective action in modifying or improving plants and animals. This was direct rational action. No doubt often, even with man, it operated unconsciously, that is to say, without a deliberately set purpose, but in many cases we behold it as the result of deliberate aim and plan, and where such did not exist there was always at least the vague idea of getting something more desirable in some form.

Natural Selection, indeed, which, after all, means essentially *adaptation*, seems to be (after a certain stage is reached) the only way by which, under the necessary laws of life, species could have been fully evolved and organic life carried forward and perfected. But nothing leads us more directly to see the presence and all-controlling action of Reason in Nature than just such action as we witness in Natural Selection After showing the power of " modifying selection " possessed by man, Darwin asks, " Can the principle of selection, which we have seen so potent in the hands of man, apply in Nature ? " and he goes on to show that there it acts " most effectually." Yes, it is the very same *principle*, only there it is the manifestation of a Reason outside of man. When we see this principle of Natural Selection watching, seizing on, and fixing even the smallest changes that will be for the benefit of the organism

[1] Dr Wallace compares the work of Darwin in the establishment of this factor with Newton's demonstration of the law of gravitation, "which established order instead of chaos" (*Darwinism*, p. 9)

and its offspring, acting to those ends, as Darwin said, "on every internal organ, on every shade of constitutional difference, on the whole machinery of life," surely we behold the most intimate presence and working of Reason in Nature. Take as a further illustration, Wallace's description of Natural Selection as a "rigid selection at every step of progress that has led to the preservation of every detail of structure, faculty, or habit that has been necessary for the preservation of the race"; and again—"variation and natural selection are ever-present agencies, which take possession, as it were, of every minute change originated by these fundamental causes (those of growth and variation, of correlation and heredity), check or favour their further development, or modify them in countless varied ways, according to the varying needs of the organism." Where could we have clearer evidence of an all-working and all-controlling *Reason* which has regard to the welfare of both the individual organism and the species? (see *Darwinism*, pp. 103, 442, 444, etc). The fittest to survive (as individuals) are, he shows, the fittest to meet the conditions of their life; "the fittest survive to continue the breed," and the peculiarity (which gives this fitness) "will go on increasing and strengthening *so long as it is useful to the species.* But the moment it has reached its maximum of usefulness, and some other quality or modification would help on in the struggle, then the individuals which vary in the new direction will survive" (pp. 9–13).

What is this but the manifest working of Reason? It is not, as is sometimes said, that the appearance is *as if* Reason were working there Weismann says that the wonderful result (in Evolution) is brought about "as though it were guided by a superior intelligence." But when he shows "how, in a purely mechanical way, through the forces always at work in Nature, all forms of life must conform to, and adapt themselves precisely to, the conditions of their life, since only the best possible are preserved, and everything less good is continually being rejected" (*op. cit.* ii. pp. 56, 391), we make bold to say that, in this, we have the actual presence and working of that one and only *Reason*, whose continuous working fashions all things, and constitutes us, ultimately, rational beings. It would seem that nothing but a misconception of *the manner in which that Reason is present and acts* prevents its recognition as the supreme Cause in all Evolution. It is there, not as something *separate* from the process, but working in and through it, conditioned in it all, and dominating it all for the purpose of the creation.

The Analogy of Individual Organisms

As we have seen, it is in the development of individual forms of life from the germ to the full-grown animal, that we can best witness the working of an evolution—it is this that gives us the very idea of evolution in the wider sense. Here, as well as in the conservation and upholding of individual forms of life, we see the whole process proceeding under the influence of a principle of *unity* in the organism. All life is from the germ, and we behold all its varied forms continually evolving, not indeed, Science now assures us, from an absolutely structureless germ (as used sometimes to be said), but from an infinitesimal speck of protoplasm distinguished by certain indications of structure, from which emerges, now a mouse, now an elephant, now a tiger, and now a man; and we behold all the parts of the organism so evolved, working together under some influence which makes the organism a unity, and under which all the parts subserve what can only be called *the idea of the whole*. As Professor Tyler has put it, "It is the whole organism, one and indivisible, which controls in germ, embryo, and adult, in egg and owl. This individuality, or whatever you call it, impresses itself upon developing somatic cells, moulding them into appropriate organs, and upon germ cells in process of formation, moulding them so that they may continue their sway." And he notes that Wilson, Whitman, Hertwig, and others urge the view "that the organism as a whole controls the formative process going on in each part" of the embyro (*The Whence and Whither of Man*, pp. 302, 303). We cannot describe this principle of unity and control—this formative principle—better than by calling it "the idea of the organism." This "idea" (or complex of ideas) is not to be thought of as if it were a separate entity, and doubtless it has its material representation in the germ from the first, but although it thus has (like all ideas, even in the mind itself) a material side, the spiritual side is manifestly there and is dominant. So is it in all Evolution. The spiritual side or element is always first and deepest, and is that which governs the process, according to necessary, rational laws, which are in themselves, of course, the very expression of Reason.

A most important confirmation of this Ideal conception of organic evolution will be found, as we shall show immediately, in that which Mr. Benjamin Kidd has termed "projected efficiency." A further confirmation comes from that "mutual aid" which Prince Kropotkin and others have set forth as a factor of even superior importance to Natural Selection, and which has to all appearance its foundation deep down in the very nature of life Still another support is derived from the tendency to see in variations, not only something predominantly due to the environment; but something *definite*, instead of "fortuitous." But to these and other recently emphasised important factors in Evolution we shall devote a separate chapter.

Plant Life

(3) In the sphere of *plant life* similar laws hold good, although here we cannot affirm the operation of a con-

sciously felt want. We seem rather to see the marvellous working of mechanism as it approaches to Consciousness— a perfect, though unconscious, rationality, may we not say? so that actions which we witness in some aspects of plant life have all the appearance of conscious, rational actions. There seems to be only a step to the actual manifestation of Consciousness as we see it begin to show itself in animal protoplasm. Though there is no conscious feeling, yet the way in which the requirements of the organism are met forces us to believe in the action of a Reason, both as conditioned in the organism, and as outside it, by which Matter has been, or is continuously so constituted as to answer continually to the needs of the living plant. Reference has been already made to the *plasticity* which characterises plant life.

We add that, both in the animal and in the vegetable worlds, we seem to see "life" breaking out, in almost endless varieties of its lower forms—parasites and micro-organisms included—but which have all a useful (rational) purpose to serve in relation to the maintenance of particular organisms and of the balance of life as a whole (see Wallace, *Darwinism*, pp. 18, 25, etc).

Inorganic Evolution

(4) That which we witness, or may rationally infer, in relation to that *Inorganic* sphere which is farthest from us, obliges us to carry forward to it the same principles. We cannot tell *how* matter is formed so that it becomes the servant or the other side of Spirit (the "other side" is, of course, just the *manifested* side) But when we picture to ourselves that which is achieved in inorganic evolution, when we follow in thought the process as it advances from stage to stage, when we behold matter taking on itself those definite characters through the infinitely varied actions and interactions of which the world is gradually built up, the

atmosphere formed in such a way, and with exactly, to a nicety, such constituents as are requisite for life, and the needful moisture provided, when we see, at the appropriate moment, life itself appearing and proceeding steadily on its upward way in obedience to wants felt within itself, and under the influence of the pre-formed environment, which is at the same time constantly increasing in complexity and up-lifting power, till it reaches its goal in man, we cannot see more plainly anywhere, as it seems to the reason in ourselves, the action of an Omnipresent, all-working Reason with a purpose in view.

Let us endeavour to set before our mental vision the process of the world's development as Science shows it us. Of course, we know of no absolute beginning, but there was a beginning to this actual world. "This solid earth on which we tread," Science tells us, was not always the solid earth, but "in tracts of fluent heat began." There was a time when no life was possible on its surface or in its waters —when there were *no* surface and *no* waters, properly speaking—when not even chemical combinations were possible. We are invited to extend our imagination still backwards into a far distant past, when the elements that form our solar system existed only as a widely diffused gaseous cloud, or rather as an immense tract of extremely tenuous invisible vapour extending over millions of square miles in space. The "atoms" of matter were potentially there, and it was all in movement; but the most recent Science leads us to deem it unlikely that the atoms had as yet received those definite and unvarying qualities which constitute them the "elements" and make them "the foundation stones and building bricks of the Universe." There may have been, it is supposed, at first, only the primitive basis of matter. But it is widely diffused and in rapid motion, its basis is electrical. "Well," it may be said, "we have here only *matter*, we see nothing that can be called God." So it has often been said. But wait a little. There is much more there than " matter " as we may think we know it. Even were there nothing more than matter— what is this wonderful " matter "? Whence comes it? Who or What endows it with such marvellous world-forming potencies? But Science tells us that there is much more than ordinary matter. The Ether is there, the equally marvellous medium of radiant Energy, Light, Electric action, and Magnetism, and, perhaps, even of Gravitation itself. *Energy* is there, not only as the basis of matter, but also in the form of Heat (or whatever the corresponding power may have been) which has driven the primitive particles so far apart, ready to show itself anew in the form of Gravitation which will bring them in on themselves again. Whence this original expansive Energy, apart from which there could be *no* beginning? Nay more, " Law " is there, not a " thing," or a " force," or something to be evolved, but *a principle of order* and a most real, though spiritual, *Power*, under whose influence the Cosmos shall, in due time, appear.

But to proceed: First, gravitation[1] begins to act, the particles of the extended vapour-cloud are drawn together, a spherical form is assumed, which begins to rotate on its own axis. Heat is again generated by the clash of atoms; the Ether is thrown into those vibrations which shall yet be the light of physical life to men. As the movement increases in rapidity, portions of the great mass are thrown off and take on movements similar to those of the parent globe; circling around it as a centre—the genesis of the solar system.

Confining our attention now to our own world, we behold it a whirling fluid globe of fire, in which, owing to the intense heat, chemical combinations are impossible.

[1] The most recent studies of " Evolution in the Heavens " tend to show that other agencies have been operative ; that repulsive action has had a share in the process (see article by Miss A. M. Clerke on " Evolution in the Heavens " in *Monthly Review* for November 1905, and Professor Darwin's address to the British Association, 1905).

But it is constantly radiating out its heat; gradually it cools down; chemical forces begin to operate, and, just as the temperature decreases, the elements as we know them are gradually formed. Chemical combinations now take place, the elements are welded together in various definite ways, rocks and minerals are formed, an atmosphere gathers around; with the cooling there is a shrinkage, a pasty crust is formed, with many undulations; water falls into the depressions, seas are formed, mountains are heaved up, and, as Æon after Æon goes by, the solid earth as we know it, the scene of life, the abode of man, takes form.

"Well," you say, "this is Evolution, not Creation; we can see no trace whatever here of a God or a Creator." Yes, it is Evolution, but the evolution of *what*? It may be that of matter, up to the point at which the elements are formed, but from that point onward it is the evolution of *an ordered world*—of a cosmos, and, as we have already seen, in the evolution of matter itself definite order rules. Is there not something more than what we *see*, or can be described by Science, revealed in such a process? There may have been no *external* power working; the fact that the formation of the elements went on steadily *just as the temperature was lowered* (see Duncan, *The New Knowledge*, p. 206 f.) shows that the all-working Reason was *immanent*, but none the less, a spiritual Power has dominated it all. That "*God* is *Spirit*" is a truth which many of us have been slow to learn. We seem to think that there is no God at all if we do not see, or are unable to picture to ourselves, the action of some external, or semi-material Being.

It is true that all has proceeded by the action of "the Forces," and under "the Laws," of Nature—Gravitation and the rest. But what are these Forces and Laws? Modes in which Energy acts according to rational necessity. Gravitation, for example, is not something that starts into action from nothing, or for *no reason*, or for some arbitrary reason, such us an external appointment. Rather is it the very action of Reason itself. Reason is behind it all and in it all. The whole evolution has proceeded under, not blind, but *rational* necessity. There can be no *blind* necessity. It could not, in the circumstances, have been other than it was. There is *a reason* for the existence and mode of action of every single form of force in the Universe, and its action only reveals that Divine rationality which governs all things. Reason, Thought, Mind, Spirit, has been the unseen influence under which all Forces have acted. We know the reality of Reason in our own consciousness, and we know it as the only Power that can account for the rational Universe So that what we have witnessed has been the *Evolution* of a Divine rational *Thought and Purpose*, which, as it unfolds itself, becomes the rationally constituted world that we know and that reveals itself as Reason and Spirit in ourselves. Its principle throughout has been a Divine *Reason*, and Reason has governed the entire process. It has been as truly a *Creation* as an Evolution, proceeding in the only way in which it could proceed, under the supreme influence of Reason. *This* is the living Power that is manifested in Evolution. This it is that is really *alive*, and that unfolds and expresses itself in the universal and eternal process of the Worlds.

Just as in the evolution of individual organisms we see the whole process proceeding under the influence of what is, on its spiritual side, the Idea of the organism as a definite unity, so here we behold it all comprehended under one vast ideal unity, under which all things are working and which they are for ever tending to realise What we have before us is just the unfolding of a great *world-organism* under the influence of a dominating Idea, and through the action of powers such as suggest the thought that they are but the manifestation of that which we call "Reason," *conditioned* for the time being for the purpose of Creation. The whole process shows itself to be emphatically a rational one, proceeding under rational laws and having a rational end in view.

When we confine our thoughts to organic evolution, we are tempted to see in the action of such causes as "Natural Selection," which, while it is not recognised as the action of Reason in Nature, is often spoken of as if it had a vaguely conceived quasi-purposive activity that can account for things—something that becomes a substitute for a Creator. But in inorganic evolution we are introduced to a different sphere, one in which such action cannot be imagined, the countless adaptations and balancings in which we surely cannot but ascribe to an all-embracing Reason, which has the whole within its purview and sees the end from the beginning. These adaptations have been often pointed out We see them very noticeably in such seemingly simple and commonplace matters as the constitution of the atmosphere, the proportions of land and water in relation to life, the balance of animal and vegetable life in its relation to the atmosphere and to the material of life, and in those mutual ministrations apart from which life would not be possible on the earth.[1] Is it too much to say that the Power which so constituted *material* things and evolved the inorganic world had life on the earth in view in its action? It is just because the inorganic world is what it is that life appears, persists, and progresses: shall we say then that there was no prior thought of it all, *no purpose* at all in it, no Divine Reason behind it all and in it all?

[1] It is, Weismann points out, solely to "adaptations" of life to its conditions that its development from the lowliest forms, up to man, is due.

EVOLUTION

Illustration

One very striking proof of the Reason that governs Evolution—one which embraces also the *living* world—may be quoted. It is to be seen in what has been termed "a third kingdom of existence," viz., that of the *Bacteria*. As was said by Dr. Griffiths in his Presidential Address to the British Medical Association at Swansea (July 28, 1903): "We now find that these micro-organisms have a definite and important place in the scheme of Nature. They are distinctly separate from both the animal and the vegetable kingdom. They form a kingdom of their own, which we may call the bacterial kingdom. Their very existence appears to be antagonistic both to animal and vegetable life. Their object in Nature is evidently one of destruction—the breaking up of the complex molecules of animal and vegetable substances into simpler combinations. They are Nature's scavengers, and undoubtedly they are the causal agents of all the communicable diseases to which flesh, and not human flesh alone, is heir" (*Glasgow Herald* report, July 29, 1903) Now, in whatever way these forms of life may have been evolved, they are a *necessity* for higher forms of life. Yet their function is quite different from that of the ordinary evolving life. They are there as *destructive* agents, to minister to the general life by their very destructiveness. Their existence implies, therefore, some *wider Reason* acting in view of the general life, and in some way providing it with that strange, destructive, yet most beneficent and necessary agency.

But why look for particular instances? Nature is *full* of such examples Science itself is based, as we have seen, on the intelligibility of the Universe. Are not all its laws rational laws? Do we not find, wherever we can look, with telescope or with microscope, in the farthest fields of Space and in the lowliest organisms alike, the operation of the very same Reason as that which shows itself in conscious form in ourselves? The necessary movements of distant planets can be so accurately predicted as to lead to the discovery of new planets; the necessary laws of matter in its interior constitution are so certain as to lead to the discovery of new elements. It is an undeniable fact, relied on implicitly by every Scientist, that wherever we can reach to, in the immensities of Space, or in the almost unfathomable depths of the *sub-material* world, we invariably find the same laws operating, constituting the same *order*, so that Nature never deceives the truth-seeker: if we but interrogate her truly and patiently, she ever returns us a rational answer. We no more look for another kind of answer from her than a child expects an unkind response from his mother. If we seem to get a different answer, we are sure that we have not heard aright. What more than this should we require in order to be certain that the evolution of the world has proceeded under the influence of a Divine Power which is, in one aspect, perfect Reason itself?

The Monistic Position

But what are we to say regarding the specifically Monistic affirmation that the spiritual element exists originally only in an imperfect, undeveloped state, so that mental elements are formed out of elements not yet mental in the sense in which mentality appears in conscious beings; that it is only in the course of evolution that Spirit reaches its complete development and full expression? We shall have to return to this subject when we come to consider specially Haeckel's Monistic position. Meanwhile we remark that there is a sense in which the above affirmation is true, and a sense in which it refutes itself. *Spirit* as it is manifested in ourselves, can never be reached in that way, it cannot be derived from a wholly unconscious source.

What such Monists begin with is not really *Spirit*; it is really neither one thing nor another It is quite true that elements as yet insentient and unconscious come in the course of Evolution to be the organs of the manifestation of life that is sentient and conscious, it is true also that our conscious mental life rests on elements in themselves unconscious. But it is at the same time manifest that, while these last must be considered as belonging to the spiritual or subjective side of things, to call them *Spirit* is entirely unwarranted. *Spirit* cannot be something insentient or unconscious. To assert "Spirit" at the beginning in this way is merely surreptitiously to introduce that spirituality which is known to appear in the long run, and which *has* to be accounted for. Yet, at the same time, there is a sense in which it is correct to say that all matter has a spiritual side from the first. It has this, not because it is "Mind-stuff," as Clifford held; or because it has the imperfect elements that develop into the spiritual side of our personality in some mysterious way attached to it, but because matter is from first to last *the expression of Spirit*, it has a rational meaning, and serves rational or ideal uses. The Power which acts through matter, which appears in the external world conditioned by matter as "force," and which manifests itself as Spirit in ourselves, is in its essence spiritual; it is the Divine Reason itself. And it is because matter has, *in this sense*, a spiritual side, that, as it comes in on itself, as it were, with increasing complexity (as it shows itself to us), the Power which animates it appears in ourselves as spiritual. We have in this fact the explanation of much that is otherwise inexplicable. There is a sense in which it is true that in themselves the elements of our rational life are, as Clifford said, "not rational, not intelligent, not conscious," and it is wrong, in this aspect of them, to speak of them as "Spirit." But they are ever the expression of Reason, dominated by rational laws, and fulfilling rational purposes. In *this way* they have a spiritual side from the first This whole subject will be more fully dealt with in subsequent chapters.

All Monists, however, do not, by any means, regard Evolution after the manner of Haeckel. Dr. Carus lays emphasis on the "formal laws" that rule everywhere: "We must . . . emphasise that the formal laws according to which these not-feeling, not-rational elements combine into higher structures endowed with feeling and reason, are also a part of reality. The formal laws which are the *raison d'être* of all cosmic order, are omnipresent in every particle that exists, and we can learn to understand that nothing will stir, or change, or be, unless it be in conformity to the law of causation which is the law of change, and to the laws of form in general" (*The Soul of Man*, p 15). It is under these laws that the whole evolution proceeds. Brought together as *a unity*, and having regard to their source, Dr. Carus names them "*God*" (p 438) What are these potent "formal laws" but just the laws of Reason, the expression of Reason?

Professor Lloyd Morgan, who declares himself a Monist, and proceeds on strictly Monistic lines to build up the conscious life, sees in Evolution as a whole the action of "a *selective Synthesis*" which is higher than all and deeper than all, and "finds its expression in the primary laws of nature and mind." He shows its action in the inorganic world in crystallisation, in the chemical sphere in the selective synthesis of the atoms in a definite and determinate manner; and he shows that synthetic action is a distinctive quality of Mind. It is probably, he holds, through the action of this selective synthesis that living matter is formed and that the variations which play such an important, though obscure, part in Evolution are due. It is through its action that germs develop, each in its own particular form—mainly through an inherited difference of what he calls "their vital spin," due primarily to inherent and determinate selective synthesis of the vital molecular vibrations which constitute the "spin," and secondarily, to the conditioning of the "spin" in harmony with the environment. "To this is owing the development not only of the Body, but of the Mind." "An activity which is selective and synthetic is disclosed throughout all the operations of nature, and in psychology is an essential factor in mental development" (*Intro. to Comparative Psychology*, pp. 332, 333, seq.).[1]

What is thus stated is very interesting and suggestive. But *what* is this all-pervasive selective synthesis but just that which we have described as the action of an all-pervading Reason in the Universe? It is there as an "intrinsic activity" because it has so conditioned itself. Our very conception of such a synthesis is derived from the action of Reason in ourselves in the "activity of apperception and in the building up of our rational life"; it is *here* that such a selective synthesis is first known, and what Professor Lloyd Morgan does is to show that this selective activity is universal—common to all known aspects of Nature and in nowise restricted to the inner realm of Mind.

Thus, on the testimony of these two eminent Monists, we have the assurance given us that Evolution proceeds under the influence of a Power which is neither Matter, nor Force, in its ordinary manifestation. Spencer, as we shall see, has the same implication. That Power we can only describe as an Omnipresent and all-working *Reason*.

[1] As already mentioned, Professor Lloyd Morgan argues for a Theistic conception of the Universe.

CHAPTER VI

NEWLY EMPHASISED FACTORS IN EVOLUTION

WE are assured on high authority that, "while the *fact* of Evolution forces itself upon us, certainty in regard to the *factors* seems as far off as ever" (Thomson, *The Science of Life*, p. 228). These factors as stated by Professor Le Conte are, first, the four well-known ones: (1) The physical environment, affecting function, which again affects structure, both of which as changed are inherited by offspring, and so increased from generation to generation; (2) Increased use and disuse of organs enforced or permitted by change in the environment, physical or organic or both, also inducing changes which go on increasing in successive generations, (3) "Natural selection" or "survival of the fittest" among divergent varieties of the offspring—the distinctive Darwinian factor, (4) "Sexual selection," added by Darwin, who, however, laid the main stress on Natural selection in the struggle for food, or means of living. The first two factors are Lamarckian, and on these the chief stress was laid by Spencer. (5) In 1886 a fifth factor was added (suggested by Mr. Catchpool and elaborated by Mr. Romanes), viz., *Physiological selection*; otherwise called "isolation," which prevents the commencing varieties that tend to pass into species from being swamped by cross-breeding This is an important factor from our point of view, because, as

Professor Le Conte points out, "natural selection is intent only on preserving the best individuals, physiological selection on preserving *the kind*. Natural selection continues the direction of progress unchanged, physiological makes for new directions" (*Evolution in relation to Religious Thought*, pp. 73, 79). In both respects, therefore, this principle acts distinctly *with a view to the future*. To these Professor Le Conte adds another factor, characteristic of man alone: " This is the conscious, voluntary co-operation of the thing evolving—the spirit of man—in the work of its own evolution. This may be called the *rational* factor." We have already dealt with some aspects of the operation of this "rational factor," although, strictly speaking, all the factors operating are "rational", only, not consciously such (to us) in their operation. "With reason," says Professor Le Conte, most truly, "another and infinitely higher factor is introduced, which, in its turn, assumes control, and not only again quickens the rate, but elevates the whole plane of evolution. Moreover, this voluntary, rational factor not only takes control itself, but transforms all other factors and uses them in a new way and for its own higher purposes" (p. 87, f.).

Since the above was written, other factors have been brought into prominence.

1. There is that principle of "*projected efficiency*" which Mr. Benjamin Kidd has emphasised in its bearing on Social progress, but which is of equal importance from a Theistic point of view, and in our endeavour to find a rational interpretation of the World. In this respect, although Mr. Kidd does not deal with this aspect of it, it is not too much to say with him, that while "the Darwinian hypothesis as it left the hands of Charles Darwin, remains in all its main features unshaken . . . it has already been overlaid by a meaning which carries us almost as far

beyond the import of Darwin's contribution to knowledge as the Darwinian hypothesis itself carried us beyond the more elementary conceptions of Goethe and Lamarck." We have, in fact, by reason of the recent advances in the study of biological evolution, entered "a new era of knowledge"—one which will yet be seen to "dwarf into comparative insignificance other features of contemporary thought upon which attention has been concentrated to a far greater degree" (*Principles of Western Civilisation*, p. 32)

The new discovery (if it can be called such) is simply that Natural Selection has in view, not merely the interests of the individuals living at any given time, but the interests of the greater number yet to come—of the species as a whole. This indeed might have been inferred from Darwin's own statement of the facts (as Mr Kidd notes), for individuals were always passing away after a relatively brief existence, and the advantages which they had gained in the struggle were handed down by inheritance, so that real progress was the result. Their success was never limited to their own individual welfare merely, but had always in view the betterment of those who should come after them. When we find Darwin saying that Natural Selection is "daily and hourly scrutinising throughout the world the slightest variations . . . rejecting those that are bad and adding up all that are good; silently and insensibly working, whenever and wherever opportunity offers, at the improvement of each organic being in relation to its organic and inorganic conditions of life" (*Origin of Species*, chap. iv.), we feel that surely there must be a *purpose* in all this beyond the life of the ephemeral beings who are the immediate subjects of these operations, and who are being continually succeeded by other beings bringing with them the advantages gained by their predecessors, to be in turn the subjects of the regard and working of this wonderful

"Natural Selection."[1] The *future*—the life of the *present* day, indeed—has, surely, always been in some way in view. The very object that Darwin had before him was to explain how *the present* had arisen out of the past.

This species-regarding aspect of the process has been pointed out by various writers; but it is to the continued Biological study of Weismann especially, Mr. Kidd holds, that the establishment of this principle on scientific grounds is due. To summarise as briefly as possible, the evidence as presented by Mr. Kidd,—

1. It has been shown by Weismann (1) that the lengthening or shortening of the life of individuals in a species was determined primarily, neither by external physical conditions nor by molecular causes inherent in organic nature; (2) "that throughout the higher forms of life, so far from Nature tending to secure the longest life to the individual, the tendency, on the contrary, was, other things being equal, rather to shorten its duration"; and (3) "that duration of life had no ultimate relation to self-realisation in the individual, but was really dependent upon conditions which involved that its length, whether shorter or longer, was governed by the needs of the species" (pp. 46, 47).

2. He has explained the origin of *death* to the individual members of the higher forms of life—an experience which cannot be rightly said to exist in the lower forms which perpetuate their existence by subdivision—because of "its *utility* in the upward progress upon which life had entered." It afforded "the most favourable conditions for the existence of as large a number as possible of vigorous individuals at the same time," and worn-out individuals are not only valueless to the species, but are even

[1] In Dr Wallace's statement of the action of Natural Selection in his *Darwinism*, it is clear that it is not the individual merely, but the *Species* that is in view.

harmful, for they take the place of those who are sound. And, as Mr. Kidd points out, it gave immensely increased opportunity for variations and for that action of Natural Selection to which progress is due. "With individuals occupying their places in Nature indefinitely, there would have been no room for variation, adaptation, and progress as we have come to witness these phenomena among the higher forms of life. . . . The individual must die to serve the larger interest of his kind in the immense process of progress upon which life had entered" (p. 54).[1]

3. Similarly, the entire development of the process of reproduction (with all pertaining to it) has had, underlying and dominating it, this regard for *the future*. Apart from all disputed elements in Weismann's theories of heredity, "to combine together the hereditary qualities of two distinct individuals, and thereby to secure the advantage to be obtained from the mixing together of the individual tendencies to vary of the whole species," it was always necessary to return to the single cell. This principle has "controlled an immense range of modifications in character, function, and form," giving "the ever continued progress towards increasing differentiation in function and complexity of structure in the adult individual." We here witness the immensely important functions of parenthood arising, and "the burden of the future continuing to press with ever increasing weight as these functions develop under the stress of Natural selection." Lower forms of life and forms that fail in the forward march are left behind. The interval that requires parental care is ever lengthened out more and more, until, largely under its influence, humanity in the true sense of the word is reached.

Thus, as Mr. Kidd remarks, "The centre of gravity in the Evolutionary conception can no longer be regarded

[1] Dr Wallace notes that the same ideas had occurred to himself (*Darwinism*, p 437, note)

NEWLY EMPHASISED FACTORS IN EVOLUTION 123

as being in the present." "The condition under which development has proceeded in life throughout measureless epochs of time has been, in short, a condition in which the shadow of the future has continually rested upon the present, growing and deepening as the upward process has continued. In the course of this process, we must consider that it has never been the welfare of the infinitesimal number of individuals at any time existing which constitutes the end towards which Natural selection may be regarded as working. It is always the advantage of the incomparably larger number of individuals yet to come towards which the whole process moves."

The application of this principle to Social Science is manifest, and its bearing on a Theistic interpretation of the Universe is no less evident. How can we conceive of such a process save as dominated by a *purpose*? If, throughout it all, *the future* was ever in view, there must have been some *Mind* in which that view was held. We have here, therefore, a fresh illustration of our contention that it is *Reason* that is the real power in the developing Universe. We know that there was no such purpose as is affirmed consciously present to the individuals engaging in the struggle for life, only their individual requirements were in any measure present to them, or, at most, the more immediate wants of their offspring But in all that they did they were governed by a wider and far-reaching purpose *that used them* as its instruments. We do not need to suppose that that purpose was present as a personal, directive agency. The nature of the process, as well as its more immediate results, forbid the thought. But there was (and is) an *inherent rationality* dominating the whole process of Nature, beyond, and often in spite of, immediate individual desires and actions—a rationality which has been from the first working steadily onwards, realising and manifesting itself ever more and more clearly. Individual purposes have been embraced in, and overruled by, a higher rational purpose which had the ultimate end in view. Its action in Nature, we have already said, is imaged to us in that which is seen in the evolution of an individual organism under the principle of its unity after its kind. While this principle is not a conscious purpose *over* it, as it were, it is really there; it is *inherent* in it, and it governs the entire development. So it is with reference to the greater organism of the World itself. From the first it has been governed by Reason; it has had a rational *purpose* inherent in it; and this rational purpose and inherent rationality of Nature evidences the reality of a rational Source, which contains the whole, and which has, in some way, entered into this process of Creation, conditioning itself in various forms to that end, and progressively realising itself, or its purpose, in the process. "Projected Efficiency" inevitably implies foresight and purpose somewhere.

2. There is the principle of *Mutual Aid*, as set forth, most notably, by Prince Kropotkin in his *Mutual Aid among Animals and Savages*. Failing to find in his actual observation of animals in a state of nature, in circumstances likely to have produced it, that condition of a struggle for life amongst the members of the various species which came under his notice in his Northern journeys, on which so great stress was laid by Darwin, he was led to doubt the supreme value of the great Darwinian factor, which some of Mr. Darwin's followers had carried to a much greater length than their master. A lecture by Professor Kesseler, Dean of the St. Petersburg University, inspired him with the idea that "besides the law of mutual struggle, there is in Nature a law of *Mutual aid*, which for the success in the struggle for life, and especially for the progressive evolution of species, is far more important than the law of mutual contest." This had been suggested by

Darwin himself in his *Descent of Man*. When the same idea was presented to the mind of Goethe, he said that, if there was such a law in Nature, it would be capable of solving many an enigma. In various works the subject had been more or less dealt with, especially by Buchner and Espinas. But Buchner had jumped too readily to the assumption of "Love" among animals: whereas the roots of mutual aid and sociability must be found deeper down, resting on the wider basis of solidarity. Kropotkin set himself to gather evidence of the facts which he believed to exist proving the reality of feelings of kinship and sociality, and of the exercise of mutual helpfulness, amongst animals and men, beginning with the lowest savages. His papers first appeared in the *Nineteenth Century Review*, at periods during some six or seven years, and they created a deep impression at the time on many minds. Subsequent writers, notably Professor Henry Drummond in his *Ascent of Man*, Mr. Alexander Sutherland in his *Origin and Growth of the Moral Instinct*, and Mr. Giddings in his *Principles of Sociology*, have treated of certain aspects of the subject, with, at least, the human side of which, Mr. Fiske had previously dealt in his *Cosmic Philosophy*, as he did still more fully in his later writings.

Prince Kropotkin's book presents a large amount of evidence to show that the condition of perpetual and pitiless struggle for life that some have depicted does not really exist in the animal world, that, as far as we can judge, it never has existed either amongst animals or primitive men, but that, on the contrary, "mutual aid is a law of Nature and the chief factor of progressive Evolution", that "the war of each against all is not the law of Nature," that mutual aid is as much a law of Nature as mutual struggle.

Beginning with the Colonies of ants and bees among the invertebrates, he goes on to show the existence among *birds* of hunting and fishing associations, of sociability and mutual protection among small birds, of bird associations at times of breeding and migration, and their friendly autumnal societies. Amongst *mammals*, the unsociable species are but few. There are associations of wolves and lions, of deer and buffaloes, of many smaller creatures and of monkeys, and mutual aid is given in many ways in the common struggle for life. "Life in societies," he says, "enables the feeblest insects, the feeblest birds, and the feeblest mammals, to resist or to protect themselves from the most terrible birds and beasts of prey; it permits longevity; it enables the species to rear its progeny with the least waste of energy and to maintain its numbers, albeit a very slow birth-rate; it enables the gregarious animals to migrate in search of new abodes," where abundance of food may be found. It ministers more than anything else to the development of that intelligence which, all will agree, is the most effectual aid in the struggle for life and "the most powerful factor of further evolution." If it were only conflict in times of calamity that resulted in survival of "favoured" individuals, *retrogression*, not progress, would be the rule; for these are "neither the strongest nor the healthiest nor the most intelligent" Besides, the individuals would come out of such a conflict with health weakened instead of strengthened. The conclusion is that "competition in the animal world is limited to exceptional periods." Through Mutual aid, Natural Selection finds better fields for its activity, "better conditions are created by the *elimination of competition*, by means of mutual aid and mutual support; and amongst almost all kinds of creatures, Nature seems to seek out these ways, and by uniting the individual members of a species, and often of more species than one, in a common interest, leads them to the pleasantest life and along the pathway of progress" "The mutual protection thus obtained, the possibility of attaining old age and of accumulating experience, the higher intellectual development, and the further growth of sociable habits, secure the maintenance of the species, its extension and its further progressive evolution. The unsociable species, on the contrary, are doomed to decay" (p 293).

Coming to the human species, Kropotkin shows how erroneous is the common idea that primitive men lived either in isolation or in families constantly warring and struggling amongst themselves. Ethnology, he holds, in the hands of Bachofen, MacLennan, Morgan, Edwin Tyler, Morse, Post, Kovalesky, Lubbock, and many others, has proved that men originally lived in "bands" or societies which were the natural development of those which still exist amongst the higher and more intelligent animals. As Darwin himself saw, man could never have been descended from apes that lived in isolation, but from a social species (*Descent of Man*, chap. ii).[1] Man, standing alone, or struggling in families merely, could never have surmounted the conditions that were opposed to him and have grown in language, intelligence, and social life as he did in early times. Therefore, if we go back as far as we can—to the later glacial, or to the early post-glacial period—we find in the assemblages of flint implements evidences of man's social life: these are rarely found in isolation The caves which palæolithic man inhabited give evidences of life in communities. So do the traces of the Lake-dwellings of later times, and, in times still later, of the shell-heaps or kitchen-middens of Denmark. Observation of primitive tribes still existing show us the same thing. The family is, Kropotkin holds, a late institution; men are first found living in a kind of social organisation in which rules pro-

[1] In the last edition of *The Descent of Man* Darwin says. "Judging from the habits of savages and of the greater number of the Quadrumana, primeval men, and even their ape-like progenitors, probably lived in society" (p. 94). He gives many examples of Sociality, etc.

motive of the general good have to be submitted to. The marriage customs of savages prove the existence of such early organisation. The universality of the clan system—prevailing amongst the early Semites, the Greeks of Homer, the Celts, and still persisting amongst Red Indians and other tribes—supports the view of the originally social nature of mankind. It is true that some recent writers, such as Starcke and Westermarck, have contested these views concerning marriage and the family, but Kropotkin gives a large amount of evidence in favour of the more generally received conceptions (see Appendix VII.). The entire contention is further supported by facts observed amongst those tribes which are still in the lowest stage of development—Bushmen, Hottentots, Australians, etc.

Now, all this has a very important bearing on the question of the nature of the Power to which Evolution is due. The Sociality and Mutual aid which were thus such important factors in the process (and which Darwin himself laid stress on in his *Descent of Man*) divest the picture that we form of the evolving world of much of the gloom which the reign of strife as represented by the advocates of Natural Selection as the supreme cause of development threw over it, and at the same time bring into clear light the action in those far-off times of a cause which, in its complete manifestation in the life of to-day, we agree to regard as the highest of all. The Sociality and Mutual aid amongst animals and savages are the expression of something, not physical, but *spiritual* in its essential nature. They belong to the subjective side of Nature. They are the expression of rationality *in the relationships* in which creatures stand to each other, and of the feeling which is evoked by common participation in a life which is spiritual in its ground or basis. The close alliance of these elements with Intelligence is seen in the fact that it has always been where they were dominant that Intelligence has been most highly developed, whether in animals or in man. They are, in short, the expression of that Reason, as it rises in manifestation, which we maintain has been deepest and dominant in the whole process.

3. The importance of the *Reproductive factor* in Evolution has been emphasised by several writers, notably by Thomson and Geddes in their work on the *Evolution of Sex*. We are here specially interested in the fact that by them in particular, the *altruistic* or *ethical* aspects of the process have been made prominent—" that increase of reproductive sacrifice which at once makes the mammal and marks its essential stages of further progress—that increase of parental care ; that frequent appearance of sociality or co-operation, which, even in its rudest forms, so surely secures the success of the species attaining to it, be it mammal or bird, insect or even worm,—all these phenomena of survival of the truly fittest, through love, sacrifice, and co-operation, need far other prominence than they could possibly receive on the hypothesis of the essential progress of the species through internecine struggle of its individuals at the margin of subsistence " " We see," they say, " that it is possible to interpret the ideals of ethical progress, through love and sociality, co-operation and sacrifice, not as mere utopias contradicted by experience, but as the highest expressions of the central evolutionary process of the natural world " (pp. 311, 312 ; see also *Ideals of Faith and Science*).

Mr. Spencer had already shown that Altruism is founded deep in the very nature of life, " being in its simple physical form absolutely necessary for the continuance of life from the beginning." " From the dawn of life, Altruism has been no less essential than Egoism—self-sacrifice is no less primordial than self-preservation " (*Data of Ethics*, pp. 201, 203, etc.). Mr. Fiske also has given great prominence to this feature of Evolution in his *Through*

Nature to God and other writings. Indeed, the principle that shows itself in Altruism has its roots in the very nature of living matter, with its "anabolism" and "katabolism," rising into reproductive sacrifice, and showing itself ever in higher and higher forms In their recent paper in *Ideals of Faith and Science*, Thomson and Geddes do not hesitate to say that "the greater steps in advance in the organic world compel us to interpret the general scheme of Evolution as primarily a materialised ethical process underlying all appearance of a gladiatorial show."

Now, we have already seen that this "species-regarding" element implies a *purpose* in the whole movement,—beyond anything in the individual organism,—and a "Mind" which entertains that purpose and looks onward to the result to be secured. But what we are concerned with at this point is the distinctly *Ethical* character that is now discerned in the process—which is seen to have such a deep foundation and to be so all-pervasive. An ethical character of the process has, of course, been often affirmed *from the results*, but now it is seen in the actual working out of the evolution and at the very foundation of life. What does it imply? If the process of Evolution can be truly described as "a materialised ethical process," surely we cannot find a stronger evidence of that *rationality* which we have affirmed characterises it all and dominates it all. The ethical is simply the "practical reason," in Kant's phrase. It is, as already said, the expression of the rational relationship in which beings stand to one another. It is the underlying Reason in all things that brings it about, and when it appears, we behold that same Reason manifested in a higher form than it could possibly be, in the absence of such natures as have now been produced. Of the element of *Feeling* involved we shall have to speak farther on.

4. As already remarked, the tendency amongst

students of Evolution is more and more towards the recognition of the importance of the *Environment* Natural Selection must have something to work on. it could not operate at all apart from "variations." These variations, Darwin held, occurred indefinitely, indiscriminately, to all appearance fortuitously, and it was this, more than anything else, in his theory, that seemed to banish creative action from the world. It is being increasingly perceived, however, that these variations are due to the environment, and that they do not occur fortuitously. With respect to plant structures, Mr Henslow holds that he has proved that those variations in structure that are the source of varieties in plants, and, hence, of new species, are "due to the responsive power of Protoplasm, which, under the influence of the external forces of the environment, builds up just those tissues that are best fitted to be in harmony with the environment in question" Darwin, he maintains, confined himself too exclusively to plants under culture in which such indefinite variations do occur. But in Nature the variations are always "definite and always in the direction of adaptation to the environment itself, and it is in this, not in Natural Selection, that we have the real origin of species." "Natural Selection, at most, only weeds out the unfit," and its action in this respect has, as we have seen, always respect to the *future* of the species (see *The Origin of Plant Structures* by the Rev. G. Henslow). The whole process is one of continuous adaptation to an ever-increasing environment under the influence of an all-governing purpose.

In De Varigny's *Experimental Evolution* many examples are given of the effects of changes in the environment in creating variations, physiological as well as morphological, in both plant and animal organisms, and the conviction cannot be resisted that these variations are really of the nature of *adaptations* to the changed conditions when these are not such as to cause death. They seem to be direct, definite, and purposeful, with the view of maintaining life under the altered conditions. For instance, "while tadpoles soon die when introduced into water containing some amount of common salt, it is easy to enable them to survive by using at first very dilute solutions to which a small quantity of salt is added every day or every second day." And so completely may they adapt themselves to their new environment, that if they are suddenly transferred to their original element, they will die. External influences may not only modify breeds by direct, though, it may be, very gradual, changes in the environment, internal and external, but abnormal plants and animals may be in this way created. It is not the *external* environment merely that we must think of. Variation of food may induce physiological variations most important in their character. The slightest change of chemical composition may sometimes have remarkable effects (while on the whole the organism admits of much " physiological elasticity "), which, although they may not be manifested outwardly, are really definite variations in adaptation to the changed conditions. As regards external characters, there are many familiar examples. " Merino sheep lose their wool in warm climates and recover it under cold skies . . . the silky covering of the common hen in Guinea, becomes transformed in Europe into the feathers we are accustomed to see on our domestic fowl, etc." These are *definite* variations of a truly *rational* character in adaptation to changed conditions; and we believe that the more closely the examples of variation given by Darwinian writers are studied, the more clearly will they all be seen to be the result of definite adaptation to changes in either the external or the internal environment, and *all*, in this way, " rational " in their character.

Professor Lloyd Morgan, in his work on *Comparative Psychology*, also maintains the probability of *definite* varia-

NEWLY EMPHASISED FACTORS IN EVOLUTION 133

tions. "The observations of Schmankewitsch," he says, "appear to show that by gradually altering the salinity of the water in which certain brine-shrimps live, one species can be transformed into another species differing *determinately* in the form of the tail-lobes and the character of the spines they bear." So with certain Texan moths, a difference in feeding gave "new and *determinate* characters such as to justify, it would seem, their being regarded as different species." "The recorded experience of breeders shows that the material offered to artificial selection is not the result of fortuitous, but rather of determinate variation," and he quotes Weismann as saying, "We are undoubtedly justified in attributing the cause of variation to the influence of changed external surroundings" (these may act upon the germ-plasm of all organisms). "The necessary variations from which transformations arise by means of selection must," Weismann says, "in all cases be exhibited over and over again by many individuals," and this, Professor Lloyd Morgan remarks, is just what we should naturally expect if the variations are not indeterminate, but the outcome of selective synthesis (*Intro. to Compar. Psych*, pp 348, 349)

We may, perhaps, safely take a step farther. As Mr. Henslow reminds us in the work we have referred to, the question which lies at the bottom of all changes is that which Dr. Croll asked in the *Philosophical Magazine* for July 1872, viz., "*What determines molecular motion?*" "If one plant or animal differs from another, or the parent from the child, it is because in the building-up process the determinations of molecular motion were different in the two cases; and the true and fundamental ground of the difference must be sought for in the cause of the determination of molecular motion."

We can answer the question so far as to say that the motion involved must depend upon *some previous motion*. And this answer carries us directly to the Environment. It has been something operating in the surroundings of the plant or animal that has set up those molecular motions that issue in variations. Whether these variations arise in the germ itself or otherwise, and whatever may be the precise function and mode of operation of Natural Selection, we are no longer face to face with those fortuitous or indiscriminate variations which seemed for a time to banish all rational purpose from our conception of Evolution. The simple and certain fact that molecular motion, whether in the germ or in the structure, can have no source save in preceding molecular motion in the environment, by bringing supposed "fortuitous variations" back into the order of Nature, delivers us entirely from the spectre that seemed to arise out of the old conception of a mindless Evolution. As already said, we do not need to imagine any *special* or *separate* directive Agency, vital force, or other. But for the complete answer we are carried to the *entire environment*, which (as we have seen) is ever ordered and rational and dominated by the pressure, so to speak, of an all-controlling purpose—a purpose which has ever the *future* before it, and which must be mental or spiritual in its nature.

Note on Weismann's Theory.—Since the foregoing was written, we have been enabled to consult Weismann's most recent work on *The Evolution Theory*, and find strong support therein "The roots of all the transformations of organisms," he says, "lie in changes of external condition." If these had remained alike, "then no variations of any kind and no evolution would have taken place. But as this is inconceivable, since even the mere growth of the first living substance must have exposed the different kinds of biophors composing it to different influences, variation was inevitable, and so also was its result—the evolution of an animate world of organisms" (II. p. 380). Again, "The ultimate forces operative in bringing about this many-sided evolution are the known, and—although we do not recognise it as yet—perhaps the unknown—chemical-physical forces, which certainly work only according to laws, and that they are able to accomplish such marvellous results is due to the fact that they are associated in peculiar, and often very complex different kinds of combinations, and thus conform to the same sort of regulated arrangements as those which condition the operations of any machine made by man. All complex effects depend upon a co-operation of forces" It is like the working of a machine contrived by human intelligence, and " If it be asked, what replaces human intelligence in those purposeful combinations of primary forces, we can only answer that there is here a self-regulation depending upon the characters of the primary vital parts, and this means that these last are caused to vary by external influences and are selected by external influences—that is, are chosen for survival or excluded from it." " Thus in our time the great riddle has been solved" (*The Evolution Theory*, ii. 380, 381, 391).

In relation to a religious view of the World, Weismann presents a strong contrast to Haeckel. He expresses the belief that " in all likelihood the time is not far distant when the champions of religion will abandon their profitless struggle against the new truth, and will see that the recognition of a law-governed Evolution of the organic world is no more prejudicial to true religion than is the revolution of the earth round the sun" (i. 8) " To those that fear that Evolution will destroy their faith " he says, " let them not forget that truth can only be harmful and may even be destructive when we have only half grasped it, or when we try to evade it. If we follow it unafraid, we shall come, now and in the future, to the conclusion that a limit is set to our knowledge by our own minds, and that beyond this limit begins the reign of faith . . . the need for an ethical view of the world, a religion, will remain, though even this must change its expression according to the advancing knowledge of the world" (ii. 395).

Weismann's theory of Evolution is often misunderstood from the religious standpoint. He is said to exclude "design"; but it is only particular design *over* each individual form that he excludes · the whole is embraced in a wider design, although that does not give effect to itself in the manner once commonly supposed. It is true that he says that the great riddle has been solved—"the riddle of the origin of what is suited to its purpose—without the co-operation of purposive forces" But all was from a given beginning, and it is only the action of "purposive forces" *apart from such as are actually expressed and operative in the Universe* (such as used to be maintained) that are thus shown to be unnecessary. "Everything," he maintains, "is adaptation, from the smallest and simplest up to the largest and most complex, for, if it were not, it could not endure, but would perish" (see ii. 378). Again he says: "What the breeder does within the narrow limits of human power is being accomplished in free nature through the conditions which allow only what is fit to survive and reproduce, and thus bring about the wonderful result—as though it were guided by a superior intelligence—the adaptation of species to their environment" (p. 391).

Now, all this is just the operation of *Reason* as it has conditioned itself in the Universe as a whole. The "superior Intelligence" is really there, although in a different form from what was once supposed. The whole takes places in a "law-governed" Universe, and is the outcome of the whole complex workings of its rational laws. A law-governed or law-ordered Universe is really, as we have sought to show, a Reason-ordered, or rational Universe It ought to be emphatically stated that "Law" or "Order" is *the only way* in which Reason can be

NEWLY EMPHASISED FACTORS IN EVOLUTION 137

manifested *in a physical Universe* What we come to see, culminating in man, is the result of the presence and working of this Reason as expressed in the whole and in each part of the whole. Organisms are, as it were, Weismann says, "cast into a mould" (although there is also the "substance of life"). What is this "mould" but just *the rationally constituted environment?* The whole result is the product of an all-working Divine Reason as self-conditioned for the creation.

CHAPTER VII

Spencer's Evolution Doctrine

WITH marvellous perseverance and ability Mr. Herbert Spencer has depicted the course of Evolution on its physical or material side, showing how it is all due to, and may be deduced from, the simple principle of "the persistence of Force, or Energy." It has become fashionable in some quarters to decry Mr. Spencer's work and to speak of his System of Synthetic Philosophy as already belonging to the past. The present writer does not share that feeling. While unable to comprehend the "persistence" of Mr Spencer's Agnosticism, felt by himself, at the last, to be so unsatisfying, he regards Mr. Spencer's books as amongst the most remarkable ever given to the world, and believes that he has rendered real and lasting service to Philosophy and to Religion. He has reason to know that there are some who have been greatly helped by that writer's insistence on the reality of Religion as a product of Evolution, and on the certainty of the existence of a Power that is manifested in all phenomena—one with that which wells up in our own spiritual consciousness. If Evolution was the product of the working of this Power, which, Mr. Spencer held, must be greater than aught that we know in ourselves, the firmest ground seemed to be laid for a Theistic conception of the Universe. And although Mr. Spencer himself disclaimed all *knowledge* of that Power, if it was really manifested in some measure in all things, the conclusion did not seem difficult to reach, that it was, at least, most highly known in its highest manifestations. He was thankful, therefore, to find Professor Flint in his recent great work on Agnosticism treating Mr. Spencer in a much more generous way than is common on the part of Theologians. " His services," he says, " have been of inestimable value alike to Philosophy and Theology."

The first part of Mr. Spencer's *First Principles* has often been severely criticised, and many effective points made against his reasonings therein ; but, as he has said himself in a postscript to the last edition of that work, it is really quite unconnected with the soundness or the reverse of the System which the second part of that book presents. We have long felt that all that Mr. Spencer has in the second part so well described in physical terms might be equally well described (as he himself has acknowledged) in spiritual terms, and this we shall attempt to show in the latter portion of the present chapter.

I

If we grant Mr. Spencer his starting-point, it seeems impossible to deny his conclusion as regards the physical Universe. Granting the existence of the matter that he assumes, in a widely diffused condition, of the qualities ascribed to it, of the environment in which it is placed and of a persistent Force, all the steps in Evolution seem to follow naturally and necessarily. Gravitation first begins to act, bringing the diffused particles together (although, as already noted, other agencies are now supposed to have been operating), and, owing to their different exposures, they coalesce in different ways leading to a diversity of results, and from this point the evolving process goes steadily on, issuing in the wonderful Universe that we live in.

But, while we are able to accept Mr Spencer's account of a continuous evolution under the influence of a single constantly acting Principle, we may differ seriously from him in our ultimate definition of that Principle. There are three things at the beginning *assumed* by Mr. Spencer and unaccounted for by him—the three essential things, indeed, viz., the *matter* through which Power acts, the *force* which drove the particles out into that extremely diffused condition, and which shows itself again in the form of Gravitation, and the *environment* in which the whole is placed. So that, even though we accept all that Mr. Spencer says, we can reach no ultimate explanation of the Universe in this way. The Matter, Motion, and Force, and the Universe around them—the essential constituents of the problem—are as far from being accounted for as ever. Beyond this, there are, of course, the questions of the origin of Life and of Mind.

Granting that the persistence of Force does all that is claimed for it, Matter, with a certain definite constitution, is assumed to begin with. Apart from *such* matter, the actual results could never have been reached. Just as, to revert to a favourite analogy suggestive of the whole theory, there is in the case of each individual organism, not only the action of Force, but a certain definite constitution of the germ which makes each organism what it is, so must it be assumed with respect to the original matter of the Universe. These definite qualities which give its character to each germ, and of which the organism becomes the expression, are ideal or spiritual in themselves, although they are materially expressed. Reasoning from this analogy, the Universe has a spiritual side from the first.

Mr Spencer's theory of the passage from "the homogeneous" (although, as we have just seen, it cannot be really homogeneous in the strict sense of the term, as he himself has acknowledged) is purely mechanical, and does not in itself account for what takes place. It shows how, under the pressure of Force, *some* and *varied* combinations were the necessary result; but it does not show why these particular combinations which form the Universe as we know it were the outcome. So far as the mere necessity of passing from the homogeneous, and the mere variety of effects are concerned, the combinations formed might have been of *any* similar atoms. Why should they be those that we know? He himself says that it was owing to the presence of certain *affinities*: the particular combinations, therefore, are due to those *affinities*. Why there should be these, and what constitutes them, are the real questions to be answered even on the physical or material side.

If we turn now to "Force," we must ask *what* this Force *is* which persists with such wonderful effects. It is not anything material or physical. At a certain point of the diffused matter, as truly as at the end of the swing of a pendulum, it has no positive (physical) existence at all; it is what is termed "potential" only. It cannot be separated from the matter through which it acts and of which it seems to be a quality, while, on the other hand, matter itself, in the form in which we have to do with it, is constituted by it. If we abstract all that we may describe as "the forces and qualities of matter," what have we left? We seem to have nothing left at all—nothing physically effective, at any rate Power, no doubt, is real; but Power is not material or physical, although it may have physical effects. This persistent Force (if it is not to be merely persistence of persistence) must be at bottom something *spiritual* Mr. Spencer himself affirms that that which persists is not Force as we know it in its conditioned forms, but "an unknown and unknowable *Power*, which we are obliged to recognise as without limit in space and without beginning or end in time" (Statement prepared for Professor Youmans by Mr Spencer, see Clodd's *Pioneers of Evolution*). Mr. Spencer acknowledges that we are forced to think of it in *subjective* terms—our only conception of force being drawn from our own sense of muscular effort. But we are not merely obliged so to think of it; our thought is true force is not anything material, but is spiritual, and, as we have already seen, it is revealed in its true character in our own consciousness. The only force that we *know* is the only force that exists and persists, viz., that which has a spiritual origin and is spiritual in its nature. It is the same, Mr. Spencer says, as that which "wells up in our own consciousness" The only difference is in the different ways in which it is *conditioned.*

Mr. Spencer thus fails to show how, on the ground of mere "persistence of Force," the world comes to exist. Granting all that he says about Force on its physical side, we can in no way account for this rationally constituted Universe, culminating in reason in man, save by regarding — the "Power" of which Force is a manifestation as Spiritual—that is, *Divine.*

II

We have been long convinced that what Mr. Spencer terms "the persistence of Force" may be shown to be *the persistence of Reason.* This may be fully illustrated from his own works. That which Mr. Spencer describes so well on its physical or mechanical side has also a rational or spiritual side, on which it may be equally well described. If Spirit or Reason is to operate in the physical world, *it must take on itself a physical side,* and, of course, it is only *this* that we directly observe. But all the progressive action that we witness in Evolution—arrangements and re-arrangements, adaptations and re-adaptations — with progress as the result—going steadily onward till conscious reason appears in ourselves, is exactly what we understand by rational action (although it is necessarily through matter that the Power operates in the external world), and, as we must say once again, it is to this very action in the world

SPENCER'S EVOLUTION DOCTRINE 143

outside of us that the presence of reason in ourselves is due. The Ideal element is not only there throughout, but, reasoning from all that we know, it is ever first and deepest, formative and supreme Behind the whole process and *in* it all there is the Divine Reason, which simply expresses itself or works itself out creatively in those necessary and rational ways that are described by Mr. Spencer on their mechanical side The result that is reached is due neither to matter nor to force, but entirely to that Divine Reason which makes matter and force to serve it. It is because *this* is the source of the worlds that the evolution is what we know it to be; the process is that of the evolution of this primal Reason, or creative thought, in its world-forming action

Mr. Spencer himself distinctly affirms that the whole process has *a spiritual side*, although he chooses (for reasons which he states) to exhibit it on its material side; but he says, were he forced to choose between the material and the mental, he would choose the mental mode of representation. This fact is strangely overlooked by many who quote that writer, whether in the interests of Agnosticism or in opposition to the Materialism with which they mistakenly charge him. We can best follow out our argument by quoting largely from Mr. Spencer himself. In the concluding chapter of *First Principles* he says, " The reasonings contained in the foregoing pages afford no support to either of the antagonist hypotheses respecting the ultimate nature of things. As before implied, their implications are no more materialistic than they are spiritualistic; and no more spiritualistic than they are materialistic. The establishment of correlation and equivalence between the forces of the outer and the inner worlds, serves to assimilate either to the other, according as we set out with the one or the other term." He goes on to say that neither term can be taken as ultimate, that "though the relation of subject and object renders necessary to us these antithetical conceptions of Spirit and Matter; the one is no less than the other to be regarded as but a sign of the Unknown Reality which underlies both" (last edition, p. 446).

Now, here it will be observed it is affirmed that we may form either a spiritualistic or a materialistic conception of the World according to whichever of the two terms we set out with, yet by Mr. Spencer both are left behind as being but signs of an Unknown Reality underlying them both, landing him inevitably in Agnosticism. The mistake that Mr. Spencer makes is to regard these two terms as being of *equal value for* the explanation of the World He avers that we may set out with either Mind or Matter equally. Surely this is not the case. Not to speak of the fact that we only know that there is such a thing as "matter" through Mind, we cannot begin with Matter, Motion, and Force *merely*, so as to get the actually existing world of Spirit, Mind, Reason, and Consciousness. This would be to attempt to do what Mr. Spencer elsewhere shows clearly to be impossible, viz., to get something from nothing, or the greater from the less. The Mind that knows matter is surely greater than the matter that knows nothing, and cannot be produced by it. On the other hand, we know Mind as that which is competent to produce the world, and we need seek no other source for it. While matter cannot conceivably produce Spirit, Spirit can conceivably produce matter, and is competent to produce all that we behold in Nature—revealing itself in our own consciousness as Spirit—which assuredly matter could never do.

In his *Principles of Psychology* (third edition, 1881) Mr. Spencer seems to go further towards a spiritual explanation of the Universe. He there writes· " Nevertheless, it may be as well to say here, once for all, that were we compelled to choose between the alternatives of translating mental phenomena into physical phenomena or translating physical phenomena into mental phenomena, the latter alternative would seem the more acceptable of the two." The mental activities of which we are conscious must, he has said, be the activities of something real, and the activities outside of us can be thought of only in terms of that Mind through which they are known. "We may go farther towards conceiving units of external force to be identical with units of feeling, than we can towards conceiving units of feeling to be identical with units of external force. Clearly, if units of external force are regarded as absolutely unknown and unknowable, then to translate units of feeling into them is to translate the known into the unknown, which is absurd. And if they are what they are supposed to be, by those who identify them with their symbols, then the difficulty of translating units of feeling into them is insurmountable; if Force as it objectively exists is absolutely alien in nature from that which exists subjectively as Feeling, then the transformation of Force into Feeling is unthinkable Either way, therefore, it is impossible to interpret inner existence in terms of outer existence." Not only so, but he goes on to show that thus a spiritualistic interpretation of Nature becomes "a conceivable hypothesis" Those activities which exist outside our nature may, although really the same in essential nature as those within consciousness, be antithetically opposed to consciousness simply because they exist outside. "Consciousness cannot, as it were, run through them, and so they come to be figured as unconscious—are symbolised as having the nature called material as opposed to that called spiritual." These are certainly very large admissions. Not only is it declared quite impossible to conceive Spirit in terms of Matter, but it is affirmed to be *possible to conceive Matter in terms of Spirit*—possible "that units of external Force may be identical in nature with units of the Force known as Feeling" (I. pp. 159, 160, etc).

Yet it is affirmed that we get no nearer thus to the comprehension of external Force The resolution of Mind into units of Feeling leaves us unable to think of the substance of Mind as it exists in such units, and so, "could we really figure to ourselves all units of external Force as being essentially like units of the force known as Feeling, and as so constituting a universal sentiency, we should be as far as ever from forming a conception of that which is universally sentient. Hence, though of the two it seems easier to translate so-called Matter into so-called Spirit than to translate so-called Spirit into so-called Matter (which latter indeed is wholly impossible), yet no translation can carry us beyond our symbols." If we speak of "substance of Mind," we need to remember that "we cannot think of substance save in terms that imply material properties Our only course is constantly to recognise our symbols as symbols only, and to rest content with that duality of them which our constitution necessitates. The Unknowable as manifested to us within the limits of consciousness in the shape of Feeling, being no less inscrutable than The Unknowable as manifested beyond the limits of consciousness in other shapes, we approach no nearer to understanding the last by rendering it into the first. The conditioned form under which Being is presented in the Subject cannot, any more than the conditioned form in which Being is presented in the Object, be the Unconditioned Being common to the two" (pp. 161, 162).

This last quoted portion seems clearly to contradict what has been already said by Mr. Spencer in the first quoted portion. He there affirmed that we *did* come nearer the conception of the Force without by regarding it as assimilated to that which is *known* within, because, while the outer was assuredly incapable of producing the inner, the inner might conceivably be able to produce the outer; and he has just said that it is *wholly impossible* to translate Spirit into terms of Matter. It is quite true that we can form no conception of unconditioned Being from its conditioned revelation within, in the sense in which Mr. Spencer uses the word "conception." No Theologian will affirm for a moment that we can *so* conceive God as to be able to picture to ourselves the form or mode of His existence. No more can we picture to ourselves the substance of Mind, or the mode of the existence of " a universal sentiency " But these incapacities constitute no real objection to our interpretation of external activities in terms of inner, or spiritual activities as regards their source and essential nature, or to our believing in the existence of a Being who is competent to produce both series of activities No one will claim to *know* the Unconditioned in Mr. Spencer's sense of "knowing"; yet, all the same, we may know that there *is* such a Being, and we may also find ourselves compelled to think of Him wholly in terms of Mind or Spirit, and not at all in terms of Matter (which last Mr Spencer himself declares it to be quite impossible to do)—regarding Matter as being only something constituted by Him, or through which He manifests Himself to us and effects His purposes. Such Unconditioned Being need by no means remain the Unknowable of which Mr. Spencer speaks If we know that such a Being exists at all—and this Mr. Spencer affirms we may be absolutely sure of (it is " the certainty of certainties ")—we only know of His existence through His manifestations, and these same manifestations surely tell us something of His nature. Mr. Spencer indeed, as has been often pointed out, ascribes a good many qualities to the Unknowable Being—Power, Eternity, Infinitude, Omnipresence, Self-manifestation, etc.,—most of which, however, he maintains we cannot "*conceive.*" Yet we know what they mean, and we can certainly think of the Ultimate Reality in such terms. Mr. Spencer himself says that we *must* do so. If we think at all, it can only be in those human modes with which the Source of our being has furnished us. To say that we cannot know God beyond human modes of knowledge, is the merest truism That is the knowledge that is afforded to man, and it is sufficient for all human purposes. Any other form of knowledge is, in fact, utterly impossible, to seek for it is to attempt to go beyond our humanity.

It has, moreover, to be remembered that what is revealed in consciousness is more than mere "Sentiency", it is Reason and Will and Love, and we find in these, extended to Infinity in God, not only the powers competent to produce the Universe, including our rational selves, but *the only Power* that can conceivably do so Mr. Spencer acknowledges a spiritual side to the Ultimate Reality, although he exhibits a mechanical process of evolution only. Can we believe that the spiritual side, acknowledged in the Ultimate Being, remains *wholly quiescent* throughout the process, and is not rather the actual Source of all the power that works therein? It only manifests itself by means of matter, but to put the material side on the same level as the spiritual is contradictory to all that we know.

Elsewhere—in his chapter on "Results," in his *Principles of Psychology*—Mr. Spencer affirms that "the antithesis of subject and object, never to be transcended while consciousness lasts, renders impossible all knowledge of that Ultimate Reality in which subject and object are united" (p 627). Here it is to be noted that we have the affirmation that there *is* an Ultimate Reality in which subject and object are united What more do we want for *God*? Subject and object in God do not, of course, necessarily mean "Mind" on the one side and "Matter" on the other. But if for the moment we regard the subjective as Mind or Spirit and the objective as matter, we can surely have no doubt respecting the relation of the two in the Ultimate Being. We know Him to be Spiritual, and we cannot for a moment suppose that "matter," or its substratum, has the same value in the Divine existence as the spiritual. Nay, how can we conceive of any source of Spirit save Spirit, any more than we can conceive of any source of power save Power? Conditioned Spirit can only be derived from unconditioned Spirit—its manifestation, indeed, under conditions, whereas, on the other hand, we can easily conceive of that which we term "matter" as the product or exteriorisation of Spirit, or the means of its manifestation and operation. Mr. Spencer's mistake throughout, we repeat, is to regard the two sides as of equal value, and to ignore the revelation that is given within ourselves as the highest product of the Power that works all in all. But, further, we would ask, Is it only in the Ultimate Reality that the antithesis of subject and object is transcended? Do we not know them as one in ourselves? My Thoughts, my Will, my Brain, my Body with all its material combinations and movements, are objects to myself. I know these as *mine*. I as self-conscious am object to myself. Both subject and object are united in me, and I know Mind as revealed within myself to be supreme. We know Mind in ourselves as that which employs and uses matter to effect its purposes, as that which can all but create matter It is true that both are *united* in us, and that, as Mr. Spencer says, we cannot think of Mind save as being substantive. But may not Mind be ultimately the only *real* "substance"? It is certainly not true that we can only think of Mind in terms of matter. As we have seen, Mr. Spencer himself declares this to be an impossibility. It may seem that Mind in us depends on matter, but we have already seen it to be certain that Mind was acting in the Universe before ever matter became organised in us, and that the reason why

Mind in us is related to matter as it is, is simply because it is through the organisation in us of that which Mind has wrought in external Nature that finite Minds are enabled to appear. As we have seen, Mr. Spencer maintains in this same book, that "Intelligence has been shown to have the same nature and the same law, from the lowest reflex action up to the most transcendent triumph of reason—from first to last its growth is due to the repetition of experiences, the effects of which are accumulated, organised, and inherited" (p. 507). But we must ever think of Mind as being before matter, as being, both logically and chronologically, that which is first and deepest. If the Power that persists, and to the persistence of which the Universe is due, reveals itself, as it is acknowledged to do (on one side at least), *as Spirit*, we have no need to go behind this for some hypothetical source of both Spirit and matter. We have found in Spirit that which is competent to explain matter as that which is necessary for the external expression of Spirit and for the carrying out of its purpose in the Creation, and we simply wilfully turn away from the explanation that is thus given us, when we attribute both matter and Spirit to an unknown and unknowable Reality that is supposed to underlie them both—as if anything *could* underlie *Spirit*. Spirit, as it exists in us, is certainly not Spirit as it exists in itself in unconditioned form; it is Spirit in a conditioned form of existence, but none the less is it *Spirit*; and unconditioned, but self-conditioning, Spirit is its only conceivable source.

But, finally, all that we contend for is covered by the affirmation made by Mr Spencer in his *First Principles*, that the Ultimate Reality cannot be less than Personal. In words the substance of which is familiar, he says (we quote from the last edition): "In the estimate it (his Philosophy) implies of the Ultimate Cause, it does not fall short of the alternative position, but exceeds it. Those who espouse this alternative position assume that the choice is between personality and something lower than personality; whereas the choice is rather between personality and something that may be higher. Is it not possible that there is a mode of being as much transcending Intelligence and Will as these transcend mechanical motion? Doubtless we are totally unable to imagine any such higher mode of being But this is not a reason for questioning its existence; it is rather the reverse" (p. 80). This is all that Theology need ask from Science; it is all that is required for our faith in God, or our confidence in Him. No Theologian will affirm that personality in God is not something higher and greater than it is in us, where we know it to exist under necessary limitations; no one will deny that it is something greater than we can conceive, but if it is *greater*, not less, than what we know as personal in ourselves, our faith may well rest contented. When Mr. Spencer goes on to ask,—seeing that the Ultimate Cause is in every respect greater than can be conceived,—" May we not therefore rightly refrain from assigning to it any attributes whatever, on the ground that such attributes, derived as they must be from our own natures, are not elevations but degradations?" (*ib* p. 81), we answer that, on the very same ground as enables him to affirm that the Ultimate Reality cannot be less than personal, we are bound to ascribe to that Ultimate Reality all that is highest in ourselves, in infinite degree. Intelligence, Love, Will in God are certainly not held and exercised in the same way as they are in us, under conditions and limitations, but they are essentially the same realities in their *unconditioned form*. We cannot conceive the *mode* of their existence in the Ultimate Cause, but we know that they must be there in their perfect, unconditioned state, else they could never be here in conditioned form in ourselves, and, in Mr. Spencer's own words, our inability to conceive the mode of that existence "is not a reason for questioning that existence, but the reverse."

Mr. Spencer's doctrine thus not only leaves us our belief in God, but places it on an immovable basis as "the certainty of certainties"; his Evolution theory may be as truly stated in terms of Spirit as in terms of Matter, and we believe that the day will come when Theologians will be thankful to Mr Spencer for having set forth with such fulness a description, on its mechanical side, of that Evolution which he at the same time maintains has also a *spiritual* side, on which it may, with equal truth at least, be represented.

Note.—In a Postscript to Part I. of the last edition of *First Principles* (1899), Mr Spencer says that the "account of the transformation of things" to be given in Part II. "is simply an orderly presentation of facts; and the interpretation of the facts is nothing more than a statement of the ultimate uniformities they present—the laws to which they conform"—and that, therefore, neither Atheist nor Pantheist, neither the believer in Divine immanency nor he who believes in a Deity who has given unchanging laws to the Universe, will find anything at variance with the beliefs he may hold. Although this is largely negative, it makes the distinct statement that his System is *consistent with Theism.* How it can also be consistent with Atheism is difficult to imagine. He seems to think that it is so because he only gives account of "ultimate uniformities or laws," but it is just—after all that he has said—those uniformities or laws that have to be accounted for. To explain everything save that which makes everything what it is, is no philosophical explanation of the Universe. It is just these "uniformities" or "laws" that proclaim the omnipresent and all-controlling action of Reason in the Universe

CHAPTER VIII

HAECKEL'S MONISTIC EVOLUTION

ALTHOUGH Haeckel proceeds on different lines from Mr Spencer, he too lands in an "unknowable Reality" which he terms "Substance," with the threefold attributes of "Matter, Energy, and Sensation." But, while Spencer avowedly wrote to uphold Religion in his understanding of it, Haeckel as avowedly denies the existence of God, of a Spiritual world, of Freedom and of Immortality. We do not find in him that acknowledgment which Spencer makes of the possibility of a spiritual interpretation of the Universe. While he maintains a spiritual side to the one only Substance from the first, it is originally unconscious. Although he speaks of a "Monistic Religion," he is frankly Atheistic. Pantheism is claimed by him as the system most in affinity with his own; but it is declared to be a Pantheism which is only a more polite name for Atheism His only object of devotion is the Trinity of the True, the Good, the Beautiful. While he explains from a scientific standpoint some of the particular world-riddles, he gives us no ultimate explanation of the Universe; after all that he says, the riddle remains as great a mystery as ever. This by his own confession. His great merit, according to his able English defender Mr. McCabe, and apparently in his own opinion also, is that he has traced the development of Mind from its unconscious antecedents. The value of this achievement will be discussed immediately.

The eminent services of Haeckel to Biology, Zoology, Anthropology, etc., are beyond dispute, and there is much in those writings of his which have recently been translated into English—one of which, *The Riddle of the Universe*, has had such an enormous circulation—of a suggestive and instructive character. This is true especially of *The Wonders of Life*, which is written with remarkable clearness and is free from those ebullitions against Religion which disfigure *The Riddle of the Universe*. We cannot but sympathise with his desire to reach a truly Monistic Philosophy, and it must be acknowledged that the practical moral and social Ideal which he erects is, in many respects, one to be desired. At the same time, however, there is a tendency to justify suicide, a lightness of regard for infant life, and an inclination to weaken the marriage tie, which, in spite of all protestations to the contrary, are the natural outcome of what is really, if not " Materialism," a *materialistic* system. Haeckel speaks of Buchner's " Materialism," but his own system seems to be at bottom as truly deserving of that appellation as Buchner's, who, equally with himself, protests against such a designation. Buchner was not a Materialist. He was a writer from whom one may learn much.

Although Haeckel fails to give a satisfactory explanation of the Universe as we know it, his *method* is a sounder one than that of mere Positivism or Agnosticism He maintains the rightful place of philosophical thought in addition to the mere observation of facts He is strong on the supremacy of Reason, and on the value of the principle of Causation. He is right also when he says that speculation cannot stand when it runs contrary to fact. He excludes " Emotion " and " Revelation." Why these should be totally ignored is by no means clear. It is, he says, because they demand belief in " the Miraculous." Why Emotion should do so is not at all obvious—" the heart has its reasons as well as the head " Nor does " Revelation " necessarily involve "the Miraculous" in his sense of the term. All our knowledge may be revelation, and it may not be confined to one plane only.

He bases his Monism on what he terms "the two chief cosmic laws—the chemical law of the constancy of matter, and the physical law of the constancy of force." Matter and Force (or Energy) are the two aspects of that which he calls "Substance," the law of which (really, nothing more than simply the persistence of Force) determines everything in the Universe and accounts for its entire Evolution, culminating in rational man. But since a subjective, sensitive, mental, and spiritual side to the Universe is also directly known within ourselves—that through which we know anything at all, indeed—he divides the "Force-side" of Substance into two aspects, "Energy" and "Sensation." Sensation as well as Force, he holds, belongs to all Matter. "This Trinity of Substance," he thinks, "provides the safest ground for Monism." "I may formulate it," he says, "in three propositions (1) No matter without force and without sensation (2) No force without matter and without sensation; (3) No sensation without matter and without force," "these three fundamental attributes are found inseparably united throughout the whole Universe, in every atom and in every molecule" (*The Wonders of Life*, p. 465). Given this marvellous "Substance," the Universe is the outcome of what he terms "the law of Substance," which is really, as we have said, simply the law of persistence. This magical phrase is merely an expression for what is elsewhere laid down as the foundation of the system, "the constancy of matter," and "the conservation of force," with the addition of the affirmation of a spiritual side to matter and force from the first. This latter assumption is clearly necessary in order to account for the spiritual element which is so manifest in the outcome, the failure to account for which doomed the old Materialism. Haeckel however, does not in this way really account for the spiritual element in the Universe, and for that very reason his form of Monism must also fall. Let us look at it a little more closely.

1. Haeckel bases his system on the constancy or conservation of matter and force. Our first remark is that the most recent Science does not give support to this position, at least so far as the conservation or constancy of matter is concerned. The recently observed phenomena in connection with Radium have even thrown doubt on the validity of the assumption of the conservation of Force or Energy. It depends entirely on how the marvellous energy constantly emitted by a minute particle of Radium is to be accounted for, whether that doctrine can stand or not. The dissipation of Energy *in the material system of the Universe* has also been established on other grounds. But, certainly, recent Science does away with the belief in the constancy, or conservation, of *matter*. Strictly speaking, the only statement that Science was ever warranted in making was that " mass " is conserved in any system of change that is dealt with. To carry this into the sweeping statement of the eternity of matter is quite another thing. According to Haeckel, matter is eternal, unchanged in its substance and unchangeable. Of course, he has no means of knowing this, and Science is now, through many voices, assuring us that matter has been, and perhaps is now being, evolved— brought into existence as " matter "—and, instead of being eternal, or constant, is actually disappearing. In the words of Professor Crookes at Berlin, " This fatal quality of atomic dissociation appears to be universal, and operates whenever we brush a piece of glass with silk; it works in sunshine and in rain-drops, in lightnings and flame, it prevails in the waterfall and stormy sea " Matter is consequently " doomed to destruction " (see article in *Edinburgh Review*, October 1903, " The Revelations of Radium "). Matter has

HAECKEL'S MONISTIC EVOLUTION 157

had a history, an evolution, and it is having a dissolution too. Instead of being a constant thing, it seems to be nothing but "a relation." "An electron as a unit of matter is a particle of negative Electricity. So it is really a transient expression of a relation. When a negative and a positive charge of Electricity have met and satisfied their 'affinity' for each other, they cease to be" (Dr. Saleeby in *Academy*, Feb 11, 1905). If then matter is not conserved, one side of Haeckel's Monistic ground falls in, only Energy is left, and even this, so far as the physical Universe is concerned, is being constantly "dissipated." We have argued that, in any view of it, Matter must be regarded as being the creation of some Power and as the vehicle of Energy. Haeckel's last book shows that this view—the reduction of matter to Energy—is being taken by many German students at present. Matter, that which reveals itself as the tangible side of "Substance," so to speak, or to go back to Spinoza, whom Haeckel follows, as the "extended" side of Substance, may not, in any of its forms, have permanent existence. It simply serves the purposes of the underlying Energy or Power. It cannot be conceived save as the product of Power. It is reducible to the play of energies (electrons), and these again may be nothing but temporary relations. Haeckel himself ought to be the first to admit this. He will not hear of any origin of *life* save the play of chemical forces. These alone, he maintains, could form the primary basis of life, there is no other power that could build up the life-molecule. Is it not at least *as* certain that the atom, as well as the molecule, must have been built up by some kind of Energy, and that it is essentially the expression and vehicle of Energy?

2. The inclusion of a spiritual element from the first is so essential to Haeckel's Monism, that we must devote special attention to it. He attributes "sensation" to all matter, and it is only in this way that he can embrace the

subjective or spiritual side of the Universe in his system. The spiritual is most assuredly here in the outcome, and it is seen to be useless to try to account for it without assuming its presence from the first. This is certainly a step in advance of the old Materialism. Whether the assumption is warranted, in the sense in which Haeckel makes it, and whether, supposing it to be granted, it is adequate to account for the Universe as we know it, are perhaps the most important questions to be determined in relation to this Monism

There is a sense in which a spiritual side must be ascribed to matter from the first; but it is not the sense of Haeckel The spiritual side of matter is with him at first something wholly unconscious. We too affirm that matter, as the expression and instrument of Reason, has a spiritual side to it. But with Haeckel the spiritual side of matter appears simply as the " Force " that is inseparable from matter, which Force, under certain conditions, becomes *developed* into conscious Mind or Spirit. Conscious Mind or Spirit, we are assured by him, has no existence till the vertebrate form is reached and Brain has attained a certain measure of development. He twits certain Theists with making God a " gaseous vertebrate." Now, the assertion of the constant presence of Force or Energy with matter is one which Science makes, quite independently of Haeckel's theories, but that it can be called *Spirit* in any true and intelligible sense cannot by any means be affirmed. Force (that is Energy) may be—we believe it is—spiritual in its essence, but this is not to say that Force can be rightly termed " Spirit." Spirit, as the word has hitherto been used, and as Haeckel requires to account for it, always implies conscious Mind, Feeling, Thought, Will. We may rightly speak of something lower than this as " spiritual "— a thought, a feeling, an emotion, a sentence with a meaning in it—but it is not " Spirit " as we know it in the highest outcome of the creation. If there may be feeling and thought and other psychical elements existing and operating without consciousness, these are still, in that form, less than "Spirit" While, therefore, Haeckel may be entitled to affirm "force" as present and operating from the first, and while he may rightly trace the gradual evolution of Mind or Spirit in finite beings from lower unconscious forms, he has no right to identify the unconscious energy which is all that he really acknowledges as existing in prior states, and which he calls the other side of matter, with that *spirit which is only reached in the way that he himself professes to show.* It is simply an assertion—one that *has* to be made because of the actual presence of Spirit in the outcome. In *The Wonders of Life*, however, Haeckel does not term the other side of matter "Spirit" (as it is rendered in the E.T. of *The Riddle*, and as it is employed by Mr. McCabe in his Defence of Haeckel); he speaks simply of "sensation," and explains it to mean "unconscious sensation." Has he any greater right to ascribe *this* to all matter, and does it serve his purpose to do so?

1. It must be pointed out, in the first place, that the question has no bearing on *living* matter; it is not whether we are always distinctly conscious of sensations, nor even whether sensation can be said to belong to the plant world; but whether it can be rightly ascribed to inorganic or non-living matter Is chemical reaction, for instance, an example of sensation? There may be, of course, it is universally admitted, sensations of which we are not directly conscious—that is, to which we are not attending—as in the automatic playing of a piece of music, but the consciousness is always there, and attention can be directed to the sensations. There may also be stimuli so slight, that, while they make an organic impression, do not awaken sensation proper until they reach a certain degree of force; but the present question is not really concerned

with what happens in the case of organised or living matter, but whether there is any warrant for speaking of "unconscious sensation" *apart* from living organisms. To call it "Feeling," as Haeckel sometimes prefers to do, makes no real difference.

Haeckel seems to think that unless sensation be ascribed to all matter, he is shut up to the Dualism of Kant and others. But Dualism is not the only alternative. In his chapter on "Sensation" in *The Wonders of Life*, and in *The Riddle of the Universe*, chap. x, he has done his best to prove that sensation belongs to all matter; but it cannot be said that he has succeeded. He says that he cannot conceive the simplest combination of chemical elements without attributing to them an element of feeling; it is necessarily implied in "chemical affinity," the elements must have a *feeling* towards each other of attraction or repulsion, it must be "pleasant or the reverse", in short, he endorses "the loves and hates of the atoms" of Empedocles.

Chemistry, certainly, gives no support to such a theory. It can do quite well without the word "affinity" It speaks of structures and weights, not of loves and hates. What brings the atoms together it does not profess to know. Chemical union, it tells us, " may be brought about by an attractive force between the atoms, it may be due to the force of gravity, conditioned by the forms and the motions of the atoms; but it is more probable that the forces between the atoms are electrical forces" (Muir, *The Story of the Chemical Elements*, see also Duncan, *The New Knowledge*). The Electrical theory is now the most widely accepted one. " Chemical affinity," says Professor Duncan, "is Electrical affinity." But whatever it may be due to, it is really too absurd to attribute to the atoms anything that can be rightly called "sensation." Ridicule is not argument, but when Haeckel does away with the highest faiths of man on the ground of such a theory as this, it is not unfair to exhibit the ridiculous side of it. The atoms, certainly, do not always come together "pleasantly." It often needs a tremendous force to effect their union, and the same is required again to separate those once-reluctant atoms. Their dislikes are sometimes unaccountably violent. Carbon plays a great part with Haeckel, and Goethe has spoken of the affection of carbon for oxygen; but chemists tell us that this same carbon is a rather inert substance, only uniting with oxygen at a considerable degree of heat. Occasionally these loving atoms are violently torn asunder. Their loves must in some cases be very wide and in other instances very narrow. For, while some atoms can afford to take six outsiders into their embrace, others are so narrow-minded that they will only give hospitality to one What a virulent "hatred" of organic matter some of those flesh-burning acids must entertain! If we are to attribute anything at all like real "feeling" or "sensation" to all matter, what an extension of suffering we will have in the creation! A sensitive soul will scarce dare to strike a blow with his hammer, lest in pounding he should be wounding. This "sensation," Haeckel tells us, rises higher in the plant world If so, there must be some very real feeling in its members. Does it actually pain the flowers when we cut them? In that case, we had better cease gardening. Perhaps it gives them "pleasure," and they yield themselves up with real grace and goodwill for the joy or consolation of humanity. But, with their important function of reproduction to serve, we can scarcely suppose that they can find pleasure in their destruction. Haeckel even associates "sensation" with gravitation. He speaks, in this connection, of "the falling stone." Does the stone then *feel* something when it is attracted to the earth? What must its feeling be when it is dashed to the ground and smashed in pieces?

Of course, he will say that this is all nonsense, that he

does not mean this, that he speaks only of "*unconscious sensation.*" It is only at the first, he says, unconscious sensation Well, then, it is not *sensation* at all; and, certainly, to attribute *such* "sensation" (even if there be such a thing) to matter is nothing to his purpose. "Unconscious sensation" is *not* sensation as we know it as a feature of the subjective side of the world. It is not unconscious sensation merely that Haeckel needs to account for, but *conscious* sensation, or sensation as an element in mental life. It is sensation in this sense that he must embrace in his Monistic system, not something different that has to be distinguished from it by the epithet "unconscious" In short, he uses the word "sensation" in two quite distinct senses. What he attributes to matter is not that which we know in experience as "sensation." By no means can he get the spiritual element in the world embraced within his Monism except by attributing to all matter the lowest form of it—sensation. But it is in name only that he has it; for what he terms "sensation" in matter turns out to be no real sensation at all. His failure to include true sensation, and the spiritual element in general, in his Monism is its condemnation as a system. Language can scarcely be too strong in reprehension of a "philosophy" (not of the person) which would on such a basis deny God, substitute mechanism for Freedom, take away from suffering humanity all the consolation and help of Faith, and rob it of the hope of Immortality. The wonder is that so many can be, even momentarily, carried away by such a scheme. We can only regard it as a testimony to the deep-seated feeling for *unity* in the human mind.

2. But let us ask, in the second place, whether—supposing we should grant the right to give the name of "Spirit" to the unconscious element, which, according to Haeckel, is from eternity the other side of matter—it is

possible to derive the world that we know, culminating in conscious Mind or Spirit in ourselves, from this unconscious element as its source?

Haeckel himself, although he has a great deal to urge against belief in God, scarcely discusses this question of questions; but Mr. McCabe, in his *Haeckel's Critics Answered* (Mr. McCabe is the translator of Haeckel's recent works), is obliged to face it, although his treatment of it is all too brief, and far from satisfactory. It needs to be emphasised that, supposing Haeckel's preliminary contentions were granted, this is the real question on which everything turns with reference to his doctrine: *Can we get the world of conscious Mind or Spirit, as we know it, from unconscious elements as its original source?* The real question is not that on which Mr. McCabe lays so great stress and employs his powers so earnestly to meet—whether *over and above* the one Substance with its two sides, a Divine *directive* power must be affirmed. We do not by any means assume the "blindness" of the "laws of Nature," or of the forces which act through matter; we believe and affirm them to be throughout the expression of Reason itself. But is it possible, starting from what is in itself *unconscious*, ever to reach by any process of evolution the rational world culminating in consciousness—in self-consciousness in man? We maintain that it is wholly impossible to do so.

Mr McCabe gives an admirable resumé of Haeckel's Evolution doctrine, which, for the sake of clearness, we will quote. "An illimitable substance revealing itself to us as matter and force (or spirit), is dimly perceived at the root of this evolution as a simple and homogeneous medium (prothyl), associated with an equally homogeneous force. Then the continuous prothyl, by a process not yet determined, forms into what are virtually or really discrete and separate particles—electrons: the electrons unite to build atoms of various sizes and structures, and the rich variety of chemical elements is given, the base of an incalculable number of combinations and forms of matter. Meantime the more concentrated (ponderable) elements gather into cosmic masses under the influence of the force associated with them; the force evolving and differentiating at equal pace with the matter (with which it is one in reality). Nebulæ are formed; solar systems grow like crystals from them; planets take on solid crusts, with enveloping oceans and atmospheres. Presently, a more elaborate combination of material elements, protoplasm, with—naturally—a more elaborate force-side, makes its appearance, and organic evolution sets in. The little cellules cling together and form tissue-animals, which increase in complexity and organisation and centralisation until the human frame is produced, the life-force growing more elaborate with the structure, until it issues in the remarkable properties of the human mind" (*Haeckel's Critics Answered*, pp. 68, 69).

In the presence of such a statement as this, many questions suggest themselves, but we content ourselves at present with pointing out that the weakest part of the statement is in its foundation, viz., the affirmation of an original "*homogeneous* medium (prothyl) associated with an equally homogeneous force" as the source of the Universe. "Homogeneous" here means "purely simple"; otherwise its affirmation is nothing to the purpose.

1. Now, in the first place, the assertion of such a homogeneous medium is a pure assumption for which there are no sure grounds in fact. It cannot be called even an hypothesis. it is a pure supposition. No one knows that there was or is such a substance. If it exists, Science brings us no tidings of it, and it can never bring us any. It cannot do so for the simple reason that, as Mr. McCabe admits, we never reach an absolute beginning, we must always start with such matter and force as cannot possibly

be (if the history of the Universe be that eternal cycle of birth and decay and re-birth of worlds which Haeckel maintains) homogeneous in their character. The past history of some portion of the Universe, at least, is bound to be represented in the matter and force with which we start. So that we can go farther and positively assert that the matter and force from which this actual world has been evolved were *not* homogenous. Haeckel's foundation is thus seen to be an assumption which, so far as this world is concerned, rests on nothing. We have far more warrant for saying "In the beginning God," than Haeckel has for his assertion of a primitive homogeneous matter and force. This is not to deny that there may have been a primitive prothyl, but to show that there is no warrant for asserting its homogeneousness, in the sense intended. We may think of particles of matter of extreme simplicity, but if we take along with these, the forces associated with them, acting on and through them, we are very far from homogeneity. The tendency of Science proper is to throw us back on Electricity—on electrons or electrical units, and these must have at least both positive and negative poles. Thousands or even millions of these may go to make up an atom.[1] The atom is now known to be a structure of great complexity. Far from reaching simplicity at the foundation of the material world, a new world of wonders opens upon us. As a German Scientist has put it, "there apparently is, behind the world of phenomena as we know it, an entirely unknown region, the very first coast lines of which we are only just beginning to perceive" (quoted by A. Zimmern, *Nineteenth Century and After*, Jan. 1904)

2. But, in the second place, supposing there was a

---

[1] Professor Lodge, speaking in the Birmingham Town Hall in January 1905, said that while 300,000,000 atoms could be in a row side by side in an inch, electrons were 1,000,000,000,000,000 times smaller; they were to atoms as a grain of duck-shot to Birmingham Town Hall.

primitive prothyl, the Universe that we know could never have been evolved from it unless it contained in some form the *potency* of its highest constituents as these are manifested in the outcome This implies, of course, that there was something more than a purely homogeneous matter and force; that there was something that had the power, as its potencies evolved or unfolded themselves, in the environment in which the matter was placed, to produce the rational Universe culminating in man.

Mr. McCabe perceives this; for, after he has argued away the idea of an external directive Power, he says: " The only possible conception of telic action on a cosmic scale is when we descend from grandiose phrases to practical ideas, that from the start the matter-force reality was of such a nature that it would infallibly evolve into the cosmos we form part of to-day." Clearly, this *must* have been so: the real question is, What is implied in the fact?

After Haeckel, Mr McCabe argues that the absence of any primitive design is proved by certain features, with which the world is crowded, that forbid the thought of it. Mr. Mallock is quoted in support of this, and a fearful indictment of Nature, on account of the evils which abound in it, is given from Mr. Fiske's *Cosmic Philosophy*. It ought to have been said, in fairness to that gifted and truth-loving writer, that in later writings he sought earnestly to show how, even in the face of all these evils, we might still believe in a God of Love (in his *Through Nature to God* these " evils " are specially dealt with). We are not at this point to enter on a discussion of the " evils in Nature "—we shall deal with them in a subsequent chapter; meanwhile we would refer to Mr. Fiske's little book just mentioned But we would here point out a very common mistake concerning these evils that even writers like Haeckel and Mr. McCabe fall into. It is the supposition that on the assumption of a Divine Being these evils could have been avoided. On the contrary, on the assumption of a God who is identical with the perfect Reason, they are *inevitable* nowhere in the Universe, even in the things that seem most irrational (as Huxley has said) is " Law " absent (or the Reason, which expresses itself in the " laws of Nature "). " Nature," said Huxley, is " a perfect logical machine." All these things occur in the working out of Reason ; and not one of them could possibly be other than it is, except where the free reason in man could take up the work. It is astonishing to find Mr. McCabe, notwithstanding all that he says about the *necessary* unfolding of the one only substance, affirming that a Universe " without carnivora " is conceivable enough !

Let us see what Mr. McCabe has to say in reply to the argument we have stated. He touches it in his answer to Dr. Iverach's assertion in *Christianity and Evolution*, that " if thought has come out of the Universe, if the Universe is a Universe that can be thought, then thought had something to do with it from the outset." " That," he says, " is the favourite form of the argument that 'you cannot get out of a sack what is not in it.' It is a long discredited fallacy. We have seen how out of a simple matter and force have come an immense variety of things. These things were only *implicitly* in the primitive prothyl. Similarly, the evolution of thought only shows that thought was implicitly in the first cosmic principles. Moreover, consciousness evolves out of the unconscious every day—in embryonic development " (p. 79).

This is not much, but is perhaps about all that can be said. We find it continually repeated in one form or another, and the fact that it goes down with many as unanswerable must be our apology for dealing somewhat fully with it. Scarcely a sentence in the above reply will bear examination.

(1) We are still simple enough to believe that we cannot get out of a sack what was never in any form in it or in any way put into it This is but the assertion of that axiom which has guided all thinkers from the beginning down to Spencer, "*ex nihilo nihil fit*" We are compelled to believe that by no conceivable means can something be got from nothing, or, what comes to the same thing, the greater from the lesser. Wherever we think that we see this feat accomplished, we may be certain that we are making a mistake. Some hidden wizard is playing us false. Whatever we may get out of the sack when it has been opened, was either there *in some form* when it lay unopened beside us, or it has all been put into it in some way, however obscurely to us. This is none other than that principle of *Causation* which Haeckel himself so strongly maintains and on which all Science is built.

(2) We have already seen that the assertion that out of a "simple matter and force" have come an immense variety of things has no foundation in fact, and its adduction here is simply a begging of the question at issue. That question is really *whether* there was a *simple* matter and force in the beginning.

(3) These things, it is said, "were only *implicitly* in the primitive prothyl." But why "*only*"? Their being there, even implicitly, is the real mystery. This as much needs to be accounted for as their explicit presence in their developed form. When we sow seed in our gardens the *flowers* are "only implicitly" there, but they cannot be there, even implicitly, apart from the seed; and the presence and potency of the seed needs to be accounted for quite as much as the flower that grows and blooms explicitly It is this alone that accounts for the explicit presence of the flowers, their roots stand in that implication which is thus acknowledged, it is essential to their existence.

(4) "Thought," it is admitted, was "implicitly in the first cosmic principles" What a marvellous thing we have here—confessedly. Thought, Mind, Conscious Spirit with all its powers, was implicitly present in the cosmic principles There is a sense in which this is true, but it is not the Haeckelian one. How wonderful these cosmic principles must have been! Where did they come from? How did they arise? Whence came this implicit Thought? These are just the great questions which remain entirely unanswered, and it is surely much more reasonable to say "from God" than to say from nowhere, or to put the question aside on the plea of such inevitable Agnosticism as Haeckel himself repudiates.

(5) But, says Mr. McCabe, we see the thing done every day. "Consciousness evolves out of the unconscious every day—in embryonic development"

We have here the cardinal fallacy (already referred to) which misleads many who would substitute an evolving Substance for God. In all that we know of Evolution there is no warrant whatever for the assertion here made. There is no such process to be observed anywhere in Nature as the development of the conscious from the unconscious. Embryology shows us nothing of the kind. There is always present the egg or germ *that has proceeded from a prior conscious being or parent*, and which contains the potency of the entire future development under the influence of the environment. Hereditary characters are assuredly in some way expressed in the germ from which each creature derives, not only its origin, but its distinctive form and individual peculiarities. Evolution itself has been aptly defined as "Heredity modified and influenced by variability." Haeckel, although even he speaks in one place of "*the simple ovum*" (*Riddle*, p. 48), says in his chapter on "the Embryology of the Soul," "It is well known that every child inherits from both his parents peculiarities of character, temperament, talent, acuteness of sense, and strength of will," etc. (*Riddle*, p. 50). All these physical and psychical qualities must be conveyed by, and, in order to that, must be in some manner expressed in, the germ. What nonsense then it is to speak of "the simple ovum" or "simple cell," or of "the homogeneous beginning" of our being! The germ has a distinctly spiritual side from the first—that which Haeckel calls the "cell soul"—many "cell souls," of course. This fact needs to be specially emphasised, although it ought to be obvious to every one. It was common at one time to speak of the protoplasmic germ as being entirely structureless, although Scientists like Professor Allman showed that it could not possibly be such, but that the sources of all the distinguishing features that characterised each creature must be expressed in some way in the molecular constitution of the germ. His words in this connection are still well worth quoting. "To suppose," he said, "that all protoplasm is identical where no difference cognisable by any means at our disposal can be detected, would be an error. Of two particles of protoplasm between which we may defy all the power of the microscope and all the resources of the laboratory to detect a difference, one can develop only to a jelly-fish, the other only to a man, and one conclusion alone is here possible—that deep within them there must be a fundamental difference which determines their inevitable destiny, but of which we can know nothing and assert nothing beyond the statement that it must depend on their hidden molecular structure" (British Association Address, 1879). The ever-advancing study of Biology and of kindred sciences has fully confirmed this statement. The constitution of the nucleus and surrounding protoplasm of an animal cell is now much better understood, and is seen to be of an extremely complicated character, so that Sir William Turner could say in his Presidential Address to the same Association in 1900, in which the whole subject is lucidly set forth · "By the researches of numerous investigators on the internal organisation of cells in plants and animals, a large body of evidence has now accumulated, which shows that both the nucleus and the cell plasm consist of something more than a homogeneous, more or less viscid, slimy material. Recognisable objects in the form of granules, threads, or fibres can be discovered in each. The cell plasm and nucleus respectively are therefore not of the same constitution throughout, but possess polymorphic characters . . . In short, the homogeneous, absolutely simple matter of which we hear so much is nowhere to be found in Nature." Nothing exists that can warrant the affirmation that something can come from nothing.

It may be thought, however, that if we go to Phylogeny instead of Embryology, we shall see the development of the higher forms of life from the lower, and, in the last resort, from mere structureless specks of Protoplasm. It is to this that Haeckel himself goes back, especially in *The Wonders of Life*. But, as we have seen, protoplasm itself, even in its simplest form, is an extremely complicated combination, in which "matter" has attained to such elaboration that it possesses those qualities of irritability, nutrition, etc., which under the influences of its environment in the rationally-constituted world make possible the development which ultimately manifests itself so marvellously. As Sir Henry Roscoe has said, protoplasm is itself a structure. Even here we have something far from homogeneous. In this wonderful protoplasm we have the outcome of the action of a great variety of cosmic forces, acting together for millions of years, and it is only under the continued action of these and similar forces (all of which are wholly rational in their character and action) that any development can take place Take away either this plainly "manufactured" specimen of matter called Protoplasm, or the forces which continually play upon it in an ever widening and ever rising environment, and no such development would be possible. This is not the getting something from nothing, or the greater from the lesser; it is the creation, or, if the word be objected to, the production, of something higher by the continuous action of certain powers which can be definitely traced on a previously specially prepared material There was *in the sack* at the beginning this prepared substance, with the potentiality of growth, of feeling, etc., and with the capacity of receiving constant additions from without, so that as the process proceeds the sack is being constantly filled up with something new. We never do, and we never can, get out of the sack anything which was not in some way in it, or put into it.

It must be said that Haeckel himself does not (in the later book at any rate) attempt, in this connection, to perform this feat of getting something from nothing. He attributes—however illegitimately—"sensation" to the primitive matter, and, while he carries us back from the cell, which as a Biologist he acknowledges to possess structure, to what he affirms to be the as yet undifferentiated protoplasm of "the Monera," he himself makes it evident that this primitive "plasm," far from being homogeneous, possesses a most complicated chemical structure. We refer especially to *The Wonders of Life*, in which he contends for a purely chemical origin of protoplasm, but, he says, this does not exclude "a very complicated chemical structure" (p. 142). "Chemists," he says, "tell us that the molecule of plasm is very large and made up of a great number of atoms (over 1000), combined in smaller or larger groups, and in a state of very unstable equilibrium, so that the life process itself causes constant change in them" (p 140). It is certain, therefore, that in this original substance, with its very complicated structure, with its natural capacities, and with the powers that are acting on every portion of it, there was the *potency* of the entire development, and Haeckel leaves us as far from any explanation of this primitive plasm as ever we were. To attribute its presence to chemical and physical forces, instead of to some hypothetical " vital force," or to some special supernatural agency, does not lessen the mystery one whit, nor make it the less a Divine work; it only throws us back upon the play of those wider, law-ordered forces which constitute the Universe, through which the Divine Reason acts. The higher can never be explained by the lower, nor the greater by the lesser. As already pointed out, on the evolutionary theory the potency contained in the original substance of any particular world that began in time may have come from a pre-existent world. And if, keeping before us the analogy of evolution from a potential germ under the action of cosmic forces, we seek in thought to carry back the process into Eternity, or try to conceive an absolute beginning, we can rest in nothing short of an Eternal Source which contains in itself, and could impart to the *monon*, the potency of the entire Universe.

3. The evolution of the worlds, we are told by Haeckel, is an eternal process, so that, of course, we can never reach any absolute beginning. The ultimate question therefore is, Whether there has been from all eternity a matter and force (or spirit, in the sense affirmed), which by its very nature is for ever evolving itself and for ever dissipating itself, or dissolving its evolutions, to form for ever fresh ones,—the eternal Substance rising to the height of self-consciousness in man, but ever falling back again into elementary matter and force, with no final purpose discernible in it all,—*or* a Divine Being who eternally constitutes or gives rise to matter, so that it shall be the medium of a purposive development under the influence of the

infinite Reason that He is? The answer to this question, whether given by Haeckel or by any one else, cannot be gained from direct observation; it must rest on such *inferential reasoning* as Haeckel himself vindicates. The question is really this: What will adequately explain the Universe culminating in man? Haeckel's affirmation of a primitive eternal "Substance" such as from its nature unfolds into the infinitely diversified and rational Universe, is purely suppositional. He has no means of knowing that such a Substance exists. If it does exist, it is more difficult to account for than the existence of God. Haeckel acknowledges that the great riddle of the Universe remains unsolved as long as the nature of the Substance from which everything is evolved is shrouded in what is apparently "impenetrable mystery." "We grant at once," he says, "that the innermost character of Nature is just as little understood by us as it was by Anaximander and Empedocles 2400 years ago, by Spinoza and Newton 200 years ago, and by Kant and Goethe 100 years ago. We must even grant that this essence of Substance becomes more mysterious and enigmatic the more thoroughly we study its countless phenomenal forms and their evolution" (*Riddle*, p. 134) This is a strange solution of the world-riddle—one, too, that is put forward as a substitute for faith in God and hope of Immortality—by the affirmation of a Substance which is not even positively known to exist in the form which is given to it, and which if it does exist, with all the powers that are ascribed to it, as surely needs explanation as the world itself does. It is the explanation of the riddle by proposing a new and harder one. The original basic Substance, we are told, in some way not understood, breaks up into ponderable and imponderable matter. If so, it must have in itself the potency of both and of all that is produced in the course of the long development—vital and mental, or psychical, products included. It must be able to split itself up, at a certain stage, into objective and subjective being; and it has all these powers eternally; they come from nowhere, and they work towards no discernible rational end. And this is what the intelligence of the twentieth century after Christ is asked to accept as a "rational" substitute for God. To Haeckel and to those who follow him, this "Substance" is a substitute for God, because it seems to them to do all that God is supposed to do. At the centre of the Universe, or at its foundation, they place this unconscious, irrational "Substance" which unfolds itself under a blind necessity, with no rational end in view. Reason can never accept such a substitute for God, or such a solution of the world-riddle.

But Haeckel quite misunderstands what is meant by *God*. "Only one comprehensive riddle of the Universe now remains," he remarks in his concluding chapter of *The Riddle of the Universe*,—"What is the real character of this mighty world-wonder that the realistic Scientist calls Nature or the Universe, the Idealist Philosopher calls Substance or the Cosmos, the pious believer calls Creator or God?" Here he speaks as if "Nature," or "the Universe," or "the Cosmos" were the proper equivalents of God. The Christian believer has a very much higher conception of God than that. He does not confound God with the Universe, either in its original substance or in its developed form, and no synthesis of all its forces can ever be to him *God*. God, he believes, is *Spirit*, not matter in any form, or mere force, the matter that is employed to form the Universe, he believes, is in some way Divinely produced, so that, under the action of the laws of Reason, the Universe that we know is the result. The real question Haeckel never once seriously considers, viz., Could this marvellous eternal Substance (matter-force, or matter-spirit, as some call it), which, according to its law of persistence, develops into this Universe of Life and Thought, do all this of itself under a blind necessity, with no reason for or in its action? If we ascribe anything like "sight" or "reason" to it, we are at once carried beyond Haeckel's "Substance." Could that unconscious, non-rational Substance of his ever of itself produce the conscious and rational Universe? No one lays greater stress on the *supremacy of Reason* than Haeckel does. And no one has argued more strongly or (in our opinion) shown more clearly that this Reason in man is the result of a long experience of ancestral life in relation to its surroundings. Why does he not see that the Reason in man has therefore been derived from his relations to a rationally constituted Universe, and that the "pure Reason" for the reign of which he pleads, means really only man's sharing in that Divine Reason from which the whole Universe proceeds? In man, according to Haeckel, Reason proclaims its supremacy. It therefore *is* supreme. Reason in its fulness is but another name for God.

Surely an Eternal *Being* is more credible than an Eternal Substance of the kind affirmed. If it be said that God Himself would need to be explained, the remark surely applies with much greater force to an eternal "Substance" with the attributes ascribed to it. All forms of manifestation, Haeckel says, "pass away, but Substance itself remains." It is therefore, in itself, something *different* from *the forms* of matter and energy which are at any time its manifestation. What *is* this wonderful Substance in itself which is only *manifested* in those transient forms? That it is different from its passing manifestations is a notable admission. But, of course, *God* does not need to be explained. We affirm Divine Being as that sufficient explanation of all things in which alone the rational Mind can rest We have in this affirmation an explanation behind which we cannot go, and there is no need to go.

We have found that "sufficient reason" which Haeckel says we must seek in all things. The finite reason can rest in this and in this alone; there is nothing more to be sought or found. If we say "substance," that, with its attributes, has to be explained; if we say "God," that can explain even this substance, if it exists. That the process is an eternal one does not in the least render needless the Theistic explanation. An eternal God is as much required to explain an eternal Universe as to account for the rise of one in time.

Nor does this explanation necessarily land us in such a Dualism as is repugnant to modern cultivated Thought. There may be a temporary Dualism, set up in the creation, as between it and the Creator, which shall yet be transcended, since all things proceed from an original Unity There may indeed be truly only one ultimate "Substance"— a word, however, which, although "derived," as Mr. Illingworth remarks in his *Personality, Human and Divine*, " exclusively from our own experience of a permanent self underlying (or under-*standing*) all our affections and manifestations," has come to have materialistic suggestions, and ought therefore to be avoided , " Subject " or " Being " is much to be preferred; but this cannot be the merely physical and unconscious spirit Substance of Haeckel, it can only be an eternal, living and conscious, *ethical Being*, who has the reason and the power of His existence in Himself alone, and who, not blindly or irrationally, but with a wise and good purpose, gives eternally life and being to that Universe in which we see the two-sided manifestation of His Power. We are ready to grant that there is a sense in which the whole Universe may be spoken of as *alive*—here with the highest form of finite life in ourselves, and there, in the physical world, with a lower form of life , it is perhaps to this conception of the Universe that Science is leading us. But such a conception does not lower the vital as we know it; it rather elevates the physical, and leads us back to the fundamental powers of the creation. It is, further, always a finite and derived life imparted by Him who eternally gives rise to the Universe, and who is leading it onward and upward towards its completion in Himself. What we may venture further to suggest on this subject we reserve for a subsequent chapter.

Much more might be said in criticism of Haeckel, but we have confined ourselves to the most essential points. Haeckel denies *Freedom* in man, although he has no special argument on this subject But if men are not free, why all this argumentation and condemnation of error and of evil? Men cannot help it, and are not to be blamed. If they are not really free to choose and form their beliefs and to frame their course of action, why reason with them and seek to persuade them to take a truer view of things and to pursue a more rational course? Does Haeckel suppose that it is "the weight" of argument in the physical sense that carries conviction? Indignation, such as Haeckel sometimes shows towards that which he deems erroneous and evil, is entirely out of place in a world where Freedom is an illusion.

He speaks of the evolution of both Morality and Religion. But, while *Morality* is to remain and be further developed under the influence of "pure Reason" towards a balanced Altruism and Egoism, *Religion* is to be thrown out as superstitious merely. Yet *both* have been evolved in man under the influence of his environment. Surely there has been something *real* operating in the evolution of Religion as well as in that of Morality. If Religion has been sometimes low and mis-directed, so has Morality. Why the one should go and the other be left is another "riddle" which we do not attempt to solve.

CHAPTER IX

SPIRITUAL MONISM

General: Relation to Idealism, etc.

"MONISM" is a term that may be understood in various ways. There is, we believe, a true Monism, as well as a false and misleading Monism. When it is attempted to account for all things in the way that Haeckel pursues, such a "Monism" is, as Dr Edward Caird has said, "the grave of Philosophy." "Scientific Monism" affirms the working in the Universe of a single Power, which is revealed in the two aspects of Mind and Matter. It ought, therefore, to give, *at least*, equal value to the two sides or aspects It is only in their union that we can have a real Monism

Haeckel fails to give even this equal value to the two sides. His Monism is none other than thoroughgoing Atheistic Pantheism, baptized with a new name. He plainly acknowledges this, indeed. Everything is accomplished by Matter and the Energy associated with matter: the part that is played by the spiritual side affirmed to belong to matter and force is simply *nil*. Sensation is attributed to matter in an impossible way, and from matter and energy thus endowed, the entire world, objective and subjective, is derived. But, till conscious life appears, the "sensation"-side *does* nothing. Matter and energy really account for all that is accomplished; the sensitive side is passive merely, and is only gradually raised by the working of matter and energy to higher manifestations.

Spencer also, as we have seen, while acknowledging explicitly a spiritual side to the Universe, really makes "Force" do everything and account for everything It is evident that a genuine Monism cannot be reached in this way: these systems are as truly Dualistic as those which they oppose; but one side of the Dualism is left entirely inoperative and quite unaccounted for. It *has* to be acknowledged, but it is of no practical account in the working out of the process up to man, or at least up to conscious life. There is indeed an unknown "Substance" or "Reality" behind it all, and in attributing all to this underlying third element the *name* "Monism" may be justified. But this Substance or Reality in their systems does nothing of itself; it is its *manifestations* as matter and energy that accomplish everything

To some extent a similar line of remark applies even to Professor Lloyd Morgan's much superior statement of Monism in his *Comparative Psychology*. He attributes all to an underlying "activity"—which is "not a product of evolution," but "that in and through which evolution is rendered possible." "Object and Subject are the co-relative modes of manifestation of an underlying activity, one in existence, but none the less fundamentally distinct in aspect" (*Intro. to Compar Psychology*, p. 10). But, like Spencer, he leaves this underlying activity practically an unknown Something (although he has elsewhere made it plain that it is to be taken in a Theistic sense) In the statement now referred to, while, like Spencer, he recognises both sides, he seems also to make the mistake of attributing *only* equal value to the two sides of the manifestation. He rejects, he says, "the psychism" which says that "mind is the reality, and body the mere phenomenal appearance." There is (or has been), no doubt, a one-sided psychism which must be rejected. But if, as he at the same time reminds us, it is the analysis of experience by " Mind " that is the foundation of all our knowledge, surely, in this very fact, Mind proclaims its superiority. " These views " (of Psychism), he says, " depart from the cardinal principle of Monism, which is that practical experience is the fountain-head of reality They give to one product of the analysis of this experience a validity superior to that of another product of this analysis." But surely here the fact is overlooked that *Mind* is known to us, not merely as a *product* of the analysis, but as that which itself *makes* the analysis. Apart from Mind, we should not know that there is such a thing as " body " or have any experience at all. Manifestly, the two cannot be placed on the same level. And as long as the two aspects remain merely side by side, or are only related in an unknown " Substance," " Reality," or " Activity," a genuine Monism, such as will account for the world that we know in experience, cannot be reached. We have still a Dualism which is not reduced to any intelligible Unity.

The same remarks apply to the Monism of Dr. Carus, which is also of a much higher type than that of Haeckel, but almost equally unsatisfactory in the end. To take one example: " Dualism," he says, " assumes that the gulf between the two empires, the thinking and feeling on one side and the not-thinking and not-feeling on the other side, is insurmountable, Monism, however, maintains that there is no gulf, for there is no reason for such an assumption Both realms, the feeling and thinking on the one hand, and the unfeeling and unthinking on the other hand, are not at all distinct and separate provinces. The transition from the one to the other takes place by degrees, and there is no boundary line between them." All this may be quite true, there is indeed no " gulf " between the physical and the psychical, but the truth will appear, at least equally well, if the one be considered as being simply the instrument or means of expression of the other—its "other side," in this sense. We surely reach a truer *Monism* in this way. This relation of the two is really well illustrated in the sentences which immediately follow the above quotation:—" The atoms of oxygen which we inhale at present are not engaged in any action that is accompanied with feeling, but some of them will be very soon active in the generation of our best thought accompanied with most intense consciousness. After that they are thrown aside in the organism and pass out as waste products in the shape of carbonic acid" (*The Soul of Man*, p. 43). Is not this that is true of *this* particular "matter" just that which is true of all matter? It is there only to serve temporary purposes of Spirit. After having done so, it may, *in that form*, pass away. It cannot, therefore, have the same value as that which it so *serves*.

There is, however, a *true* Spiritual Monism, and it is very desirable to see how it can be reached and stated in harmony with both Science and Christian Theism. Science is certainly leading us to some form of Monistic conception of the Universe, and the harmony with religious faith of such Monism as can be scientifically established needs imperatively to be shown. The very wide and ready reception which Haeckel's writings have met with gives evidence of the tendency of thought in this direction amongst all classes of people.

Even those Scientists who are most strongly opposed to Haeckel's Monism hold that the ultimate explanation of the Universe must be Monistic Thus,—to quote one or two examples,—Sir Oliver Lodge in his criticism of Haeckel says: "But philosophically we cannot be satisfied with Dualism, we are all inclined to look forward to an ultimate Monistic view" (*Hibbert Journal*, January 1905, his views are more fully stated in his recent work, *Life and Matter*). Similarly, we find Professor McKendrick saying in his "Murtle Lecture": "The determination is no doubt towards Monism, the old Dualistic theory of Matter and Mind being unsatisfying, but it is not to a material Monism, but rather there is an effort, as Professor Lodge puts it, 'to elevate Matter and all existence to the level of Mind and Spirit, that God may be all in all.'" And Dr. J. A. Fleming says in his valuable little book, *The Evidence of Things not Seen*, "The insight we have gained into the fundamental principles underlying the operations of the material Universe, into the nature of matter and the relation of matter and energy, tend more and more to abolish the old dualism between matter and mind or spirit, and to move us in the direction of a spiritual Monism which regards both the laws and realities of the external world as the laws of an Eternal Mind" (p. 33).[1]

The same tendency is observable in Philosophy. Professor Ward, in his "Gifford Lectures" on "Naturalism and Agnosticism," rejects Dualism, and seeks, from a philosophical standpoint, to reach what he terms a "spiritualistic Monism." "Once Materialism is abandoned and Dualism found untenable, a spiritualistic Monism remains the one stable position." He says very truly, "It is only in terms of Mind that we can understand the unity, activity, and regularity that Nature presents"; and he concludes that "in so understanding, we see that Nature is Spirit" (Pref. p x, and Lectures XVIII.–XX.). But although this is no doubt the ultimate truth, it is not the Monism which needs to be affirmed for the world of Science and Experience Here we have what is fundamentally Spirit presented in a material form, and the only Monism that can satisfy Science and Experience must be one which shows the *unity* of Spirit and matter in the

[1] Similarly, Weismann, while recognising "Spirit," speaks of our being secured "in the advantage and the right of looking at this world, as far as we know it, as a unity" This, he says, "is the standpoint of Monism" (*The Evolution Theory*, p 393)

phenomenal world. There we have Spirit as embodied in and expressed by "matter." Dr. Ward says we cannot "have God *and* interminable mechanism as His medium and instrument really, fundamentally, ultimately, we shall have God only and no mechanism." "It is verily a case of all or none" (ii. 274) We cannot have both. "Above it all there can be only God as the living unity of all, and below it, no longer things, but only the connecting, conserving acts of the one Supreme." Now, ultimately true though this may be (although we should prefer to use the Scripture-expression "all is *of* God" rather than say "all *is* God"), yet, so far as the phenomenal world is concerned, this Monism seems to be reached, not by explaining or unifying the two sides that are actually presented to us, but by *dropping* one side of the manifestation with which we have to deal, or by explaining it away. It seems to be (if we may coin a word for the moment) a *Soleism* rather than a real Monism.

The late Professor Ritchie, however, in his *Darwin and Hegel*, sought to show that, although "Idealism and Materialism are commonly spoken of as antagonistic types of Philosophy,"—"which in one sense they are,"—there was "one form of Idealism quite compatible with that materialistic Monism which is nowadays the working hypothesis of every scientific explorer in every department, whatever other beliefs or denials he may, more or less consistently, superadd." Materialistic Monism seemed only to become false "when put forward as a complete theory of the Universe, because it leaves out of sight the conditions of human knowledge, which the special sciences may conveniently disregard, but which a candid philosophy cannot ignore" (*Introduction*, p vi). Again, criticising Dr. Ward, he says "'Either the Universe,' says Mr. Ward, 'is mechanical or teleological ; it is not likely to be a mixture of the two' (ii. 63). May not the Universe be both at once, through and through, mechanical when regarded in its material or spatial aspect, teleological when regarded in its spiritual aspect," etc. (*Philos. Studies*, p. 109).

So Professor Wundt speaks of the "justifiable endeavour after a Monistic world-theory." "It is the mind that breaks the world up into objective and subjective, and the mind seeks to reconcile them again" (*Human and Animal Psychology*, p. 448).

We take the following words of Professor Flint as pointing in the same direction· "What is the relation of physiology to psychology? No man can be so intellectually blind as to fail to perceive what a momentous question this is. Every thinking man must answer it in some form or way; yet if you answer it in one way you must be a Materialist, if in another, a pure Idealist; and it is to be hoped that it can be answered in a third way which will make you neither, which will not compel you as a rational being to deny the existence either of matter or of Spirit, either of your bodies or souls" (*Philosophy as Scientia Scientiarum*, pp. 26, 27).

A quotation that will shortly be made from the late Professor Adamson's writings reveals the same tendency.

Religion itself leads of necessity to a Monistic conception of the Universe. Theism derives all from God; but God is *Spirit* If everything proceeds from this spiritual Source, then *everything*, Matter as well as Energy, must be spiritual in its origin and essence There is really no other alternative. If we do not hold a spiritual Monism, we leave one side of the Universe unaccounted for, or unrelated to God. The Spiritualist leaves out the material side, and the Materialist the spiritual side. We must maintain all that is true on both sides—all that the Materialist can justly claim, but we must, at the same time, see "matter" to be but the expression and instrument of Spirit. If it be said by the ultra-Spiritualist that God *creates* matter—as if working from without—such a view will find small credence at present, "matter" seems to be too essential for the *manifestation* of Spirit in its operation in the world, to be regarded in such a way. It must be seen to be spiritual in its essence or origin, the very *expression* of Spirit. Science has now brought us to " Energy " as the essential thing in the physical world, but we must go behind this to *rational Power* if we would account for the rational world. It is only in this way, by beginning with Spirit as the *prius* of everything, that we can account for Spirit in the outcome of the evolution; and it is only in this way, by reducing, or rather, raising, all to Spirit that we can reach a true Monism.

To such a Monism we are also drawn by the *Unity* of the creation. The manifold is here, but it is also *one*—united under a single, all-controlling, all-concatenating Principle, the presence and influence of which alone makes the multiplicity of things an ordered Universe. We cannot conceive of this unity as if it were given from without—stamped upon the Universe, as it were—it is manifestly an *immanent* unity, the unity of Reason and of Spirit. We have, moreover, the constant witness to the reality of this Monism in the unity of Body and Mind in our own selves, and, at the same time, the proof of the higher value of Mind than Body.

There is still another reason why a true spiritual Monism should be set forth. The chief reason is, of course, because it is that to which the study of Nature and of man really leads us But we believe also that Faith would find a readier and a surer footing on it than it can on any system of "Dualism," or even on some forms of the current Idealistic philosophy which might justly resent the attribute of "Dualistic."

It is no part of our present purpose to enter on a

criticism of Idealistic Philosophy. Deeply sensible of the high service it has often rendered to Religion, and revering the great names with which it has been associated, it is with diffidence that it is touched on at all. With its main conclusions we are at one; but we think that they must be reached by a different and more empirical way—one that can give full acknowledgment to the external world, and that will carry conviction to the ordinary man as he moves about and acts in the world of his daily experience. A thoroughgoing *subjective* Idealism may, of course, lead to the most complete Agnosticism or even Scepticism.

We certainly cannot reach an effective Idealism by bidding men shut their eyes to the external world and affirming that we are shut up within our cerebral organism, confined to sense impressions and to a world wholly within ourselves. It is true that we receive our knowledge of the external world through impressions on our organism, and that "things are not what they seem"; but the ordinary man will never be convinced that he does not, in his everyday experience, *see* and *touch* and *move about in* an external world of things and beings, as certainly as he receives cerebral impressions from it which he interprets in mental terms. He is not conscious of these *impressions*, but he at least firmly believes himself to be conscious of moving about in a very real external world.

1. In venturing to make some observations on "Idealism" and Idealistic arguments, we notice first the fundamental subjective-Idealist position. Founding on Berkeley, it assures us that we know nothing directly save changes of consciousness. "When I see this paper I am aware of a change in my consciousness and no more." We are directly conscious only of mental states, not of anything that can be rightly described as an "external world." This, if it be real, is only an inference. Some decline even to draw this inference, and affirm that the external world

has no reality at all; but of this extreme form of Idealism we need not here speak.

Now, when the plain man is assured that it is impossible to prove the existence of that external world which he thinks he knows is all around him; when he is told that he has no direct knowledge of anything beyond sense impressions as reported in his consciousness, that he is practically shut up within his cerebral organism, with not even as much power of getting outside himself as a "peeping Tom", when you tell him that, although he sees you there, standing before him, hears you speaking to him, or holds your book in his hand, reading the printed page, and conscious that he might throw it into the fire if he chose, he has no immediate knowledge of anything save what is subjective only, he suspects the very basis of your argument, and your reasoning, if it "admits of no reply, produces no conviction." This is one reason why Idealistic arguments for Theism have so little weight generally, logically constructed though they may be. Their *Basis* is suspected. Philosophers may think themselves into convictions based on these arguments, and into the belief that the ground they stand on is firm, but the ordinary man is totally unable to do so.

The statement on which this Idealism is based Monism shows to be an unsound one. It is one which can only be made on the assumption of such a complete Dualism of Mind and Body, of man and Nature, as Science makes it impossible to hold to-day. Monism really brings us back (in a new way) to the belief of the ordinary man, to the doctrine of "common sense," virtually as held by Reid and Hamilton and the "Scottish School" of Philosophy, and upheld by Dr. Martineau It shows us that the internal and the external are *both* given us in one act of sense-perception; that you can no more get away from the external world than you can get out of your body (and

SPIRITUAL MONISM

just because you cannot get out of your body); that it is constantly given you as the "extended side" of your "thinking self," that there can be no knowledge which is not that of a subject and object in unity, no such thing as "subjectivity" possible apart from "objectivity." What the subject and the object *are* is, of course, a matter for inquiry.

This Idealism says that we know nothing save "changes of consciousness." But *What is consciousness? how do we come to have any consciousness?* Consciousness is ever related to our bodily organism. I can never have any consciousness whatever (in this life) apart from my bodily organism If in my ordinary waking state I have any consciousness at all, it is as an organised being and through my bodily organism My personal consciousness is simply "the thinking side," while my organism is the extended side of *myself*. The external world, in the form of my Body, has always been with me: I can never, by any possibility, get away from it.

Again, when it is said that we become aware of changes in our consciousness, *how do we do so?* There is, first of all, a vague consciousness arising from the bodily condition in general, and, of course, we become aware (sometimes painfully) of changes in the general organic condition. And, in the sense specially intended, it is always through certain special organs of sense that these changes of consciousness come to us. We never know them as separate from these sense organs. No doubt, they sometimes arise from *internal* sensations, but they are still inseparable from the organism, and, whether they come from without or within, whether what they bring us be correctly interpreted or not, whether our experience be real or hallucinatory, they can never come at all except through some affection of the bodily organism. An external world is thus always with us, and it is not true to say that we are conscious of mental states *only*, with no immediate knowledge of an external world, or of anything objective to the spiritual self. My consciousness is, of course, always *spiritual*, but it is there through an affection of my organism, of the presence of which I am always (while in a normal condition) more or less aware. The organism, as the other side to the consciousness, is the real presence to it of the external world.

Further, although Psychology shows us that there is much involved in our sense-perception that the ordinary man does not take into account, he is perfectly right in his belief that he actually touches and sees, moves about in, and deals effectively with an external world. If this was not true for his consciousness when he was a baby, he has not remained a baby. If at one time in his history an object seemed merely an indistinct "blur," with no definite sense of "outness," it is certain that he has no memory of that experience—real enough though it was—and that he has outgrown it. As Dr. Carpenter said in his *Mental Physiology*, "The *apprehension*, or the formation of an elementary notion of the *outness* or *externality* of the cause of sensational change, is an operation which the Mind seems necessarily to perform when it has attained to a certain stage of development; instinctively or intuitively making a definite distinction between the self and the not-self, the subject and the object" (p 177). Doubtless it is through a marvellous process of unconscious mental workings, in which not only touch and vision, but all the senses (including muscular and internal sensations), have a part to play, along with the feeling of resistance to effort, that we reach the position of the grown-up man in relation to the external world as a whole. (Its primary form is, perhaps, the perception of "power," outside ourselves—resisting our motions, as Dr. Wyld maintained in *The World as Dynamical*, etc) But we *do* reach it, and no normal individual fails to reach it. No doubt, even vision is the result of "interpretation," but the interpretation comes to be automatically made, with the consequence that we directly discern, live, move, and act in a real external world. And it is just the fact that a spiritual Monism insists on, that all throughout our life there is a spiritual or mental side to the organism (though not always rising to personal consciousness), that makes such unconscious working, learning, and interpretation possible as results in our immediate perception of the world as external to our spiritual selves. The case is most probably the same as that with respect to our "innate ideas," or the structures that lead to their formation. It is due to the experience of the race, briefly recapitulated (as in embryology) in the history of each individual member of it.

The Monistic position is thus stated by Professor Lloyd Morgan: "We are thus driven to the conclusion that throughout the whole range of experience from the most primitive sense-experience to the highest ranges of conceptual thought, subject and object are inseparable. There is no subject without an object. There is no object without a subject. We may distinguish the objective from the subjective aspects of our experience; but we have no grounds for regarding them as divisible or separable. We must not, therefore, picture to ourselves, or conceive the subject as something that is self-subsisting and independent; or the object as part of an external independent world, into which the subject may or may not be introduced, and the problem of Psychology as the question how these two can be brought into relation. We must rather regard subject and object as inseparably united in experience; and the problem of Psychology as the question how this two-faced unity has had its origin" (*Intro. to Comp. Psych.*, p 310)

The late Professor Adamson, in his *Suggestions towards a Theory of Knowledge, based on the Kantian*, came to what is practically the same conclusion He suggests that, with Subjective Idealism, there is probably a confusion between the proposition that "knowledge as a modification of consciousness is necessarily of the nature of consciousness, and is therefore subjective experience," and the other proposition that "knowledge is not only conterminous with consciousness in range, but has only consciousness as its object" (*Modern Philos.*, i. 285).

The foundation of our sense of the distinction between subjective and objective is to be found, he holds, in the "broad distinction in our experience between two features of its content—on the one hand that of extension, on the other hand the negative thereof—the absence of extendedness, with, probably, as its positive associate, the element of feeling." "Nowhere," he writes, "do we find psychical life save in conjunction with highly complex forms of that external reality which we represent to ourselves as under mechanical law. . . . All the evidence we have from experience would tend to lead us to represent the psychical as in the closest dependence on certain forms of change in the mechanical. It is undoubtedly true that we cannot represent to ourselves the psychical as itself a change of the mechanical kind; but it is a question which Psychology has hardly ever raised, whether we do apprehend the psychical as a series of distinct events, whether the mode of describing the mental life which gives it the position in our consciousness of a realm of existence distinct from, and, as one puts it, 'metaphorically outside' of the mechanical, is not a misreading of the actual nature of the inner life itself" (*Modern Philosophy*, i. 354).

2. Coming now to Idealistic arguments for Theism (not those of *Subjective* Idealism merely), while, of course, they contain much that is true and important, their common weakness seems to be that they assume that what is true for *us*, or for the finite Mind, must be true universally. It is affirmed, for example (as by Dr. Rashdall), That all "things" exist for Mind only, that apart from Mind there

SPIRITUAL MONISM 193

could be no "things," and that, therefore, there must be a universal Mind for which the things which we know existed, before the human mind had any being had their existence. But it is not proved that things can only *exist* for a Mind. Nothing, indeed, of the existence of which we can *know*, or that has *meaning* for us, can exist for us except as it exists for our minds. This fact, on the lines of a spiritual Monism, would certainly lead on to the affirmation of *a mental origin of things* But the Idealistic argument does not prove that nothing can *exist* save for a Mind It does not meet, for example, the materialistic assertion of a self-originating World which only comes to consciousness in *us*. We can certainly picture to ourselves "the dance of the atoms," which in their fortuitous coming together form the worlds, without thinking of any *Mind* which is watching them. Even in the argument as stated, "*things*" are said to exist, and it is only because they exist that we are asked to believe in a Divine Mind. To base the existence of a Divine Mind on that of "things" seems a dubious procedure. We can surely get a better argument for the reality of a Divine Mind than to affirm it as necessary for the knowledge of things to Mind. We want to reach a Mind that is the *Source* of things and of finite minds as well. Besides, if things exist *for* our thought they also certainly exist *before* our thought, and so it might be argued that "*things*" must exist before there can be any Thought !

The desired conclusion can be reached in a surer way by proving that all things that we know have *a meaning*, express some thought, are construable in thought, and therefore imply Thought as their fundamental reality—as that which gives them existence; therefore, a Divine Mind as the Source of things and of the finite minds to which they yield up their meaning.

So again, when, in another form of the argument, it is said, on the ground of our experience, that "nothing can exist which does not presuppose Thought," this is true in another and most important sense, but, in the sense intended, it does not necessarily follow from the premises on which it is based. It is most true that before *we* can conceive things as existing we must *think* them, nothing can have existence for us which does not exist for our thought. But does this prove anything with respect to the existence of things in relation to the Absolute Thought? "The priority of Thought," says Principal Caird (in his *Introduction to the Philosophy of Religion*, p. 157), "or the ultimate unity of Thought and Being, is a principle to doubt which is impossible, seeing that in doubting it we are tacitly asserting the thing we doubt," and "to say that Thought can think an existence behind Thought, or which has no relation to Thought, is a contradiction in terms" (p. 236). But it is—directly, at least, on the ground adduced—the priority of *our thought* to our conception of anything that it is impossible to doubt. It can be proved that no object can be *known* as existing save in relation to a thinking subject, but may there not be existence *not known*, or not *conceived* to exist? What needs to be shown is that there can be no existence which is not also *known* or *thought*. This cannot be proved by a reference to our own thought.

Is not Materialism more effectually met when we can say, not merely "your atoms, etc., have no existence apart from your thought," but that "they are manifestly in themselves, in their relation to us, and in all that they do, the expression and the agents of Thought"? On the ground of a spiritual Monism, while we do not undertake to prove that nothing can have *existence* which does not presuppose thought, we can prove that nothing can have existence *as thought* in us that does not presuppose Thought. And this surely leads us back, with certitude, to an Ultimate Mind.

SPIRITUAL MONISM

So, once more, when it is sought to base the reality of a Universal Consciousness on the human consciousness as containing the three elements of a self, a not-self, and a relation between them (as in Dr. Edward Caird's *Evolution of Religion*, etc.), the actuality of the third element, the relation,—on the reality of which the Divine Existence is based (which *is*, indeed, the *Divine* Consciousness),—is by no means clear to the ordinary mind. A philosophical thinker may, doubtless, build up a splendid structure, basing it on that ground. But it is not clear that the reality of a Divine Consciousness is not simply *assumed* at the outset; at most it is *inferred*. We are certainly conscious of the self and of the not-self, but it cannot be said that we are directly conscious of the relation between them as a third reality that can be extended into the being of a universal Consciousness. The relation that unites subject and object *in my mind* is simply Thought, Consciousness, the Mind itself. We cannot immediately identify this with God without identifying our own mind with the Divine Mind, our own consciousness with the Divine Consciousness. But we never know the self and the not-self even for a moment as in *opposition*, and, as already stated in the quotation we made from Professor Lloyd Morgan, the real question seems to be, not what *relates* them, but how they *both* come to be in that unity in which they are known to us Following this line of inquiry, we will ultimately reach a Divine Mind as their origin.

We stand on firmer ground when we say that there must be a Divine Consciousness—an all-comprehending Mind—that unites all objects and all finite minds, as well as all finite minds to each other. In this way we can get to the idea of God.

If we take for further illustration Dr. Hutchison Stirling's recent book, *What is Thought?* the difficulty is, How do you pass from the I-me, the finite subject-object that each one is, to the Absolute I-Me = God? *If* God is, He must be Object to Himself,—we certainly have this in the I-me (Thought, says Dr. Stirling); but the *if* seems still to remain.

Or, if we take Mr. Haldane's *Pathway to Reality*, we find the same difficulty of the relation of the finite self to the Infinite or Absolute Self or Subject. It seems clear that, although I am subject-object, I am not Infinite or Absolute (although I may be potentially one therewith). Evil alone shows that there must be experiences which are *mine* and do not belong to the Absolute—if we identify the Absolute with God. If we follow those who, by another pathway, land us in an all-containing Absolute to Whom everything in the phenomenal world in some real sense *belongs*, we seem really to have got to the end of everything—of all real goodness, morality, and religion, at any rate. Our own experience, however, shows us that there may be an Absolute Consciousness of the Universe without any need for supposing that all the contents of the Universe actually *belong* to it. We are continually conscious of thoughts and feelings which come into our consciousness and which yet we do not make our own, but positively reject and, it may be, condemn.

3 We certainly receive everything in terms of "thought," or as "spiritual experience." Hegel's fundamental doctrine that Thought and Being are one is true, and in our thought we know Being as far as it is revealed to us But to set up the movement of thought in ourselves as that by which we can describe the movement of the primal Divine Thought and construe the Universe, does not seem to have the same warrant. Inasmuch as we derive all *our* thought primarily from the world, we can only deal with what is thus given us, and with what we may rationally infer from it. We must look for the actual methods of Reason in that world, and from it seek

the verification of all our deductions. Above all, we must remember the new element that enters the course of Evolution when beings gifted with free-will appear. In view of that fact, the actual course that the World, from that stage onward, has taken, may be far from the Ideal, or the truly rational course.

Is not the oneness of Thought and Being and of subject and object best proved by the facts that, not only do we know them as one in our own immediate consciousness, but that all our thought about the world is derived from the world itself; that *thought* would be impossible—nonexistent, in fact—were not the world essentially a rational world? Are not thought and reality most effectually brought together by showing that it is our ancestral and our personal relation to Reality that creates the power and the very possibility of thought, with all the categories that thought employs (remembering always the *spiritual side* that is present throughout, which comes to its highest expression in ourselves); that "the web of categories which thought throws over the world" is really, in all its threads and in its entire texture, woven in response to a rational environment; that thought, in so far as it is true, is but a mirror of the world; that reason in us is the product of a Reason that is first of all in Nature? Here we seem to see the *unity* with the utmost clearness. We only express in terms of human reason what a higher Reason expresses to the reason it has developed in ourselves. We translate our perceptions into terms of Reason solely because they are primarily the expression of Reason in the world around us, of which (and of the Power that works all therein) we are the product. It is solely for this reason that what appear to us as objective things can be apprehended in terms of thought

4. The Hegelian Philosophy also rejects Dualism and subjective Idealism, and finds the self and the not-self present

in one act of self-consciousness. "The consciousness of self," says Principal Caird, "is given only in relation to the consiousness of that which is not self—subject and object are correlatives as indivisible as the notions of outward and inward, motion and rest, parent and child," etc. (*Introduction to Philosophy of Religion*, p. 130). With its doctrine that the real is the rational and the rational the real, that the Universe is the manifestation of Reason to reason in ourselves, that it "can be nothing but the revelation or manifestation of Intelligence;—that matter is the necessary object and counterpart of Spirit in which Spirit reveals and through which it realises itself; and that indeed the material world only shows its ultimate meaning when we regard it as the natural environment and basis of the life of spiritual beings" (Dr. E. Caird's brief summary in *Chambers' Encyclopædia*), Spiritual Monism is in entire agreement.[1]

---

[1] Dr. Caird gives clear statement to what is truly a spiritual Monism in various passages of his writings. For example, we quote the following from his *Essay on Metaphysics*: "In Hegel's language, that which presents itself as other than mind is *its* other—'an other which is not another,' whose difference and opposition to itself it overreaches and overcomes. We must therefore regard the independence and externality of nature, its indifference, and even, it seems, opposition, to the development of the moral and intellectual life of man, as merely apparent. For man, in this point of view, is not one natural being among others, but *the* being in whom nature is at once completed and transcended.

"Such an idea of man's relation to the world is necessarily involved in any theory that goes beyond that subjective Idealism or Sensationalism which denies to him every object of knowledge except his own states of feeling, and every end of action except his own pleasures and pains" (*Essays*, ii. 525, etc) In like manner Principal Caird sets forth the principle of unity in more than one brilliant passage in his *Introduction to the Philosophy of Religion* and other works. "The gulf between the two is not intellectually impassable, seeing that in knowing or taking cognisance of material phenomena, the intellect actually passes it. If ever we are to get at the true explanation of the world, it will doubtless be one according to which there will be no irrational gap, or breach of systematic continuity between one order of existences or one class of forces and another," etc. (see pp 112, 116 especially).

As Dr. Hutchison Stirling says, " Hegel sought the one principle to which he might reduce all. To be in earnest with Idealism, Hegel said to himself, is to find all things whatever but forms of Thought."

But the mode of argumentation by which these conclusions are reached seems not only difficult to follow, but (as has been already suggested) dubious, and it seems desirable to try to reach them in a simpler and more direct manner. When it is said that "the ultimate unity which is presupposed in all differences is the unity of thought with itself, the unity of self-consciousness, and that in this unity is contained the type of all Science and the form of all existence; in other words, that $I = I$ is the formula of the Universe,"—however true and illuminative this may be when once grasped, many ordinary minds endeavour in vain to grasp it with a confidence that will uphold their faith.

We would fain attempt to show empirically that, to quote Principal Caird's words, " Neither organisation nor anything else can be conceived to have any existence which does not presuppose Thought" (*op cit.* p 156), and would follow out his suggestion of such a possible extension of the Design argument as would show us "in the world the manifestation of a kind of Design to which the objections urged against the ordinary Design argument would no longer be applicable ; for what we should then have before us would be one vast, self-consistent system, one organic whole, one self-evolving, self-realising idea, infusing the lucidity of Reason into all things, potentially present in the lowest order of existence, slowly advancing itself, without cleft or arbitrary leap, from lower to higher, the higher the explanation of the lower, and the highest of all that in which the meaning, end, or aim of the whole would be clearly seen " (p. 148 ; see also p. 116)

Spiritual Monism does not begin with what is *within*

merely, and proceed to deduce the world in terms of the laws of thought as these are known to ourselves; it does not find in the "world," or the "object," something alien to ourselves, only to be united in virtue of a higher unity which is inferred. We find the world to which we belong *directly reporting itself* as a rational and spiritual world within our own consciousness. We do not merely look out on it and interpret it thus: it *declares itself to us* as a rational world by means of an organism which has been formed in direct continuation of the working of the Power that is manifested therein, and as its highest objective expression. Instead of regarding matter or the world as in any sense the opposite of Spirit, we see them to be but the expression of Spirit, which comes to be conscious of itself (in the finite world) in man, who realises his life as a spiritual being by means of the world, dying only to what is lower in his nature than that to which the Spirit within him seeks to uplift him, and so bring him into full possession of himself and of the world. We find in the unity of the conscious subject with his organism an immediately revealed subject-object; we witness the same subjectivity and objectivity manifested in the whole external world, although not always with consciousness, and when we seek the origin of both we can only find a resting-place in the thought of the self-conditioning of an all-containing and all-working Reason.

The remarks that have been made regarding Idealism do not affect the general argument. They have been made mainly because many who are anxious to accept its general conclusions find themselves unable to feel sure of the grounds on which they are based, and because we believe that a spiritual Monism leads more directly to these conclusions. Its advantages may be here briefly stated as follows: When we find everything in the external world given in our consciousness in spiritual terms, we are *receiving from the world itself* its interpretation in these terms. When, looking out, we find the same subjectivity and objectivity as we know in ourselves manifested everywhere, although not always with consciousness attached to it, we are not only logically entitled, but bound by the world itself, to interpret its whole phenomena in terms of Spirit. It is only because they are fundamentally spiritual that they *can* be interpreted by us as they invariably are interpreted. When we find ourselves in our organism standing in direct continuation of the external world and that world becoming conscious of itself in us, we *must* seek a spiritual origin for both that world and our spiritual selves. No other origin is conceivable or possible. Thus in a direct line we are led up to the spiritual Source of our being in God.

Spiritual Monism

Let us now endeavour to state in general terms the characteristics of that Spiritual Monism to which we are led by the study of Nature and ourselves. Afterwards we shall seek to show somewhat more fully than we have done in chap. iv., how, basing ourselves on actual observation, it is reached.

Thoroughgoing Materialism and thoroughgoing Spiritualism are, of course, both Monistic; the one affirms that Matter is the one principle of the Universe, and the other that it is Spirit. A completely Idealistic system, therefore, such as that of Hegel, may be described as a spiritual Monism. But, according to Spiritualism in general, Matter appears as the opposite of Spirit· Spiritual Monism, in the sense in which the term is here used, sees matter to be but the other side of Spirit—the manifested side, or the means of its manifestation and expression in its finite or conditioned form. *Science* is largely Monistic, in its setting forth of facts, apart from all inferences that may be drawn therefrom. The term "Spiritual Monism" is adopted in order to set forth both *agreement* with Science in acceptance of its facts, and *difference* from the interpretation which some in the name of Science give to these facts. It acknowledges the two-sidedness that is everywhere manifested, and sees everything and every being in the world to be the result of the working or unfolding, or development in its conditioned form, of a single Power manifested as both material and spiritual. But, instead of giving the predominance to the material side, or equal value merely to the two sides, or leaving them both unexplained, it regards the spiritual side as that which is logically first and deepest—that which the material side only expresses and serves —that which manifests its supremacy in our own consciousness.

"Scientific" or Physical Monism (which, however, goes beyond Science and becomes an interpretation) lays the stress on the material side or aspect, the spiritual being sometimes regarded as a mere accompaniment, although it may be at the same time affirmed to be present in some sense from the first. In Spiritual Monism the dominant side is Spirit—the mental side, not the material; it sees, in short, in the world a complete mechanical system which is at the same time a complete spiritual system and the manifestation thereof.

"Scientific" Monism is *deterministic*, refusing to acknowledge the reality and action of spiritual personalities; Spiritual Monism regards the process of Evolution as *culminating* in such spiritual personalities; it is just in them that that spiritual element which is deepest comes into its fullest manifestation in relation to matter and shows itself openly.

"Scientific" Monism affirms the material and the spiritual as seen in the phenomenal world to be two different manifestations of one underlying Reality, "Substance" or "Activity." Spiritual Monism maintains that in the phenomenal world, or the conditioned world of Science, there are not three elements to be taken into account, or two elements that find their unity in an unknown "Something," neither Matter nor Spirit, but the underlying Reality of both, which stands unresolved, like a "thing in itself", but *one sole element* which is revealed in *two aspects*—the material and the spiritual. The material side, it holds, is simply the *expression* of Spirit, although the finite Spirit only appears when matter has reached a certain degree of complexity.

Perhaps the simplest illustration is *the spoken or written word*, in which the material side is, clearly, only the symbol or the expression of the spiritual thought or meaning. There is not some unknown third thing or activity underneath them both. The only sense in which we can think of a third element is that which is implied in the very important distinction between the Conditioned and the Unconditioned. But in the world of Science it is not with unconditioned Being we have to do, but with Being in its conditioned form. We have the two sides in ourselves and in the whole Universe. That which unites them in ourselves is not some underlying Reality, but simply the *self* which as spiritual holds them both. It is the same as with the written or printed signs and their meaning. That which has united them is the Mind which has expressed itself in them. With respect to the Universe *as a whole*, that which unifies it is the Divine Mind that is over all, and that is, in some measure, expressing itself in everything

There is thus no mystery at all in that which we term "Spiritual Monism." It is not an Idealistic construction, but a conclusion to which we are led empirically and objectively. We have it constantly before us when we listen to and take in the meaning of words which come to us as aerial vibrations, or when we look at the written or printed page and mentally receive and assimilate the thought which the material signs before us express. Clearly, we have the two sides there, and with equal clearness we can see that they are not of the same value, nor the expression of some underlying, unknown third thing. The material symbols which are employed to express the thought may, in that form, pass away, it was the thought they expressed that gave them their value and their very existence, and that thought endures as the one underlying Reality—as a thought, of course, not as a personal existence. It is the same in all that we experience and in all that we do in the world. We live and move and have our being in the midst of, and by means of, a Monism in which the material is ever simply the symbol, the instrument, the expression of the Spiritual.

CHAPTER X

FURTHER ILLUSTRATIONS OF SPIRITUAL MONISM WORLD-BUILDING; CONSCIOUSNESS, MORALITY AND RELIGION, NOT PANTHEISTIC IDENTITY

IN seeking to set forth more fully the way in which, in harmony with the facts of Science, we reach the Spiritual Monism described in the previous chapter, and in attempting to clear up some difficulties that may be felt from a Dualistic point of view, let us begin with what is quite certain. Leaving aside for the moment the question of spiritual Being, it is acknowledged on all hands that everything on the earth and around it, every form on its surface, every structure and tissue in every form, is built up by the combinations of a certain number of definite atoms, according to their kind, their numbers, and their arrangement—the whole being really dependent on their "weight." These never vary in their constitution or in their modes of action. The description of these atoms, which are the "building stones of the world," by Sir John W. Herschell and Professor Clerk Maxwell, already quoted, as having "all the characteristics of manufactured articles," recent Science has by no means detracted from, but has more completely proved its truth, and given us a glimpse of *how* they are made. It shows us that the atoms of which the molecules of every kind of body are composed are themselves the products of evolution. It does more: it shows us—what Chemistry has for long assumed—that the molecules of every kind of body are in constant motion, and that even the atom itself has a structure which can only be compared to a miniature solar system. The particles (electrons) that compose this atom—minute beyond all possibility of perception by the most highly magnifying microscope—are in constant, orderly movement [1] It is in all probability their *movements* that constitute their reality. Though we speak of atoms, therefore, what is really revealed to us is *Power*—Power operating through these atoms to build and to maintain the whole structure of the Universe. Whatever is done is effected, not by the material atoms as such, but by the Power that forms them and works by means of their instrumentality. Now, this cannot be *mere* Power; that were an entirely empty notion; it is a Power that by these means forms the intelligible world which Science knows, which serves our human purposes, and which rises to rational thought within ourselves—a Power that reveals itself as Spirit within our own consciousness. It is, not "matter" or "force," but *this Power* that works all in all. It is *Reason* working.

The question of the *special* origin of *Life* comes thus to be quite unimportant. If at a certain stage of the continuous working of Power in Nature, Protoplasm was formed as the chemical base, and Life came into manifestation and action, this would only be in keeping with all that had gone before. *Nothing* is owing to "chemistry" or to "matter" merely, but everything is owing to the Power that forms the atoms of matter and that works through them. *We know of no other instrument that it possesses save those chemical atoms and the ether.* Since it has

[1] *Vide* Muir, *The Story of the Chemical Elements*, and Duncan, *The New Knowledge* "Chemical union," Professor Duncan says, "is nothing but electrical union" As certain "types of atoms are free to move, they unite together and neutralise each other electrically Chemical valency is simply a measure of the corpuscles more or the corpuscles less than the atom will hold in a stable condition" (p. 248).

formed the almost infinitely varied and often extremely complicated inorganic chemical combinations, it is not difficult to believe that the same Power could, under due conditions, in the continuity of its working, form that combination of elements which shows itself as protoplasm or living matter, and which thus becomes a higher revelation of itself. Substances the formation of which was once believed to be possible only to vital forces, have been formed in the laboratory, although living matter has not been so produced. The conditions under which it arose cannot, perhaps, be repeated. It is believed to have had its commencement in the waters of the sea. Sir J. W. Dawson believed its earliest animal form to have been what he termed *Eozoon Canadense*, which lived on alone at first in the deep undisturbed waters and built up the "Laurentian" rocks. But the organic remains of the earlier periods of life show that this living matter must soon have existed in enormous quantities both in vegetable and in animal form. Our coalfields and many of our rock formations are the evidences of this. Any *special creation* of Life is thus the less likely. And, in any case, it could only be derived from the working of the same Power which we affirm *did* produce it. As Sir J. W. Dawson remarks, it is possible that an enlightened Theism may enable us to hold *both* the opposing theories concerning the origin of Life or all that is true in either. "Undoubtedly we must hold that a higher Spiritual Power or Creator is necessary to the existence of life; but then this is necessary also to the existence of dead matter and force So that if physiologists think proper to trace the whole phenomena of life to material causes, they do not on that account in any way invalidate the evidence for a Spiritual Creator, nor for a Spiritual Element in the higher nature of man" (*The Origin of the World*, etc., p. 383).

A spiritual Monism, however, enables us the better to understand the nature and the appearance of Life. Sir Oliver Lodge maintains that Life is an entity coming in from without, interacting with the material world, becoming incorporated therein, and, probably, passing out therefrom again as something still existent, it may be, with an individual form; and he shows the advantages of such a theory in view of the scientific explanation of the world. But when we think of Life in all its varied forms, in plants and lower animals, it is extremely difficult to entertain this conception of Life as an entity. Dr. Bastian, on the other hand, contends with equal earnestness for the uprising of Life from within, in line with the working of the Energy in Nature, and sets forth very reasonably the advantages of that theory. When we remember that a *seed* may retain its *capacity* for living for very long periods, and then either lose it or actualise it as it comes into contact or not with the required physical conditions, or when we think of an *egg* retaining for a time the same capacity, and then, it may be, becoming decomposed, we cannot conceive of Life as a separate or separable entity. The "*direction*" that is claimed for it is *immanent*. But it is undoubted that we have in Life something different from Energy in its lower forms, which it seems to control for its own purposes. Life appears as something *spiritual* rather than physical; there Sir Oliver Lodge is in the right, and, we may add, it is just for this reason that there is no *physical* energy to be looked for after death as the equivalent of Life.

But if we conceive the real Power at work in Nature as one which is *fundamentally spiritual*, with matter only as its expression, and coming gradually into higher and higher manifestation, we have a possible view of Life in which both theories can be reconciled. Life is in this view midway between physical energy and conscious Mind.[1]

Once Life has entered the world, the advance to real *Sensation* as the foundation of mental life is not so difficult on the theory here advocated as it would otherwise be. If we think only of matter and physical energy as the foundation of the Universe, then it is impossible to understand how Mind could appear. But if we keep in view the essentially mental and spiritual nature of the all-working Power, the new manifestation is not of something *different* from what has existed all along (as Dualism would make it appear), it is only the fuller manifestation of that subjective side that has been present from the first, only not yet revealed as conscious in finite forms. Here the subjective side of the Universe comes into clear manifestation.

An essential quality of protoplasm is "irritability," or "sensitiveness." (It is here that the real wonder lies—in this capacity of "experiencing" irritation). In the vegetable world it is not yet true sensation, but only the result of the extremely fine organisation of matter in the structure of the plant, so that the response to very nicely *adapted* stimuli is so perfect that it simulates sensation. We witness the same thing in countless animal adaptations and in reflex actions, gradually rising into real conscious sensation. We see it in that rise of unconscious mental action to conscious mental action which is now universally acknowledged. It has been truly said that "the whole of essentially the same actions as those which we usually

---

[1] Professor Duncan says · "The great law of continuity forbids us to assume that life suddenly made its appearance out of nothing, and tells us that we must look for the elements of life in the very elements of matter, for the potentiality of life should exist in every atom" (*op. cit* p 213) This seems also to be the view of Mr Butler Burke, who believes that he has found in his "radiobes" the representatives of transition forms between the inorganic and the organic worlds (*The Origin of Life*, just published).

term intellect, viz, perception, observation, attention, comparison, judgment, etc., appear to occur automatically in the human brain in a lower degree when we are unconscious than when we are conscious, and they only rise into consciousness when their activity is sufficiently great" (Gore, *The Scientific Basis of Morality*, p. 244). In all the revelations of Science there is nothing more remarkable than what it has shown with respect to those mental workings beneath consciousness. It is only in virtue of that prior unconscious but intelligent working that our conscious knowledge or our perception of anything becomes possible. Unconscious Mentality has been silently laying the foundations for the appearance of conscious Mentality. Consciousness is just the blossoming of this into flower; or, better still, it is like the appearance above ground of the "darkling seed" which has been long below, not "sleeping," indeed, but steadily working till the sprout appears

At what stage true Sensation or Consciousness appears is extremely difficult to tell—the passage from the unconscious to the conscious is so finely graduated that it is hard to say when the latter is reached.[1]

[1] The gradual advance of the working of Reason in the unconscious form to conscious Reason was clearly set forth by Dr J J Murphy in his work on *Habit and Intelligence* (second edition, 1879), in which he sought to show "that the Intelligence which organises the body is the same which becomes conscious in the mind, and that animal instinct constitutes the transition between the two" Amongst other illustrations, he gives that of the structure of the iris, enabling it to contract involuntarily and unconsciously in order to protect the retina against too much light. The *structure* is an example of unconscious Formative Intelligence, and its action in closing one of unconscious Motor Intelligence. "From this there is a perfect gradation to those motor actions which are accompanied by consciousness and directed by the will The action of the eyelids in closing is sometimes voluntary, but is oftener performed spontaneously without consciousness or will The motion of the eyeballs is more decidedly under control of the will than those of the eyelids. And to complete the evidence of a perfect gradation between the involuntary and the voluntary actions, it is asserted that

But there is not only no need to suppose any special *creation* of animal consciousness, there is no possibility of conceiving it. How could *Mind* or Consciousness, a spiritual reality, be *created*? It can only be caused to appear, or to come into manifestation. It undoubtedly begins in extremely lowly forms, and "irritability" seems to stand just on the border-line. (If plants can be said in any true sense to "feel," as some believe, we have here the subjective coming into higher manifestation —approaching towards an individual consciousness.) Conscious Sensation is not a prerogative of man alone, but belongs to the humblest creature. If we think of consciousness in *man* merely, we may be tempted to seek for some special external origin of it; but the human consciousness is assuredly a development out of much lower forms of consciousness, and we must remember that, in all its forms, it is the product, not of matter, nor of energy merely, but of that rational Power which has been working all along, and becoming more and more completely manifested as the creation rises into higher and higher forms of being In other words, it is the outcome of its self-evolution as *conditioned* for the creation. Except as the product, or manifestation, of a spiritual Power, Consciousness can never be accounted for. Neither Matter nor physical Energy could ever produce it. But that

in some few men the iris is capable of being opened and closed at will" The same gradation is seen between the unconscious and the conscious actions in connection with the digestive system A familiar example is found in the passage from "unconscious cerebration" to conscious cerebration or voluntary, active thinking He shows the harmony of this view with Theism, since all " Intelligence is the result of the Divine Wisdom, but there is not a fresh determination of Divine thought needed for every new adaptation in organic structures, or for every original thought in the mind of man," any more than a fresh exertion of Divine Power is needed every time that a stone falls or a fire burns. Now that unconscious mentality has become an accepted and a prominent fact, there should be less difficulty in accepting the view thus set forth (pp 406-414) *spiritual Power* has been gradually becoming able to manifest itself more and more fully in its true character as Spirit. It appears first in the sensitiveness which manifests itself in protoplasm, then in the more distinct *feeling* which characterises organic beings, and it reaches at length its goal in man, in whom we have, not only sensation, but thought, reason, and self-consciousness. It is, in one aspect, a *self-impartation* of *Spirit* through a long evolutionary process.[1]

Once conscious feeling is awakened, the organism stands in such a relation to the rationally constituted environment that intelligent or rational qualities enter into it in ever-increasing degree, and, as organisms are by various means (rational necessity and natural selection included) carried along the upward pathway of life, higher and higher forms are reached, which, owing to their relation to the environment—which is now not only physical but psychical as well (*all* true "experience" being, as Professor Lloyd Morgan points out, psychical)—become ever more fully participant in the rationality that is expressed therein, and in their relation to it, till (as we have seen) Reason, that is first expressed in the external world, becomes so organised in the human brain that man stands forth as, in his own person, a rational being. In its experience the organism is always taking into itself more and more of an ideal element, and at the same time working itself more and more free from the chain of physical causation (see Hobhouse's *Mind in Evolution*; Lloyd Morgan's *Habit and*

[1] Weismann remarks that "we have no knowledge, not merely under what external conditions the origin of living matter can take place, but especially how the one substance should suddenly reveal qualities which have never been detected in any other chemical combination whatever— the circulation of matter, metabolism, growth, sensation, will, and movement" "Much," he says, "points to a gradual rise. Even inorganic material may contain them, although in an unrecognised expression," and that "their emergence in living matter is, so to speak, a phenomenon of summation" (*op. cit.* pp. 392, 393).

Instinct). All along there is a material side to our mental and spiritual life, but it is there, as it has been from the first, instrumental and subservient to Spirit.

Consciousness has, of course, never been "explained," but all are agreed that it cannot be derived from matter. As Dr. Saleeby remarks, "the difference between Mind and Matter is greater than all other differences" ("The Problem of Consciousness" in *Harper's Magazine* for June 1905) Yet when we see the material and the spiritual in constant combination, the former but the expression of the latter, we can recognise that, while Consciousness differs from matter as truly as the letters we form with pen and ink differ from the thoughts they are intended to convey, its appearance, as already said, is not really *different* from *one side* of that which is manifested in all things; it is but the spiritual coming to a clearer expression of itself—to consciousness of itself in finite form, may we not say. It has to be remembered also that Consciousness (as known to us) can never be considered as a separate thing in itself, it must always be the consciousness of some organic being, it does not hover above us separate from an organism; it is, in other words, always *a state of a self*; it is the organic being, no longer under blind mechanism merely, but conscious of *itself* in a greater or less degree. The once "blind" response to stimuli becomes an illuminated or conscious one. The "blind" response in its highest forms was the very perfection of mechanism as expressing an *underlying reason or purpose*; it is the same "Reason" that underlay and that formed that mechanism that now appears and acts consciously. Consciousness thus comes *in a direct line of continuity*, and is but a higher manifestation of an underlying spiritual Reality which has, in some form, been present from the first.

Therefore, when it is said that "consciousness arises

naturally," that it is "an accompaniment of nervous process," that "consciousness merges through sub-consciousness into unconsciousness," that it is "dependent upon the same fundamental condition for its existence as the various physical and chemical forces," etc. (a collection of such statements is given in Dr. Gore's *Scientific Basis of Morality*), it detracts nothing from the reality of consciousness as spiritual, and is no contradiction of its Divine origin. It only shows all the more clearly that it truly belongs to and is a manifestation of the universal Energy or Power. Even if it should be said that it is only an "incidental" manifestation or experience, it still remains true that, under certain conditions, it characterises, or is associated with, the universal Power. If it be further affirmed that the necessary conditions of the appearance of consciousness are the complexity of the matter of the Brain and its organisation, this is no objection to the existence of a primal Divine consciousness. That consciousness appears at all in finite beings implies that it belongs to the Infinite Source of their being. Nor do the conditions of its appearance in finite beings imply, as they might at first sight seem to do, an aggregation of matter at the Source of the Universe, but the reverse of this. Consciousness begins to appear in the created world only when matter has reached the highest differentiation and the greatest complexity of constitution There is nothing so fine as the matter of the Brain, *e.g.* that of an ant, which Huxley described as "the most marvellous morsel in the universe." Professor Trumbull Ladd says of the human Brain: "As to the delicacy of this wonderful piece of apparatus: one observer claims that the passage of a cloud over the sun will change the rhythm in breathing and the pulse-rate of a sleeping child, and if we expose the brain, its whole bulk can be seen to swell when a lamp is approached to the patient's eyes. The incredible delicacy of some of the senses can be accounted for only as it is due to the delicacy of the structure of the brain" (*Primer of Psychology*, p. 23). Of course the brain is still material and consciousness is spiritual. But, as it has been reaching this fineness of texture and complexity of constitution, the matter of the brain has been (1) leaving more and more completely behind it all that we may describe as grossness, and becoming increasingly fit to express the spiritual; (2) by reason of its growing complexity—the consequence of "experience," which is spiritual—more and more of the thought-element that finds expression in the world is being taken up into it—is being organised in it, in fact. In both ways the matter has been *spiritualised*, if we may so speak. Therefore, if consciousness is essentially spiritual and belongs to the spiritual Source of our being, its appearance in finite beings comes about precisely in that way in which we should expect to see it,—as matter returns on its spiritual origin—becoming spiritualised The manner of its appearance, indeed, bears witness to the essential spirituality of its origin. As the process of evolution proceeds, matter is becoming more and more completely the expression of the spiritual, till at length consciousness shines forth in organisms. This is certainly how, from its lowliest forms, consciousness is *developed*—rising higher and higher as experience becomes physically organised. In other words, the spiritual Power which is deepest of all in the Universe is becoming ever more and more able to manifest itself in the finite forms through which it is moving on towards the complete realisation of itself, or of the creative thought and purpose in the world.

It is beyond our present purpose to trace in detail the evolution of *Morality* and *Religion*. But the Environment has now become, not only a psychical, but a *social* one as well, and it is under the influence of that social environment, including family relationships, that Morality is developed.

We do not require to imagine a leap from a purely animal condition to that of a moral and religious being. Man stands at the head of a long line of development of Life, which ascends as it comes into adaptation with, and takes thereby into itself, ever more and more of what is contained in an ever rising environment. In man we behold the realisation of that which was always *possible* for Life as it followed its upward pathway. No Evolutionist supposes that man is descended from any existing animal form. The "gulf" that is often said to exist between "mere animal Intelligence" and Morality has no real existence, and it is not merely by reference to moral tendencies in animals that morality in man is to be explained. In the line of ascent the culmination of which is represented in man, the whole of those qualities which become ultimately manifested were slowly maturing. As we have seen, there is, deep down in the very nature of Life, an altruistic as well as an egoistic principle; the latter never stood alone; the former had of necessity to act also, and in that social environment in which Life came to stand, and of necessity to act in harmony with, it is not difficult to comprehend how a sense of Duty towards his fellows, first of all in the tribe, perhaps, formed itself in man. When Intelligence became the most effective power in Evolution, while *Feeling* was at the same time growing in intensity and in scope, the dawn of Duty and of Religion could not be far off.

We do not begin with "bestiality," and from that rise to Morality and Religion, nor do we have to attempt to develop unselfishness from pure selfishness. We would emphasise the fact that it is not "a mere animal" that becomes a moral and religious being, but the *human ancestor* with his distinctive qualities, tendencies, and capacities. Undoubtedly, man stands based on what we can only speak of as "an animal nature": he does so *now*. But we must not confound this with the purely animal natures that we know, even though we may discern in some of them an approach towards the human. The distinctive quality in an " animal nature " is such self-centredness or egoism as enables the being to exist and persist on the earth But along with that there is, even in pure animals, an altruistic element equally necessary for the family and the tribe, and we may not be far wrong in believing that it was *the strength of this quality* in the " human " line, and not the purely intellectual, that was its most distinguishing element, which, gradually enlightened by Reason, made man ultimately, in his social environment, the moral and religious being that he became.[1]

Man also became gradually conscious of another than his earthly environment—Something beyond himself on which he

[1] In the *Nineteenth Century and After* for March 1905, Prince Kropotkin sets forth a theory of the origin of Morality well worthy of attention. While not disputing Kant's reference of the origin of Morality to Reason, the question is, Why should man obey the moral law or principle formulated by his Reason? Whence the feeling of obligation, etc.? The answer is, in brief, that in man the self-assertive principle did not stand alone, but there was, even stronger in him, the social principle, still more essential for men in the struggle for life. Its benefits were manifest in even the animals around them *Nature* was thus the first ethical teacher of man (just as we have seen it was from Nature he derived his reason). " The social instinct innate in man as well as in the sociable animals, is the origin of all ethical conceptions, and all the subsequent ethical development " " It was (originally) *We*, not *I*,—the men of the tribe. In this identification, or we might even say absorption, of the *I* by the tribe lies the root of all ethical thought. The self-asserting 'individual' came much later on Even now, with the lower savages, the individual hardly exists at all It is the tribe, with its hard and fast rules, superstitions, taboos, habits and interests, which is always present in the mind of the child of Nature. And in that constant, ever present identification of the unit with the whole, lies the substratum of all ethics, the germ out of which all the subsequent conceptions of justice, and the still higher conceptions of morality, grew up in the course of evolution."

We only add that the "*individual*" had to develop (the necessity for which is shown by the fact that it is only among savages that it is otherwise), and then the merely individual interests to be consciously and freely transcended in the interests of the whole. This is what Christianity aims at.

was dependent, and above himself to which he owed obedience. He was becoming more and more conscious of it as that very sense of obligation of which we have spoken grew within him, and his rational nature and experience of life led him to infer the presence of higher Powers. All this formed for him a *spiritual* environment, and called forth corresponding feeling and action. According to his belief respecting the nature of the Powers above him, so was his religion. And just as the real nature of the supreme Power was more and more clearly perceived and come into harmony with, Religion developed.

At the centre of all this course of working, and at the centre of each man's personality—the Source and Ground of it all—there is the all-working spiritual Power. Every living form in the creation partakes in some degree in this primal Source of being; but in man it has become so imparted as to be in him, not only the source of his physical, emotional, and rational life, but the principle of an ever-rising spiritual life:

"In man begins anew a tendency to God."

"Your bodies," says the apostle, "are the temples of the Holy Spirit, which ye have of God." This is true of the Spirit in the creative sense as well as in the more distinctively Christian sense. At the centre of each man's life there is something of God—verily, "a Divine spark," as the Mystics used to say—a spark which in man has glowed into, or blends with, "the light of Reason" and "the sense of Duty," and,

"As fire uprising seeks the sun,"

has become the aspiration towards an ever higher and fuller life, capable of rising into ethical and personal union with God as He is in Himself, and only in its return to its primal Source finding its satisfaction.

Not Identity

It is not Pantheistic Identity we thus reach It may be asked, If the sole all-working Power thus rises in self-manifestation till it appears as consciousness in ourselves, is not this to deny the reality of separate human personalities and to make man merely a manifestation of God? In that case, not only would there be no room for freedom, for moral responsibility, or for religious union with God, but we should have the Divine Power directly responsible for, and actively participant in, all the evil and irrationality in the world. But the consciousness which is caused to arise in finite beings, while it is truly a manifestation of the Divine Power in its working and nature, is *not* the Divine Consciousness *itself*, but a *separate* consciousness that has been imparted or caused to arise. Otherwise, there would be no creation or production of finite, conscious beings at all, but only *a Divine movement* without meaning for us, or discernible purpose in itself. The world is not the scene of the evolution of God, but of His Thought for man and of His Power as it has been conditioned for the creation. The Divine Power works on, as it has so conditioned itself, and it issues in giving rise to spiritual personalities; but the fact that they *are such* makes it certain that, while they are manifestations of that Power in its working, they are separate from that Power in itself Otherwise, they would not be spiritual beings at all.

The first stage in the result is reached when a being has a consciousness of itself. It is necessarily of *itself* (in relation to the world) that it has that consciousness, not of God, or of the Power that has been working. There is, therefore, *a separate self* arising here. That *self* is being gradually formed with increasing fulness, till in man, personal and free, it reaches its completion. It is in this way that the Divine Spirit manifests itself in the creation in ever ascending degree. It is not (we repeat) the self-realisation of *God* as He is in Himself that the world bears witness to, but of the Divine, creative thought and purpose, or of Himself as He has conditioned Himself for the creation, and as He increasingly imparts Himself to it. The whole process proceeds (as we shall see more fully afterwards) *in* the Divine transcendency. Moreover, when the spirit of man is caused to arise in its freedom, with a personal relation to God in His transcendency, a new spiritual world has come to birth, and the Divine Spiritual Power continues its work in and on man in a new form. Not only does the evolution become now predominately a psychical, instead of a merely physical, evolution, but in that very fact a new *spiritual* evolution begins to show itself. The Divine Power is at the foundation of every man's life. As conditioned in his organism, it is the source of every truly natural feeling, *e g* of the mother-love that rocks the cradle. But the light of Reason and Duty in man is also something of God in him, and it is in that light that all natural feelings must be regulated. Man has become susceptible of higher Divine influences—perceptive of an ever ascending ideal of life, and capable of rising above the lower "natural" self to a higher life in free personal union with God. It is truly "something of God within that seeks for God without." But in our spiritual personality we are *ourselves* only : we go on freely forming ourselves, man is still man, and God is for ever God. Tennyson puts the matter well when he says in his " Higher Pantheism ".

> " Dark is the world to thee thyself art the reason why ,
> For is He not all but thou, that hast power to feel I am I ? "

The distinction between man and God is real, though as it exists in Nature it is yet to be transcended in a higher ethical unity, without loss of personality.

It is not Pantheism ; for man is a free spiritual being. If we were not personally free, we should not be spirits or persons at all. The Monism that denies freedom in man is landed in insuperable difficulty when it attempts to rise from the world to anything that can be called God, as will yet appear more fully. It may get to a Source of being which is Mind of a kind, but certainly it is not God. It is just here that the essential difference between Spiritual Monism and that which is merely naturalistic is seen.

When Mr. Mallock says in his article on "The Crux of Theism" (in the *Hibbert Journal* for April 1905) that it makes no difference whether the determination be material or spiritual, whether we be the puppets of Nature or of Spirit, he shows that he entirely misapprehends the nature of Spirit. There can be no such thing as *spiritual* constraint or determination. Spirit is not a *force*, but an influence The difficulty which many feel on this subject is created just by the fact that it is with *spirit* we have to do when we come to personality. The reality and the marvel of creation consist just in this—that it culminates in the production of spiritual beings, who, as such, are in the image of God, and the highest manifestations of the Divine creative working. As already said, the very essence of Spirit is freedom, spirits would not be produced at all unless man were created a free being It is only in this result that the creative Power reaches the goal of its working and most fully manifests itself. If finite spirit is to be produced at all, then, in order to be *spirit*, it must be *free*. And yet it must depend on the universal ground.

The distinction that must be made is really that between God as Unconditioned and God as He conditions His Power for the creation of the world. The Divine Spiritual Power as it passes out and becomes conditioned, works on in the forms in which it has become so conditioned. Matter and Force are the same to-day as they were at the beginning of their creation and action. In *Life* we have a higher manifestation of that same Power, and, *as Life*, it continues to work in the world. In *Sentiency* we have a still higher manifestation, and, higher still, in the personal self-hood of individuals. But just as neither Matter, nor physical Energy, nor Life, nor Sentiency, can be identified with *God*, so no more can our personal self-hood be identified with Him. It is still only God's spiritual Power as He has *conditioned* it in that form—as He has lent out, as it were, so much of that which eternally belongs to Himself to us; and the whole stands in a relation of dependency on, and (in man) of responsibility to, God in His transcendency, as will be stated more fully when we come to speak of the relation of God to the world and of the Divine Transcendency. Further illustrations will be given in the next chapter. Meanwhile, we maintain that in this way, basing ourselves on the actual observation of the World as Science shows us it, we reach a true *spiritual Monism* which can fully incorporate all the teachings of Science, and in which the Divine is not lost in the human, nor the human in the Divine It is at the same time a genuine Idealism; in the highest sense of the phrase, it is a " transfigured Realism "—transfigured, that is, into its ultimate source in Spirit. We have in it the reconciliation of Materialism and Spiritualism, for it holds all that is true in both systems But we go behind Matter and behind Energy in its physical form to the Power that expresses itself in Matter and Energy in all their forms We see everything in the world, from the crust of the earth up to the marvellous human brain, from the lowliest sensitive creature up to the highest spiritual nature, to be the product of one Divine, spiritual Power in an orderly and continuous course of working, or perhaps we should rather say, of unfolding, proceeding onward ever

" Without hasting and without resting."

We find the explanation of the World, crowned by humanity, not in the gradual rise of a suppositional "substance" to this high altitude, nor in the mere persistence of a motiveless "force" or "energy," or of an unknown agent, but in the gradual working, or unfolding, of a spiritual Power which contains within itself the potency of all that is to be, and by slow degrees imparts ever more and more of itself to the creation, without ever losing itself therein or becoming identified with it. If ever we are to reach Spirit in the end, we must have it in the beginning. While there is no *sensation* belonging to matter, there is, none the less, a real spiritual side to everything from the first. Everything in the creation is the product and the manifestation of an all-working Reason, or, if we say, "power," of a Power that is revealed as Spirit within ourselves. Matter has from its first formation (and we know now that it *is* formed) a spiritual side, inasmuch as it is the expression of *Reason* which has conditioned itself in material forms, expressive of some measure of its energy, for the very purpose of creation. And, as the evolution of the creative purpose proceeds, this essential spiritual element reveals itself more and more fully, till at length, when the necessary conditions are reached, it constitutes us spiritual beings, and thus reveals its spiritual nature within ourselves. As we have already said, we cannot go behind *Spirit* to seek some more ultimate reality, we can only go beyond the finite spirit to its Infinite Source. In a word, for the explanation of the Universe culminating in ourselves, we are, on the grounds of scientific fact, led back to God, " of Whom, through Whom, and unto Whom are all things, to Whom be glory for ever, Amen."

CHAPTER XI

FURTHER ILLUSTRATIONS OF SPIRITUAL MONISM: CON-
SCIOUSNESS, FEELING, WILL-POWER; SUMMARY
AND CONCLUSIONS

THE importance of gaining a right conception of the kind of Monism to which the study of Nature and man really leads us, is so great, at the present time especially, that we add some further remarks by way of fuller illustration.

1. We have already repeatedly pointed out the misunderstanding which arises from the idea that matter and force in themselves do anything, or that one kind of force " becomes," or is " transformed " into, or " produces " another and higher kind of energy. Throughout, it is the working *of a Power*, in its highest manifestation *spiritual*, that we behold—a Power that gradually reveals itself in higher and higher forms till it is revealed as Spirit within ourselves.

2. The chief difficulty will be felt with respect to the rise of *Consciousness*, or of the first faint feeling that develops into Consciousness. We will therefore, next, at the risk of some repetition, endeavour to sum up in somewhat different terms some of the most important considerations bearing on the subject—in contrast with the Dualistic view of Consciousness.

Consciousness is not something that appears full-orbed all of a sudden, it has its dawn as truly as the sunrise. As far as we know, finite consciousness or feeling is never manifested apart from living protoplasm. Its manifestation is confined to that which is endowed with the marvellous qualities of *life*. That quality of protoplasm which makes it the basis, not only of life but of Mind, is its capacity for experiencing (we cannot get a more exact word) and responding to *irritation* This irritation may not at first be consciously felt. Vegetable and animal protoplasm are to all appearance identical, but we have no good reason for believing that in the plant world there is any sentiency. There is response to irritation, but the irritation is not as yet consciously experienced. In the case of sensitive and insectivorous plants we witness a remarkable response to stimuli,—a near approach, it seems, to conscious feeling,— but it is most probably to be explained on purely mechanical principles. In very low forms of animal life, however, genuine sentiency appears. What occasions the difference? The most probable explanation is that it arises mainly from the fact that the protoplasm that takes the vegetable form is so situated that it develops early a comparatively hard cell-wall, which shuts it up within itself, while the protoplasm which is left free to act in response to its environment becomes ever more complex and more highly organised. It becomes endowed, not only with the capacity for experiencing irritation, but of being conscious of what it so experiences, and of retaining something like a memory of its experiences. " Memory," we are assured, " belongs to all organised matter." As these experiences continue, with the responses to them, a nervous system comes gradually to be formed, and, as this is developed, consciousness rises and mental life becomes increasingly complete.

We must keep clearly in view the fact that consciousness or sentiency cannot be awakened at all except in living protoplasm of a certain type. It is not due, therefore, to the action of any one external force, but to that of the

Power that has formed this living protoplasm and elaborated it to that degree which makes the manifestation of consciousness possible That Power is itself, so far, *in* that which it thus produces. We have a manifestation of it, not at a distance, but in its actual working, just as the *seed* is present in every part of the plant and flower. Consciousness is not explained by saying that this or that Force which plays on the living protoplasm is "transformed" into consciousness. Apart from the pre-formed, living protoplasm in a certain condition, there would be no consciousness. On the other hand, the awakening of consciousness is dependent on something external to the conscious being. Not that it is due to the action of any external force causing a "shock," or such like. In any living creature capable of consciousness, there is a feeling arising within itself from its own body and from its relationship to the medium in which it lives. Wherever there is feeling—true *feeling*—there is consciousness. In the plant form of protoplasm, and probably in the lowest forms of animal life, there is something very like feeling, but which is not yet *feeling* in the full sense of the word; it is not conscious feeling But we see a gradual rise from mere unconscious sensitiveness to external stimuli, leading to an appropriate response, up to conscious recognition of these stimuli, which goes on increasing in fulness till it reaches its culmination in man. Consciousness we may therefore truly say, is something produced, on the one hand, by the Power which constitutes living protoplasm susceptible of experiencing "irritation" and capable of such development as culminates in conscious feeling; and, on the other hand, by the action of those forces which affect this living matter as stimuli, which are, of course, other forms of the working of the same all-pervading Power. On both sides, therefore, it is an actual manifestation of the all-working Power itself. That Power reveals itself ever more fully in that which it produces, or in the successive forms in which it is, so far, conditioned It is never physical forces that are transformed into consciousness. Light, *e.g.*, falls on the surface of a portion of living matter and sets up certain movements in it. As a consequence the living creature has the sensation of " sight." These vibrations are not themselves transformed into consciousness; yet apart from them there would never be that consciousness But equally certain is it that, apart from the prepared living protoplasm which receives these vibrations, the consciousness would never exist So that, in any way that we can take it, Consciousness, whilst always a spiritual phenomenon, is as clearly produced by the one all-working Power, and is as truly its manifestation, as are Heat or Electricity, or any physical phenomena. But it is a much higher manifestation of that Power than anything physical; it is the culmination of all its working and its self-revelation within ourselves. A merely physical non-spiritual power could never produce our spiritual consciousness, or make its appearance in even the faintest form of consciousness. If it be asked, What is it that is conscious? and the answer be given that it is "the organism," then we have revealed in the organism something *more* at the foundation of things than matter and physical energy. But it is really the *self* that is conscious. In the lowliest conscious creature there is a *self* which is not material but spiritual, the revelation of a *subjective* side to the Universe, in other words, the revelation of Spirit as deeper than "matter" and "energy." Basing ourselves, therefore, on the facts of evolutionary Science, we hold that Consciousness appears as the outcome of all the working (or evolution) of the one world-forming Power in its various forms, and that in its appearance within ourselves as Consciousness we have the highest revelation of the nature of that Power. In the outer world it is manifested in physical forms : in Consciousness as spiritual.

It has been, of course, the position of a spiritual *Monism* that we have endeavoured to set forth. There is a certain attractiveness in the *Dualism* which speaks of consciousness as something that in some way "comes" from another source, something that is in some way "transmitted," or in which we come to "share"; especially when it is represented as our "sharing in an eternal Consciousness." It seems to give us Mind independent of matter. But we must, first of all, be loyal to *fact* if we would recommend Religion, especially to men acquainted with Science. Take away the living matter that composes the body of amœba or of man, and the forces that play upon their bodies, and where should we find this consciousness? The theory which we believe the facts lead to, however, does much more than give us Mind independent of matter. it gives us Mind *formative* of matter. There is, of course, an eternal Consciousness, and in a true sense we are made sharers in it. But unless we think merely of the bare capacity of *feeling*, this can only be accomplished through a long process of evolution,—this is indeed just the great world-process, and the reason why it is necessary. In what sense can a lowly organism be said to be a sharer in an eternal Consciousness (save as barely possessing *feeling*)? In order to be "consciousness" at all, it must have some *content*. There can be no consciousness of *nothing*. How can the amœba share in the content of the eternal Consciousness? It can only be made a conscious being, and only very gradually can finite beings come really to share in the eternal Consciousness.

Some profess to rest contented with affirming the two sides—the spiritual and the physical, which they are unable to bring into any real relation. The physical is a "closed circuit" complete in itself, and the mental is another "closed circuit," also complete in itself. There is no action of the one side on the other; there is no passage from the one to the other; there is only parallelism or concomitancy We are thus left with *two* unexplained systems before us. The tendency, however, often is to lay the stress on the physical side, the mental being so illusive that it is sometimes spoken of as a mere by-play of Brain-action—the Mind being compared to the shadow that accompanies the Body. It thus leads to something like automatism, and if not to virtual Materialism, then to a hopeless Agnosticism. The Mind is completely baffled in the presence of these two orders which cannot be causally related, nor both related to a common Cause.

In opposition to this view, Professor W B. Carpenter in his *Mental Physiology* maintained, with a clearness of reasoning and fulness of illustration, the *correlation* of all the forces, mental and physical—which. we have seen, really means *the unity of the Power* that operates in all these various forms; not, as it might *seem*, the transformation of *physical* energy into mental. "Nothing can be more certain," he says, "than that the primary form of mental activity—*sensational* consciousness—is excited through physiological instrumentality", *eg*, "Light excites Nerve-force (or its equivalent), and the transmisson of this Nerve-force excites the activity of that part of the brain which is the instrument of our visual consciousness." We cannot tell in what way the physical change is translated into the psychical change we call "*seeing* the object," " but we are equally ignorant of the way in which Light produces chemical change, and chemical change excites Nerve-force "; and "there is just the same evidence of what has been termed *correlation*, between *Nerve-force* and that primary state of mental activity which we call *sensation*, that there is between *Light* and *Nerve-force*, each antecedent, when the physiological mechanism is in working order, being invariably followed by its corresponding consequent."

So, from the other side, Dr. Carpenter says: " The

like correlation may be shown to exist between Mental states and the form of Nerve-force which calls forth *motion* through the muscular apparatus · each kind of Mental activity—Sensational, Instinctive, Emotional, Ideational, and Volitional—may express itself in bodily movements, and it is clear that every such movement is called forth by an active state of a certain part of the Brain which excites a corresponding activity in the motor nerves issuing from it, whereby particular muscles are called into exercise." Hence · "That Mental antecedents can call forth Physical consequents is just as certain as that Physical antecedents can call forth Mental consequents, and thus the correlation between Mind-force and Nerve-force is shown to be complete in *both ways*, each being able to excite the other" (pp. 12–14).

To this we add the expression of Professor Wundt's opinion as given in his latest work, *The Principles of Physiological Psychology* "The assumption that there is no such thing as psychical causation, and that all psychical connexions must be referred back to physical, is at the present day nothing else than it has always been, a metaphysical assumption. More than this, it is an assumption which on its negative side comes into conflict with a large number of actually demonstrated psychical connexions, and on the positive raises a comparatively very limited group of experiences to the rank of a universal principle" (p 9).[1]

This subject will receive further illustration when we come to speak of "the Will"; but we see from such statements very clearly the *unity* of the Power in all its manifestations. Spiritual Monism, which holds that the two sides are never separate, shows how it is possible for what

[1] Weismann also speaks of the spiritual—"thought"—as "able to react on the material parts of the body and as Will to give rise to movement" (*op. cit* p 392).

was predominantly physical in its manifestation to become, in its manifestation, predominantly spiritual [1]

Feeling, which is fundamental in Consciousness, is something *ultimate*; it cannot be *derived* from anything else; it can only be imparted, or caused to arise. It belongs to the eternal Source of Being, and by slow degrees it has been caused to appear in finite beings. In *this* sense, of course—as possessing feeling—even the lowest conscious forms of Life may be said to "share in an eternal Consciousness." Taken thus, we are, practically, at one with Mr. Green, although he seems to draw too sharp a distinction between consciousness and self-consciousness. It is true that "the distinction between change and consciousness of change is absolute," and that in self-consciousness we have something much higher than in simple consciousness. But in even the humblest consciousness there is some "consciousness of change"; without this it would not be consciousness at all, while the experience is not yet referred to a definitely conceived self, as it is in our own case. But,

[1] Mr. Mallock says very truly that the doctrine of mere parallelism, unless it is meant "to mask an admission that Consciousness is altogether distinct in origin from the Brain, which is the very theory Huxley and his school deny," "is merely a misleading re-statement of the old unmanageable doctrine for which it is put forward as a substitute. It is like saying that the redness of a red-hot poker is not caused by, but is parallel to, the condition of the heated iron." He gives a very good illustration of how the interaction that is affirmed is possible, which is well worth quoting in full. "States of Consciousness cannot as independent things re-act on the Brain—so much we admit—any more than the Brain can act on them as things independent of itself; but tracts of the Brain, when they come to be in such a condition that Consciousness emerges from them, like the glow that emerges from the iron, or the flame that breaks from hay when it has been heated in the stack, are different in respect of their own internal behaviour and the effects which they produce on the other Brain-tracts surrounding them, from what they are when in such conditions that the phenomena of Consciousness are absent, and there is thus specific interaction between conscious and non-conscious Brain-tracts, though there is none between Brain and Mind considered as two separate entities" (*The Reconstruction of Belief*, p 63).

given simple consciousness, we have in it the appearance, in a finite form, of the Spiritual, and it is wholly in keeping with Evolution that this should yet develop into such self-consciousness as we know in ourselves. This, as Mr. Green himself indicates, while it raises the animal, does not degrade the man.

3. In *Will* and in our capacity for making *Effort*, we seem to have a clear revelation of the nature of the Power that works all in the world and of the *continuity* of its working. Not in Will alone; for we may strongly will what we never do. Will in itself—that aspect of the *self* —is purely spiritual, belonging to the subjective order, although at the same time it is never really *separate* from the physical order. That we can control and direct our activities, not only those of the outer life but to some extent our thoughts and desires and inner life generally, especially through the command we have of the faculty of attention, seems to be a clear deliverance of the consciousness. Multitudes of thoughts are for ever passing through the Mind and desires of all kinds arising. We have, while sane and sound, the power to attend to or to ignore these as we choose, and to select what thoughts we shall follow and what desires we shall cherish Consciousness indeed, Professor Lloyd Morgan says, has for its "primary aim, object, and purpose—control" (*Comp. Psych.*, p. 182). In its service there are certain parts of the Brain to be distinguished as "control centres."

It is just in this power of attention and direction that the difference between mere automatons and responsible, moral, and progressive beings consists. And if the Mind has this capacity, while it may not be rightly termed a "Force," it most certainly shows itself to be *a Power*, and, as is generally admitted, it is just our experience of such will-power that gives us, more than anything else, the very idea of power. Will is the only real Power that we directly know. In our faculty of willing we are revealed to ourselves as centres of power, and power is seen to be spiritual in its essence.

We are further conscious of putting forth *effort*—in other words, of exercising *power* in action. We know that we originate, not physical energy, but *movement*, and we know no other *source* of movement than that within ourselves. The energy that is stored up in our brain and nervous system can be liberated and set in action by a simple act of volition. Just as stimuli come to me from without and make themselves known in my consciousness in certain spiritual forms, so they may excite in me such feelings and desires as prompt to action. There is a physical side to both the incoming stimuli and the outgoing power; but the consciousness in which the stimuli are received and from which the power goes forth is spiritual. I will to strike a blow, perhaps. My volition in its relation to my cerebral organism sends a current of "nerve energy" down to the muscles of my arm, or, what is the same thing, causes such a current to flow,—for it certainly would not go down in such a case without the volition (conscious or unconscious), and a different volition may inhibit or restrain it,—and through the consequent contraction of the muscles I move my arm and strike the blow. Here we clearly see that which is Mind in me appearing as a very real *Power* even in the physical world by means of the energy stored in the mechanism created to serve my purposes, which is also part of *me* in another aspect, and from which the conscious self is never really separate. Physical energy is never created by the will, but it is there in the brain and nervous and muscular system to serve it. Thus in our voluntary action we seem to have the clearest evidence possible of the continuity of the Power that is manifested in the external world with that which is manifested from within ourselves. We show ourselves to be centres of power—to be powers indeed. Whence has that power come to us but from the one Power that works in the world to which we belong? it is that very Power revealing itself within ourselves in its true spiritual character.[1]

To take a fuller illustration of the personal forth-putting of power: A heavy bar of iron is lying on my pathway. It is certain that it will never be removed unless some power be put forth to effect its removal It is unsightly, and the *mere sight of it* moves me to put forth that power. But I may be tired or lazy, and I allow the disinclination for effort which thus arises to overcome the desire to remove the obstacle. I thus yield myself quite freely to this other feeling and suffer it to sway me. But all the time there is the *power* dwelling *in me*, and other powers are working *on me*.

Suppose, now, that I resolve that it must be done. Nothing has compelled me. But I have remembered— that is, the *thought* has come to me—that some one may fall over it and be hurt. Here is a fresh (spiritual) power operating on me. It may be some one I love. With this reflection the power that is moving me grows in intensity Yet it does not *compel* me: I am still disinclined for the exertion. But I allow the thought of danger to the loved one to dwell in my mind, till at length I identify *myself* with this motive force and set about removing the obstacle. I believe that I have the power, and in making the effort I am now conscious of putting forth what we term *physical* power. It may be insufficient. In that case I reason, and

---

[1] In a suggestive article on "Thought and Force" in the *Hibbert Journal* for October 1905, Dean Ovenden affirms that "Thought, or Will power, is the originator of all voluntary force exercised by the body A sleeper, whose thought is dormant, sends forth no voluntary force, but when he wakens, the living thought fills his whole body with energy and activity. A thought transferred to another mind may be expressed in a word or a gesture, but the word or the gesture is not the thought, it is only the medium by which the thought is perceived " " Recent discoveries point to the conclusion that infinite force emanating from Eternal thought may be the ultimate explanation of the structure of the Universe."

search for something that will aid me. I find a lever and apply it, and soon the obstacle is removed. But all the time I have been putting forth *power*, and when the work has been completed I am so exhausted that I feel I have not the power to remove a second similar obstacle; but I know that if I rest and refresh myself the power will be restored internally. Now, clearly, while I act freely, there is a regular line of power here, acting continuously, at the one end *spiritual*, at the other end *physical*. The spiritual powers and the physical are manifestly *one*.

If we think of the information that moves me to remove the obstacle as coming from some *Mind*, who through the bodily organism sets up certain aerial vibrations which I interpret as intelligent speech, the power is seen to be spiritual at both ends, while, in both directions, it passes through physical phases.

A whole host of illustrations might be given tending to show how what come to us as mental influences affect the Brain, the Heart, the Blood, the Life itself. Mere *belief* in anything, or even pure *imagination*, may have the strongest physical effects, according to the nature of what we believe or imagine—may lead even to the cessation of life itself. The influence of "expectancy" and of "faith" in inducing the cure of disease, and the obverse fact that "holding the thought of fear, jealousy, or hate tends toward disease," are being increasingly recognised by physicians.[1]

[1] For illustrations we may refer to Dr Carpenter's *Mental Physiology*, Moore's *Power of the Soul over the Body*, etc. As M. Jean Finot says in an interesting article on "The Will as a means of prolonging Life" in the *Contemporary Review* for January 1906, "It would take whole volumes to state the case for the effect of Mind on matter—that is to say, the effects of our ideas, sensations, and sentiments on the body One incontestable fact stands out—viz, psychic influences frequently produce the same effects as stimulants or mechanical influences" Several examples of the power of suggestion, belief, etc., are therein given, and it is shown how auto-suggestion may contribute to efficiency and well-being, and even to the prolongation of life.

All this is contradicted by those who tell us that we only deceive ourselves when we imagine that in acting out our volitions we exert power of any kind; that all that happens is that in certain physical conditions certain physical effects follow which are strictly dependent on these physical conditions. The Mind, they say, is something entirely apart—an uninfluential accompaniment, a helpless spectator, or it may be a miserable victim of these physical processes. In certain physical states of the Brain, certain physical currents flow, with action as the result, and the starting of these currents, or their direction, depends on nothing mental at all, but on purely physical stimuli. We have already dealt with this view as parallelism. It is quite opposed to consciousness and experience, and seems to reduce men to mere automata deserving of neither praise nor blame. As Dr. Saleeby remarks, "Material changes will cease to affect mental states when opium ceases to cause sleep and music delight, not before"

But the theory claims the support of Physical Science in its doctrine of the conservation of energy, which declares that the quantity of energy in the world is always the same, that energy can never be annihilated nor created. If the mental facts were the product of energy, so much energy must have disappeared, and if the will can influence physical processes, so much energy must be created. All the energy that passes into the nervous system can be accounted for, we are told, as physical energy, quite apart from mental action. It has been pointed out more than once of late that this doctrine of conservation is true only of a "closed system," and does not make the creation of energy an impossibility. But, for the sake of illustration, let us take the statement of the dilemma in which we are supposed to be landed as it is given by Mr. Balfour in his *The Foundations of Belief* (p. 291, note) · "Every theory of the relation between Will, or, more strictly, the Willing

FURTHER ILLUSTRATIONS

Self and Matter, must come under one of two heads: (1) Either Will acts on Matter, or (2) it does not. If it does act on Matter, it must be either as Free Will or as Determined Will. If it is as Free Will, it upsets the uniformity of Nature, and our most fundamental scientific conceptions must be recast. If it is as determined Will— that is to say, if volition be interpolated as a necessary link between one set of material movements and another— then, indeed, it leaves the uniformity of Nature untouched; but it violates mechanical principles. According to the mechanical view of the world, the condition of any material system at one moment is absolutely determined by its condition at the preceding moment. In a world so conceived there is no room for the interpolation even of Determined Will among the causes of material change. It is mere surplusage. (2) If the Will does not act on Matter, then we must suppose, either that volition belongs to a psychic series running in a parallel stream to the physiological changes of the brain, though neither influenced by it nor influencing it—which is, of course, the ancient theory of pre-established harmony; or else we must suppose that it is a kind of superfluous consequence of certain physiological changes, produced presumably without the exhaustion of any form of energy, and having no effect whatever, either upon the material world or, I suppose, upon other psychic conditions. This reduces us to automata, and automata of a kind very difficult to find proper accommodation for in a world scientifically conceived. None of these alternatives seem very attractive, but one of them would seem to be inevitable"

Now, the normal man cannot believe himself to be an automaton, and serious consequences to morals as well as to religion seem to be bound up with such a view of humanity. Various arguments have been used to rebut the assertion, and to remove the difficulties, which we need not repeat. We have already seen that Mind is not the product of mere physical energy, that there is a spiritual element deepest in everything, and that the ultimate Power is spiritual But we would point out how Monism, rightly understood, brings the solution. Mr. Balfour's alternatives are not exhaustive. The whole difficulty arises from thinking of Body and Mind as if they were *separate* existences instead of the *unity* which we know them to be. It arises from the conception of Will or Mind as if it stood apart from—over against—the Body, as it were, so that it acted *on* it. But Mind and Body are *one*—the mental side and the physical side are both aspects of *me*. " Since the total content of my consciousness in any given moment constitutes the empirical *me* of that moment, it is clear that this empirical *I* controls the activity in question. In automatic acts, in so far as they are accompanied by consciousness, such consciousness is a mere spectator, but in controlled activities consciousness is more than a spectator, it takes the helm and guides" (Professor Lloyd Morgan, *Compar. Psych.*, p 189) It can do this because the physical and the psychical in us are in life *in inseparable unison*. When, *willing* to do a thing, I exert power, there is a side to my subjective life which enables me to do this without any creation of " force," or fresh physical energy whatever, and without any exercise of " force " as something acting *upon* the physical side as if from without. The willing acts by means of the energy stored up in the organism. All the energy imparted to an organism is not immediately used by it ; it does not all just go out again as in reflex action ; it remains in a large measure latent as potential energy. There is a reserve of energy from which the mental life is never separable any more than it is separable from its active energy. This the Will liberates in its volition, and through it acts; but there is never any addition to the sum total of energy in its *physical* form in the Universe so far as the action of our Will is concerned. While the Will is a real and free cause, it can only exert so much physical energy as is stored up on its physical side. Experiments, moreover, show that the energy which the Will can use at any time may be so completely expended that the Will cannot draw farther upon it, and, as a consequence, we have on the spiritual side the *feeling* of exhaustion.[1] After a succession of blows, or of similar, although it may be much slighter, exertions, the *Will*, Experimental Psychology shows, may become, not only fatigued, but paralysed (see Dr. Scripture, *The New Psychology*). It is quite a familiar experience that we may will to do something which we cannot accomplish, solely for lack of the requisite energy to carry our volition into effect, or because, as in paralysis, the connection between the Will and the motor mechanism is for the time cut off. But as long as the organism continues in a normal condition, the Will, or rather, strictly speaking, the spiritual self, abides in an inseparable union with the excessively fine and extremely unstable combinations in which physical force is stored up, and, by an exertion so slight as often to be wholly beneath consciousness, can cause such alterations in that energy as results, it may be, in tremendous action in the external world.

But if the mental side of our being thus shows itself, in unison with the physical, to be such a real *Power*, the conclusion is irresistible that it has come into existence as the result of the working of that one only Power which is operating in all the Universe, and is a manifestation of that

[1] As Dr. Wyld states the facts "We always observe these peculiar features in connection with animal exertion, viz, that the intensity of the *mental effort*—the amount or strength of the *muscular sensations* —and *the quantity of the work done*, are proportioned to each other When a large amount of work is to be effected, the mental effort is often violent, and sometimes painful and distressing; and so are the corporeal sensations which accompany it. And if the efforts are long continued, they are generally succeeded by exhaustion, both of mind and body" (*The World Dynamical*, p. 169).

Power in a finitely conditioned form. There could be no power in us save what is derived therefrom, and when we find ourselves as spiritual beings made thus centres of power, we cannot fail to see in this fact the revelation of the Power that works in other forms outside ourselves *as spiritual in its essence*.[1]

[1] The Newer Psychology adduces nothing that is adverse to what we have said. It acknowledges the two sides—the physical and the mental in constant association It has traced the nervous currents that are constantly flowing, and has thus shown more clearly the connection of our mental life therewith It has made manifest the fact that much that really belongs to our mental life is sub-conscious, or even infra-conscious originally. It has also shown the relation of *thought* to the action that takes place in *willing*. But, while some of its representatives may take up the position of mere concomitancy, others are ready to affirm a real inhibitory and active power of Will, exercised chiefly through the faculty of attention. And if the mental life thus shows itself on the one side as a power, its continuity with the Power that works externally cannot well be doubted

After stating the opposing view, Professor James in one of his latest publications says, "But from the part played by voluntary attention, Volition, a belief in freewill and purely spiritual causation is still open to us" (*Talks to Teachers*, 1902, p. 191). Other authorities might be quoted to the same effect. Wundt, *e g*, says . "There can never be an external act save as the result of a previous inner selection, and this holds both of the impulse and of the act of choice" (*Human and Animal Psychology*, p. 225) In his latest work, he says . "The subjective criterion of the external voluntary action, as directly given in introspection, is that it is preceded by feelings and ideas which we take to be the conditions of the movement" (*Principles of Phys. Psych*, 1 28). If, as some affirm, it is the *thought* of the action to be performed (or the end to be gained), or the mental picture of it, that is the cause of the act, or of the effort to effect it, this is still to affirm a spiritual power, although it is ascribed to thought instead of to will—both being simply aspects of the "*me*." So, when Sir Oliver Lodge speaks of *direction* of physical energy rather than of *exertion* of energy (*Nature*, April 23, 1903, etc), while it may be correct to say that "guidance and control are not forms of energy," yet *such* guidance, direction, and control as are exercised by the Mind consciously or unconsciously, in willing or in inhibition, are impossible without the exercise of *power* in some form. The solution of the difficulty may be found if we remember that it is *spiritual* power we have here to do with—spiritual power *never separated* from physical energy. In our possession and exercise of such power we have the revelation of that which is the real nature of all power, even of that which is manifested in the external world.

Summary and Conclusions

Our argument has been that, as there is only one Power working in all Nature, and as our whole being is due to the working of that Power,—its working thus far culminating in ourselves in our spiritual consciousness, personality, and mental will-power,—the nature of the all-working Power is directly revealed as spiritual in ourselves. Underlying all the forms in which Energy is manifested in the physical world there is this spiritual Power. "Force" or "Energy" is spiritual in its essence. The various correlated forms of physical Energy are only modes, or phases, of the manifestation of a Power which is spiritual in essence—which we know to be spiritual in ourselves It passes from form to form, according to the various modes in which it is conditioned, but it is one sole Power that is operating in all. "Matter," whether we think of solid points or of mere force-centres, is certainly constituted by some form of Power, and is thus seen to be spiritual in its essence also. The lower is thus explained by the higher, as that which to us seems lower (as it works in the external world) is revealed within ourselves in its higher form.

To say that there is a rational Power which in the course of its working is able to condition itself in us in finite form, seems quite in keeping with that form of Idealism which affirms (as by Mr. T H. Green) that there is but "one eternal Consciousness which uses the animal organism as its vehicle," or which in some way imparts itself to finite beings But we have sought to show *how it is* that this result is effected, viz, through a gradual process of evolution, rising from the dawning consciousness of the lowliest organisms up to full-orbed self-consciousness in man.

We thus escape from an unwarranted kind of Dualism, and find the ground of that *unity* which is so manifest in

Nature, and which Philosophy is impelled to seek for its satisfaction. The unity of Nature arises from the unity of the Power that works all in the Universe. We can further understand how it is that what is expressed in matter can be interpreted in terms of Spirit: the whole is spiritual and rational in its essential nature. We find thus also that which the Theistic argument, as commonly stated, needs for its completion, or we may even say, for its basis on the firmest ground of knowledge. Our spiritual experience has often been adduced as that which leads to the truest conception of the Power that is manifested in the Universe— especially our own consciousness of voluntary energy. But there was no bridge to be found from the internal to the external world. We were left in an unconnected Dualism, and had simply to leap across the chasm between the internal and the external, the spiritual and the physical. Dr. Tyndall spoke the language of Dualism when he said in oft-quoted words that there was "no passage from the physics of the Brain to the corresponding facts of consciousness." There is indeed "no passage," if we begin with Matter. But if we begin with Spirit, of which matter is but the expression, it is different. We then see that there is no *need* for any such "passage"; there is no *room* for it, because the two are really *one*. It is like inside and outside. As the one Power wrought on physically, it became also *manifested* in its real character as Mind under the appropriate conditions. There was no possibility of any "passage" between the two, for they were inseparably united, and could be sundered only by abstraction or in imagination. Throughout the whole creative working the spiritual is ever that which is but so far expressed in, and served by, the various forms of matter and physical energy, the spiritual is ever first and deepest as it shows itself to be in our own conscious power of attention, direction, volition, and effort. This is not to explain mental phenomena by the two-sided substance of most forms of Monism, but to affirm that the same Power that is manifested externally in the form of "physical energy," or under its conditions, is manifested internally as spiritual, and that the energy that works in the physical world is thus shown to be spiritual in its real nature. Of course, in the physical Universe it is materially expressed, but in our own consciousness it declares itself to be spiritual. In whatever forms of matter it may clothe itself, it is ever a spiritual Power that is acting or evolving. In the perception of this fact we have, it would seem, the solution of many a long-standing difficulty—the possible reconciliation indeed of Materialism and Spiritualism. There need be no disharmony between the two as long as it is held that the spiritual is first and deepest, and the material but the organ and manifestation of Spirit—the Monism of *Thought* and its *expression*.

CHAPTER XII

THE RELATION OF GOD TO THE WORLD

WE have seen the all-working Power so far revealed in the Universe as Reason, and as Spirit within ourselves. The doctrine of an all-working Reason is a very old one, but it is not as old as belief in God. We have it in Philosophy as early as Heraclitus and Anaxagoras, and it comes right down, through Plato and Philo, the Stoics and the Schoolmen, to Hegel and to our own times. We find it in the Bible itself, in the Psalms, in the Proverbs, and still more fully, in the *Wisdom Literature* of the Apocrypha. We find it in the New Testament, most notably in the opening words of the Fourth Gospel "*In the beginning was the Logos, and the Logos was with God, and the Logos was God.*" We find it in the most modern books dealing with the Philosophy of Theism. What we have specially sought to do is to show the Scientific grounds for it, and that on grounds set forth even by writers supposed to be, or who actually are, hostile to Theism, Reason in man is due solely to the pre-existence and working of Reason in Nature—thus placing the doctrine on such a basis as cannot be removed without denying Reason in ourselves. It finds in this way, not merely a metaphysical, but a scientific basis in universal experience on which to rest. For it is demonstrable beyond cavil that Reason in man comes originally from his relation to the Universe around him, which, since it constitutes us rational, must be itself rationally constituted—the expression of Reason in all its laws and parts.

But something more requires to be done. We cannot but ask ourselves, Why is it that the argument from Reason, which seems so plain, is so often doubted? Why does not the mind universally rest in it? We might answer that this is partly because it has often been based on such metaphysical grounds as have seemed uncertain, or have, at least, been difficult for the ordinary understanding to apprehend It is only the more recent Science, and the doctrine of Evolution especially, that has made it possible to place it on the plainest and most secure foundation. We might also suggest that it is perhaps, in one aspect, too simple to be readily accepted as sufficient; that the secret of the world is too much an "open secret." Perhaps it seems, like the Gospel, not only too simple to believe, but too good to be true. There is, undoubtedly, this other reason—the difficulty of reconciling with it the appearances and events of the world as it exists for us and goes on from day to day. There is so much that *seems* contrary to reason in the world, and in our experience of life there are so many things that happen that we cannot understand and which our reason thinks should be different. We must therefore endeavour to clear up these difficulties; which, however, exist all the same, whatever may be the nature of our Theistic argument. It is, we believe, the line of thought that we have followed that enables us to deal with these difficulties most effectually.

I

The first and most important fact to realise is that the Power which is manifested as working in the Universe as Reason is never, at any stage at which we can perceive it, God *as He is in Himself*. God is, of course, Love as well as Reason, as we shall yet endeavour to show. But our present point is the distinction that must be made between

God as He is in Himself and His rational Power as it has been *conditioned* so as to work out His purpose in the Universe. The distinction is the same as that between God as immanent in the world and God as transcendent It is manifest that our world is only one of innumerable scenes of creative activity, and that it bears witness to a constant process of development, the end of which is not yet reached. The whole of that which God is cannot therefore be present and working at any given moment in any particular world—only *so much* of the Divine rational Power can be at any moment so working or expressed in any particular world, while, of course, God is behind it all, the *Source* of all the working—which really takes place *in* Him as transcendent. The Divine rational Power is working *in* the world only as it has *conditioned itself* for the purpose of creation. The failure to make this distinction is, we believe, an error of much of our modern thought concerning God in His relation to the Universe, and the source of most of the difficulties that are felt to-day to militate against a Theistic conception of the Universe The most real difficulties are those arising from the actual world as we know it in individual experience and as the history of the evolutionary process reveals to us the course of its development; we seem to see much that we cannot reconcile with the thought of God as the Perfect Reason and Love, or as a Power personally present and working *in* the world. We have seen how completely Haeckel misunderstands the nature of the Christian conception of God, and his error is shared in even by some of the defenders of Theism. It was not shared in by Spencer, who, while he erred in declaring God to be wholly "unknowable," drew a very clear line between the Ultimate Reality as it was manifested in *conditioned* form in the Universe and that Power as it is in itself, or in its *unconditioned* Being. The distinction is one of the highest consequence, and we have in it a real contribution to Theology. God, in Himself, is neither the "Substance" of Spinoza[1] or of Haeckel, nor the all-working "Energy" of Spencer, in its conditioned forms; nor is He the "Reality" or "Absolute" of which all the phenomena of the growing and changing world are passing appearances. That there must be some Reality which underlies these phenomena is certain; but we make a great mistake when we take this for God as He is in Himself. No doubt God is, as Goethe said, Being itself, real Being, needing, in this aspect, no proving. But if so, we can never find this real Being in its truth and fulness in any finite, *developing* world. *Reality* cannot be God realising Himself as for the first time in His creation. To call that the Absolute or the Real would be, not only a serious limitation of the idea of God, but a contradiction in terms. So far as it is only realising itself it is clearly not yet *Real*. God must be the Absolute Reality *in Himself*, apart from the developing creation. It is out of His fulness that we all receive. The world is the scene of an evolution, but it cannot be that of the evolution of *God*. It can only be the scene of the gradual self-impartation of being from the Infinite Source *because* of His possession of perfect Being in Himself. It is an evolution, not of God, but of the Divine as self-conditioned for the sake of the world. What we have in the world is something *of* God or *from* God, but it cannot possibly be *God* as He is in Himself. It cannot be so, because the entire manifestation (till we come to Christ) is finite, and under necessary conditions or limitations. God in Himself is Infinite, Unlimited, Unconditioned, Perfect Being. It is impossible for such a Being to be confined in, or adequately manifested by, the finite world.

[1] Spinoza, however, distinguished between God in His infinitude and God as manifested in the World. The distinction is well stated by Dr. Hunt in his *Essay on Pantheism*, pp. 222, 226.

The same mistake is made by those who speak of "*the immanence of God*" as if it were an actual presence of God *in* the world. The Divine Reason and Love, *as conditioned*, is certainly the immanent principle of the world's life; this alone can account for the development. God, in this sense, is immanent in the world, and this immanence is never to be *severed* from its Source in the Infinite Being. There is thus a real immanence of the Divine creative Reason and Power, and there comes to be an ever-increasing entrance of God into the world. But God Himself, as the infinite all-perfect Being, while Omnipresent *Spirit*, cannot possibly be personally *in* the finite world; still less can He be in that world conceived as material, or in it in the vague manner in which some speak of the Divine immanence. God becomes thus simply "the Soul of the world"; He is practically identified with "Nature." Those who speak thus loosely of Divine Immanence lay themselves open to the retort of Mr. McCabe that, in this latest phase of Theology, God merely means "a principle in Nature and not distinct from it"; "God slowly sinks again into the life of Nature. Great Pan is alive once more."

To think of God as personally present and directly acting in the forces of Nature and of Life, would make Him the immediate Agent in all the dreadful things that happen in the world—storms and earthquakes, shipwrecks, famines, pestilences, diseases, etc., and the *direct* Inspirer of all the appetites and passions of beasts and man, the Former of animal weapons of attack on fellow-creatures. It would, in short, make Him directly responsible for all the evil in the world, and the very idea of *Freedom* would be impossible. The world would be the scene of the evolution of God, not His *Creation*. We need not wonder that we can never get at *God* in that way, or so "show to men the Father." For all that we can tell, the Universe may be infinite, but we can never grasp it in its infinitude. Much of it can give *no*

THE RELATION OF GOD TO THE WORLD 249

moral manifestation of God at all; and at its best and highest it is always limited and imperfect. So that by the utmost stretch of vision it is only a partial manifestation of God that we can behold in the Universe.

It will be said that God is *both* immanent and transcendent. True, but it is as He limits Himself in the act of Creation that He is immanent in the physical world. His Thought or Reason is there as a spiritual principle, as the power of the world's evolution, but in no other sense can God be immanent in the world. If we think of the history of the evolving world we shall see this clearly. When we picture to ourselves the almost infinitely minute and almost infinitely diffused original matter, we may seem able to imagine a kind of Divine immanence therein. But when we think of this diffused matter coming together and becoming the molten globe, or the red-hot whirling sphere, how can we think of the immanence of *God* in that? As we follow up the history of the earth through its varied phases of heat and cold; as we picture to ourselves the ice-bound land, or the steaming atmosphere, or as we call up to our mental vision the succession of strange, uncouth, fierce, and savage animal forms on its surface or in the waters, or as we think of man's slow rise from pre-human forms, how can we seriously speak of the immanence of *God* therein? The same may be said with respect to the world around us to-day, with its physical catastrophes, its unrelenting laws, its hordes of wild animals preying on each other, its millions of equally wild men, not only poor untutored savages, and heathen *groping in the darkness after God*, but the many unprincipled representatives of a high civilisation—many of them with no thought of a God at all,—when we think of the world with its wars, its crimes, its selfishness, its irreligion, what evidence is there of the immanence of God in it? There is a way of speaking of the Divine immanence that only saves the *Name* of

God, and tends really to perpetuate unbelief, because, say what we may, men cannot shut their eyes to facts patent to universal observation. And when this idea of Divine immanence is made, as it sometimes is, a substitute for Christianity, a strange *bouleversement* is effected from the standpoint of Christian Theology. The Scripture passages that are quoted to prove or to support the idea of the immanence of God are often misunderstood. The 139th Psalm, for example, really affirms the Divine transcendency. So does St. Paul's famous saying at Athens, " For *in* Him we live and move and have our being." To Christ, God was, indeed, always near, and working all in the creation; also, by His Holy Spirit within us; but it was always as " our Father in heaven" that He spoke of God. The only Divine immanence we find in the Bible is that of God by His Power in Nature and by his *Holy Spirit* in man.

Moreover, if the Power that works in the world and that rises to conscious Spirit be identified with God as He is in Himself, no real distinction can be drawn between the Divine and the human; no real freedom can be attributed to man. In the presence of error and evil we are landed in insuperable difficulty, such as is illustrated in Mr. Mallock's attempt to get to God on the lines of scientific determinism, in which *everything*—all the evil thoughts and deeds of men included—has to be embraced in the Divine Purpose, and in some way initially expressed in the primal matter of the World. In short, there is no escape from a throroughgoing Pantheism, even though we may affirm in words a Divine transcendency. But we cannot thus identify the Power that works in Nature with God as He is in Himself. God in Himself is *Spirit*, infinite, transcendent Spirit; the Universe lives and moves and has its being *in Him*, not He in the Universe. As that infinite Spirit we shall see that He is near us ever, moving within us, the very Life of our higher life; but *as the Power that works in the physical world* He is self-limited and conditioned, moving on ever towards self-realisation in that form in the world. What we witness in the world's evolution is a constant *striving*, even *struggling*, upwards of the immanent life such as we cannot attribute to God as He is in Himself, but which manifests to us the Divineness of that principle of the world's life which comes into full expression in Christ. While, therefore, God is by no means *absent* from the world or a mere Spectator of its life, but is the living Source of its onward movement—realising, or rather reproducing, His Divine life therein—we cannot think of Him as being personally *in* the evolving world.

As has already been said, God is indeed at the centre of each man's life. But it is not as a physical force that He is there, or in the way in which His power is conditioned so as to form and uphold our physical organisms. He is the Principle of our higher life, inasmuch as we have, on the intellectual side, been caused to share in the Divine Reason, and, on the emotional side, in the Divine Love, and at the same time to have a consciousness of our relation as free, rational personalities to the Infinite Reason and Love. Through the process of development in adaptation to the environment, and the experience of Life generally, the Divine Reason and Love has so risen within us, and the Divine Power has so imparted itself to us, that we are spiritual personalities in the image of God, and may also reflect His moral character. There is thus something of God Himself at the centre of our lives, which, as our true "nature," would lead us ever upward if we would only follow it—even toward the Infinite itself. But we are really thus brought into relation with God *in His spiritual being*— with God in His *Divine transcendency*.

The true doctrine of the relation of God to the World is neither Deism nor Pantheism; it might be better described as a form of "Panentheism," all things in God, who is at once transcendent and partially, but increasingly, immanent in the World. The Divine Reason is the immanent principle of the whole But when the physical world has been formed, and the goal of Nature-Evolution reached in man, capable of receiving Divine influences from his environment, a new order of Divine *spiritual* operation begins, and as men are receptive of the influences that thus come to them, there is an ever-increasing immanence of God *in man*. And while the Power that is working in Nature is revealed as being in its essence Reason and Spirit, the complete evidence for the being of *God* is only found in religious experience, as men are brought into union with God and become the organs of His Holy Spirit. His fullest manifestation shines forth from the spirits that are so in unison with Him, in whom the Divine Spirit dwells in a greater or less degree, or, it may be, "without measure," as that Spirit dwelt in Jesus Christ. We do not really see *God* till we behold One who can truthfully say, "He that hath seen Me hath seen the Father." When we stop short of this, we always find ourselves with something *less* than *God*. We must rise "from Nature up to Nature's God," if we are truly to find *God*. Theism must become *Christian* Theism, if it is really to "see" and to "show" men "the Father." In other words, we can only truly behold or know the nature of the Power that is working in the world when we see it in its highest manifestation, just as we can only know that of a flower when it has bloomed—when its immanent principle has found its complete expression.

Such a manifestation can only be given when there is in the world a moral and spiritual nature that can truly express the Ethical character of God.

II

It is in this light that we can hopefully approach those difficulties which are so widely felt with respect to the

THE RELATION OF GOD TO THE WORLD

actual world, and which have found such strong expression in recent times from J. Stuart Mill, Professor Huxley, "Physicus," Haeckel, McCabe, and others, which also constituted the chief difficulty to the mind of Darwin. Indeed, probed to the bottom, the real source of doubt and difficulty concerning God is the appearance of the actual world, and the experience of conscious beings therein in the past and in the present.

The chief points to be kept in view are these :—

1. That it is a Divine *Reason* that is working everywhere, so far immanent, and finding expression, in each particular world, but in itself transcending all worlds.

2. That this Divine Reason is present in each world only in *conditioned* form.

3. That the process of creation is an *Evolution* or gradual unfolding of the content of that Divine Reason as it has become the principle of each world and is self-conditioned in each.

4. That the evolution and the conservation of both the physical and the living worlds is ever by means of invariable "laws," which are really the laws of Reason, and therefore unchangeable. At the same time, these laws, as formulated by Science, are simply the expression of what is found to be the actual order of things, and there may be law-ordered powers or forces of which Science has not yet taken cognisance.

5. That there is no other method of creation conceivable save this *rational* one.

6. That when conscious reason appears in free personalities, a new element enters the world, a new order of (relatively) free originating causes makes its appearance, and a new course of Evolution begins.

1. If we would see our way through those difficulties which most of us feel in view of the actual world, we must

not think of our own world, or of our Universe merely, but of an indefinitely wide creation, never ceasing, going on towards infinity. The Divine Reason and Love is for ever creating, and, in order to do so, must be for ever conditioning itself in the creation, and for ever realising itself (or the Divine Thought) therein, in finite forms. If we say "it," it is because we must ever remember that Personality in God is something wider and greater (not less) than the limited personality we know in ourselves Behind the whole process there is the Infinite Reason and Love, but the Love *cannot possibly appear* till there are forms capable of expressing it, nor can the Reason be manifested in all its perfection unless the *whole* can be embraced and the creative movement consummated. While it is Divine Reason that is working everywhere, it is as *conditioned* in the forms necessary for the creation in view. It must begin at the lowest before ever it can reach the highest: the whole process will be one of gradual realisation of a Divine Idea or Purpose, in its highest aspect one of Self-realisation in finite forms of being. All the forms in which the Divine Reason so conditions itself in the physical world will continue to work on according to necessary, rational laws, and can never cease so to work. "Law" reigns everywhere, there is no such thing as lawless chance or happenings.[1] There is no "unreason" anywhere in the Universe, till we come to free beings who are permitted to enter as Causes and may act "unreasonably." This is simply to affirm that everywhere *Reason* reigns (God reigns) according to the "nature" which has been given to everything, and with scope for the freedom that makes man, *man.* There

[1] "Chance," ascribed to Nature, is simply a name for our ignorance In other apparently "fortuitous" conjunctions there has been the action of *a Will* on the one side, or on both sides, *e g*, in the illustration of the stone falling on the statesman's head, given by Mr. Mallock, there was "order" on the one side and the action of *a Will* on the other.

THE RELATION OF GOD TO THE WORLD

is a constant movement onward and upward; the all-working Reason becomes continually expressed in new and higher forms, and the old forms are left behind to work on according to the nature given them; in other words, as the creative Power has conditioned itself in them. This holds good throughout the entire physical Universe. When Life appears, the same principle rules, the same reign of law continues; life comes into being, develops and rises higher and higher according to the necessary rational laws of life, or of living matter. This accounts for all the varied strange and often ferocious forms which we see appearing in the living world, which are left behind as life rises to higher forms—each form continuing to act and to maintain itself according to the necessary conditions of its nature. This is all just the working of Reason. There could be no life on any other terms, and no advance in any other way. Natural selection, after all that has been said to mollify its aspect, seems a hard process, and we cry out against the seeming "waste"; but it is an inevitable one if life is to rise. In like manner we view with horror the "ravine" and suffering that mark the animal world But, as Dr. Wallace has shown, much that we imagine is "the very reverse of the truth." There is "the maximum of life and of the enjoyment of life with the minimum of suffering and pain. Given the necessity of death and reproduction—and without these there could have been no progressive development of the organic world—and it is difficult even to imagine a system by which a greater balance of happiness could have been secured" (see *Darwinism*, pp. 36–40). Yet the process is not such as we can conceive a God, *personally* present and working, carrying out—destroying continually the work of His hands it is not an external working, but an *Evolution*. So, just because *human life* can only be developed in rational ways—in the hard but salutary school of experience—do we see such a slow progress, so great suffering, and so much that is still backward in the world of humanity. For

> "life is not as idle ore,
>
> But iron dug from central gloom,
> And heated hot with burning fears,
> And dipped in baths of hissing tears,
> And batter'd with the shocks of doom
>
> To shape and use"

2. *Moral Evil* has its root, not in God, but in man. It is man's want of thought, selfishness, or inhumanity to man,

> "makes countless thousands mourn"

Man must be free if he is to be moral, and *man*. Hence there is always, not the necessity, but the *possibility*, of moral evil or sin. Man must rise from a semi-animal condition, and will inevitably be long weighted by his "animal inheritance" on its egoistical side. For, while both the altruistic and the egoistic are present, and the former perhaps the stronger in man as compared with the animals, the latter is first and most deeply rooted, and although the altruistic claim might make itself felt in man's rational nature with a clearness it could have in none other, disobedience to it in its higher claims—those most remote from self—was practically certain. Even in man the egoistic element must have developed itself first, and the altruistic claims of the family and the tribe were still closely allied to it. The call to go *beyond these* must have met with opposition. The root of all moral evil or sin is *selfishness*, in opposition to the claims of a wider love. Standing, therefore, of necessity, deeply rooted in the older and stronger, lower nature, man was, and is, "weak" in the presence of the higher ideals or law, and he refuses to follow them as he ought. We see the same thing to-day as must, still more manifestly, have characterised the remote past. The course of development thus became, not an undeviating upward and onward one, but one in which failure and bitter

THE RELATION OF GOD TO THE WORLD 257

experience of the effects of evil are made educative and saving powers, and in which full salvation can only be found through access of the all-environing Divine Spirit to the human spirit. All the discipline of life, however hard it may seem, is wholly rational, absolutely necessary, if man is to be lifted into a truly ethical and spiritual existence. Man cannot be *created* good ethically, else he were no more man. While evil thus (humanly speaking) cannot but arise, in a Reason-governed Universe it cannot but be overruled for good in the long run. Indeed, the problem is not that which has so greatly exercised many minds—why evil should appear in the world, but how there could have been a world of finite developing beings without the appearance in it of evil. Of course, what is evil for the higher nature was not evil for the lower. But it must become known to man as evil, it must be transcended by him, and, in the fulness of time, it must cease to be. God who begins the world must also be its Consummation; God who is the deepest Principle of its life must yet be all in all.

3. *The presence of God a spiritual presence*

It is true that there is not only the conditioned Reason working on in the ever-rising world, there is also the all-environing Reason and Love in which the whole process takes place But God, so conceived, is purely *Spirit*. As such He can find entrance to our spiritual nature, but no interference with the materialised world or its laws, or with the creative processes as such, is possible except through spiritual influences touching the human spirit. This follows from the fact that the *whole* is the working of *Reason*. Such higher influences as reach the human spirit must also act themselves out by means of the organism which relates man to Nature and to his fellow-men. If we think of the transcendent Deity as we would of a *finite* rational being, embodied in some *form*, working, now here and now there, at this point or at that, in this particular constituent of the Universe or in that other, merely, we shall meet with insuperable difficulties when we look out on the actual world. If God were such a finite being, moving from place to place, now here and now there, with a power of acting on Nature as a man can act, only in a greater degree—interfering with the actual order His Reason has instituted; or if He were present in Nature as that personal *directive* Mind—over and above that Reason in Nature (which is His own Reason as it is conditioned in Nature) —which has often been affirmed, there are many things which we may well think might be other than they are. But then *the whole* would not be that rationally connected whole that it is, which in its ordered completeness declares to us the presence and working of Reason. The Reason is *immanent*, not an external directive Power. If we try to take *the whole* into view, rather than certain isolated parts, and conceive all to be embraced in one rational purpose, we shall be convinced that nothing in the external world of Nature could possibly be other than it is, or could act otherwise than it does—save, of course, so far as human action could modify it. It is just this rational connection, this inviolable order and unvarying law, never turning aside for a moment *on any account*, that makes the rational world, and, however hard the action may sometimes press on the individual, however great the suffering that may come to him therefrom, it simply *could not be otherwise*, if there was to be a "rational" or "law-ordered" world at all, except, we repeat, in so far as reason in man is free to act and to modify the train of physical consequences. In fact, when we sit as critics of the creation, we show that we fail to understand what God really is, that we expect impossible things from Him. Though He is all-mighty, He is the Almighty *Reason*; though He is the Infinite Love, He requires adequate organs for the expression and action of His Love in the created world; though He is truly Omnipresent, He

THE RELATION OF GOD TO THE WORLD 259

is Omnipresent *Spirit*. In short, we forget the great Christian truth that, in Himself, "*God is Spirit.*" The Divine Reason always works in the only possible way, because it is the only rational way, and we may well be sure that it is always the best way, on the whole.

"Would you seek in an order reversed and amended a Hand Divine?
Nay, the wonder of wonders lies in unchangeable design.

Should God break His Laws, as He might, should He stoop from His Infinite skies
To redress that to us seems wrong, to lift up the life that dies;

Should He save from His wolf His lamb, from His tiger His innocent child;
Should He quench the fierce flames as they burn, or the great waves clamouring wild,

I think a great cry would go up from an orderless Universe,
And all the fair fabric of things would wither as under a curse"
                                                SIR LEWIS MORRIS

But when Reason has, as it were, risen out of its limitations in physical Nature as the conscious Reason that shines in ourselves, it has reached a higher stage of self-realisation, and there are many things in Nature which it is for us in obedience to that Reason and in response to our higher nature to check or alter, or, it may be, bring altogether to an end. But the action of Reason in Nature is practically the same thing as that of Cause and Consequence—one thing necessarily following another in rational order. If this rule did not hold good everywhere, there would be no rational world at all, and no such thing as Science or the ever advancing life which Science promotes, would be possible. There would be no security for anything, as far as we were concerned, it would be chaos, not cosmos. The Reason that God is is an absolutely perfect Reason, with Him there "can be no variation, neither shadow that is cast by turning." For this cause there never is or can be any changing or altering of laws, or interference between cause and consequence The finite reason of man (so much of Reason as he makes his own) might suggest that such things were desirable, but the Infinite Reason knows better. Cause and effect, antecedent and consequent, must inevitably follow each other. We repeat that it is just this that is the manifestation of *Reason,* that it is just this that constitutes the rationality of the Universe, and makes us the rational beings that we are. This, at the same time, by no means shuts out prayer, or excludes the *spiritual* (transcendent) action of God in the world, or that of other spiritual powers.

Mr. Mallock represents the question of the relation of God to the individual, in view of the actual experience of life that many individuals have had, and that many still have, as one side of the great " Crux of Theism " (*Hibbert Journal* for April 1905). Suffering, he admits, may work good on certain natures, but what of the others ? He forgets that God can only reach the individual through the creation of a *race* that must receive and hold its life according to inevitable laws, and that, if God is to give rise to a World at all, the experiences that seem so dreadful could not possibly be avoided, save in so far as free finite causes have had to do with them. This fact leads us to believe that the ultimate experience of the individual may be far more intimately bound up with that of the *race* than we have been in the habit of imagining, and to entertain the hope that, in some way, in the final perfecting of the race, the Divinely intended good shall be made possible to each individual member of it.

A brief extract from one of Augustine's soliloquies, prefixed to Whittier's poem, " The Shadow and the Light," may fitly conclude this part of the discussion. Augustine asks, Whence is evil, and Why is it not caused not to be, if God is Good and Almighty ? " And admonished to

THE RELATION OF GOD TO THE WORLD 261

return to myself, I entered even into my inmost soul, Thou being my Guide, and beheld, even beyond my soul and mind, the height unchangeable . . . And I beheld that Thou madest all things good, and to Thee is nothing whatsoever evil. From the angel to the worm, from the first motion to the last, Thou settest each in its place, and everything is good in its kind. Woe is me, how high Thou art in the highest, how deep in the deepest! and Thou never departest from us, and we scarcely return to Thee." And so the poet sings—

> "the Sphinx sits at the gate of life
> With the old question on her awful lips
>
> In paths unknown we hear the feet
> Of fear before, of guilt behind,
> We pluck the wayside fruit, and eat
> Ashes and dust beneath its golden rind.
>
> From age to age descends unchecked
> The sad bequest from sire to son,
> The body's taint, the mind's defect,—
> Through every web of life the dark threads run
>
> Oh why, and whither?—God knows all;
> I only know that He is good,
> And that whatever may befall
> Or here or there, must be the best that could
>
> . . . . .
>
> Shine, Light of God! make broad thy scope
> To all who sin and suffer, more
> And better than we dare to hope
> With Heaven's compassion make our longings poor!"

III

How then are we to think of the rational Power that shows itself working in the world, in its relation to God, the world and ourselves?

1. We may think of it after the Biblical and Philosophical conception of " the *Logos* " (Reason and Word) that was *with* God, and that *was* God (that is, essentially

Divine), that, dwelling eternally *in* God, yet goes eternally forth *from* God (while God Himself, with equal truth, goes forth in that) to become the Principle of the world's life and the Power of its entire development; always bearing in mind that it is not of this one world merely we have to think, but the entire creation. This is really God going out from Himself into the creation, and it is solely because this is at the foundation of the Universe that it can rise, not only as we know it to have risen, but to a height at present inconceivable. It is at the same time just this that creates the real " Riddle of the Universe " from a religious point of view—that is, the difficulty of believing in a Divine Creator.

2. From the standpoint of Science, the form which this Biblical conception takes, on its mundane side, is that of *the Principle of the World-organism.* (The term " a Soul of the world " is liable to be misunderstood.) We have already seen that it is impossible to think of the immanent Power as that of a Being personally acting *in* the physical world. Our most helpful thought of the Universe—one to which we are directly led in many ways—is that of *a great organism*, analogous to the many smaller organisms which abound in the world. Every organism that we know is dominated by a principle of unity which is also the idea of its being, and it is under the influence of this ideal principle that its entire development proceeds. This is its " soul," unconscious at first, but truly there, and initially expressed in the living matter of the germ. " The Soul " only comes to a growing consciousness of itself at a certain stage of the process, when it can freely and consciously direct the actions of the organism, so far as these are left to its control. So we may think of the great World-organism as animated by a Divinely imparted principle of life, and dominated by a Divine Idea and Purpose which slowly unfolds in the course of that which we term " Evolution "—the Reason and Love at the foundation of the whole coming to a consciousness

THE RELATION OF GOD TO THE WORLD 263

of itself *in finite form* in man as a person, in himself so rationally constituted that he is able to direct such of the elements as are open to his manipulation and control, and on grounds of consciously perceived rationality and rectitude to carry onward and complete the process. The development of an organism under its principle of unity, idea, or purpose, is perhaps the best way in which we can represent to ourselves the relation of the Divine all-working Power to the world. As this principle originally proceeds from God, and *is* God going out from Himself for the sake of creation, this conception to which Science directly leads us is identical with the Christian conception of "the *Logos*," reaching complete Incarnation in Christ.

3. May we not go farther? We know that somehow in the living matter of the germ of each organism are expressed the hereditary qualities of genus, species, and individuality—qualities often not only physical, but intellectual, moral, and spiritual — of each creature. However little we are able to understand it, the result in each particular case shows that these potentialities were actually *there* in some influential form. May there not have been something similar in the case of the primal matter of the World-organism? If we think that this was impossible with ordinary matter, is it not conceivable that we are in error in supposing that "*living* matter" is only something of comparatively recent date? Is not this the reason why we never can behold its beginning, nor even conceive how it could ever appear in the line of the working of merely physical and chemical agencies? Is not this marvellous "matter of life"—in its invisible constituents—in some way deepest of all that is material, most original of all, and as capable of becoming the expression of the Divine Thought or Idea of the world as the living matter of organic germs is capable of expressing the Ideal of each form of living creation—as it undoubtedly is? Perhaps Protoplasm, *as*

we know it, could not have existed when the earth was in a molten state. But perhaps this is true only of the *chemical* combinations in which it appears to us; its real essence may lie deeper. We must further ask, whether the *entire matter of the Universe* was at one and the same time in such a condition as to make the existence of living matter impossible? May it not rather have been, in the case of each particular world, only a portion of the original material that passed into that condition that we know as ordinary matter? We have the *Ether* always present, and, doubtless, always, in some way, operative; it is, Science now teaches, actually formative of ordinary matter, and we do not yet know what it is that gives to living matter its peculiar and quite unique quality and capacity. Does not the Ether have a most intimate relation to life? Or, once more, we may repeat the question often put in our day— Is not all matter in some real sense alive? May it not be in its ultimate constituents as capable of bearing the impress of the creative idea of the world as the matter of individual organisms is assuredly capable of bearing that of the idea of the organism that is to be developed?[1] Or, if we think rather of modes of energy, of different "vital spins" (with Professor Lloyd Morgan), it makes no real difference.

---

[1] We are encouraged to allow the text to stand by reading the following remarks of Dr Flint "Apparently there were many long ages before there was any life and intelligence on the earth, but, conceivably also, the sources of consciousness and knowledge may have been present in the cosmic ether before our world became a globe differentiated from all other worlds Nor is it entirely certain, perhaps, that vegetable and animal vitality may not have had, in an incalculably remote age on earth, their origins in the same protoplasmic substance What is alone indubitable is that conscious life has had an exceedingly long history on earth That it was preceded by a vastly long history of entirely dead matter does not seem to have been adequately proved either in the affirmative or negative Even a molecule of matter would appear to have a history, in or behind it, which the chemist and biologist, geologist and palæontologist, have failed entirely to decipher" (*Philos. as Scientia Scientiarum*, p 49).

THE RELATION OF GOD TO THE WORLD 265

Physical Science has recently suggested a view of "matter" which might be truly described as *organic*. Each *sub*-atom is supposed to be as truly " a system " (in the Ether) as the planetary system is one in Space. The whole Universe would thus be *a vast organic system*, and if we carry to it that conception of a principle of unity which we derive from our knowledge of living organisms, we come within sight of a possible way in which the primary Reason may be originally related to that Universe, which, at every point and as a whole (as far as we know it), shows itself to be a rational Universe. The primary matter of the Universe, it must be remembered, is of inconceivable minuteness or fineness, and if, as we believe, Mind in ourselves can influence matter and set up motion, it is not incredible that the primal Mind can so express itself in, and give motion to, " matter " as through it to form the Universe, as that which is thus initially expressed unfolds or evolves. In any case, the only possible metaphysical explanation of Matter seems to be to regard it as that by means of which the Infinite Reason so expresses itself that the rational Universe is the result.

But, finally, we must ask, Whether it is needful to suppose anything more to be necessary in the working out of the Divine Reason in infinite Time and Space in innumerable worlds, each one manifesting in its outcome some worthy phase of that Reason and Love in finite forms, than just such an arrangement of " matter " as Mr. Spencer *assumes* to start with, seeing the results to be inevitably accomplished through that " persistence of Force " which we have already seen to be, viewed on its spiritual side, " the persistence of Reason "?

If the primal arrangement, *whatever it may be*, represents *Reason*, the subsequent working is bound to be a continuous manifestation of the Reason that is so represented in the beginning. If it is the expression of the Divine Thought, or of the Divine self-conditioning for the creation, the result is bound to be the rational Universe that we know, culminating in the self-realisation in man of the Reason that so conditioned itself, in the manifestation of God in Christ; and, ultimately, in the complete realisation of the Divine Purpose in the creation

For the beginning we need only *Reason* giving expression to itself in order to work out its purpose, and for the continuous development of the Universe we need only to think of the continuous, ever-advancing expression of that same Infinite Reason. There is, in this way, in the World a parallel development of matter and Spirit—not of Spirit in its *essence*, but in its *manifestation*. It is the Divine Reason, never ceasing in its self-expression, and gradually realising itself in free, personal, rational, and spiritual beings.

Throughout, it is with *Reason* that we have to do. God is Omnipotent; but He can never act irrationally. His method is a gradual Evolution or Unfolding of His creatively conditioned Thought or Reason. Instead of criticising, let us have confidence in the all-perfect Reason that God is, let us *wait* and *work* with that Reason as it has been caused to shine in our own consciousness, and as it is, in its Infinite Reality, the spiritual Environment of our entire being.

CHAPTER XIII

THE ALL-WORKING POWER AS LOVE

I

THE Power that reveals itself as working all, or slowly unfolding itself, in the Universe is not a mere "cold Intellectual Principle," forming the world as a logical necessity merely. It is "Reason" in the wider sense of the word—that which is revealed within us by means of our entire "rational nature," although it is only gradually that its true character can appear, as forms come into being capable of expressing it. As we have seen, it is manifested as life, as feeling, will, desire, love, as personal—in a word, as Spirit, the constituent elements of which are generally held to be Thought, Feeling, Will, Personality. As far as we have gone, it is in Reason and *Will* that the nature of the Power that works all is most clearly revealed to us It is in Will alone that we have any knowledge of *Power*. Outside ourselves we see only succession—what from our own experience we *believe* to be the results of moving power; but of moving power itself we know nothing apart from Will in ourselves. And Will is only known to us as an active power that has, through the working of the creative Energy, become centred in a living and sensitive being With the lowliest manifestation of animal life, *feeling* and *desire* make themselves manifest. With all our perceptions an element of feeling is associated. "Sensation," on which our perceptions depend, is itself a "feeling." Except in the chain of purely logical or mathematical deduction, we never know Reason as something absolutely severed from Feeling, Sentiment, Desire. Even in such a process there is a feeling of interest or of satisfaction. Our rational life has always an emotional and a voluntary element in it. In all our movements we are animated by desire; we wish, and we will what we wish. Life itself may be described as the constant expression of a want, of a desire. This may often lead us astray in our reasoning and in our practical life, because, unconsciously to ourselves, the emotional and volitional element may predominate, and we may thus reach the conclusions, or attain the ends that we desire, rather than the true, the right, and the really good. But in the perfect Reason and Love there is no such possibility. There they are perfectly balanced, truly *one*.

Schopenhauer was so far right, therefore, when, for Hegel's (supposed) logical deduction of the Universe from "Thought" he substituted "Will." He would have been still nearer the truth if he had simply *added* Will to Thought, although even then he would have stopped short of the whole truth. As is usual, he was right in what he affirmed and wrong in what he denied. Taken together, we have a *rational Will*, which is the only true *Will*, a blind or irrational Will would be no true Will at all; it would be simply a Force that might work anyhow and produce any kind of result. The emergence of Reason in man, and, indeed, the production of the rational world, forbid the supposition that a merely blind Will is at the foundation of the Universe.

But further, an *unmotived* Will would be no true Will; apart from a *motive*, we should still have an irrational Will only. Will is always the expression of desire or motive, which always seems to the creature *willing* directed towards something *good* for it, whether it be really such or not. Feeling grows into desire, and desire may become affection *or love* such as moves the Will to action. In this way there

THE ALL-WORKING POWER AS LOVE   269

is always a *reason* for that which is willed,—Reason and Will are inseparable,—and the chief motive of Will is a desire for, an affection towards, or a love of, some thing or person, which may be, in the finite creature, only more or less clearly perceived.

If then God be Will, He must have a reason for His willing—a *motive* for His action in creation. But if He is the Perfect Reason, what can His motive be but the perfectly *good*? This alone is the perfectly rational Will The truly rational and the truly good are *one*. The truly good for us—the Ideal—is what in Reason *ought* to be, nay, deeper still it is what it *must* be. It is what *is* in God. *Perfect Reason and Perfect Love are One.*

II

But we are not left to our "reasonings" on this subject. The Love that is implicit in the Reason that forms the world makes itself manifest as the process of unfolding proceeds. What was implicit in the beginning becomes explicit in the end. Unlike the "Reason," which can be made manifest in even purely *physical* arrangements and relations, the Love (like the Feeling and the Life) can only appear as a substantive reality when there are sensitive organisms standing in such relationships as shall call it forth. Love cannot find expression in what is physical merely. Of course, if we believe that God has created the world for the sake of man, then, in this very fact, and in all that is made to minister to our life, we behold the manifestation of His goodness and love. The Universe is, in this light, their manifestation But till a certain stage is reached, we can never expect to behold the very presence of Love in the material Universe, in the same way that we can see *Reason* in everything We need to bear in mind that it is an *Evolution* that we have to do with— a gradual unfolding of that which is implicit from the first.

We have already seen (in chap. vi) the "physical basis" of Love in its manifestation, in the very nature of the life-substance. We see it manifested more and more clearly as true Feeling shows itself and as the psychical life develops. We need not here recount the story of the evolution of Love in detail. It has been told (so far) by Mr Spencer in his *Data of Ethics*, by Mr. Fiske in his *Cosmic Philosophy* and later writings, especially in his *Through Nature to God*, by Professor Henry Drummond in his *Ascent of Man*, by Mr. Sutherland in his *The Growth of the Moral Instinct*, and by other writers [1]

It is true that, as Kropotkin remarks, in its earlier animal stages, it is not yet *Love* that we witness, or even sympathy in the proper sense, but "a feeling infinitely wider than love or personal sympathy" It is something that flows out of the deep fountain of the *solidarity* or *unity* of Life, and its appearance in this way is all the more impressive and declaratory of its Source. As we have seen, one of the earliest forms of feeling going beyond the self seems to have been that of the *unity* of life amongst the members of the same species in the same place. We witness this very low down in the animal world, in animal colonies, in the communities of ants and bees, and in the

---

[1] Dr Saleeby, in *The Cycle of Life*, has written impressively concerning this "Coming of Love" In the first division of the living cell we witness something more than Egoism, and see how "intimately entwined are the roots of the moral sense with the very first principles of living matter." The appearance of sex—the female—the mammal, with the necessary care for the young, both before and after birth, the later the birth, the more helpless, the more for the mother to do Here we see care for something *other than self*. In mother and child we have "two distinct agglomerations of matter and energy, which are the manifestations of the Eternal to us, and one of these objects has developed within itself certain specialised portions in which its life-blood is transformed, at no small cost, into a wonderful fluid designed for the use of the other Verily, this is a striking phase of the struggle for existence. Here is a living thing struggling, and at no small cost, that something else may live."

THE ALL-WORKING POWER AS LOVE

flocks and herds in which various kinds of birds and animals associate. Out of this arises the instinctive sympathy which shows itself in mutual care and aid Whether we hold that this life in association preceded the narrower life of the family, or believe that the family life was first, there could never have been a time when the human infant did not call forth the special care of the mother, awaking " the mother-love that rocks the cradle " and the answering love that from the cradle watches the mother's face. As the family relationship becomes established, we see a higher love appearing — higher, because it is a step more removed from self and from what is physical We see it still rising in tribal and social regard, and still higher in that friendship which has its origin so deep down in the animal world. We witness its gradual ascent till, from common tribal feeling, it becomes a wider, national, and then a racial, sentiment. We see this Love shining in Conscience as the supreme Law of Life—a Law which has come to be inwardly acknowledged by almost every one, whatever his theological or philosophical creed may be, or whether he has any such creed at all. Just as truly as Reason is supreme in the intellectual life, Love shows itself to be sovereign in the moral sphere. In this Supremacy of Love over the practical life we have the sure revelation of the deepest nature of the Power that fashions our life, and that has carried up this evolution of Love in spite of the natural (and for its temporary purpose necessary) Egoism which opposes it, or which gradually unfolds in created forms that which essentially belongs to it. We see in this the unity of Love with the Reason that rules the other side of our being In countless forms Love is manifested, not only as the highest, but as the mightiest Power in life, doing that which no other power can effect, leading to acts of heroic self-sacrifice and of triumph over every lower form of power. In the religious sphere we behold it moving in human hearts as a power that can rise (as shown in Christ) even above all that is of the finite self and make the human form a veritable manifestation of God in the world. In this religious sphere we see it showing itself as a spirit of charity which can transcend all individual interests and all personal relationships, and go out to all mankind. We behold it rising into a love which ascends to the Source of Being Himself, and seeks the realisation of a higher life by losing the merely individual self in God—becoming one with the Universal Love and Life.

It is to be noted that in all its manifestations this Love is never separable from " Reason," although in free natures it may often be severed from the truly rational; it is always that which belongs to the *relations* in which beings rationally stand, or believe themselves to stand, to each other.

In this gradual rise of nascent feeling into Love we have the revelation of the nature of that which is the true " substance " of our being. The evolution of Life is the evolution of this *Love*, which (one with Reason) is therefore deepest in the creation In one aspect, Reason may be regarded as that *in* which the evolution takes place—that according to which and by the necessity of which it all proceeds, just as Reason in ourselves may be regarded as the *Light* in which we live rather than as a personal possession. But there must be something *deeper* which is the real *Substance* of Being—something which in this rational way becomes increasingly explicit as the evolution goes forward. We say that this is *Life*—that mysterious something that makes the living world—and we now see that, in its deepest nature, this Life is the *Love* in which, in its unity with Reason, the whole process of Evolution has its source, and in the production of which in finite beings it finds its goal. In God, of course, the " substance " of Being must be *ethical*, not physical, nor intellectual merely.

THE ALL-WORKING POWER AS LOVE

We are thus led back to *a primal Love*, which, just because of its nature as perfect Love, for ever gives itself to the creation, which, just because it is the perfect Life, for ever seeks to spread that Life abroad in finite forms, and to reach beings to whom it can wholly impart itself. Even as Reason, God must be for ever manifesting or expressing Himself, but it is in the Love that is one with the Reason that we find the deepest motive of the creation. The Divine Life conditions itself so as to give rise to innumerable worlds on which shall stand rational, emotional, ethical, and spiritual beings, who shall be able to perceive and respond to the Reason and Love thus manifested in the creation, and by becoming one therewith in their spiritual being, be sharers in the Divine Life itself. The perfect Love that God *is* thus for ever, literally, goes forth, giving itself that it may find itself in others to whom it imparts itself, and in whom it finds the satisfaction of its life of perfect Love. It is an eternal process of Love, and it is thus by for ever giving Himself that God for ever maintains His Divine Life of Perfect Love—not *realises* Himself as if for the first time, but maintains and sheds abroad His Life. Giving Himself, He is for ever finding Himself. The whole creation in this way becomes the manifestation of an Infinite, self-giving, self-sacrificing Love, it is a constant appeal, and, rightly read, a real Gospel to men, although it is only the revelation that is made in our own highest selves, read with clearness in the light of the Divine self-manifestation in the Cross of Christ, that enables us so to interpret it.

The reconciliation of the actual world, of the process of Evolution, and of the appearance of countless individuals whose lot seems to have been mainly one of hopeless misery, constitutes, as has been said, one side of what Mr. Mallock calls "the Crux of Theism," and we have already seen, so far, the answer to it. If we regard God as a present Actor in the natural world, endowed with all the might of

Omnipotence, and deliberately choosing His actual method out of many possible alternatives (as has been often done), the problem will be a hard one indeed But, as we have already pointed out, the fact that God is the perfect *Reason*, who can only in rational ways (surely *the only possible* ones) realise His purposes, and who, in order to create, must *condition* His being in the forms of the Universe, to be therein as a self-realising Power,—having many adverse tendencies to contend with if conscious life in finite beings is to be realised and developed,—while life can only be possessed according to certain necessary laws, and by the individual only through the race,—so far meets the difficulty. Believing God to be the perfect Reason, we must not (and we need not) hesitate to say distinctly that the external world and the laws of life *could not* be other than they are. If they *could* have been different, then the world is not that Revelation of *Reason* which all knowledge must assume it to be. But, left to Nature alone, we should still be dissatisfied. It is only when we come to the full revelation of the eternal Love in the human form of Him who gave Himself up to the Cross for the accomplishment of the Divine purpose in the world, that we behold such a manifestation of the Divine Love as shows that God actually gives Himself to the World, that creation is no easy work of an Almighty Being, but involves an eternal sacrifice on the part of God, and that He will withhold *nothing* He can give or do in order to realise the purpose of His Reason and Love. What more can man ask of God? In the presence of such self-sacrificing Love our criticisms seem poor indeed. Of course, it is implied that this present life is not the whole of human existence. But the fact that this is the light in which it is so necessary to set forth the Cross to-day shows how far we have travelled from the earlier modes of thought and feeling. To St Paul, the Cross was primarily that whereby the Sovereign Deity reconciled *judicially* the sinful World to

THE ALL-WORKING POWER AS LOVE 275

Himself in order that men might be saved, to-day we must employ it to reconcile men to God in a very different sense This does not imply that there was not a deep truth underlying Paul's thought, it only shows us the more clearly the *infinite* significance of that Cross. Both aspects belong to it, we believe. On it there was manifested that which was both necessary and sufficient to "take away the sin of the World," to reconcile the sinful World to God and save men from sin; and there was, at the same time, declared a *Love* the reality of which in God is sufficient to meet men's doubts for ever.

CHAPTER XIV

THE DIVINE TRANSCENDENCE

FROM the revelation of the power within ourselves we are led to look for the same Power without and beyond ourselves. We find it in some measure in the Universe around us, but we cannot stop there. The Universe and the Power that works in it must have a Source beyond themselves. The Power that works in the Universe is, as we have seen, *conditioned*—self-conditioned, we believe— and we are forced to look beyond it, as it appears, to that which has become so conditioned. It is manifested in the Universe only in finite forms, and we are impelled to rise to the Infinite. Account for the idea of God as we may, nothing short of Infinite or Perfect Ethical Being can satisfy it. Underneath all the phenomenal manifestations, underneath the Power itself that produces them, there must be some Ultimate Reality which transcends the evolving and ever-rising Universe—not only our world, but all worlds, and all universes Only *this* can be *God.* It is true that we cannot argue logically from the finite to the Infinite, but the finite necessarily implies the Infinite. It is suggested on every hand in both the physical and the living world The boundless sky, the limitless space, the thought of Eternity, the endless variety in the world—the leaves of the forest—the faces and natures of men and women, no two of all the many millions exactly alike,— even these suggest the infinitude of the Source of Being.

THE DIVINE TRANSCENDENCE

Although *conditioned* in the Creation, it is the Infinite Reason that is the constant Source of it all We rise to the conception by an inevitable intuition. It is *given* us " in that knowledge of our finitude in which we at the same time transcend it."

By no one has the necessity we are under of rising to the thought of a transcendent Reality been more clearly expressed than by Mr. Spencer The existence of an Infinite and Eternal Reality from which all things proceed, which is not, as it is often taken to be, the Power that works in the world in its conditioned form, but the Absolute, Unconditioned Reality, is with him " the certainty of certainties." It is well worth while giving yet another quotation, stating, as it seems, in incontrovertible terms this truth, although he denies that we can *know* the Ultimate Reality : " The momentum of thought inevitably carries us beyond conditioned existence to unconditioned existence . . . we are by the laws of thought . . . prevented from ridding ourselves of the consciousness of absolute existence; this consciousness . . . being the obverse of our self-consciousness . . . this which persists at all times, under all circumstances, and cannot cease until consciousness ceases, has the highest validity of any " (of our beliefs)

He affirms also, as we have seen, that since that Reality is the Source of personality in us, it cannot be less than Personal. The Ultimate Reality is thus, in the truest sense of the word, Super-natural as well as Super-personal. It is this *transcendent* Being Who has been the *God* of all developed religions except such as were Pantheistic. From the power that is conditioned in Nature and in ourselves we are directly led to the thought of this wider Power, this ultimate Source, this unconditioned Being, and we can be certain that this Ultimate Being cannot be less but must be greater than the highest manifestation of the conditioned power that works all in the Universe and finds its highest expression in ourselves. It is this *transcendent* Being Who is the God of Christianity, and it is to be feared that the tendency to substitute for Him a merely immanent Deity has militated against Religion. While recognising all the truth there is in immanency, we must pass beyond that to the *transcendent God and Father. God is Spirit,* God is Reason, God is Love, and as such, He is Infinite, Omnipresent, and Eternal. *In* this Infinite Reason and Love we and the entire Universe " live and move and have our being " Only in rising above the Universe and all that is therein, do we really rise to God. While He is never to be *severed* from the Power that works all in Nature, He is not to be identified with it so as to be in Himself limited by it or confined to it. That Power *is* God in one aspect of His Being, it is God as He has conditioned His Reason and Power for the realisation of His Thought of the World and as He works in Nature. We may, in this sense, speak of His self-realisation therein; for His Thought of the creation cannot be less than the realisation of His own essential Being in finite beings, yet to be brought into full ethical union of life with the Infinite Reality that God is. But in order to create at all, to form or evolve the world, He must have prior existence in all the fulness of the highest life that can be realised in finite forms of being. In order to create, He must, as it were, eternally go out from Himself into the creation. It is this alone that is the source of the Power that works on in the developing, ever-rising world. And it is here that we have the supreme instance of His perfect Love. We are not troubled by the question, How to give rise to the World? The Love of God, one with His perfect Reason, solves the problem. Just because God is the perfect Reason, He must manifest Himself and spread His life abroad Just because He is the perfect Love, He cannot but do so. This is a necessity which is one with the most perfect freedom. In each particular world there

THE DIVINE TRANSCENDENCE 279

comes to be *so much* of the Divine conditioned as becomes the principle of its life, and this is bound to be manifested in the outcome. But the whole thought of God in His creation need not be embodied or conditioned in the evolving world. The entire process takes place *in* God, it is a spiritual as well as a physical process, God is the spiritual Environment of the world, and as the entire process proceeds, He is continually entering more and more completely into the creation. A Monism, whether "physical" or "spiritual," which makes no distinction between God and the World, cannot rise above Pantheism, or really give us *God*. "Monism," as Science leads us to it, we repeat, applies only to the phenomenal world. Yet there is also a higher, all-embracing Monism. The apparent Dualism that is set up in the initial act of creation is for ever being transcended, it is not an absolute but a strictly relative Dualism, and, as we have said, the evolving world is never separate from God in His transcendency. God is in some degree within it, and it is always contained in His Omnipresence. The seeming Dualism will be completely transcended when the Divine Thought has fully realised itself, when the separate beings to whom the Divine Life has been imparted become one with God. Of course, as we have in former chapters sought to show, there is no Dualism, but a strict Monism, in the actual working out of the Power that has become conditioned in the world for the creation.[1]

[1] We have compared the evolution of the world to that of an organism under the influence of its idea. But we may also, without departing from the fundamental principle of continuity, or of the continuous working and ever-rising expression of the Divine Reason that is behind it all, think of a succession of organisms ever higher in kind There is, first of all, the physical world necessary as the scene of life There *may* have been at first only so much of the Divine Thought impressed, as it were, and so much potency imparted, as to form, through its rational working out, after the analogy of the development of an organism, the physical world The living world may be regarded as a higher organism

Since God is Spirit, His self-realisation in the creation can be reached in spirits only, and freedom is of the essence of Spirit. Therefore man is made in his inner self a free being, who can only be gradually and freely developed into his full manhood, with the necessity of learning from experience, with the possibility of living to his lower self, or to the world merely, and of, for a time, holding himself even in opposition to God, instead of rising to his true life in union with Him. There is, not only the Divine, immanent at the centre of our being, but there is the transcendent Being, "from whom" (to use St. Paul's phrase) the Divine Power that works all in the world has proceeded. And, as we have seen, the immanent Power, even as it rises in ourselves, merges into the transcendent. Man as a rational and spiritual being rises out of Nature and comes into direct relation to God in His transcendency— Whose Spirit is the true Spirit of his higher life. It is only when a life rises into complete union with the transcendent God, that *God*, as distinguished from that which, although "of God," is always less than God, can be revealed in the world. This, as we shall see, is what we have in the Incarnation of God in Christ.

God, as Spirit, is ever very near to us. But, as has been well said, He "never invades our freedom." If He did so, we should no longer be spiritual beings such as He has made us. His creative work would be annulled.

into which enters a new measure of Power from the all-environing Source, which should work on till *man* appears as its realisation. But the process does not end here The world of *spiritual beings* may be looked upon as a still higher form of organism, and just as the human individual derives much of the ultimate content of his being, not merely from the original germ, but from the Universe around him, so men as spiritual beings may be considered as continuously deriving the elements of their spiritual life from the all-environing Divine Being, until His thought of Himself in finite form is fully realised in them A new stage in the spiritual evolution would thus appear in Christ as the Centre and Source of a fully spiritual humanity.

THE DIVINE TRANSCENDENCE 281

It would be as disastrous to the world as a new "flood" would be. This is why to many God seems to be absent from the world. They say "God never *does* anything", that they look for Him on the right hand and on the left, in the heavens above and in the depths beneath, even in the depths of their own being, yet cannot behold Him. They forget what God is, and what man is. God is for ever near us, feeling for us, sympathising with us, longing to help us He is nearer than we can understand or imagine. But, on the one hand, man must stand in freedom and freely develop, if he is to be *man*, and, on the other hand, it is as *Spirit* that God is thus near us, and it is only spiritually, to the spirit in us, that He can communicate Himself, or make Himself known.

There are ways, however, in which He, in His transcendency, does communicate with us all and impart more and more of Himself to us. Religion rests on this presupposition. Not Christianity merely, but all religions, believe that God can and does communicate with the spirits of men. The "Holy Spirit" is the Christian term for the Deity in that form of manifestation or self-communication, in harmony with our freedom and with our place in Nature The belief in a Holy Spirit that visits men is not confined to Christianity, but is to be found in some form almost everywhere.

Our Relation to God in His Transcendency

1. In order to set forth more fully our relation to God in His transcendency, let us begin by pointing out that, when Spirit has realised itself in us in self-conscious form—that is, as *spirit* in man (which, we repeat, must be *free* spirit, else it were not *spirit* at all)—a new order of being has made its appearance, a spiritual world has begun to arise out of the physical, and a new mode of Divine self-

communication commences to operate. When Reason becomes conscious Reason in us, we are no longer limited to the actual expressions of Reason in Nature around us We can rise into the Universal Reason, and by intuition and logical processes (which in themselves bear witness to the rationality that is supreme) we can reach conclusions concerning matters not directly brought to us through the senses. The light of Reason that shines in us is, as Culverwell puts it, "an ascending light"—a light that seeks its fulness by rising to and blending with the uncreated light—the Infinite or Perfect Reason that God is. In Reason, as it is organised in us, there is so much of the Divine light shining, but we instinctively feel that there is a fuller measure of that Light beyond us, and we seek to rise into it, so as "in Thy light to see light." In Malebranche's phrase, "we see all things in God" But in order to do so in full and perfect vision, we must rise to the Reason that transcends us all, or suffer it in its fulness to enter into us. It shines in some measure within us, and the more we seek and follow this Divine light, the more of it we shall receive. None of us can find in this life a full participation in this Divine Light, but in the measure in which we do find an entrance into it we come into Intellectual union with God in His transcendency, and there is more of the Divine Life, in this aspect of it, entering into us.

2. The Reason that becomes conscious in us shows itself in us as a *creative* Reason. This is the source of Imagination and of human creative Art in all its forms. In the possession of this faculty we participate in that creative power which is essentially Divine, as far as means have been put within our reach of giving expression to it. We may use this power wisely or unwisely, rationally or irrationally, but in its possession we are sharing in the power of the transcendent Deity A true artist, in

whatever form, is a creator; his work is something added to the Universe, and it remains to send forth influences for good or for evil. Forming us in His own image, God entrusts this power to us. Therefore Art, in all its forms, should be deemed a sacred thing.

3. Again, the Reason that becomes conscious in us shows itself as a *perfecting* Reason. In virtue thereof we can take up and freely carry to completion the creative work which has, so far, culminated in ourselves, and, as it were, committed its immanent work to us. We can do this only as we come into ever fuller unison with the Reason in Nature, as we rise into participation in the Perfect Reason and Love that is above and beyond us all, and as, in this way, we come to recognise the true, rational Ideal of human life. We thus become the conscious agents in and through whom the Divine transcendent Reason carries on and completes the work which that Reason by its self-conditioning began. The future is, as it were, put into our own hands; the progress and well-being of the race rests with itself. There is very much that Reason as it shines in us can do in the way of perfecting and completing the work of Reason in Nature. Much that is presently existing and working there, or still kept up and carried on by man, has served its purpose and may well be left behind, or done away with. For example, to many sensitive minds it seems a cruel thing to breed dumb animals only to slaughter them for human food. We do not need to be vegetarians to sympathise with this feeling. But the advances M. Berthelot has already made in organic Chemistry justify his hope that this practice may become unnecessary. Creative agencies absolutely necessary in a certain proportion for life itself must be controlled and modified by the Reason in man, *e g*. the *bacteria* that are essential to life, but are also the sources of disease As Mr. J. A Symonds has well

said, the lesson of Evolution is not just "Whatever is is well," but "Whatever is is well, but nothing really *is* which is not in progressive and militant movement. In a similar way we may think of warfare, once, perhaps, inevitable, but surely now to be superseded by methods of Reason. So also of the Ideal organisation of Society in harmony with universal Reason, Justice, and Love. The whole process of material advancement, of social amelioration and organisation, of human unification, of, in a word, the making the world what it ought to be, is committed to us, and can only be accomplished as we rise to and participate in the Reason and Love that is above and beyond us all, which, shining within us, *seeks* us as its organs or instruments.

4. Further, the Reason from which we have derived our being reveals itself not only as an Ethical Inspiration within us, but also as an *Ethical Authority* over us. In the course of the evolutionary process a moral Law makes itself known as supreme over men. A Conscience has been evolved which bears witness within each man to the supremacy of the law of Righteousness, which is also the law of Love. It is at the same time the law of Reason; for it is only the expression of that which ought rationally to rule in the relationships in which we stand to one another. But we have in it a knowledge given us transcending all that comes to us from observation of "the Cosmic process" merely; although it is that process that has wrought it in us, so that the moral order is in no real contradiction to the Cosmic order, as Huxley affirmed it to be. But it transcends it, while continuing and completing it. In Conscience and the Moral Law we are brought within clear sight of absolute and universal, rational and moral principles, capable, as Kant said, of becoming "Law universal." An Ideal comes to shine before us, which calls on us to rise above ourselves as we have been formed by *Nature* merely.

The Ideal of Duty which appears on our spiritual horizon is nothing less than Infinite If we strive to reach it, we find that there is always a beyond, still to be striven towards. We can never find mental satisfaction save as we are endeavouring to realise that Ideal. And in our endeavour after it, in obedience to this ethical call, we discover that we are entering into fellowship with a Higher than ourselves, Whose approval or blame seems to be made to shine upon us in that Conscience, which has, it would seem, one side turned towards ourselves and the other towards the transcendent Authority that calls and commands, or invites us in the name of a Perfect Righteousness. In this ethical life we can certainly know ourselves as being uplifted by that which transcends the Universe.

5. Again, in the *Love* which declares itself to be the supreme law of our life—the deepest principle of the moral Law—we have a revelation given within ourselves of a Love which is Infinite and Perfect; which seeks to inspire our lives, to dwell within us, and to act through us. It is higher than aught that comes to us from Nature merely It seeks to carry us entirely beyond our " natural selves " into a life of which *universal* Love is the principle and the inspiration, in which we shall transcend all that is individual and personal merely, and find the full realisation of our true selves in a life which we know to be the very life of God living in us. Surely here we cannot fail to see our visitation and uplifting by the transcendent God and Father.

6 There is still something more. The Divine Life as it has conditioned itself for the sake of creation has so far realised itself in our natural life as spiritual beings. The Divine element that is deepest in the creation is at the foundation of our life, and rises up within us in conscious personal form. For this reason there arises in us what we term " religious aspiration." Its source is the Divine within

us which seeks its fulness of life in the Divine above us. There is in us all, as the deepest principle of our being, an immanent Divine life that seeks its unity or its return to itself in its completeness in the unconditioned, transcendent Being, and to raise us, as finite beings, into that life. This is the very essence and meaning of *Religion* This is why we have "a religious nature," why we seek for "union with God," and "can never rest till we have found Him." In whatever form Religion comes to us, this is its essence— union with God in His Holy Spirit of Truth and Love. The religious aspiration is not something of man merely, but of God, who is at once in some degree immanent in us and also the spiritual environment of our life. Not only do we seek God, but God is in all things seeking us, and as we yield ourselves to His Spirit, we can, in prayer, in spiritual communion, and in life devoted to His purposes and at one with His will, come into real and growing union with God in His transcendency. It is in full ethical and spiritual union with God in His transcendency that the creation finds its completion, and the temporary Dualism is for ever transcended In this experience Spirit returns to itself, and the finite individual life is perfected in God. This *complete* union with God has only been realised once in time in Jesus Christ, and in its realisation in Him we have that incarnation and revelation of God in Christ to which we shall devote a separate chapter.

Stated from the Divine side

We have stated all this mainly from the human side, but we may with equal truth state it also from the Divine side. It is indeed, primarily, from the Divine side that it ought to be stated, for it is all the result of the working of God in Nature and in ourselves. Nature becomes to us the medium of spiritual influences. In its Beauty and

Sublimity it touches and uplifts the soul. Ocean, sky, and starry heavens speak to us of the Infinite, of the boundless room there is in the creation, of the mighty Power of God, of the endless Hope there is for the World in the Infinite Love that is its Source, of the confidence we can place in the all-perfect Reason. By the sterner aspects of Nature and the darker experiences of life we are also "taught of God." Both the goodness and the severity in our life-experience are meant to lead us above the world and above ourselves to the true end of Being in Whom alone we can find an Object of absolute worth and the satisfaction of our spiritual nature. God in His transcendency is ever near us; as St. Paul said at Athens, " He is not far from each one of us." When men ask, " Where is God ? " we answer that He is in some real measure at this moment within yourself, and as the all-containing Spirit, in the Perfect Reason and Perfect Love that He *is*, He is the environment of your being. What we need so much to realise is that this Perfect Reason and Perfect Love, which are *one*, *is* God, that in so far as these enter and possess us, *God* really enters and possesses us, and that by an act of reasonable *faith* we can rise to our rest in this God.

> "'Yes, write it in the rock,' St Bernard said,
> 'Grave it on brass with adamantine pen !
> 'Tis God Himself becomes apparent, when
> God's Wisdom and God's Goodness are displayed,
> . . . .
> For God of these His attributes is made.'"

God is essentially an *ethical* Being, and His entrance into man is described as His work in " the Holy Spirit." Ever since man became a conscious spiritual being, the Holy Spirit of God has been shining in on him, illuminating, visiting, inspiring him. Very much more has gone to the " making of man " than the " cosmic forces," or the action of the immanent Power in Nature only. There has been also all along a Divine Spiritual action, both through the manifestations of the Divine in Nature and the experience of life, and through the more direct action of a Holy Spirit in ways which we may fail fully to comprehend. God has been no mere idle Spectator of His unfolding Universe Not only does He for ever give Himself to be the immanent life of all His worlds, but in His transcendency He watches over them, "fosters them in Himself," visits them in His spiritual influences The evolutionary process was not the result of blind necessity. There was a rational and loving purpose in it. The process has all gone on *in* God, we must repeat, and as it has advanced God has been entering more and more fully into His world, ever expressing more of His Divine fulness of life, and at the same time seeking the satisfaction of His love therein. For, while there can be no quantitative addition to that which is perfect, the very quality of Love is its capacity of infinite increase The World thus *means* something to God. Just because His nature is perfect Love, He seeks and finds His Life in the impartation of it to finite beings. The Sacrifice of creation has not been made for nothing. The Creator, as truly as the Saviour, looks to "see of the travail of His soul, and be satisfied." There are many who seem to think that God might have done more for His world. They forget what God *is* and what He has already done. He has given Himself to be its immanent life, and in Christ He has repeated the sacrifice. He has been for ever seeking to find a fuller entrance into man in the Reason and Love that He is, without over-bearing our freedom, and so unmaking us. What does the world need to-day for individual and social "salvation," but just *response* to this Divine Reason and Love? The deficiency is not on the side of God, but wholly on that of man. From the moment that man rose out of Nature, capable of receiving and of responding to spiritual influences, these have not ceased to play upon him, but the response has been painfully slow, because of man's inevitable relation to the natural world and his necessary grounding in a sensuous nature, which, however, given the capacity of obedience, does not make his attitude the less sinful and unworthy.

While the influences of God's Holy Truth and Love have come to all men, some individuals and races have been more open and susceptible to them than others. There have been poets and artists on whom wondrous Ideal visions have arisen, and to whom an extraordinary insight has been given. Higher still, some men have been so specially open to the perception of ethical and spiritual truth that they stand forth amongst others as inspired men—prophets and teachers, reformers and founders of religions. Whether those inspirations come to men through "the sub-conscious," as some believe, or in a more direct way, makes no real difference Special openness to them depends fundamentally, no doubt, on something in the physical organisation; but that again depends, ultimately, on the working of a Divine Spiritual Power.

As we have said, some *races* also have been more susceptible to those higher Divine influences than others; there has been in them a greater openness to the incoming of the Divine. It was this that constituted Israel "the people of God," and through that nation, with its prophetic men and women, its poets and legislators, there came to be a fuller entrance of God in His ethical attributes and power into the world. Here was found the "line of least resistance" along which the new spiritual evolution proceeded, the whole process, both on the natural and on the spiritual sides, culminating in Jesus Christ, in Whom we have the supreme revelation of God in a finite form, in which, nevertheless, the merely finite is transcended, and man becomes wholly one with God. What was represented in His humanity is Divinely meant to be realised in us all.

The Records of the revelations that have thus come to men—of Divine manifestations and experiences—constitute the "Bibles" of the race. But these records have always mingled with them (as there was, of necessity, with the experiences themselves) much that is human merely. The records of the Christian revelation, although not absolutely pure from such merely human elements, stand forth as unique in their purity, and in their power to bring men to the knowledge and experience of God. This is owing to the exceptional purity and fulness of the Divine revelation in Christ. But, at the present time especially, when so much is heard of the application of Criticism to those records,—a process inevitable, to be welcomed, not to be feared,—it is very necessary to remember that *the religion* was before the record, that it was not the record that made the religion, but the religion that made the record. However valuable and helpful in many ways the record may be, our faith does not depend on books, but on the *experience* that came, and that still comes to men, in ways that may be recorded in books, but which has been more lastingly engraved on human hearts, and passed on in the direct and living line of human beings, in whom the same experience has been ever anew repeated.

Note.—Of course, this subject of the Divine Transcendency might be well illustrated by reference to the Ideals of the True, the Beautiful, and the Good, the supremacy of which even Haeckel acknowledges. These Ideals, as they arise within us and *reveal themselves* to us, necessarily imply their *Reality* in a transcendent Being. Others, however, have set this forth so fully that repetition is unnecessary.

CHAPTER XV

THE INCARNATION OF GOD IN CHRIST

CHRISTIAN THEISM affirms a special revelation, even an Incarnation, of God in Jesus Christ. We shall take no serious notice of such Monistic criticism of Christ and Christianity as we find in Haeckel's *Riddle of the Universe*. It has been sufficiently replied to In some parts it is quite unworthy of notice: the treatment is so inadequate to the subject, it is so full of misconceptions, that we can only wonder at it as coming from a man of Science. Yet even he admits that in regard to "the idea of the good, which we call virtue," even "Monistic religion" can reach nothing higher (p. 120). This is a very large and most notable admission, coming from one who, in the twentieth century after Christ, believes himself to have transcended the errors and superstitions which have, up till now, hidden the truth from men. The "idea of the good which we call virtue" is certainly the highest thing in the practical life of men. To have given expression to *this* in its supreme and abiding form, so many centuries ago, surely gives to Jesus Christ a unique position in the human world, even if, as Haeckel maintains, He should have derived His teaching from the scattered precepts of "earlier religions." How came it that He, to all outward appearance a peasant of Nazareth, who had never been in the schools of the Philosophers had such an insight into the highest practical truths, that He could bring them together in a way that has made them authoritative for all the succeeding generations of mankind? Science has a problem in Christ which must be faced and solved, if possible; and it is one to a clearer understanding of which she has, unconsciously, done not a little to help us. In the light of modern Science, Christ, far from becoming a receding figure, seems to be brought nearer and made more real to us as the veritable Incarnation of God in human form. It is easy to speak of Him as possessed of "supreme ethical and religious genius"; but how is this to be explained as arising in that person, in that place, and at that time?

But it is not in the verbal teaching of Christ alone that Christianity sees in Him the supreme revelation of God. It beholds this also, and still more impressively, in *the Person and Work of Christ*. In ignoring these, the modern critics of Christianity leave out of account its most important elements Christianity has always seen in Christ the very Incarnation of God Himself in human form—"the Word (Logos) that was with God, and that was God, become flesh," "God manifest in the flesh." It is from the life of Christ, as a manifestation of the life of God in human form, that Christianity derives its fullest knowledge of God and its supreme inspiration: it is really on this foundation that it rests. The question we have now to deal with, therefore, is whether this doctrine of the Incarnation of God in Christ can be maintained on a rationally Monistic basis and in harmony with Evolution. We may go farther, and ask, Whether modern Science does not help us to a clearer apprehension of such an Incarnation?

To many who are familiar with the teachings of modern Science, the Incarnation of God in this world, even admitting that there is a God, seems something quite incredible, an idea to be ignored rather than reasoned about. And

THE INCARNATION OF GOD IN CHRIST 293

to not a few who hold in words the orthodox doctrine it lacks vitality, if not reality. The enormous extent of the Universe and the seeming insignificance of man, "like a microscopic insect upon an enormous balloon," makes it seem, they say, even ridiculous to assert that—to quote Mr. Edward Clodd—"Some sixty years after the death of Lucretius there happened an event for which all that had gone before in the history of the planet is said to have been a preparation. In the fulness of time the Omnipotent Maker and Ruler of a Universe, to which no boundaries can be set by human thought, sent to this earth-speck no less a person than His Eternal Son." A moment's reflection, however, might well convince any one that relative *size*, bigness, or bulk has nothing to do with the matter. The human brain is of very small bulk as compared with the earth or the sun, but how much higher is it in value than the most huge aggregation of matter! If the earth is but a speck relative to the Universe, this, the mightiest and most valuable thing on the earth, would be but a point, quite invisible.

But the mode of the evolution of the world—the *continuity* of the process—the denial of which, Mr. Clodd says, is "the one scientific heresy," makes it also seem incredible that at some moment of time a Divine Being entered into the evolving world, as is supposed to be necessarily implied in the Christian doctrine of the Incarnation.

We shall endeavour to show that, carried out, a rationally Monistic conception of the World and of its evolution helps us greatly to a clearer apprehension of the reality of the Incarnation, that it shows not only its possibility and what we may term its naturalness, but even its inevitableness. If God as the Divine Reason and Love is the Principle of the world's life, that Principle *must* realise itself and become expressed in the highest life of the world. Given God at the beginning, then, on the principles of a Monistic Evolution, God must be manifested at the end.[1]

The distinction between God as *conditioned* for the creation, and God in His Unconditioned Being, between the immanent, self-realising Divine in Nature and the transcendent Deity, must not only be taken into account but helps us greatly here. We have seen that the idea of a "Logos" going forth from God and becoming the immanent life of the World, finds support in a rational conception of the Universe, with its process of Evolution. The World, conceived as an organism, has this as the ideal and effective Principle of its life, and just as truly as in the case of any other organism the principle must come into manifestation, and appear in its truth in the culmination of the process of development

God, however, is also transcendent, and for the true Incarnation of God in man *both* the immanent and the transcendent Divine must be represented. And it is this that we have in Christ. In one aspect, He is the highest product and supreme manifestation of the Power that works all in Nature, along the lines of natural evolution. The Divine principle of the world's life finds, as such principle, in Him its fullest expression.

But Christ was not the product of Nature merely; He was, as Christianity has always in some form maintained, also "the Child of the Holy Spirit," and as such, "the Son of God" — not merely as His Reason and Power are conditioned in Nature, but as He is in Himself — the

---

[1] It may be of interest to note in this connection that Dr. Paul Carus, in his Monistic *Primer of Philosophy*, speaks of "the conception of a God-man, of a Saviour, of God revealed in evolution," as a reality which can be seen and grasped on the Monistic principles which he advocates Nevertheless, as we shall see, we can never reach the full Christian conception of Christ on the lines of merely "natural" evolution, or by regarding Him as the product of such evolution only.

THE INCARNATION OF GOD IN CHRIST

"Eternal Son," *i e*, the Son of God as above time, or of God in His transcendency.

But we have seen that *no man*, regarded in the light of His highest life, is the child of Nature only, but is also the product of those spiritual influences which have been, in various ways, operating on Humanity from God in His transcendency — the influences of "the Holy Spirit," in virtue of which God has been increasingly entering into Humanity. Just as each organism in the world is not the result of the presence of the life-principle alone, but also of the influences of the environment, so man in his highest truth is the result of spiritual influences that have been operating on him from his spiritual environment. There has been a *spiritual* as well as a *natural* evolution. The complete Divine Thought of man as a son of God goes on realising itself through *spiritual* influences that succeed the natural. In Christ we see man as he has become through this process of *spiritual* evolution, which is continuous of the merely natural evolution, and, as such, He becomes the veritable incarnation of *God* Himself in a human form

Failing to remember this twofold relation of God to man—the transcendent as well as the immanent—there are not a few Christian thinkers at present, who, in the revolt from the common conceptions of the "miraculous," and in their reasonable sympathy with scientific teachings, believe they can get at Christ along the lines of natural evolution merely. But it is not the Christ whose appearance gave birth to Christianity that is thus reached, it is not the Christ who is the revelation of *God* Such a Christ would only be the highest revelation of the *conditioned* Power that works in Nature He could not hold that unique relation to God on the one hand, and to Humanity on the other hand, which is occupied by the Christ of the Gospel. He does not satisfy us when we have so found Him, because He does not take us out of the circle of the merely "natural life." If, however, we can see in Christ the product, not of Nature only, but also of that transcendent Power which as Spirit in many ways works on man, we have in Him the revelation not only of Nature, or of man as Nature makes him, but of *God*, and of man as man is conceived and made by God. This is what Christianity has always seen in Christ—not Nature only, even at its highest, but God Himself revealed as incarnate in human form.

For this we do not need to step aside from the pathway of Science We do not require to affirm a physical miracle, in "Virgin-birth," or "miraculous conception," or otherwise. Whether these are facts or not, we can behold quite clearly in Christ the fully, Divinely formed Child of the Holy Spirit, the product of *all* the Divine working in the world, expressing, not merely that which is individual, but that which is universal. Nor is it necessary to suppose that God, or "a person in the Godhead," in one moment of *time* so emptied Himself of the Divine attributes, or so put off the Divine "form" (as some say), as to be able to clothe Himself in human flesh. It is not necessary (were it possible) to think of God as coming into the world-process at some definite point of time, as if from without, and becoming incarnate. The real incarnation of an *ethical* Being cannot be so conceived, it can only be the result of a gradual, progressive process of entrance into, and self-expression in, Humanity God, as we have seen, had been from all eternity conditioning His Being so that it might be the Life of finite worlds. It is *there*, in the Eternal, not in the Temporal, that we must look for the Divine *Kenosis*, or self-conditioning of God, or the going forth of the *Logos* (meaning both Reason and Word), or of God from Himself so as to give rise to the world. God was, *in that form*, already so far *within* our Humanity—

THE INCARNATION OF GOD IN CHRIST

as the Power to which our natural human life was due God, *in that form,* realised Himself so far in man as man. But the all-perfect Reason and Love was behind it all, never separable from the process, and it went on, ever entering more fully into man, till in a perfect manhood the Divine Ideal of the creation should be realised. This Ideal could be nothing else than the realisation of Himself in finite form, but with infinite ethical content—that of God as existing for Himself, God as Son.

God, in His transcendent Being, had been, ever since man appeared, entering through His Holy Spirit, more and more fully, into our Humanity. When man appeared, there began (once more to quote Browning) "anew a tendency to God." God alone could meet, develop, perfect, and satisfy that tendency. There was no longer merely natural evolution, but a new, Divine, Spiritual evolution, carried on by means of the operation of that aspect of God which we know as "the Holy Spirit." That Divine working found, as we have said, its most open field in the Hebrew nation. The Old Testament is the record of the gradual development, deepening, and uplifting of the Divine Life in man, which was still continued after the record was closed. It is this alone that gives its unique and permanent value to the Old Testament. The line of progress is quite clear and unmistakable, and it culminated in Christ. After Old Testament times, after "prophecy" had ceased, fresh elements were made to contribute to the process from Greek and Roman, and perhaps from Oriental thought and life. A hard experience deepened in men's hearts the sense of their need of God, and made them more and more receptive of Him in His truth. There was a line of ever-deepening piety and devotion, represented for the most part by "the humble poor"—poor in heart, at least, but increasingly rich with the entrance of the Divine in its highest ethical qualities. The results of all this Divine working were preserved, stored up, and handed on, with increase, from generation to generation by means of that "tradition" which forms an ever-enlarging and uplifting intellectual, moral, and religious environment, to successive generations, and by those same laws of Heredity which (however they may work) carry forward other elements of progress. Just as increasing Rationality and advancing Morality become *organised* in men, so do the results of advancing Religion. Just as a truer and wider Conscience comes gradually to be formed, so does a truer and fuller religious consciousness—a rising God-consciousness. The newer Psychology helps us here also. There is nothing in man's whole experience that does not have a physical side, every spiritual emotion and every religious experience has its physical expression just as truly as has every intellectual thought and every moral feeling. It is this that makes religious development or progress as truly possible as intellectual and moral development and progress —along with the ever-increasing religious environment in which each successive generation stands. Just as truly as we have in a Plato or a Shakespeare the product of a rich preceding intellectual life—something quite impossible apart from past racial experience—so do we have in Him whom we dare not name beside others standing on quite lower levels of life, the product of an ever-deepening ancestral *spiritual* life. That life was God's working by His Holy Spirit, as it deepened in men, God Himself was entering ever more and more fully into Humanity, and the product of all this Divine working was that which became expressed in the wondrous Child that Mary bare in Bethlehem (if it was in Nazareth, as some believe, it surely does not matter). This was the Divine method of *incarnation*, in harmony with, and in continuation of, the whole Divine working in the world and in man It is, as already said, the only conceivable method of the incarnation of an *ethical* God in man—by means of a *process*, at once spiritual and physical (according to the Monistic constitution of the World), by means of which the Power which is at the foundation of our life, not only as it works self-limited in Nature, but as it is in its ethical truth, becomes expressed in a Person, at once human and Divine.

Therefore, what we behold in this Child of the Spirit is the appearance, not merely of an ordinary human self-consciousness, nor that of a dawning or imperfect consciousness of God, but a fully formed God-consciousness, as natural to Him as was His human consciousness. It was just as natural for Jesus to think of and feel towards God as His *Father* as it is for an ordinary man to think of and feel filially towards his father in the flesh. As in man a new tendency toward God appeared, so in Jesus Christ was manifested in Humanity a new complete consciousness of God as the basis of a higher life of sonship towards God. In Christ we behold the full uprising of man above the flesh, above the merely natural man, above Nature and all that is external merely, above the individual self entirely, to the Universal Life of Love, which is the Life of God; in Him we see, not only the human Son of man, but also the Divine *Son of God*.

The ground of the life that rose so high was thus laid in that organism which represented all the previous working of God in man both through "Nature" and through "the Spirit," in that line which proved most susceptible to the Divine influences; and throughout His entire history we see Christ standing constantly in this relation of Sonship towards the transcendent God and Father. Not only has the Divine risen *in* Him to such a degree as to constitute the basis of a life in perfect union with God, but we see how, in His whole experience, that life is developed and perfected till complete ethical unity with the Father is the result. Such essential and eternal union with God,

Whose Being is essentially *ethical*, was necessarily ethical in its nature, and therefore it was only realised by Christ in its fulness as the result of a life-process or experience. "Though He was a Son, He yet learned obedience by the things which He suffered," He "was made perfect through suffering." God, through that Holy Spirit, which Christ Himself affirmed to be the Divine Presence and Power within Him, was ever entering more and more fully into His spiritual being, until the consummation was reached and the human consciousness became merged in the Divine consciousness. Here the immanent Divine returned into perfect unity with the transcendent Deity, and the Person in Whom this was realised was truly both God and man in one undivided personality. Back beyond time, He could truly speak of Himself as having "come from the Father"—as having "proceeded forth from God and come into the world." Above all human paternity, He could rise to God as His Father in a fulness of meaning which no one else could reach, and could say, with a truth to which His whole life and works bore witness, " He that hath seen me hath seen the Father."

The full unity of Christ with God was manifested in the sacrifice of the Cross. In that complete sacrifice of Himself, in obedience to the will of the Father, and in response to the movement of the "Spirit of the Father" within Him, for the universal good and the accomplishment of the Divine purpose in the world, the individual self was passed beyond entirely, and the *man* was wholly one with God. In the Love that was manifested in that sacrifice, the finite was wholly transcended ; for it was nothing short of the Infinite Love that God is, which gives all and holds nothing back. Greater Love could not have found expression, whether in human form or in any other. In that love of Christ, therefore, which flowed forth in obedience to what He believed to be the Mind and Will of the Heavenly

Father, and as giving expression to the movement of God within Him, we have the completest manifestation of the Love of God that can possibly be given to Humanity —given also, as it must needs be, *through our Humanity* as it is raised to the highest expression of its life. We witness, as already said, a finite form with an infinite ethical content. And it was the revelation of God, not only as Love, but as the perfect Reason which can never turn aside from its rationality. This is really what is implied in the statement that the Cross was the manifestation of the Holiness or Righteousness of God as truly as of His Love. There was a rational and ethical necessity for that sacrifice, in view of the need of the salvation of men from sin and self, and it must be met, even though it involved the sacrifice of God's own beloved Son. Just as in common life the rationality of the Divine procedure inevitably entails individual suffering and sacrifice, so was it in this supreme example. But there, as ever, it was the means of higher individual life, and of universal good. That Cross of sacrifice became the source of a higher life to the world. Christ, in His Person and Work, became the Mediator of a new relationship between God and man.

In relation to Humanity, Christ, arising and standing in it as He does, becomes at once the fulfilment of the Divine Ideal of man, the Head of Humanity in its truth, and the source of a new and higher life to it. In relation to God in His transcendency, the Dualism set up by creation is in Him entirely transcended, and the immanent power returns into union with its original Source. Personally, Christ, by His complete death to self and the individual life, rises into the fulness of a higher Divine and universal life in God. The separation between the Divine and the human is in Him wholly overcome. Without losing His personality, He has passed into the very life of God. Through Him in His entire manifestation, and from Him in

His present Divine-human life, the Holy Spirit goes forth in the fulness of its power to inspire, regenerate, and perfect the individual life, and, in the unity of individual lives animated and dominated by that Spirit, to realise the Divine Ideal of the creation, the perfect and eternal Kingdom of God, in other words, that Life of God which is the life of Reason and Love, in all mankind. It is only when this is reached, of course, that the Divine idea in the creation shall be fully realised. But it had first to be realised and manifested in an *individual Person* who should be the Centre and Source of new life to Humanity.

Through the Incarnation of God in Christ, the spiritual evolution of man has received a new impetus—a fresh access of Divine spiritual power. There is now, indeed, a new immanence and transcendency—that of God in Christ, and of Christ in God. We wonder, perhaps, when we think of the slow progress of Christianity, of the many corruptions which have been suffered to enter it, of the strange and perverted forms in which it has sometimes appeared. Why does the Kingdom tarry so long? Why does the "living and reigning Christ" seem to have so little power? Why do evil and error, in spite of all that has been done, appear still to be so mighty? The answer is similar to that in regard to evils in Nature. The Kingdom, Christ taught, is like a *seed* sown in the earth which must *grow* amidst its various natural surroundings, often retarded by them, sometimes corrupted, and, to all outward appearance, almost destroyed. He planted in the world a *principle* which should be the power of a new spiritual evolution, but which can only realise itself in harmony with the laws which rule in all evolution. This we have in the entire manifestation of God in Christ.

This new principle made itself very manifest in relation to the old world into which it entered, and it is simply the truth to say that to it we owe all that is best in our

THE INCARNATION OF GOD IN CHRIST

modern thought and life The new Ideals that have arisen to shine before men have been kindled by it. To it is chiefly owing the difference between the old world and the new, and the confidence in a still better world yet to come. It has been and is still realising itself, not only in "the Church" and amongst professed believers, but in the world at large. Evil is *not* so mighty as it was before the introduction of Christianity. Christ would not be crucified in the civilised world of to-day. In the growth of the spirit of justice, of love, of charity, of Humanity in its higher feelings, attributes and aims, and in the improved condition of the peoples generally, we have abundant evidences of the potency of the new principle which Christ planted at the centre of the world's life. It was not, of course, an absolutely *new* principle, but a manifestation, and therefore an intensification, of that which had been working deepest of all from the first.

On the other hand, we have in *Christ in God* a real, new, Divine-human transcendency—a new element in the *transcendent* Divine. Christ *in God* is a real, present Teacher, Helper, and Saviour of those who look to Him in faith. In God there now lives One who has in Himself realised the true and full life of our Humanity, the true Head of the human organism, to Whom we can become united by faith, Who is able to impart that same life to all who look to Him for it, not in some wholly mysterious manner, but in harmony with the laws of our whole nature and of its development. Those who trust themselves to Him (and to God in Him) find this to be true in their experience, and it is open to all to verify it for themselves. But we need to remember that Christ's power is *spiritual*. It is like that of the transcendent Deity in relation to Nature. The spiritual life in man must be one of entire freedom, depending wholly on our free response to the Spirit of Christ. The Kingdom of God is a spiritual Kingdom: men can never be *forced* into it; it can only be realised by means of spiritual influences— men coming freely into a life-union with God. Here again, as in Nature, we are apt to expect *unreasonable* things.

The delay in the coming of God's Kingdom on the earth is, however, largely due to the failure of Christians to realise these two aspects of the relation of Christ to men—the immanent and the transcendent—and thus to see how temporally dependent Christ is (and God in Him) on the fidelity of His followers to Himself and on their efforts on behalf of the Kingdom. Christ's existence to-day, though most real, is spiritual in its character; His action is on men's spiritual natures, through His "Word and Spirit," and it is only through the response and instrumentality of His disciples that His work can be done in the world. If, as the opponents of Christianity are constantly reminding us, things are not as it might fairly be thought they should have by this time become, had Christianity really the power we ascribe to it, the fault lies to a great degree in our want of faith, in our apathy, indolence, and self-saving faithlessness, in our lack of receptivity, in our slowness to yield ourselves up to the immanent principle of Christ, and to become the free and willing agents of Christ in His transcendency. Those criticisms that come to us from our opponents have much truth in them relative to ourselves, and ought to be salutary. They affect the Truth and Honour of Him whom we own as Master and Lord. Instead of resenting them, or seeking to explain them away, let us rather profit by them where they are just, taking up more earnestly than we have yet done the great work which God in Christ has committed to us, for which the world is calling, and which He looks to us to accomplish in His Power.

Christ's disciples to-day, like those of old, long and

THE INCARNATION OF GOD IN CHRIST

pray for the "coming," or manifestation, of their Lord in His Kingdom and power and glory. The hour of "that Divine event" rests largely with men themselves; it is only "at the end," when God's purpose in the world has been realised in the race, that Christ shall be manifested in all His glory. But as we move on in the power of His Spirit towards the realisation of this end, His glory is being increasingly manifested.[1]

---

[1] For a fuller treatment of this subject the writer may be permitted to refer to his previous work, *The Spirit and the Incarnation* (Messrs T. & T. Clark, Edinburgh, 3rd edition, 1907).

CHAPTER XVI

THE CHRISTIAN CONCEPTION OF GOD

1. THE specifically Christian conception of God is distinguished by the doctrine of the *Divine Fatherhood*. God, Christ taught, is the holy and loving Father of men. It was the unseen Father who was revealed in His life as that of a perfect Son—the only form in which we can conceive that a full revelation of God could have been given to men. Any thought of God that comes short of this Divine Fatherhood comes short of Christianity, and at the same time proves insufficient to meet the wants of our spiritual nature. Man must believe in and realise his real *kinship* with God if he is to attain to the full height of his being as a son of God, or find its fulness in union with God The full sonship is, of course, ethical in its nature, something that man must rise into in his freedom. God as our Father, Christ taught, is the all-perfect ethical Being, the principle of whose life is that of universal Holy Love, and it was as such that He was revealed in the life of Christ, which was that of a true Son derived from the fulness of the Father.

This Christian truth of the Fatherhood of God finds very clear illustration from a Spiritual Monism. If there is only *one sole Power* operative in the Universe, whether in immanent or transcendent form, one Ultimate Fountain of Being that must be thought of as the perfect Reason and the perfect Love, if that one Power has for our sakes conditioned Himself so as to give rise to the material world to be the scene and the school of our life, furnishing it with all things necessary for our physical life and progress, if out of the Divine fulness Life itself has proceeded, if that Divine Power has wrought steadily onward as a perfecting Reason till man has been evolved, able to rise out of Nature and to look beyond it to the Source of his life; if his nature is such that he can share in the Reason and Love that belong to the Eternal Being, if the Eternal Spirit has so visited man as to carry the religious life to such a height that he feels he can only find rest and fulness of life in a union with God, if there is a Divine spiritual environment into adjustment with which his life must come if it would realise itself in its truth, if we are able to recognise and, in our own character, to express the Divine character, then, surely, we can get no better name for the Source of our being than that so constantly on the lips of Christ, "our Heavenly Father." A Spiritual Monism shows, without the need of any expansive argument, our direct natural kinship to God and the possibility of our rising into a still higher *ethical* sonship

Is this decried as "anthropomorphic"? There is indeed such an element in it, as there must be in all our language and in all our definite thought. Just because we are human we cannot but think and speak in human terms, even concerning God. We know all the while that God is not just like a human father He *is* our Father as the Source of our being, in what He has done for us, and in the love He bears us, but there are, of course, no human limitations or conditions in Him, His Personality is greater than ours. He is, Christ taught, our "Heavenly Father," exalted high above all that is of the earth merely, of Whom He said, "How much *more*" will He be to us and do for us all that is good, than any earthly father can be to his children or can do for them. We have already in dealing with the conceptions of God as the Divine Reason and Love, and as a purely spiritual Being, seen the reply to those objections which may be urged from the actual appearance of the world and experiences of life. In the presence of the revelation given in Christ it is made manifest that He is *such* a Father as will spare *nothing* that is for the real good of His children.

It is from faith in God as this all-perfect Father—from the assurance that we live and move and have our being in the environment of an all-perfect Reason and Love, under the sway of which all things in our individual life will be overruled for good, while the call is ever to work with the Divine Reason and Love in the great field of the world, and to live as the true children of the Heavenly Father, that the highest inspiration as well as the truest comfort and blessedness of life come to us. In this faith, not only submission to the Divine Will, but confidence in its necessity, in its wisdom and goodness, however hard it may appear, can be reached, and the soul's highest strength be derived. To be able even to say with the Stoic poet, "Lead thou me, God, Father, Lord, and thou world's Law, whithersoever I am by you appointed to go; for I will follow unreluctant, and yet should I refuse, through evilness (or cowardice) up-grown in me, none the less I shall surely follow" (*Cleanthes*, in Symonds' translation), is to be made a conqueror over the world. And surely the revelation of God's Fatherhood in Christ and in His Cross, in its sacrifice and its triumph, ought to enable us to repeat that prayer with an ardour and confidence such as no ancient Stoic could command. Christ invites us, not to a cold surrender to the Divine Reason merely, but to a loving unity with the Divine Reason *and Love*—as the children of an all-wise and all-loving Father, Who makes "all things work together for good," and beyond Whose Reason and Love *nothing* can possibly go.

We are encouraged to go to Him with the confidence of children, and to "pray always" as to One who is not only working as self-conditioned in Nature, but is above Nature and sure to hear and answer in all that is *good* and in harmony with the Reason and Love that He is.

2. But to the developed moral consciousness that seeks to realise this oneness with God and communion with Him there will come the sense of *sin* and the feeling of unworthiness. This sense of moral separation from God may become even painfully oppressive. How can *I*, conscious as I am, not only of imperfection but of sin and selfishness, draw thus confidently nigh to the all-perfect Being, and venture to repose my confidence in Him who is "of purer eyes than to behold iniquity"? And further, If I am to put my trust thus in God, I know that I must seek to live in harmony with His highest ethical and spiritual requirements. But just here I find myself to be weak. "The good I approve, I do not, the evil I would not, that I do. the law is holy and just and good, but I am carnal, under the power of my fleshly, earthly nature: I would fain live in harmony with God's requirements and be able to put in Him my trust, but, O wretched man that I am, who shall deliver me from this body of (sin and) death?" Christianity evokes the answer "I thank God through Jesus Christ our Lord, for the law of the Spirit of life in Christ Jesus made me free from the law of sin and death." In this it ministers to our greatest practical need. For God is essentially an ethical Being, and real union with Him must be ethical in its nature. And let men say what they will about the power of human reason and intellectual knowledge to elevate man and to set right the world, the real enemy to the individual and to society is that power of the fleshly or "animal" nature—centred in *self*—above which men fail to rise. It need not always find expression in the grosser and more obvious forms, and

it may be much stronger in some than in others, but the doctrine of Evolution makes it certain that it is there in some measure and in some form in us all. It is there because it was inevitable that the lower ("natural") life should be first. As St. Paul says, "that was not first which is spiritual, but that which is natural." It was not evil, but good for the lower life, but when the Ideal of a higher life shines upon us it becomes the real source of evil or sin. It is salvation from *this* that we need. Till we are lifted above the power of this lower nature, the highest life is impossible to us, till men in general are delivered from their own lower selves, no real or permanent Redemption can come to the world.

It is *man* who is his own worst enemy, and in his isolation and mere individualism the worst enemy of his fellow-men. It is therefore a special feature of the Christian doctrine of God, and, in view of the actual world, it should surely be a most welcome one, that, in and through Christ, He is revealed as *a God of grace and of spiritual salvation.* God's forgiving Love goes forth freely to sinful men through the Cross of Christ so as to save them spiritually. He in His humanity and in His sacrifice of Himself on the Cross has brought us all, in His own Person, nigh to God, or, stated from the Divine side, "God was in Christ, reconciling to Himself the world." *Theories* of the *mode* do not here concern us. Experience proves that trust in the *fact* takes away the sense of guilty estrangement, and enables men to draw near to God with holy confidence and in full harmony with their consciences. Not only so, but Conscience itself witnesses to their acceptance with God. Sin does not appear less, but more sinful; the man is not lowered morally, but uplifted. Through the Cross sin can be freely forgiven and the sinner saved—*from himself.* Through that act of faith men find that new spiritual inspiration that gives them freedom not only to will but to act out the "law of God" In that "Spirit of Christ" which, through their thus drawing nigh to God, comes to dwell in them, their own spiritual nature is so reinforced (or it may be quickened) that they are consciously lifted into a new life of sonship towards God. In the Divine Love that now finds entrance to the heart, the *principle* of the ethical "law of God" becomes the very principle of the life. And if there still remains a struggle against "the flesh," a battle with the world and with the lower self. if the afflictions, temptations, and trials which discipline life must still be shared in, and death itself be met, they can take to themselves the assurance, "My grace is sufficient for thee, my strength is made perfect in weakness," and they find it verified in their life-experience.

There is nothing in such a conception of the world as Science will justify adverse to this gracious manifestation of God to men, this fuller revelation of the Source of their being in adaptation to their needs, this continuous impartation of His power and of Himself to them. Was it not the great Apostle of Grace who exclaimed, " O the depth of the riches both of the wisdom and the knowledge of God!" adding, in words we have already quoted, " For of Him, through Him and unto Him are all things" But we go farther, and affirm that the doctrine of Evolution has not only confirmed the truth concerning, not indeed the "original sin" of the old Theology, but the fact of our inheritance of a nature with tendencies which, for man, are sinful, but that it leads us to believe it to be reasonable to expect that God would draw near in gracious help to the beings whose life as His children *must needs have* such lowly beginnings, and be realised through the knowledge of evil and through conflict with it—in such a way as should be in continuation of His working in the creation, and wholly in keeping with their freedom. Even Mr. Huxley's famous Lecture on

"Evolution and Ethics" has been well described as an attempt to show, without making any reference to the Christian doctrine, how the Pauline doctrine of Nature and Grace "answers to the needs of human life in its conflict with the workings of Nature, and closely accords with scientific principles" (T. Bailey Saunders in *The Quest of Faith*). But we agree with the writer just quoted that Huxley was wrong in opposing Ethics to the "Cosmic process" out of which they are born; and we see rather in Grace such a fuller manifestation and *impartation* of the Divine spiritual power as the progressive movement which characterises the history of life, and indeed that of the entire World-process, leads us to expect, if life is to be carried to its consummation, and if the one all-working Power—the Infinite Reason and Love—behind it all and in it all, is to realise itself in the creation. This does not make it the less "*grace*" to the individual, but it shows us that there was *Reason* as well as Love in the process, that it was not out of mere arbitrariness that, as Paul said, "where sin abounded, grace did much more abound."

3. Another distinctive characteristic of Christianity in its conception of God in His relation to the World and of the World in its relation to God, too much overlooked by our popular Theology, is brought into clearer light by Science and Monistic Philosophy, viz., *universality*. If there is only one sole principle of the world's life, we are led to see very clearly the *unity* of Humanity before God, the Source of our being and the Eternal Father of men. There can be no particularism. We see that all human beings *must* stand in that equal relation to God and most intimate relation to each other which Christianity assumes and plainly declares, that we are all "bound up" in one common "bundle of life," and that, try as we may, we cannot really separate ourselves from the others who are bound up with us therein. It thus enforces what reflection

THE CHRISTIAN CONCEPTION OF GOD 313

shows us, that a single isolated individual would be nothing, could have no existence in the world The individual could not *be* apart from the race The good that we receive and the evil that is done in the world must be referred, not to individuals merely, but to Humanity. Although individual development is first aimed at, and the individual life has real and permanent value, there is but one life and one Humanity before God, and the perfected individual must stand in, not only natural, but free, voluntary union with the race.

It is this that is the deepest ground of that real Brotherhood of man which commends itself to all as the mark of a universal Religion, but which seems to be so slow in its practical realisation. It is too much a matter of words only. Monism brings the principle home to us, as being founded deep in our common life and relation to God, and shows us how vain that religion must be which fails to recognise it practically, however good it may seem for the individual It shows us the basis of Christian morality, and of all true morality, in a universal human relationship which must find expression in universal Love, such as was manifested in Christ.

It gives us, too, the rationale of the Cross of Christ as that of the Representative of a Humanity which is as one man before God. It explains why we all suffer because of the sins of others, and, so far also, on their behalf. It shows us why the individual man can never cut himself off from a broad human responsibility. And it annihilates any *merely* individual hope that we may selfishly entertain, insisting that our hope must be one, not for ourselves only, but for the whole of the race to which we are bound by the indissoluble bond of a common life proceeding from Him whom we call our Heavenly Father.

4. In speaking of the Incarnation of God in Christ we have already made reference to that distinctive feature of

Christianity known as the going forth of that *"Holy Spirit"* which is essentially the Spirit of God, but which comes to us as "the Spirit of Christ," inseparable from the spiritual presence of Christ. As we have said, all religions (that of the Old Testament in particular) bear witness to the reality of a Divine spiritual Influence coming in various ways to men. But in pre-Christian religion this is *in itself* (not in its Source) an *impersonal* influence. One of the most distinctive doctrines of Christianity is that *in and through Jesus Christ* the Holy Spirit of God comes to men, not only with greater fulness of illuminative and inspirational power, but as a Divine-human personal Presence. It is, in short, the abiding presence of Christ as He in Whom the Dualism of Creation is transcended and our Humanity is brought into its true and full relation to God. It is through this "Spirit of Christ" received as the spirit of our own life, that we come to stand, live, and work in our true relation to God and man. While essentially ethical, it is also a personal Spirit, at once the very Spirit of God and the true spirit of man. Through that Spirit we can not only be taught, and guided into "all the truth," but be "strengthened with might in the inner man." This Spirit of Christ can so possess our spirits as to become a source of spiritual strength to us that nothing else can so supply As Paul found in his "infirmity," "His grace is sufficient for us, and His strength is perfected in our weakness." "Most gladly, therefore," said Paul, "will I rather glory in my infirmities, that the power of Christ may rest upon me" That last sentence exactly describes it. It is a Power that rests upon us, overshadows us, "tabernacles over us," makes us strong in weakness, peaceful in trouble, rejoicing in tribulation, victorious over trial and temptation. Even with respect to trust in God's fatherly care, we may find ourselves weak, but if we not only see the perfect trust of Christ, but surrender ourselves to the actual Spirit of Christ, as that Spirit was manifested in His life and is ever with us, we shall find the peace of Christ, and be enabled to live in that true relation of trust and obedience of which Christ was, in His own life, the supreme manifestation.

It is in this "Spirit of Christ" that man has his union with God, and it is *in ministering this Spirit to men* so that they may live and act in it, that Christianity fulfils its highest function. Beliefs are of importance only as they are part of this ministration. Our life is true only as it is animated by that Spirit. It is the Spirit of unity with God and with men, the Spirit out of which the creation proceeded, and in which only it can be perfected. It is that Spirit alone, therefore, that can make the world what God means it to become. For it is none other than God Himself in man.

This Spirit comes to us in the same way in which spiritual influences came to men in the past—through the Divine self-conditioning, which reached its highest expression in Christ. But there is this difference: in Him the Divine as it had gone out into the creation returned, as it were, into full union with the transcendent Divine, and therefore the Divine-human Christ becomes an abiding Presence and Power in inseparable union with God, the spiritual Environment of our being. It is possible also that what Science has shown respecting the "unconscious" foundations of our mental life, or that wider "general consciousness" which lies deeper and seemingly extends farther than our normal consciousness, may help us to understand how such inspiration and help may come to us from God in Christ, or Christ in God, and the spiritual world in general; but the most essential conditions are "*faith*" and "willingness to do His Will."

5. There is one other distinctive feature of the Christian conception of God to which we must refer, viz., *the Triune*

Being of God, the doctrine of the *Trinity*. This is at least the conception of God that has been held by the great Body of the Christian Church. To many it may seem quite unimportant, so purely scholastic, metaphysical, or even mythological, that we may well leave it behind us. To some it may appear that a reverent agnosticism is more in place than any attempt to speak of the Divine Being in itself. Now, we do not write in the interests of "Trinitarian orthodoxy"—often barren enough—or of any Church or sect, and we are far from suggesting that a man cannot get the benefits of God's self-revelation in Christ without "believing in the Trinity." We grant also that we are unable fully to comprehend the Divine Being in Himself, simply because we have no experience of the life of pure Spirit, and that beyond a certain point it is impossible for us to go But the Christianity which overcame the world, as contrasted with the more Jewish form of it, certainly believed that there was given to it the revelation of a threefold distinction in the Divine Nature. ' And even to-day, in relation to God, both in Nature and in His transcendency, as well as in Christ and Christianity, this doctrine, rightly taken, is far from being of small consequence. In a formal statement, not only of Christian truth, but of God as a living, conscious, acting Being in His relation to the World, it must hold an important place. Perhaps indifference to the Christian representation of God as distinguished within Himself, has not a little to do with the decadence of belief in a *living* God, distinct from "Nature"; for when God comes to be thought of as being something like "pure Being," whether we call it pure Reason or pure Love, or vaguely conceived "Mind" merely, He is very apt to become little more than a Name to us.

This doctrine of a Trinity in God has, doubtless, been often so stated that thoughtful men could not possibly believe it. When it is said that God in Himself is "a

THE CHRISTIAN CONCEPTION OF GOD   317

Person," and that " the Son " and " the Holy Spirit " are *also* " Persons" in the same or in a similar sense, or in the individual sense of the word " person " as applied to human beings, God would certainly seem to be, not "one," as Christ said He is, but Three. But this is a misunderstanding of the Christian truth, which is, assuredly, not Tritheism. Rightly understood, the doctrine of the Trinity is an endeavour to express an important practical truth with respect to the Divine Being which is as necessary to Philosophy as it is to Theology. Even an ardently Monistic writer like Dr. Paul Carus affirms that we *must* think of God as Triune. " We cannot even conceive of God," he says, " without attributing trinity to Him. An absolute unity would be non-existence. God, if thought of as real and active, involves an antithesis, which may be formulated as God and World, or *natura naturans* and *natura naturata*, or in some other way. This antithesis implies already the trinity-conception. When we think of God, not only as that which is eternal and immutable in existence, but also as that which changes, grows, and evolves, we cannot escape the result, and we must progress to a triune God-idea The conception of a God-man, of a Saviour, of God revealed in evolution, brings out the antithesis of God Father, and God Son, and the very conception of this relation implies God the Spirit that proceeds from both." And of course this is also *Monism*, for the three are *one* (*Primer of Philosophy*, p. 101).

We have already seen how our study of God's relation to Nature and to man leads us to what is at least a Trinity of *Divine manifestation*. This has been abundantly illustrated in preceding chapters, quite apart from the specifically Christian doctrine. It has been shown that God is at once the Unconditioned and the Self-conditioning One, as in His rational Power (the " Logos ") He goes out from Himself and becomes the Reason and Life-giving

Principle of the Universe, at once the immanent and the transcendent Deity. We must think of God as not only existing *in* Himself, the Infinite Source of Being; but as existing *for* Himself,—" the Son " in God,—and as going forth from Himself into the creation to realise Himself, as such, in finite forms therein (as He did so realise Himself in Christ),—returning to Himself in that "Holy Spirit" which is His own deepest life, but which, *for us*, proceeds from the Divine manifestations, culminating in Christ.

If it be said that this is only a Trinity that arises in the course of the Divine manifestation, or for the creation, not one in God as He is in Himself apart from the world, it is at least the *manifestation* of a real Triune distinction in God And if it be remembered that the process of creation, although, for us, proceeding in Time, must have been an *Eternal* fact to God, Whom we cannot think of save as always acting, we shall see that this Trinity is eternally real *in God*.[1]

[1] The truth and practical value of the Trinity is, of course, maintained by Hegelian and by other Idealistic Thinkers on purely philosophical grounds Amongst quite recent writings, reference may be made to Mr. Haldane's *Pathway to Reality*, Dr. Hutchison Stirling's *What is Thought?* and the late Professor Ritchie's *Philos Studies* The last-named writer says "The doctrine of the Trinity may be thought of as a mere magic puzzle to charm oneself out of hell with, but it may be, and has been, the greatest of all formulæ ever used in the attempt to grasp the relation between the universal and the particular If God be thought of as the Creator, only as the Source of all things, there can be no religion except a religion of wonder But God is also the Son—He reveals Himself in man—and man requires our love and service Lastly, through all the efforts of man moves the Spirit of God, bringing man back to Him, or what is the same thing, manifesting God in man. And this is an eternal process. God for ever is in Himself the same; for ever He goes out from Himself to become other, for ever He returns to Himself . This is nonsense, it will be said It represents the sincerest thought of the sincerest men that have ever lived—only torn apart from their lives which made it real and true We cannot get rid of mysteries, because the phrases that do well enough in space and time are inadequate with the things of Eternity There the contradiction must be met and be reconciled, the one is the many, the universal the particular" (p. 241).

THE CHRISTIAN CONCEPTION OF GOD 319

But further, if we are to think of the Divine Reason as conscious of itself, as it must be if it really is the perfect *Reason*, it must become an Object to itself, it must also go forth expressing itself, and shine forth again from that expression of itself. In this again we see imaged forth God as Father, Son, and Holy Spirit—which, of course, are the *human* terms by means of which we seek to express those distinctions which we believe must exist in God if He is to be conceived as a living, self-conscious, and active Being

So, in the very Being of God as the perfect and Eternal *Love*, like distinctions are implied. Love, in order to be Love, must have an Object, while the only adequate Object of the Divine perfect Love must be God Himself as distinguished for Himself This is the very thought that seeks to realise itself in the creation—the mainspring of its life —and therefore from its realisation in Christ the Holy Spirit of Love goes forth in all its fulness in order that the Divine Thought may be realised in the whole of mankind. We do not, however, believe that we can get a real Trinity in God, or reach the Divine Christ, by simply making " the World " the Son (even though we see the world's life culminating in Christ); the distinction must be logically thought of as existing *in God*, prior to the world, and Christ is thus seen to have His Being grounded in the Divine Nature and to be verily the manifestation of *God.*

We see further the importance of this doctrine in view of the necessity we are under of conceiving of an *eternal ethical* life in God. On Monistic evolutionary principles God must be thought of as containing in Himself the fulness, or the perfection of the life that is manifested in the creation, not in its intermediate forms, indeed, but in those highest ethical forms which reveal most fully that which there was in the primal Source of Being. There can be nothing in the evolved forms of being higher than there was in Life's primal Fountain. In other words, man cannot be greater than God. There must therefore be in God the fulness of that ethical life which shows itself to be the highest thing in man. But such ethical life is impossible *out of all relations*. A sole, undistinguished Being could not possibly be an ethical Being. It may be fairly questioned, indeed, whether He could be even a conscious being, but certainly He could not live an ethical life out of all relationship real or Ideal, and the Ideal is always *real* in God. There must therefore be *in God* the prototypes of those personal relations which make ethical life and personality itself possible to us And yet it must be *in the one Divine life* that these distinctions or *quasi*-relationships exist, else it would not be in the life of *God* at all that they existed God must thus distinguish Himself from Himself, giving rise thus to " God as Son," while both arise out of and are united in the one *Spirit* which is the deepest life, the ethical life of God, both as Father and as Son; and which proceeds from God in both aspects of His Being. It seems to be this conception of God setting Himself over against Himself as another that best enables us to think of God as that Eternal ethical Being that He is, and must be, if He is the Source of the World's life It is the realisation of Himself as another, yet one with Himself (as Son, the life of Sonship), that is the motive of the creation, it was this that was realised in Christ, and that is to be, in some real sense, realised in all in the consummation. The separate finite beings who have been evolved through the creative process and perfected by the Divine Spirit, who represent that Sonship which was the Ideal of the creation, return to God again, and are eternally united with Him in the one Holy Spirit of Life. Christ is thus, as the Scriptures represent Him, " the first-born among many brethren " God, along with Him, " brings many sons unto glory." As Christ Himself said, " The glory which Thou hast given me I have given unto them, that they may be *one*; I in them and Thou in me, that they may be perfected into one" Again we read· "Your life is hid with Christ in God When Christ who is our life shall be manifested, then shall ye also be manifested with Him in glory" "If He shall be manifested, we shall be like Him."

Christ lives in God now (and God in Him), and we shall live in God with Him, and God in us In the Divine Being or Life there may be thus an ever-increasing number of "persons" sharing in the one eternal life, while that life is still to be distinguished as that of *Father*, the Source and Goal of all, *Son*, embracing many finite sons in whom the Sonship eternal in God has realised itself, and among whom Christ has still "the pre-eminence" (see Col. i), and *Holy Spirit*, including *all* the influences that go out from God, whether immediately or mediately—that is, whether emanating directly from Himself, or through His manifestations, or through the personalities that have been brought into union with Himself.

We can only speak on these matters with a stammering tongue, and only in the light of the spiritual illumination that comes through Christ We now " see as in a mirror darkly," but if once we get beyond the *tritheistic* conceptions, which are too common in the popular thought of the Trinity, we can at least behold, in a reflected manner, something of the profound truth there is in the Christian conception of God as Triune We can see how God can be both immanent and transcendent, how He can be for ever giving Himself to be the Life of the world, and yet for ever maintaining Himself, and finding His life again in the finite forms which He causes to arise and which He brings into eternal life-union with Himself We seem to discover in this light the *Reason* of the world's life, and to be able to foresee how the creation can yet be completely unified with the Creator,—God in all and all in God, "to Whom be glory for ever. Amen."

PART II

FREEDOM AND MONISTIC SCIENCE

CHAPTER 1

THE QUESTION

IN what has been said in the preceding section the Freedom of the Will has been affirmed and so far illustrated But the importance of the question is such that a separate section must be devoted to it. In what has gone before it has been argued that the Divine creative action culminates in the fact that we are made personal, spiritual beings, and that it is in this fact that we have the revelation of the all-working Power within ourselves as spiritual. The Power that works all things, or that is constantly evolving itself as conditioned in the creation, reaches in this way its goal, realises and manifests itself, at least to this extent While God is the sole Cause of the Universe and of our own existence therein, He constitutes us so far in His own image that we become *causes* that operate freely in the Universe. Apart from this, not only would there be no moral responsibility, no morality and no religion, but the process of the Universe itself would appear a quite meaningless one, consisting only of successive manifestations of an unknown Power, but never reaching anything that had permanent worth or real value in itself. There would be no possibility of rising from such a Universe to *God*, or of reconciling the actual world with the existence and action of a Divine moral Being. As Mr. Mallock remarks, " A child can understand that unless the Will is free—unless out of different actions which are all of them possible to us we can choose to perform any one and refuse to perform others—we cannot be responsible to God for what we do or abstain from doing, and that there can between God and man be no moral relation." The question of the Will goes deeper than this; but any one can see that, unless there is in us some real element of Freedom, some power of self-control, of choice and voluntary action, there can be, not only no Religion, but no such realities as virtue or vice, merit or demerit, praise or blame, worthiness or unworthiness. There can be no affection save what is physically evoked and controlled, no attraction of friendship or of worth, no gradation of character, no character at all. We should be simply conscious automatons, pulled by countless strings, governed by physical forces, miserably self-deceived creatures, living under an illusion of freedom, responsible for nothing, worth nothing.

But the simple fact that all men have this so-called "illusion of freedom" suggests that surely there is some reality in it. It is necessary, even those who most strongly deny its reality assure us, for all that pertains to our highest life, for the advancement, nay, for the very existence of society. Strange then would it be if there were nothing real in it, if it were wholly an illusion.

The deepest ground of our belief in its reality is, of course, this universal consciousness of its possession, confirmed by all our social institutions, educational efforts, common speech and literature, everyday actions, and feelings of self-condemnation, regret, and remorse. If we have no freedom, all these are based on illusion; but certainly we would need very strong proofs that they are so.

Of course, it is said that Consciousness is not always to be relied on; that it sometimes tells us what turns out to be incorrect or false But this applies only to the *inferences* we draw from facts of consciousness, not to the facts themselves Our sense of freedom is not an inference, but the direct testimony of consciousness,—it is our " consciousness of Freedom,"—and if this cannot be trusted, what is there that we can trust? Certainly no affirmation of what is believed to happen *outside* our consciousness can have the same weight.

If this be so, it may be asked, Why go any farther? Why not simply rest in this indisputable testimony of consciousness? We *do* rest in it, and in order to be convinced of the reality of our freedom it is unnecessary to go beyond it [1]

But since the reality of our freedom is denied in the name of Monistic Science, it is necessary to show the groundlessness of that denial, and to make it plain that, on the contrary, Monism, rightly taken, gives the strongest support to our conviction of our freedom, and the best explanation of its possibility in view of certain facts that are urged against it. We do not imagine the Will to be what Dr. Bastian has called "a kind of psychological ghost," nor, strictly speaking, a separate faculty at all. It is an aspect of that *Self*, or Ego, which is the synthesis of the bodily and the spiritual viewed on the spiritual side, or, better still, an aspect of that *Self* of which, from first to last, the physical is the expression, organ, or instrument. We do not affirm a will absolutely free from all conditions, circumstances, and physical relations, or that acts without motives. A madman may so act, but no sane person will do so. But we affirm a will that is to some extent its own

[1] As M Renan says, "By establishing moral truths on the solid foundation of practical reason . . . Kant . . . assigned to them their true basis and their decisive position The notion of duty—that is to say, the rule of practical life—is thus recognised as a primitive fact, beyond and above all discussion. It is the same with free-will, without which duty would be but a meaningless word The abstract discussion which has so long been kept up between fatalism and free-will has no longer a *raison d'être*. Man feels that he is free . it is a fact which no reasoning can affect. Such are some of the great conquests of modern Science " (*Philos Dialogues and Fragments*, p. 116)

law, which can initiate action, has a power of choice, determines what motives shall prevail, and, in the true sense of the word, forms its own *character*—a will that is free to choose either to inhibit or to act, and to do this whether it is able to exercise the control it seeks to exercise, or to carry out its volitions, or not.

An important distinction must be made at the outset with respect to the meaning of the word "Freedom." It is used in more senses than one. It may mean freedom of choice, or freedom of action. A person may freely choose what he is not able to carry out in action. Again, while our choice is free, we may not be free to choose the highest. A man may be in bondage to his lower nature. He chooses quite freely to follow that nature, but in relation to the law of a higher life he may not be free. Freedom in the sense of harmony with the higher nature, and with the universal Will, may be something that can only be won through knowledge and struggle against nature in the lower sense.

In discussing the question as it stands at the present time, we cannot do better than follow the reasonings of Mr. Mallock in his strong, unshrinking presentation of the determinist doctrine. It is the most recent and the liveliest statement of the case that we know of, and it is scarcely possible that it can have a more uncompromising support than that which he gives it in his *Religion as a Credible Doctrine* and *The Reconstruction of Belief.* It will be with the earlier work, however, that we shall chiefly deal, as it contains the fullest treatment of the subject.

In the later work, the Freedom that must be claimed for man has been well stated as follows: "When most persons talk of belief in moral freedom, they mean by freedom a power which exhausts itself in acts of choice between a series of alternative courses; but important though such choice as a function of freedom is, the root-idea of freedom lies deeper still It consists in the idea, not that a man is, as a personality, the first and sole cause of his choice between alternative courses, but that he is, in a true, even if in a qualified sense, the first cause of what he does, or feels, or is, whether this involves an act of choice or consists of an unimpeded impulse. Freedom of choice between alternatives is a consequence of this primary faculty. It is the form in which this faculty is most noticeably manifested, but it is not the faculty of personal freedom itself. . . If a man is not in any degree, be this never so limited, the first cause or originator of his own actions or impulses, he must be the mere transmitter or quotient of forces external to his conscious self, like a man pushed against another by the pressure of a crowd behind him. In other words, he would have no true self—no personality at all." While some expressions in the foregoing statement are open to criticism, it is substantially correct. As we understand it, it is in agreement with Coleridge's definition of *Will* as distinct from *Nature*, than which we know nothing better, and which is well worth quoting in full. "Whatever is comprised in the chain and mechanism of Cause and Effect, of course *necessitated*, and having its necessity in some other thing, antecedent or concurrent— this is said to be *Natural*; and the Aggregate and System of all such things is NATURE It is, therefore, a contradiction in terms to include in this the Free-will, of which the verbal definition is—that which *originates* an act or state of Being. In this sense, therefore, which is the sense of St. Paul, and indeed of the New Testament throughout, Spiritual and Supernatural are synonymous"

Again he says "Nature is a Line in constant and continuous evolution. Its *beginning* is lost in the Supernatural and *for our understanding*, therefore, it must appear as a continuous line without beginning or end But where there is no discontinuity there can be no origination, and every appearance of origination in *Nature* is but a shadow of our own casting. It is a reflection from our own *Will* or Spirit. Herein, indeed, the Will consists. This is the essential character by which WILL is *opposed* to Nature as *Spirit* and raised *above* Nature, as *self-determining* Spirit —this, namely, that it is a power of *originating* an act or state" (*Aids to Reflection*, xliii. C, note; cix. C, note)

We need not argue for less than this, then. But Mr. Mallock asserts that such Freedom cannot possibly be maintained in harmony with Science—the very idea of it is unthinkable; it can only be maintained on practical grounds and on the principle of "a synthesis of contradictories."

The subject has two aspects—the psychological and the physiological: let us follow Mr. Mallock, and take first "the determinism of Psychology." He complains that "Theologians" generally run away from the real issue and seek to prove something else: we will promise at least to try not to do this, and to avoid prolixity.

CHAPTER II

"The Determinism of Psychology"

ACCORDING to pure Psychology, the case stands thus, says Mr. Mallock: "The act of will as known to us by our own experience is an act which is invariably determined by the strongest motive; and motive again is determined by two things—the talents and temperament with which an individual is endowed at his birth, and the circumstances by which from his birth onwards he is surrounded. Now it is perfectly obvious that he has, when his life begins, no voice whatever in the settlement of either of these—of his circumstances on the one hand, or of his talents and temperament on the other. How then is it possible that an element of free choice, which was, when his life began, obviously not possessed by him, can be smuggled into his nature at any subsequent period?" (*Religion*, etc , pp. 90, 91).

Here we shall only remark at present, that when the element of free choice appears there is nothing "smuggled into" the man's nature, any more than there is when distinct self-conscious thought or speech appears. These are not possessed in exercise by the new-born child any more than will, in the sense here spoken of; but there is a provision in his organism for their appearing in due time. So it is with freedom of choice. It is a well-established fact that many faculties for which provision is made do not immediately make their appearance.

Another remark may be here made. Mr. Mallock

throughout speaks of *motives* as if they were something distinct from the man himself—standing over against him and *determining* him This is a fallacy which underlies his whole argument But the motive, *as motive*, is nothing but an aspect or attitude of the man himself. As Principal Caird has said, "You may attempt, as has been often done, to apply material analogies to mental phenomena— as when moral action is represented as the result of the force of motives acting on the will. But the analogy here is a purely fallacious one. The mind that is to be acted on in volition is already present in the motives that are supposed to act on it It is the mind that is moved which constitutes or gives their constraining power to the motives that are conceived to move it. In no single moment of its experience can thought be entirely passive, for the activity to which it yields is an activity which thought itself creates and constitutes, an activity the form of which thought itself has already determined" (*Intro. to Philos of Religion*, p 115)

But let us follow Mr. Mallock into the more detailed discussion of what he terms "the determinism of Psychology." Of course, there is the assumption here that all who are entitled to be called Psychologists are determinists, which, it need not be said, is by no means the case. The present tendency is rather to emphasise the reality and importance of the Will The first point is that we always will what is desirable If we had but one desire we should will only the one thing: so "in the presence of two or more alternative objects, each of which he desires, but desires in very different degrees, the man can only, other things being equal, will to gain the object the desire for which is most intense. . . Just as water on an incline flows down the incline, not up it, so does the man will in accordance with his sole desire, or with the strongest" (pp 97–99) This "bondage of our wills in every act of willing to the sole desire or the strongest desire of the moment, is absolute, necessary, invariable   It admits of exceptions no more than does the law of gravitation itself."

This is said to be admitted by thinkers of all schools. It may well be admitted, for no other action of the will is conceivable.   But how does it come to be a "bondage"? If the will were *compelled* to will or choose something other than that which it desired most, then, indeed, it would be a *bound* will, but when it naturally, and, Mr. Mallock says, necessarily, *wills* that which it desires or desires most strongly, this is surely the proof of its freedom, rather than of its bondage.   A free will does not consist in one that is free or able to carry out what it wills   the will is behind the action or the effort to act.   The will is simply *the man* in one aspect of his being, it is the man as desiring and as free to choose that which he desires most.   Only if anything stood between him and his so willing would the will be bound.   Further, these desires are not material things over against the man, but states of the man as a spiritual Ego or person.   The process that goes on is not predominantly a mechanical one, but a spiritual one.

The usual answer to his assertion is, Mr. Mallock says, "that we are free, within limits, to govern our desires—and so to govern the will through its necessary submission to these."   What is here affirmed is true, and it raises the real question at issue.   But it is quite a mistake to speak about "governing the will"—as if it were something objective to the man.   *Self*-government is really that which is asserted, and this is certainly, within limits, possible to us.

But in order to refute this, Mr. Mallock proceeds "to consider the desires themselves—how they arise and by what circumstances they are conditioned", to see whether "any principle of freedom can be arrived at by this route."

Our desires, he says, are given us from without and depend on our constitution, *e g* the desire for food · "we are its puppets, not its masters." How this affects the question of the freedom of the will is hard to see. We must take ourselves as we find ourselves. We are not pure spirits to whom infinite desires might be possible, but embodied beings, under certain necessary conditions of life. Apart from our constitution and our circumstances, we could have no desires at all, and no such thing as *will* could come into exercise. But even our desire for food—imperative as it seems—we can govern, or, to state it more accurately, we can govern ourselves in relation to it, so that we may not simply yield to the desire to eat. The hungry man who is determined to finish his task before he eats, and whether he ever eats again or not; the starving mother who gives away the desired morsel to feed her perishing children; the drunkard whose craving is driving him almost to desperation, but who can so far govern it that he will not in order to gratify it lay himself open to the charge of theft: these are plain examples of how we can govern the most deeply-seated and imperious desires, or ourselves in relation to them. Of course, if we were to abstain from food altogether, we should die; but even to this extent can the will prevail over the most imperative natural desires. People have been known to perish of hunger rather than do wrong, and from less worthy reasons to starve themselves to death. Certainly all this is still in obedience to a desire, but it is one which the person has formed for himself, and persists in cherishing in spite of other natural desires more external to *himself*.

From our nature and from our circumstances arise innumerable desires, and they could not arise from any other source. As long as a man is free to follow his desires, whatever they may be, his will—that is, *he himself*—is in this sense *free*. The real, deeper question of freedom does not so much as arise in such a case. It is only when the natural, freely accepted and followed, course of desires is met and countered by something else that the deeper question comes into view, or becomes a conscious one. And this can only happen by the conviction arising (in whatever way) that there is something *higher* or with superior claims upon us than simply following out our natural desires or seeking our immediate gratification.

Mr Mallock comes face to face with the real question in discussing Professor W. Ward's distinction between "spontaneous impulse" and "resolve," in the last of which only, according to Dr Ward, does freedom appear. Mr. Mallock affirms that *both* are the result of circumstance and equally mechanical. Since the chief interest of the subject is due to its connection with moral and religious virtue, let us consider the illustration which he gives of St. Anthony's temptation to unchastity: " He resists the impulse by painful and prolonged resolve; and in this resistance every Christian assumes that we have a typically moral action. But what does this assumption imply?" It implies in the first place, we are told, that St. Anthony had no *bad* motive, also that his resistance was not without any motive at all; that, in short, it was from a good motive. "There would probably be more motives than one—the desire to avoid hell, the desire to attain to heaven, and the yet more specific desire to unite his life to Christ's —the last the most essential." But it is urged that if Christ had never lived, this supreme motive could have had no existence. Christ's life, then, and St. Anthony's knowledge of Him, "form part of St. Anthony's circumstances at the moment of his forming his resolve. Both of these circumstances are imposed on him by external causes. He had no voice in deciding that Christ should be born, or that he should have knowledge of Him. Subtract the two circumstances, and would the character of his resolve and resistances have suffered no appreciable change ? If they would not, Christ died and was preached in vain. If they would, then resolve is not independent of circumstance."

To the reply that might be made, that these circumstances do but furnish him with an opportunity of submitting himself to Christ's influence, which he is equally free to embrace or to turn away from, and that thus the principle of freedom remains as free as ever, Mr. Mallock urges that this is only running away from the difficulty. Granting for the moment that St Anthony (and others) had this freedom, and that the fact of his having chosen devotion to Christ as the foundation of a Christian life redounded to the credit of his free-will only, this love to Christ must make his subsequent resistance to sin easier than it would have been were this love absent. "Thus, whenever one of his resolves is struggling to complete itself, a moment must arrive at which the presence of this love for Christ carries the resolve to completion, and at which, had this love been absent, the end of the struggle would have been failure. In other words, at such a moment as this his resolve is determined by circumstances and is no longer free. Determinism has caught us up and holds us in its grip once more ; and as often as we try to escape from it, it will catch us in the same way."

He follows this up by quoting the words of Christ : " If the men of Sodom had been able to hear *me*, the men of Sodom would have long ago repented,"—an external circumstance being present, they would have resolved in a certain way. And this dependence on external circumstances is illustrated by all spiritual biographies—to St. Paul the voice comes, and to Augustine. " In one man, illness, misfortune, or the loss of a beloved friend, effects a sudden change in his sense of the relative values of things " " It is never described as an act independent of motive and circumstance." Such an act is indescribable, because not clearly thinkable. Were it possible, it would not be a normal act at all. "It would be more like that of a drunkard than it would be like that of a saint." This typical case and the reply to it may stand, Mr Mallock says, for all other arguments on behalf of freedom and the reply to them.

Now, no one will affirm that our acts of will are "independent of motive and circumstance." Constituted as we are and placed where we are, we are necessarily largely dependent on what comes to us from without, and the idea of volition without a motive is an absurdity. But the motive never can be a motive *as outside of ourselves*— determining us as if from without. It must, as feeling, desire, emotion, etc., become part of ourselves—of our own feeling at the moment. The love of Christ, for example, can only be a motive in us when it kindles an answering love in our hearts In other words, the motive is never apart from the man it moves; it is ours—part of ourselves

The real question is, How do we act when, *from whatever source*, certain desires arise within us, or when certain appeals, awakening certain desires, are made to us? Are we simply at the mercy of whatever may happen to come to us? No, Mr. Mallock admits, we will act according to that which has the strongest attraction for us at the moment, which makes the strongest appeal, creates the strongest desire or motive. But what shall so affect us and become the strongest motive, or even be entertained at all, depends on something in ourselves—depends on our *character*. But the very idea of a character implies a freedom in virtue of which we, so far, at least, *form ourselves.* This is what is of the deepest consequence, and it is this that determines how we shall act in the presence of temptation. Let us return to the case of St. Anthony. His highest motive, no doubt, came from without; but it does not follow that he did not freely accept and cherish it. The same appeals that came to St. Anthony came to others with quite different effects. It is quite possible that Christ may be preached in vain, and that men may even, as St Paul says, "receive the grace of God in vain." The question, moreover, is as regards the determining motive *at the moment of temptation*. It is not merely that *at first* St. Anthony might have resisted the appeal of Christ; there is a continuous and present question whether he shall yield to the higher motive or the lower. The love he has for Christ is one circumstance, and his own natural feelings constitute another. Both appeal, not to some abstract thing called "the will," but to the *living man*—both exist as motives in himself—and the question is, What is it that determines which he shall yield himself up to? It is surely *the man himself* as a free spiritual being that makes this determination. No doubt there is a motive for this, else it would not be rational action at all: we can never, in this sense, get away from motive But he is *not compelled* either way, but gives his free consent to the motive that thus wins the day within him. He identifies himself with it and lets it carry him. The lower motive may be a very strong one in relation to the lower, animal side of his nature. The appeal may awaken feelings or desires which might carry another man away with them at once, or by degrees. St Anthony may cherish, and so strengthen those feelings, until they dominate him, or he may, in various ways, turn away from the appeal and weaken those feelings so that higher motives may be followed. The lower motive may be, in a *physical* sense, much the stronger one, and there may be a fierce and prolonged struggle within the man's soul where the higher and the lower motives meet. And if the higher motive win the day, it will not be in virtue of any superior compelling strength, but because the man, in spite of his lower self, *chooses* to yield himself up to it rather than to the other. We can have no better illustration of freedom than just such a case. That he still does all with *a motive* does not (as Mr. Mallock says elsewhere) make the course he follows less voluntary. An un-motived will would be no will at all. "A characterless will" is not conceivable. It is not the absence of motives that would make us free; action in the absence of motives, or according to any but that which, however weak in a physical sense, becomes the strongest motive to us, is, we repeat, inconceivable; it is in the *choice* of what motive we shall *cherish* and make the determining motive of our action that our moral freedom appears. It is just in our capacity for pause, deliberation, attention and inattention, inhibition, self-control, choice and voluntary action or inaction, that the difference between freedom and mechanism consists.

Christ's saying that the men of Sodom would have repented had they heard *Him* is not to the point The necessary coming of circumstances from without is granted, it is *how men choose to relate themselves to these* that is the question at issue. It does not follow that *all* the men of Sodom would have repented at the preaching of Christ. And so with respect to the appeal to Christian experience of conversion, etc Other men have had experience of the same circumstances that have led to a radical change in some, but with no such results Did this depend in no degree on their own choice? Is the Gospel simile of the "Fisher for men" to be taken quite literally? Have those who hear the Gospel no more power of decision than have the fish that happen to be swept into the net?

Every attempt to prove that resolve is free is, says Mr. Mallock, an attempt (1) to dress up the assertion in the clothes of the truism that, at any given moment, out of two opposite courses we are free, if we will, to take one or the other, and (2) to substitute for the unanswerable objections of the determinist others which are perfectly answerable, but are not put forward by anybody.

The question, of course, is not whether we are free to act in a certain way *if we will to do so*, but the prior one whether we *will* freely or not. It is certainly not what Mr. Mallock goes on to say it is according to certain advocates of Free-will, viz., that whether I am hungry or thirsty is a question which I decide for myself—"that if, at a given moment, I am longing for a glass of water, I am able to make myself long for a dry biscuit instead." Surely nobody ever said that before. That would not be governing the desires, but entirely *changing* them—a very different thing. No, it is whether, when I am thirsty, I am free to decide whether I shall drink at that moment or not. I may come in warm from my work in the field, and long for a drink of cold, cold water. I am just about to take it, when I remember that it is dangerous to drink cold water while I am heated. What the advocate of Free-will asserts is, not that I can make myself feel hungry instead of thirsty, or that I can make myself no longer to feel thirsty, or no longer to desire that drink of cold water; but that I can pause, deliberate, revolve motives in my mind, and freely decide whether at that moment I shall drink or not. I can cherish my natural craving for the water, turning my mind away from the consequences that are to be dreaded, till the desire to drink becomes the overpowering motive; or I can so hold before my mind, or attend to those who enforce, the possible consequences, that their avoidance becomes the strongest motive, and, thirsty as I continue to be, I can resolve to wait till I have cooled down a bit. Certainly in this I act according to that which is the strongest motive at the time, but a moment ago that motive was not present to my mind at all; I myself brought it up, or when it came, from whatever source, I kept it before me, allowed it to turn me aside from my purpose—*made* it, in fact, the strongest motive.

When Mr. Mallock says that "the truism" expressed

by most advocates of freedom in the formula, "We are free to act as we will to act, and to take either of two opposite courses, if we will to take it," means, not only that we are free to behave in this way, but that "we are not free to behave in any other," and that thus "the opponents of determinism seek to prove the doctrine of freedom by representing the unanswerable proposition that our acts are necessarily caused by our wills, and our wills are in their turn necessarily caused by our desires, as identical with the proposition that our desires are not necessarily caused by anything," he shows a strange misconception of the real question. To say that we have freedom of choice is by no means the same thing as to say that our desires and volitions are not caused by anything. Our *desires* are created in various ways and of our *volitions*, their ultimate cause may be our own free choice. That *we* are causes, within certain limits, is the very essence of our contention, according to what Mr. Mallock himself says it is necessary to maintain.

Mr. Mallock denies that the determinist affirms a free act to be impossible because it is an act without a cause He admits that the cause is the will of the man who performs the act But, he says, "a man may be compared to an engine running from Brighton to London, which at Croydon takes the line either to London Bridge or Victoria. If it goes to Victoria, the cause of its going is the engine. If it goes to London Bridge, the cause is the engine likewise. But in saying this we leave the question untouched of why the engine goes to this station, not to that one." So when a man eats or drinks, or does anything, we all agree to say that his will causes it The question at issue is, "What, when one of these acts is performed, has caused the man to will this one and not the other? Why has he drunk a glass of water instead of eating a biscuit? or why has he eaten a biscuit instead of drinking a glass of water?

To say that the cause of his eating or drinking is his will, is not to answer the question, but to ignore it." All this is obvious, as far as it goes; but let us continue the quotation. "In the case of the engine, if it goes to London Bridge, the cause is its own machinery; but the cause of its going to London Bridge instead of going to Victoria is not its own machinery, but a movement of the points at Croydon. Similarly, in the case of the man's eating or drinking, his will is the cause of his doing whichever he ultimately does, but the cause of his doing the one, and not doing the other, is some determining fact amongst his own previous circumstances—either some process of which he knows nothing in what is vulgarly called his own inside, or some fact which he knows—such as the fact that ten minutes ago he had something to eat, but could get nothing to drink, or had something to drink, but could get nothing to eat. The defender of the doctrine of freedom, instead of facing this fact, shirks it." "His doctrine is intelligible or thinkable only so long as we do not look at it steadily."

This statement, with the illustrations that are given, seems to indicate that Mr Mallock fails to grasp, or to bear in mind, the real psychological question concerning Freedom. It is true that the question is, How does the will come to make one decision rather than another? but what the advocate of Free-will affirms is, that *the man's own free choice* is an element in determining what he shall will to do, as between two different courses. Take the case of the engine going to London Bridge instead of to Victoria, or *vice versâ*. If it goes to London Bridge, the cause, Mr. Mallock says, is the movement of its own machinery; but that the cause of its going to London Bridge instead of to Victoria is not its own machinery, but a movement of the points at Croydon. But surely, behind both of these, there is a prior and still deeper cause—some-

"THE DETERMINISM OF PSYCHOLOGY" 343

thing in the mind of the driver, or of those who prescribed the course for that particular engine. The points at Croydon did not move of their own accord. There was not only the act of the pointsman, but some motive, some reason, why the pointsman should shift them. So, back behind such " circumstances " as Mr. Mallock adduces as the determinants of the will, there is *something in the man himself*—in the spiritual self or Ego—which is the real determinant. As long as there is nothing arising to check the flow of the desires and their gratification, the process goes on as if it were wholly an automatic one—that is, there is no definite consciousness of volition as an act. But whenever a conflict of motives or desires arises, then the consciousness realises its function, takes the matter into its own hands, deliberates and decides. That it always decides according to the motive that is strongest—that is most influential at the time—is, we repeat, no ground for affirming determinism, in no way could it possibly act differently if it is to act sanely But that which becomes " the strongest motive," becomes such by the free choice and acceptance of the self or Ego, and is often *made* such by elements which the Ego brings forth and adds to it. So far is the freedom that is claimed from being the " dream," the " chimera," the " nonsense," which Mr. Mallock, in the last instance quoting Hobbes, declares it to be.

Mr. Mallock concludes this portion of the discussion by quoting what Kant, " as a Psychologist," said of Freedom. " If we consider human character empirically,"—that is to say, as a scientifically observable phenomenon,—" and if into the soul of a man as expressed by his inward, no less than his outward acts, we could penetrate deeply enough to know every one of his motives, even the slightest, which determine his soul from within, and if at the same time we could know with equal completeness every single circumstance which could act on his soul from without, we should be able to calculate his future conduct as certainly as we can calculate an eclipse of the sun or moon. If we look at a man's character as observation and experience give it to us, there is no such thing as a principle of freedom to be found in it."

Kant was the great master of Antinomies, and what he here states from the empirical point of view he himself refutes from other points of view. He is usually regarded as the successful vindicator of the Freedom of the Will. In the passage quoted above, he is, of course, speaking only of the empirical order which can be *observed*, but he shows at the same time that there is a higher order to which man as possessing "Reason" belongs, to which the observed empirical order is due, and in which man is possessed of "free-will" (see *Critique of Pure Reason*, p. 333, etc., Meiklejohn's Translation). But even to the passage given by Mr. Mallock no defender of Free-will need object. Of course, if we could know *everything* that would affect a man, and all about how he should hold himself in relation to it,—" if we could know every one of the motives, even the slightest, which determine his soul *from within*,"—we would know certainly how he would act. But this knowledge would not make his action the less free. What is that determination of the soul "from within," if not determination from the man's own self or soul? Therefore, when Kant says there is no such thing as a principle of freedom to be found in a man's character, we may well answer, after the manner of Leibnitz, "except the man's character itself,"—that is, the man himself as a free agent, while, of course, he stands under the necessary limitations of a finite, embodied being, in a law-governed Universe. But he can, in his freedom, will and act by means of and in harmony with these same laws.

CHAPTER III

"The Determinism of Matter"

I

In passing now to "the determinism of Matter," we have the same objection to make to Mr Mallock when he speaks in the name of "Science" as that which was made to him when speaking in the name of "Psychology." By what right does he represent Physical Science as being necessarily a system of determinism? Are all Scientists determinists? Is Monistic Science necessarily deterministic? and are all Monists opponents of the doctrines of Freedom? Such a mode of speech as he adopts is very misleading, and it is desirable to show that it is unfounded.

The late Professor W. B. Carpenter—who in his *Mental Physiology* led the way in a study that has become of increasing interest and value—while he maintained the correlation of all forces, vital, physical, and mental—was yet an earnest advocate of Free-will, and, when that doctrine was attacked by Huxley and Clifford, strenuously maintained it. "Feeling assured," he wrote, "that the sources of my belief in it lie deep down in the nature of every normally constituted human being, I cannot anticipate the time when that belief will be eliminated from the thought of Mankind,—when the words 'ought,' 'duty,' 'responsibility,' 'choice,' 'self-control,' and the like, will cease to have the meaning we at present attach to them,— and when we shall really treat each other as automata who cannot help doing whatever our 'heredity' and environment necessitate" (Preface to 4th edition of *Mental Physiology*, p. lv).

Coming to a later time, we find Professor H. Charlton Bastian, in his work on *The Brain as an Organ of Mind* (in the International Scientific Series), a writer who certainly cannot be dismissed as a "spiritualistic Philosopher,"—while he rejects the idea of the Will as "a psychological ghost,"—stating in strong terms his repudiation of automatism. While asserting that "Every higher and intellectual and moral process—just as much as every lower sensorial or perceptive process—involves the activity of certain related cell-and-fibre networks in the cerebral cortex, and is absolutely dependent upon the functional activity of such networks," he decidedly rejects "the notion which some would associate with such a doctrine, viz, the supposition that human beings are mere conscious automata." He even holds that "states of feeling may in very truth, and in accordance with popular belief, react upon nerve-tissues so as to alter the molecular motions taking place therein Feelings, whether purely personal or of the moral order, have thus, as they seem to have, an indubitable effect in modifying our Intellectual Operations, our volitions, or our movements." Of automatism as a system, he says it is "one in which all notions of Free Will, Duty, and Moral Obligation would seem . . to be alike consigned to a common grave, together with the underlying powers of self-education and self-control"

These statements by men of science whose special study was the relations of Mind and Brain, might be largely multiplied, but, coming to our own time and keeping *Monism* specially in view, we find an avowedly Monistic writer like Professor Lloyd Morgan claiming for the Will a distinct place and function He shows that there is in the organism, "besides the mechanism for automatic co-ordina-

"THE DETERMINISM OF MATTER" 347

tion, a mechanism of control," and that it is the *self*, or what he terms "the empirical me," that exercises this control (*Compar. Psych.*, p. 199). " Since the total content of consciousness in any given moment constitutes the empirical me of that moment, it is clear that this empirical *I* controls the activity in question. In automatic acts, in so far as they are accompanied by consciousness, such consciousness is a mere spectator; but in controlled activities consciousness is more than a spectator—it takes the helm and guides." It is free to guide according to the laws of its inherent nature, save in so far as it is thwarted by some external constraint—" not free," he says, " to transcend those laws, as is sometimes supposed in the Free-will controversy, to the confusion of the issue " There is a power of control, probably over the attention,—acting also through the sensory centres,—to modify and guide the flow of ideas " That same psychical *I* which takes effect through the control centres on the motor activities of the body, takes effect also through associative fibres on the sensory centres which are involved in the production of ideas" (p 190, *et seq*). Once more, he says that "as with the not-self, so with the self, there is something more than a sequence of states of consciousness, there is an activity which is selective and synthetic, which is orderly and determinative " (*ib.* p. 314).

These references are sufficient to show that it is not right to say that Science (as if with one voice), or even Monistic Science, affirms Determinism.[1]

---

[1] We need not refer to other present-day representatives of Science —such as Sir Oliver Lodge, but it is interesting to note that even Mr McCabe, the able defender of Haeckel, says, " A man can control his actions to a great extent, and will to that extent be responsible for them, on that we have the witness of consciousness " And again, replying to Mr Mallock, he writes, " The difficulty about the freedom of the will may turn out to be largely due to our slavery to language That which formerly went under the name of ' Freedom ' is disproved by Science But the fact remains—and it is a *scientific* fact, a psychological fact— that we are conscious of being able to influence our character and our

To see that there is a *physiological provision*—in the higher animals and man—for such control as is claimed by the advocates of Free-will, we need go no farther than to Haeckel himself. In *The Riddle of the Universe* (p. 46, cheap ed.), he asserts that, in addition to the provision for reflex action, "when the tri-cellular reflex organ arises and a third independent cell—the psychic or ganglionic cell—is interposed between the sense-cell and the motor-cell, we have an independent elementary organ of will." This in the lower animals remains *unconscious*. "It is only when consciousness arises in the higher animals as the subjective mirror of the objective, though internal, processes in the neuroplasm of the psychic cells, that the will reaches that highest stage which likens it in character to the human will, and which, in the case of man, answers in common parlance to the predicate of 'liberty,'" which, however, Haeckel deems "deceptive"

Here, then, we have an organ specially designed to serve voluntary action. Is the action *not* voluntary, but only seemingly so? In that case, there is no real distinction between it and the previous reflex action—the organ serves no purpose but to deceive us. If all our actions are physically determined, they might quite as well go on without this volitional organ as with it. The only difference is that in the highest animals and man it is accompanied by consciousness—not in the lower forms of life, where, while the action is real, it is unconscious But consciousness is simply a state of the self or Ego. The only difference that this accompaniment makes, according to Haeckel's statement, is that we mentally *see* what is going on, and *imagine* that we are *acting*, and acting freely. This is surely a strange purpose for an organ to serve. By what right does he

actions, and so cannot deny our responsibility within limits It is for ethics and psychology to determine those limits and to readjust our terms and conceptions" (*Haeckel's Critics*, p 118).

affirm that we are thus deceived, and that, in spite of the existence of this organ and of our consciousness of freedom, the actions are not really voluntary but determined? Is there no reality in our idea of freedom—no such thing? He has no grounds whatever for such an assertion in the *facts* of Science; it is wholly an *inference*, based, not on Science, but on a certain theory or philosophy, viz., that there can be no relation of mutual influence between the spiritual and the physical; that in all cosmic action the physical or the material is supreme. Consciousness says exactly the reverse of this, and we find nothing adduced which refutes this deliverance of consciousness. On the contrary, the actual existence of a special volitional organ is as complete a confirmation of the deliverance of our consciousness as we can expect to find.

Haeckel himself speaks of " the will " as " that momentous element of the soul which determines the character of the individual." If it really does this, surely it must be *free* and supreme in the organism. But " the human will," he says, " has no more freedom than that of the higher animals, from which it differs only in degree, not in kind " But suppose that the higher animals *do* possess some measure of freedom, what then? It differs in *degree*, we are told. In degree of what? It can only be in degree of that volitional control which in those higher animals begins to show itself in addition to wholly reflex and instinctive movements. Otherwise the words have no meaning.

II

But let us turn now to Mr. Mallock's statement of "the determinism of Matter." The very title startles us. What a marvellous thing this " matter " must be which determines all the movements of the human mind and soul, all that we have been in the habit of crediting to man as a free agent, all the actions and issues of the world! For if " the determination of Matter" be a fact, this is what we have to accept. It is not really *we* who do anything; all is done by this unknown something called "matter." "In two distinct ways," says Mr. Mallock, "Physical Science absorbs the question of free-will and reduces moral responsibility to a biological problem." "In the first place, the physicist takes the living individual as we find him, with his faculties and character given, and identifies these with the processes of the individual's own organism. In the second, he takes the physical organism as the result of its pre-natal antecedents and connects its idiosyncrasies with those of its innumerable ancestors" (p. 125).

The first method again "resolves itself into two parts, one of which presents the hypothesis of free-will to us as something essentially inconsistent with the general principles of Science, while the other presents it to us as inconsistent with particular scientific facts"

1. Free-will is affirmed to be inconsistent with the general principles of Science, inasmuch as it contradicts the universally accepted laws of ."the conservation of energy and of momentum." We have already dealt with this objection in chap. xi. of Part I., what we may have to say further with respect to it and Mr Mallock's treatment of the replies that have been given to it, will come better after we have grappled with what he describes as "the question, yet more intractable, of whether the facts of Science will allow us to regard it (Freedom) as a reality, and will not rather expose it to us as a baseless and unbelievable dream."

2. These facts of Science, it is said, are the familiar ones that show that the Mind, "its highest faculties and its most revered and sacred qualities, are notoriously at the mercy of the vulgarest material accidents, so that, whether or no the mind has any control over the brain, the brain, under certain conditions, has an absolute control over the mind."

The defenders of Free-will, however, have, it is said, "what seems to be an obvious answer to this." "The brain," they say, "is undoubtedly the instrument of mind, by which alone, in our present state of existence, it is capable of exercising any of its faculties, or revealing them to itself or others" It is like an organ of which the will is the player. if the mechanism is wrong, the music will be wrong, while the will itself may exist in all its integrity.

This argument, Mr. Mallock admits, is "plausible," and, he says, "it is perfectly easy to imagine a condition of things under which it would be a complete answer to the kind of difficulty which it is put forward to meet." We venture to think that it is not only plausible, but, in its substance, perfectly adequate, and that Mr. Mallock has done nothing to make it appear otherwise. Only, we must not think of the will as if it were a faculty *separate* from the man, or the entire organised being; something which is not, under our present conditions of life, dependent on its relation to the organism. As we have seen, it only comes into manifestation or play when an organ arises to serve it. But the fundamental facts pointed to by Mr. Mallock are neither more nor less than those that show the dependence of the mind on the bodily organism as a whole for its manifestation. They apply equally to life itself, our very existence in this world, as truly as the exercise of the faculty of will, is "notoriously at the mercy of the vulgarist of material accidents." This no more affects the reality of Free-will than it does that of our existence in this world. It only raises the wider question of the relation of Mind and Body in general

But there are certain facts, it is urged, which prevent our resting in this general answer. "Each day we are being taught in clearer and more startling detail, that our organ, the brain, is not only capable of refusing to play the tunes which the Mind or will of our hypothetical organist would impose upon it, but it is capable also, in reference to purely physical stimuli, of grinding out tunes totally different of its own." Scientific inquiry is tending to show that "the diseases and accidents to which the brain is liable, or again, certain kinds of medical and surgical treatment, may not only suspend on occasion the customary action of the latter, leaving thought, emotion, purpose, and will in abeyance, but may also, no less frequently, leave these in full activity, and yet at the same time have profoundly changed their character." Mr. Mallock gives several illustrations from Dr. Hollander's work, *The Mental Functions of the Brain.* A man who had a portion of his brain removed, so far recovered his faculties that his case was quoted as a proof that mind and brain are essentially distinct things But it was found that his moral character was greatly changed. " His intellectual powers suggested those of a child, while his animal passions became strong in proportion " Now, such an abnormal case as this proves nothing at all concerning Free-will. It only shows that the man, after his accident, had *not* recovered all his normal qualities Normally, before the accident, he was quite a different man; and it is with man in his *normal* condition we are concerned, not with man as he may be rendered by accidents The accident to this particular man had evidently affected that portion of his brain to which the moral nature is related, and, probably, that on which the normal action of the will depended.

Other illustrations are from memory, which may be sometimes either partially or wholly lost through an accident, and which is occasionally abnormally strong in some one direction in idiot children; from fear and courage, which may disappear when certain parts of the brain are removed, from " the sense of sin and the vengeance of God," abnormal thoughts of which may go at the bidding of the surgeon's knife; from honesty as dependent on a cerebral

"THE DETERMINISM OF MATTER" 353

basis, which, if affected, may make a once honest man a thief, and from chastity, which depends on the condition of the cerebellum. But there is really nothing new in any of these facts, they do not carry us one step beyond the general question of the relation of Mind and Body, unless, indeed, we regard them as exceptions that prove the rule. They are all examples of *abnormal* cases, illustrations of what happens when accident occurs to certain portions of the brain —the dependence on which of all mental functions is fully admitted on all hands. The very same thing applies with equal force to speech and sight and other faculties. As for the brain "grinding out tunes of its own," the same thing happens in dreaming and in "reverie"; but, while the brain is healthy, this can be checked by the slightest volitional effort; in the case of dreams, by the simple act of awaking—returning, that is, to the normal condition

It would be just as much to the purpose to cite the total cessation of all manifested volitional action when a more serious accident has resulted in death.

But, Mr. Mallock argues, such brain changes actually change *the character*. "If abnormal conditions of the brain affected character only by suspending the action of the will . . . so that no apparent qualities, whether good or evil, were left to it, we might . . . contend with some plausibility that the will, untouched in the background, continued as free as ever." But—in addition to this suspension of action—abnormal affections of the brain "on other occasions suffer it to remain in extreme activity, and invest its actions with a moral quality which is new to them; since it forces the Christian to surrender his trust in God's boundless mercy; since it suddenly gives to the honest the perverse intentions of the pickpocket, to the chaste those of the profligate, and to the prurient the purity of a Galahad; since, in a word, the brain is shown to control the will in those very domains of conduct in which freedom is most vehemently claimed for it,—to suppose that the will is a separate and independent force, which impresses its orders on the organism of which it shows itself so frequently to be the slave, is to indulge in a supposition for which Science not only affords no evidence, but which all the evidence collected by Science contradicts" (p. 142).

With reference to this—which looks so formidable—we need only repeat that the will is not to be regarded as "a separate and independent force which imposes its orders on the organism," remaining "untouched in the background," whatever may affect the brain, but is simply *the man* or the *self* in the exercise of volitional functions *by means of the organism* which exists for that purpose, and that, of necessity, if the organism be injured or diseased, or if, in a word, any abnormal conditions exist, the outcome will be abnormal in its character. It is not "the will" merely that is affected in the illustrations which are given, but the physical basis of the entire character. The man, as we say, is no longer "himself," and the aim of the physician is to bring him back again to his normal self, which may sometimes be impossible in this life. Mind and brain are in this life so united that what affects the one will affect the other, so that, if the brain be rendered abnormal, the manifestation of the self as related to that organ cannot but be abnormal also. The cases cited are really forms of *insanity*, but the fact that a man may become insane is no argument against the qualities of sane persons These examples of what may happen *abnormally* cannot possibly prove that the will in the normal man "is the slave of the organism"; they rather stand out as illustrations that it is quite otherwise with the normal person.

3. The final argument is drawn from *Heredity*, which it is said, not only furnishes us with "that intellectual outfit which in its essential features is practically the same for all of us"; but also "with those minute differences of

"THE DETERMINISM OF MATTER" 355

character in virtue of which no one of us is precisely like another It gives us our various characters as it gives us our various faces. It gives us, in addition to our various powers of thinking, infinitely varied assortments of thoughts, desires, and instincts, written before our birth in a species of invisible ink which the light or the heat of life gradually renders visible" (p. 144). In special illustration, reference is made to the strange recurrence of the vagaries to which amative desire is liable. These depend on a structure of thoughts, inherited, it may be, from remote ancestors—"engraved in the substance of the brain itself, that having slept through the life of one man, and again through that of his son, may in the lives of his grandchildren start into full activity." Mental character transmits itself precisely in the same way as do physical characteristics. Thus, while the desires and thoughts excited in the man by external circumstances are determined by his actual character at the moment, "his actual character, through an unbroken series of developments, has been determined by the potential character which was his when life began." At a former time it was possible for "inaccurate and obstinate thinkers" to suppose that "amongst the inevitable characteristics which God or Nature had imposed on us, the desired principle of freedom might still be lurking somehow. But Heredity has made this appear to be impossible It has thus stopped the last earth in which the phantom of freedom could hide itself It has thus supplied the last link in the chain by which man is bound to the mechanism of universal Nature—has shown him to be part and parcel of one single inexorable process, and no more responsible for any one of his thoughts or actions than he is for the colour of his eyes, or the history and temperature of the earth which have rendered his life possible" (p. 148).

Now, of course, the facts of heredity must be fully

acknowledged. Through it, in one way or another, we receive everything that we possess as our individual capital or outfit in life the one thing which we do *not* receive through either individual or social heredity is just that which Mr. Mallock says we *do* receive, namely, our *character*, in the proper sense of the word. We receive our " nature," " temperament," " characteristics," and " idiosyncrasies "—our " disposition," or what Mr. Mallock terms " our potential character," but our " *actual character* " is the one thing which the man so furnished forms for himself. Why cannot the heredity which hands down everything else transmit the capacity for self-formation? Amongst the other faculties which are handed down by heredity is that faculty of freedom for the existence of which we are contending. That power of self-formation on which personal character depends is not merely " lurking " somewhere, but is characteristic of the man as a man. The will-faculty may be much weaker in some than in others, some men come into the world very heavily weighted by their inheritance , " the fathers have eaten sour grapes, and the children's teeth are set on edge ; " " unto the third and fourth generation," and much later, these elements may descend, but the man is not utterly helpless in the midst of them Even though we grant to Mr. Mallock that certain " thoughts " of our ancestors are embedded in our cerebral matter, to come out, sooner or later, into the light of consciousness, all that we receive from inheritance forms only the *ground* of our lives. Apart from those conditions on which life itself is dependent, no utterly irresistible *necessity* is laid on any normally constituted person ; he receives as one of the most precious elements of his inheritance that power of pause, deliberation, self-control, and choice, which the advocates of Free-will contend for. Deepest of all, there is, of course, in every man a definite *nature*, which, as he has received it, may be full of evil

"THE DETERMINISM OF MATTER" 357

tendencies, but, shining on every man, there is the Ideal of his true self—what he *ought* to be—which in concrete ways calls and claims him, and which he is free to follow, or to strive to follow, or not, as he himself chooses. He is self-condemned if he fails to strive to follow it. He would not be *a man* otherwise, only, as Mr. Mallock admits, a machine—a mere wheel or cog on a wheel of the great world-machine, which drives on inexorably under the influence of purely physical forces, although in the higher animals and man the action is illumined by consciousness, and man, at least, is made to believe that he is acting freely—deceived thus by a blind Cosmic power,—and to what purpose?

It is manifest that the arguments adduced by Mr. Mallock in support of the "determinism of Matter" have weight only as representing a system which lays the whole stress on the mechanical or purely physical aspect of things: in plain words, it is that which used to be known as "Materialism," although the name (and the thing) be disclaimed by "Monistic Science" and by Mr. Mallock. But what else can the "determinism of Matter" mean?

In his closing sentence Mr. Mallock remarks that the coincidence in result of those independent lines of inquiry "is the crowning witness to this great universal truth, of which the absolute necessity of our volitions is merely an example and a consequence, namely, that the process of the entire Universe is not two processes but one, or that, even if we suppose it to be two, the two are so inexorably united that the one is just as uniform and just as necessary as the other." But as it is worked out, this becomes a purely one-sided and mechanical Monism; everything is subordinated to the physical side of things, the mental or spiritual is treated as if it were but incidental and, in its highest affirmations, illusive. Man, in whom the spiritual or subjective side of the Universe comes into its highest manifestation, is represented as wholly at the mercy of the physical side of his being. It is a Monism of the objective only — or of what seems to be objective. A Spiritual Monism acknowledges the two sides, but the spiritual side, in virtue of which alone we know anything at all about the matter, or about "matter," is held to be first and deepest, and the material simply its necessary expression and instrument—its other side, in this sense. Even as represented by Haeckel (and, as will doubtless be acknowledged, by Mr. Mallock), Monism, in some sense, recognises "Mind" from the beginning as well as matter; two sides or elements all through. According to some, these move in parallel lines; each is real, though never influencing the other. In another view, they are simply two aspects of one reality, with no kind of separation or "gulf" between them. Mr. Mallock himself has shown (in a passage quoted in chap. xi. Part I.) how conscious states can influence the organism. But with many this recognition of Mind is verbal only; the entire stress is laid on the material side, and purely physical or mechanical laws are made to govern everything. Under such a system, it is, of course, impossible that man can be held to be free —any more than that some small wheel in a great machine can set up an independent motion of its own But, as we have seen, there is another view possible, which is still Monistic. We have only to be in earnest with the acknowledgment of *Mind* from the first; we have only to recognise it as being really *Mind*; to be true to what we find in our everyday experience (and which must be true in the nature of things), that matter is but the servant, the expression and instrument of Mind, which must ever be first and deepest;—we have only to see this to be true from first to last, in order to reach a true spiritual Monism and be freed from the physical incubus. Of course, there is in the finite, developing world a gradual rise of Mind

"THE DETERMINISM OF MATTER" 359

into expression corresponding to that development of matter and growing complexity of forces which make this possible. Evolution, in short, shows us a co-relative development of both Mind and Matter, an increasing rise of matter in complexity, with a corresponding rise in the manifestation of Mind. But that growing complexity of matter is manifestly to *serve* the rising manifestation of Mind, which reaches its highest expression in man as a spiritual being, related still to a material organism, indeed; not bound down by merely physical powers, however, but capable of free self-formation.

4 It is in this light that we are able also to answer the objection mentioned at the beginning of this section from the seeming contradiction of Free-will to the general laws of Science—the conservation of energy and momentum. We need only briefly summarise what has already been said in Part I. chap xi. on this subject.

These are generally recognised physical laws, and on the theory of parallelism which some adopt, there is, of course, no contradiction of them No more is there any contradiction on the theory of a Spiritual Monism.[1] The two sides or elements are always conjoined; there is no gulf between them, or need for the "passing" of influence from the one to the other. The material is from the first but the expression of the spiritual. There is no "fresh creation of energy", the whole energy that is employed is *there*, stored up in the two-sided organism which has its centre in the "empirical me." According to the will of this central *I*, will the physical action be, not as in obedience to

[1] It is interesting to note that Mr. Romanes, in his *Thoughts on Religion*, still adhered to "Monism" as giving the best explanation of free-will in this connection "To the obvious objection that with a plurality of first causes—each the *fons et origo* of a new and never-ending stream of causality—the cosmos must sooner or later become a chaos by cumulative intersection of the streams, the answer is to be found in the theory of Monism" (p 130).

an order or effort or exertion of energy *from without*, but as the expression of the will of the one indivisible *self*.

As long as we think of the will as something entirely separate from, or standing over against, the physical organism, it may be impossible to conceive how the purely spiritual can affect the material, or how it can do so without the creation of energy. But what we have to do with is not " pure spirit " on the one hand and " mere matter " on the other, but spirit that is expressed and organised in matter, with its invariably associated force or energy. That which exercises the volition is not a separate spirit, but *the organised self or Ego*, one side or aspect of which is physical and the other spiritual. We know from familiar experience that though Spirit cannot influence matter directly as pure spirit, it can do so whenever it finds material expression, through, it may be, the influence it can exert on other spirits similarly organised. A thought becoming a word, or expressing itself by a look even, can do so. Our thought can affect matter and manipulate it as soon as it becomes embodied in an appropriate instrument. In ourselves, the material side is throughout the instrument of the spiritual self, though this self is not at every stage conscious. The physical is there solely to serve the purposes of the spiritual self, and is never separable from it. There is thus, in the free action of that self, no break in the chain of physical causation, no new creation of energy, no breach of the law of conservation.

We may fitly conclude this part of the discussion by giving Mr Mallock's summary in his later work, of the difficulties or impossibilities in the way of belief in Freewill from a scientific point of view (which he at the same time earnestly urges must be held from a *practical* point of view), and the brief replies that may now be made to them. They are four in number.

1 The first or Theological question, " How man can be free to do or not any particular thing, when his choice

"THE DETERMINISM OF MATTER" 361

has from all eternity been fore-written in the will of God," we leave over for the present

2. The Psychological question is, "How any act can be free, when no volition is possible apart from the determinism of motive ; the theory that freedom resides in the intensification of this motive or that, being merely the difficulty restated in different terms" The answer to this is that there is *no* determination of motive. The motive is always part of the self—of its feelings, desires, etc, and the person is ultimately self-determined.

3. The Physical question, "How the will which is inseparable from the action of the physical organism can interfere with the process of which it is itself a product, any more than a wheel of a watch can interfere with its own rotation?" This simply begs the question in stating it. That the will is *not* like the wheel of a watch, constrained to move by preceding physical movement, is precisely our contention. Nor does the will "interfere" with the process, it simply fulfils a function provided for it in the organism. But even if we keep to the mechanical mode of representation, it is quite possible for a wheel to have an action which, according to the design of the machine, might institute a process which would not otherwise have followed. We may see this illustrated in such machinery as continuously turns out a product by different, successive, yet connected, processes.

4. There is still another, and, Mr. Mallock says, "far more significant though little noticed difficulty. The very principle of Freedom is one which eludes thought altogether, separating itself into two ideas of which each destroys the other." Put shortly, it is this · "The man acts either for some cause or for none. If his action was caused, it is of no value, if it is wholly uncaused, it is both morally meaningless and impossible" The answer is that the cause of the action is the man's own personal self, and

that, far from being either impossible or without value, it is just in such action and in none other that moral value is found, for it is the expression of what the man *is* or at the moment *chooses to make himself*.

Before proceeding to discuss this question of Freedom with reference to God and His relation to the world and ourselves, let us endeavour to give a short summary of the rise and development of Will-power as Science exhibits it.

CHAPTER IV

THE RISE AND DEVELOPMENT OF WILL

THE beginnings of voluntary action are to be found, we believe, very low down in animal life It does not come suddenly into the world with the appearance of man, as some absolutely new thing (as Mr. Mallock seems to say), but, like every other mental faculty, it has a history and a development. Voluntary action is, indeed, so inseparable from consciousness, that Wundt in his latest work (*The Principles of Physiological Psychology*) makes it the criterion of consciousness. Of course, this does not determine *what* is voluntary action as distinct from reflex action or automatism. "The generally accepted objective criterion of an external voluntary movement," Wundt says, "is the reference of the movement to the general animal impulses —nutritive and sexual." "The manifestations of life, even amongst the protozoa, are explicable only on the hypothesis that they possess a mind", *e g.*, the amœba returning to its food; ciliated infusoria pursuing others which they kill and devour (although this may last only for a short time). These manifestations "point also in the case of the ciliata to a variation in the choice of means for the satisfaction of the organic impulses that would be unintelligible as a merely mechanical result of external influences" (pp. 27, 29).

"Sensation determining mental action," says Dr. Murphy, "is the germ of Will." The power which is manifested in the physical world as energy passing from one form to another according to the constitution of the matter with which it is associated, or through which it is expressed, becomes manifested in the animal world as a conscious power—as a *self*, feeling and acting consciously and freely (although for long beneath rationality), in or by means of the organism that has been evolved to serve it according to its "nature" or "kind." The organism is not, as some seem to suppose, the *prison* of the creature, but that which has been formed to serve it in its life, while, of course, its range of action is limited by its organism. But every conscious being, even the humblest, is a *self*, which can never be a mere *blank* or entirely "characterless." Every creature has its "nature" founded in certain feelings or wants which it *experiences* and seeks to meet and supply. It is just thus that it seeks and finds its life according to its kind. Related to the organism as it is, the seeking to supply these wants (or to realise its functions) becomes instinctive, and although the organism has of necessity a physical basis, in its efforts to supply its wants and find its life the conscious creature acts quite freely. It has "a will to live". without it it would not be a living animal at all. It is not an automaton, nor is it merely dominated by the physical side of its organism. The objective and the subjective are *one* in every normal creature. As long as an animal is at liberty to follow the law of its nature, we cannot speak of it as being in *bondage* of any kind, although each creature is limited in its possibilities by its nature.

"Reflex action," says Professor Tyler, "takes place without consciousness or will. Instinctive action may be voluntary, but it is, after all, not so much the result of individual purpose as of hereditary tendency. Is there then no *will* in the animal until it has become intelligent? I think there has been a sort of voluntary action all the time Even the amœba selects and chooses, if I may use the word, its food among the sand grains. And the will is stimulated to act by the appetite. Hunger is the first teacher" (*The Whence and Whither of Man*, p. 137). If we watch even one of the humblest of creatures, we will see it moving quite freely in search of its food, picking it out carefully from amongst other elements; if it comes into contact with something that had seemed food, but turns out not to be such, it will reject it, and it will change its course and turn aside from that which would injure it It can originate its own movements and continuously shape its course in response to what comes to it through its avenues of sense, even though these are not yet specially defined, and though there is nothing more than a vague diffused sensitiveness. We witness here something very different from what obtains under the reign of inevitable succession in the purely mechanical world. The creature in a real sense *wills* its actions, but, as Coleridge remarks, "Who would not smile at the notion of a rose *willing* to put forth its buds and to expand them into flowers?" or, to come down to the more purely mechanical, who could imagine a rolling stone, or, to take something more refined, an electric current, voluntarily turning aside from an obstacle which confronted it? We have, at least, here such freedom as Professor Lloyd Morgan speaks of as "the real freedom of the individual to control his activities in accordance with the laws of his inherent nature"

But the development of the principle of Freedom proceeds. As we have seen, at a certain stage a special control-centre is formed, and this certainly appears to fulfil a function of the creature—to minister to its growing needs As the self expands, as the possibilities of a larger life open to it through its relation to an ever-widening environment, as it comes to share more and more in Reason or Intelligence, to be able to draw inferences from other sources than the immediate *natural* environment, as new feelings, emotions, desires, and aims can become *motives* to it, and as it becomes able to resist the immediate organic or instinctive cravings in obedience to some other aim,—such as the help of a comrade,—or some higher, though not compulsory law, the principle of Freedom rises in its manifestation. As Professor Tyler remarks, "the animal that first felt fear—an emotion not *of* the organism but *for* it—took a long step in advance"; and many other emotions and feelings followed. We have at this stage, therefore, a higher manifestation of volitional power. That even animals may be trained to manifest this higher measure of freedom, no one that has paid any attention to them can possibly doubt; *e.g.*, the cat, strongly tempted to steal, but resisting under the *acquired* influences of its training, not always from fear of consequences either. Darwin, in chap. iv. of the *Descent of Man*, gives several examples. "As far as deliberation and the victory between opposing motives are concerned," he says, "animals may be seen doubting between opposed instincts, in rescuing their offspring or comrades from danger." Mr. Hobhouse (in his *Mind in Evolution*) instances the dog whose wounds are being dressed, naturally impelled to bite, but turning it into a caress; and the self-restraint of pointers, and of animals in their masters' presence.[1] As Mr. Hobhouse remarks, "In such purpose, controlling instinct, we have the germ which, as purposes are widened and systematised, develops into the rational self-control of human morality."

But the animal is still largely limited by its "nature," to which a definite physical organism corresponds. It is when we come to *man* as a rational and spiritual being that we witness the emergence of Freedom in a very much higher form, although not even with him, at first, is it found in its full fruition. In the animal, as Coleridge remarks

---

[1] Even a cat will press the finger of a friend with his teeth so firmly that it cannot be withdrawn save at the will of the animal, and yet with such restraint as to avoid penetrating the flesh

THE RISE AND DEVELOPMENT OF WILL 367

"its nature is its law, and the will is hidden and absorbed in this law", but in man the law shines upon him as Reason, commands him as Duty, moves him as Sympathy and Love, and he may give practical expression to that higher Law or not. It is when we come to a rational being, "with his faculty for and store of general ideas, and ability to construct what is not perceived,"—with his capacity of looking forward, of forming plans and purposes and of adapting means to realise them,—with his power of *choosing* his ends and course of action, that we behold the birth of the higher freedom, yet as a development from lower forms of the same power. "Power," says Dr Harris, "is constituted Will by being endowed with Reason. A rational power is a Will. Because man is rational he is able to compare all ends and methods and motives of action, and determine among them the motive he will follow, the ends for which he will act, and when, where, and how he will exert his energies for the end chosen." It is not a separate faculty, but an aspect of the rational being. "Will is the name of the Mind considered as self-determining, just as Reason is the Mind itself considered as rational The names designate two aspects or powers of the person, yet but one indivisible person. If you regard the person as Will, he is a rational Will. If you regard him as Reason, he is energising and self-determining Reason, or, as Kant says, 'the Will is nothing other than the practical Reason'" (*Philos. Basis of Theism*, p. 351).

"The Will," as something *abstract*, has of course no actual existence. As Wundt remarks, "It is not a real process at all, but a general concept gained by abstraction from a large number of concrete facts. And the concrete individual volition which has actual existence is itself a complex process made up in every case of memories, sensations, and feelings" (*Principles of Physiol. Psych*, new ed p. 212) Of course the *Self* that wills has a real existence. The essential element in Will is the power of *choice*, and nearly all Psychologists are agreed that this is rendered effectual through the faculty of *attention*, or what Wundt calls *apperception*. If in the presence of different motives, we ask ourselves how one comes to have greater power with us than others, we shall find that it is chiefly by our power, if we choose, of *attending* to it rather than to the others—bringing it into the focus of the consciousness, rather than leaving it in some part of the field merely. This is in itself an act of will. As Wundt puts it, the appearance of an obscure idea in Consciousness is a *Perception*, that of a clear one is *Apperception*. " There can never be an external act save as the result of a previous inner selection, and this holds true again both of the impulse and of the act of choice . . . So that apperception is the one original act of Will." Certain feelings are motives to the act of apperception, but—what is most important to observe—" the act of apperception itself shows all the characteristics of an act of Will" (*Human and Animal Psych.*, pp. 246, 255, etc) That is, we voluntarily *choose* whether we shall bring any particular motive into the focus of the Mind , in any case, we choose whether it shall be our determining motive or not.

Man, no doubt, has also a " nature," and it is his nature as a human being that gives the original ground or quality to his *self*, to which are added individual tendencies and idiosyncrasies, for the most part inherited. Far from there being a " characterless will," there is a most complex unity of feelings, desires, and tendencies at the foundation of his being, constituting the original *self*. But his capacity for receiving influences from without which may become motives to him, far transcends that of the highest animal. He is capable of regulating and governing the merely organic desires, instincts, and passions by reason—*capable* of it, but by no means certain always to do it. He is free

THE RISE AND DEVELOPMENT OF WILL 369

to do it or not do it as he *chooses*. He may not be able to carry his choice out into action, and even the exercise of a right or rational choice is much more difficult for some than for others, but if this power of choice, and consequent responsibility, be not within his reach, he is no longer to be deemed "all there," or responsible His condition is an abnormal one

As Professor Le Conte points out in his most valuable lectures on *Religion and Science*, man, who can influence others in harmony with law, can also influence himself. As self-conscious, "he views himself objectively, as he would another person,"—"deals with himself objectively; persuades himself, argues with himself, influences himself, marshals motives to determine his conduct in the right direction—in a word, uses moral contrivance with himself as he would with another. It is as if the free determining will were a different thing from the executive will. The executive will belongs to animals as well as to man;—the determining will belongs to man alone, the executive will lies passive under the power of motives; the free determining will, here as elsewhere, arranges conditions, and marshals forces or motives, and thus determines the action of the executive will" (p 304).

What is particularly to be noted is that man's nature is *Ideal* as well as actual. It is something always above him, to be sought after, struggled for, realised. He is conscious of a higher law for his life than the impulses of his animal nature From both without and within incitements to follow that higher law and to realise that higher nature come to him. But he may choose to *attend* to them or not in his freedom. There are other influences —desires and feelings—that would keep him from attending to the higher call and from following the better way. He is always free to *choose* the higher or the lower. In this sense he is "captain of his fate." His is a rising nature and an ever-enlarging self. He becomes a centre of self-directed action, a free agent, forming a character, impressing himself on the world. When the lower influences conflict with the higher, he can go on freely forming himself according to either. No doubt he will, as a rule, choose and act and go on forming himself according to the way in which he has previously formed himself. But this self-formation has been effected through a course of free action all throughout. "Character," says Dr. Ladd, "is the self as it has been formed by habits of will." It is not merely that we always choose according to our character at any given moment of our history, and are therefore free in the "soft deterministic" sense, but that in our choosing we have been continuously either forming our character or perpetuating it. Yet character does not in this life become inexorably fixed. It does not follow that a man *must* inevitably continue to act as he has been previously forming himself. His power of *choice* and inner free action is such that he may suddenly and quite unexpectedly, not only to others but to himself, begin to attend and yield himself up to some influence which may be in itself *physically* weak, but morally strong, that leads him from that moment to reverse his previous course of life and modes of thinking, feeling, and acting, and to begin to seek to form an entirely new kind of character, which, however, is not *foreign* to him as a man, but is his true (ideal) nature. This is abundantly illustrated in cases of conversion—religious and other, especially religious—and is not to be explained wholly by the accumulation of previous unconscious workings apart from all acts of will in relation to them.

We reach the highest point when the self becomes conscious of a call to a completely *spiritual* life in harmony with the Divine will, in which the lower nature has to be risen above entirely—so far as it stands in opposition—the lower self to be sacrificed in obedience to the highest Duty, the merely individual interests transcended in the interests of a wider, even a universal Love, and the will brought into unity with the will of God Here, again, there may be much initiatory disinclination and struggle, but the man is still free to *choose* and to strive after that Divine Ideal. He may, however, be so strongly held by the self as he has formed it that he cannot in practice rise above what Coleridge describes as "the prudential life." It is *the one self*, but there has now shone upon it the possibility of a far higher self, which makes it seem that there are two selves—a lower and a higher. The higher self, however, is really just the man's true nature, shining upon him and claiming him. But it is ever something to be freely chosen and realised.

Thus, from the lowliest beginnings, we witness a *self* with a certain nature, or with certain characteristics. But as we rise in the scale the self expands, and with it expands power of choice and of action. From the very first, there is a form of *will* and a measure of freedom this is of the very essence of the life of every conscious creature; no being is the mere slave of the material organism, which is only there to serve it. But only with the expanding self does the freedom grow, till in rational man, with his Ideal as well as his actual "nature," we find a *personal* centre of power both of choice and action He becomes a Cause— an originating Cause—in the world of mechanism, in which, of course, again to quote Coleridge, "he can only act outwardly by confluence with the laws of Nature." Man thus, while standing rooted in Nature, rises out of it as the completest self-expression of that spiritual element which has been deepest of all from the very first. Free-will, so far from being the extraordinary thing, the appearance of which in man is held by some to be so inexplicable and so incredible, is but the manifestation of a Power that has been steadily moving on toward this end and gradually rising in its manifestation.

There is, certainly, even in the highest human volitions, a physical side to them in all their working, but if we keep in view the fundamental fact of the *unity* of the physical with the spiritual, of which it is, in fact, only the expression, this relation to the physical, as we have already seen, creates no difficulty. It certainly affords no ground whatever for transferring the origination of our acts of will from the spiritual side to the physical. That can only be done on the principles of pure mechanical Materialism, however it may be disguised. On such a theory it is " matter " that rules, matter that is supreme, not spirit. But it is ever the personality that is deepest and active. It is not my brain that wills the deed any more than it is my arm that does it; it is *I* who will it; it is *I* who do it, and therefore it is *I* who am responsible for it. And inasmuch as it is I who form myself, I am responsible for what I become. I receive a certain ground or germ of character by inheritance, but at the centre of it there is that spiritual self which develops into personality— that rational self that I am, with the power of choice and free action that characterises such a self. Once again, to quote Professor Wundt: " The facts of physiological inheritance make it extremely probable that, if our investigations could penetrate to the very beginnings of the individual life, we should find there the nucleus of an independent personality, not determinable from without, because prior to all external determination." It may be said that this nucleus of personality is itself the product of the past; but if we recognise the presence and working of the spiritual element in *all the past*, we shall see that this self cannot be the product of merely mechanical working. It is the highest manifestation of the Spiritual.

We shall now resume and conclude this discussion of Free-will by considering the subject in its relation to the Source of the World and of ourselves.

CHAPTER V

FREE-WILL IN RELATION TO GOD AS THE SOURCE OF THE WORLD AND OURSELVES; THE CHRISTIAN DOCTRINE OF FREEDOM

As already said, apart from the recognition of human freedom as a new causal element which enters the world, it is impossible to rise from the contemplation of the world to an ethical God, or to reconcile its actual appearance with the reality of such a Being. When Mr Mallock (in an article in the *Contemporary Review* for July 1905, and in his *Reconstruction of Belief*) seeks to show a way "through matter to Mind," his determined rejection of Free-will lands him in an ultimate Mind of a kind that we can reverence very much less than Spencer's Unknowable, a Mind (if it be indeed a *Mind*) which it is impossible that any moral being can ever look up to as his God. He says very truly that if we accept the utterance of Science that "there is nothing in Mind and Consciousness not previously in matter, matter must contain potentially everything that is in Mind or Consciousness." Therefore, since Free-will does not come in, we are led to "two simple truths . . . one is that the mind-state or brain-state of a man, at any moment to-day, was, if we assume the processes of Nature to be uniform, fore-written in the special arrangement of a certain number of particles at the time when all matter was a diffused and nebulous mass; and the other is that this arrangement of those particular particles was implied and fore-written in, and was only made possible by, a correspondingly specific patterning of the nebula as a whole." Spencer's "indefinite incoherent homogeneity" had thus no existence: "There is no indefiniteness in Science . . and the atomic arrangement of the so-called indefinite nebula, though it may have been simpler, can have been no less precise and peculiar than that of the most complex organisms which by the process of Evolution have emerged from it." So far, the movement here is in the right direction if we wish to get "through matter to Mind" But we can only reach a truly *Divine* Mind at the beginning if we recognise a stage at which Free-will comes in and begins to act. Not only so, but we have no warrant at all for concluding to Mind or Spirit at the beginning, unless we recognise its effective causal existence at the end. If there is no *freedom* in the finite world, there is no real Mind or Spirit anywhere that we can know of or infer, and it is groundless to speak of such an existence at the beginning. Why should we talk about Freedom at all, if the thing has no existence in the finite world? How can we ever hope on scientific principles to reach it in the Ultimate Being? The question is foreclosed at the outset.

What Mr. Mallock says is true only up to the point where freedom emerges. Otherwise, we should have God —the original Mind—directly responsible, nay, deliberately providing for, not only all the good, but every form and kind of wickedness in the world For it is all—up to every event of to-day—up to, Mr. Mallock says, "every word in to-day's newspaper,"—up to, therefore, every wicked thought that has ever been in any bad man's mind, and every cruel and evil deed that has ever been perpetrated,—*solely* the outcome of that which was impressed on or contained in the original matter of the Universe. If this is what Science leads us up to, it is certainly not *God* that we find or aught that can be called Divine But this consequence only arises through accepting the denial—not by Science, indeed, but by certain interpreters of Science—of human Free-will, free choice and action. From this point onward another personal element than the Divine has entered into the making of the world and into the making of man. This also has, indeed, been provided for in the primal constitution of the Universe. It does not, as Mr. Mallock seems to suggest, give us only a God in the making, but a God *whose purpose it was* to bring into being free agents in His own likeness—the only elements of real worth or value in His creation. For, up to this point, there is *nothing but machinery*. All that we behold and experience is but the working out by absolutely necessary laws of a vast Cosmic mechanism, with no element of real personality in the whole.

We have already (in chap. x. of Part I.) pointed out the fallacy underlying Mr. Mallock's reference to such a supposed necessary relation of the individual human spirit to the Universal Spirit as involves that we are constrained by it, and are merely "the puppets of Spirit," which is as bad as to be "the puppets of Matter." The very idea of Spirit is that of *influence*, not force or constraint. And if individual spirits are produced, then, in order to *be* spirits, they must be free. But the present argument is that everything—every feeling and thought and action—is necessarily contained and ensured in the primitive material of the Universe. let us look at it as stated in *The Reconstruction of Belief*. "All that is, is implicit in all that was." "To deny this is to deny Science—the possibility of any trustworthy inference whatever" This includes what is in the brain; *e g.*, the brain of Augustine when writing the famous sentence, "Thou hast made us for Thyself, and we are restless until we find rest in Thee." "Such a brain, according to Science, were we able to observe its secrets, would exhibit in the layers of the cortex—in the pyramidal layers especially—a cellular or molecular patterning of a kind so distinct and peculiar, that the ejaculation of the saint could be read in it by the ideal scientific spectator as surely as an Egyptian inscription is read by the instructed scholar." Now, this last statement may be true, but the question at issue is, whether the human personality—the Will—has had no part in this formation. Mr. Mallock himself has shown, in the illustration formerly quoted, how conscious states can influence brain states.

The arrangement at that moment existing in the brain of Augustine is carried back by regressive steps to the very beginning. An illustration is given from billiard balls. " Let us suppose that a number of billiard balls have been set in motion by the single stroke of a cue, and continue, we will say, for a minute forming themselves into different figures. From any one change in this grouping taking place in any one second, a spectator possessed of complete knowledge of the circumstances, including, of course, the condition of the bed of the billiard-table, and the cushions, would be able to infer their position at any one of the seconds preceding it, till he reached their original collocation and the strength of the blow that started them To deny this is, in Huxley's words, ' to deny Science'" But suppose that one of those billiard balls had in it the possibility of originating action of its own, of inhibition, or refusing to be just driven in the direction in which the cue would send it, and could deflect its course, striking other balls in so doing, a new element would thus have entered, the result would be different; and although *this kind of action* would have been provided for in the original nebula, its precise character was not predetermined. Such action as we have supposed would, of course, be impossible on purely physical principles, but it is just of that kind which we claim for the free Will. A more elaborate illustration is given from the arrangements of tessera; but it is to the same effect, and we need not follow it out We can never get to God in this way. In fact, a doctrine founded on the denial of Freedom gives us *neither God nor man.*

But from the existence of free personal spirit in man we are inevitably led back *through matter and mind in their unity* to God as Spirit, the Source and the Life of all. In the Divine Being, of course, those problems that arise concerning freedom as it exists in finite developing beings have no place. In God, as the all-perfect ethical Being, Freedom and Necessity—that is, rational and ethical necessity—are one. Just because He is perfect ethical Being, He can only act in one way,—that of perfect Reason, perfect Righteousness, perfect Love,—and He so acts in the perfect freedom of His perfect nature. Man's Ideal is to attain to a like ethical union of freedom and necessity, when his will shall be so established in Reason, Righteousness, and Love that he shall only choose the true and the good and act accordingly. This leads us to state briefly, in conclusion,

The Full Christian Doctrine of Freedom

Human Freedom is implied in the assertion of man's moral and spiritual nature, of his responsibility and sin. While mere Theism has always a formidable difficulty before it in the actual condition of the world, Christianity, as a religion of Redemption, is based on the fact that the world is *not* (yet) what God means it to become. It asserts that the process of the world has not been a wholly mechanical one, that man is not nature only but spirit and free, and that, in his freedom, he yields himself up to the lower self when he ought to follow the higher—which is *sin*

The Christian "Salvation" is salvation from sin in this sense. The evil in the world is for Christianity not a mere physical necessity, the result of an inevitable mechanical process, something wholly unavoidable, but the result of man's failure to rise to his true life and to work freely with God as he ought to do and might do.

This implies that, while the will is free to choose, it may be in bondage to certain powers or influences which hinder or prevent its proper action. The same influences may also prevent its proper *choice*, but then they are *freely* allowed to do so: the man *consents* to the rule of the world or of his lower nature over him. Man, in the Christian view of him, is at once free and not free. He is free to *choose* even the holiest and the best; but he may suffer himself to be so held by his lower nature that he will not make that choice. And even if he does make the choice, he may find himself not free to act it out. He may be in bondage to his lower nature But as long as he is normally *man*, he is responsible for his choice, and in his choice of the lower is condemned, not only before God, but before his own conscience "I approve the better, but follow the worse," is a universal confession. "When I would do good," says St. Paul, "evil is present with me." With the "mind" he is free to choose, and actually does choose and "consent" to the higher Law that "it is holy and just and good", he would fain follow it; "but another law"— a more external one—brings him ever into subjection. It is from this condition that the Christian salvation delivers us, bringing us into an ever-enlarging freedom. It brings new influences to bear upon us in such a manner that our *attention* is gained for them, and they become far stronger motives than aught that comes from the world or the lower nature.

The perfect freedom of man is only gained, as Epictetus said of old, "when whatever is the will of God is our will, and whatever is not the will of God is not our will", when, that is, we freely choose and abide by the Divine Will, not merely as expressing itself in the mechanism of Nature (although that too is included), but as it is declared in Reason and Conscience, as it is revealed in Christ, and as it is indicated in the Providence, or rational ordering and overruling, that is over our life. Then only are we fully *free* in the highest sense of the word—when we are at one with the Law of our Life—when the Divine Will becomes the principle of *our* Life and Will. And the more firmly we are grounded in this freedom, the less frequently will such problems as we have been discussing arise The more completely our will is at one with the highest Law of our Life, the more complete will our freedom be; the nearer will it approach to that Divine Freedom that is one with necessity. Just as habitual acts become automatic, so shall we act at once freely and naturally.

We are not concerned to go back on the dry and wearisome discussions of Freedom in which the Theologians of bygone days engaged, beginning with Augustine and the Pelagian controversy. The earlier Christian Fathers, however, maintained the freedom of the human will. As Hagenbach says, " All the Greek Fathers, as well as the apologists, Justin, Tatian, Athenagoras, Theophilus, and the Latin author Minucius Felix, also the theologians of the Alexandrian school, Clement and Origen, exalt the autonomy of the human soul with the freshness of youth and a tincture of Hellenistic idealism, but influenced by a practical human interest." The same is true of Tertullian and Irenæus. Neander says, " The Alexandrian teachers gave the greatest prominence to Free-will as the *conditio sine quâ non* of righteous Divine judgment, in combating with the Gnostics " But, without going back to these controversies, let us notice briefly the three great difficulties into which Mr Mallock says the theological question ran up—one of which has been already mentioned

The first question is, " How God, who is admitted to be

the Author of everything, can escape the charge of being Himself the Author of Evil." This is answered, of course, by the establishment of the fact of human freedom While God is the Author of the free being, He is not the Author of that being's actions. The faculty of Freedom constitutes man a responsible Cause in God's world.

To the further question, "How, since God's will is Omnipotent, the puny will of man can act in opposition to it, as it must do if God hates sin, and man is the sole cause of it," the simplest answer is that Omnipotence is not necessarily always in exercise, just as in man there may be power the forth-putting of which is rationally withheld. If God created man free, we have in this very fact, perhaps, the highest manifestation of His Omnipotence—just at the point where it seems to withhold its action—and if man is meant as a free being to come into voluntary harmony with God, for Omnipotence to interfere would be a contradiction—an annulling of the creation when it had reached its highest point.

To the final question, " How, since God has complete fore-knowledge of everything, and sees man's future acts as clearly as if they were already committed, man is able to act in any other way than one, namely, the way by which, as if on a chart, is delineated the Divine foreknowledge," it is sufficient to reply that the Divine foreknowledge is not *compulsion*. Although God may know beforehand all that will happen, it by no means follows that He *causes* everything to happen, or that it is necessitated. Even *a man* can foresee the course of events to a large degree, but he knows that his foresight of them is not their cause, and may be convinced that men act quite freely. God, we may believe, is responsible for the world with the natures that naturally arise in it, but He is not responsible in the same way for what happens in the acting out of such natures as are gifted with freedom He is responsible, indeed, for the *existence* of the world that makes the appearance of such natures possible, and, indirectly, for the actual world, but this responsibility is not His because He has *determined* all the actions of His creatures, or because they stand in such a line of inevitable succession that no other action was possible for them. Pope's words may still be quoted—

"God,
... binding Nature fast in Fate,
Left free the Human Will"

We have also to bear in mind that Time—succession—does not exist for God in the way in which it does for us. With Him there may rather be an "Eternal *Now.*" "A thousand years are with the Lord as one day." And although He does not *determine* all the acts of free beings. "He sees the end from the beginning"

PART III

IMMORTALITY

CHAPTER I

Alternative Views

OUR treatment of Christian Theism would be incomplete without a section bearing on the survival of the soul and Immortality. Belief in a Hereafter and an eternal life in God is an integral part of Christianity. Strictly speaking, the distinctively Christian conception is that of an "eternal life" into which men may rise here and now through spiritual union with God. It has thus a higher reason for itself than the reasons which are commonly urged on behalf of the general conception of "Immortality," and the Christian grounds of belief must not be confounded with the more general arguments Apart from this distinctively Christian ground, although a general confidence in a future existence may be (as we believe it is) well warranted, there are many uncertainties connected with the subject, and alternative views are possible.

1. Although this is not the view to which we are ultimately led, it is possible to think of Immortality (or even survival) as belonging to the "fit" or qualified members of the race only. Our Lord in His teaching spoke of it as something belonging to "the righteous," His disciples, the members of the kingdom of God He spoke of "the resurrection of the just" who are the "sons of God," the "sons of the Resurrection,"—"those who are accounted worthy to obtain that Age," etc.; and although He said that man "could not destroy the soul," and that

"all live unto God," such sayings are limited by their context. In the parable of the rich man and Lazarus, we may have only such an adoption of current views as is natural in a parable In His general teaching concerning the "Judgment" and "last things," the scene is laid *on the earth*, and what takes place applies to those alive at "the coming of the Son of Man"

By His apostles the Christian Immortality is invariably represented as something to be "striven after," to be "laid hold on," to run for as for a prize which might be missed. As a general principle, it is to be entered on as the reward of "patient continuance in well-doing"; in its most distinctive form, it is to be realised through spiritual union with Christ, "who *is* our Life." And although this may be described as an "aristocratic Immortality," it pertains to the aristocracy of the highest ethical life, which is surely the true nobility, most entitled to receive what is described as "the crown of life that fadeth not away."

2. It would also be quite in keeping with all that we know of Evolution to regard the attainment of a future progressive life as something pertaining to "the fit" only— a continuation of the process which reaches its earthly consummation in man as man—the rising up of the human personality into the fulness of a higher life of sonship in relation to God. If such a limited Immortality seems repellent, it must be remembered that it embraces all, whether "Christians" or not, who have really begun to live the spiritual life in union with God, and that *there may be reasons* why, apart from the quickening of the higher life of the spirit, continuance in being may be impossible—even physically impossible. "It is the spirit that quickeneth," and it is the spirit that forms the "spiritual body." Even God, when He places Himself under the limitations necessary for creation, cannot do just "anything whatsoever"; and, for aught we know to the contrary, the

alternatives may have been (just as they are in relation to the suffering undergone by lower creatures ere man was reached) either no creation at all, or this limited Immortality and final "survival of the fittest." If it seems *hard* to us, it may be even harder for the great Source of our being and Lover of souls, but none the less, the alternatives *may* be those suggested.

3. The silence of the Scriptures with respect to the condition of those who have not risen into the new life of the Spirit, to whose operation in men resurrection and eternal life are distinctly ascribed, is certainly striking. The Judgment is always represented as taking place on the return of Christ to *the earth*, and those then living are judged and punished. But apart from the visions of the Apocalypse, only in two passages (John v. 28 and Acts xxiv. 15)—neither of which is beyond question—is there any reference to the resurrection of the unbelieving or the wicked. According to St Paul, they seem simply to be left in "death" (whatever that may imply), without any "resurrection."

4 Apart from the Scriptures, to many the thought of the countless multitudes of human beings who must be included if Immortality is universal, embracing all who have ever lived—many of them scarcely human, some even, in certain respects, apparently lower than some of the higher animals—is a most oppressive thought, well-nigh making any belief in Immortality impossible. The present writer remembers well the relief with which in days of mental struggle long gone by, he met with the suggestion in a work of "Thorndale Smith's" (*Thorndale, or the Conflict of Opinions*) that it was not necessary to affirm a future life for every human being without exception, but only for such as had attained a certain stage of development and of moral life; may we not say, only for such as had *worth?* In our ignorance of the conditions of Immortality, we cannot

absolutely affirm it for all who have ever lived. Must we not draw the line at least at the distinctly human? But again, where is that line to be fixed? Do not some of the higher animals manifest elements of worth to a degree as great as some in human form? If we include all that are human, can we exclude the whole of the lower creatures whose lives have made human life possible? But if the idea of a limited Immortality seems more congruous to any one, there is nothing *positively known* to prevent his holding to that belief. As already said, there may be even physical reasons why it cannot be otherwise.

But, on the other hand, (1) the Christian heart and mind, or may we not say, the fully developed human feeling, cannot rest satisfied in the thought of a *limited* future existence. Unless there be, unknown to us, some physical reason which makes continuance in being impossible for some, the Christian conception of God as the Universal Father, as well as our thought of Him as the perfect Reason and Love, seem to compel us to take a wider and more hopeful view of the destinies, not of the individual merely, but of the *race*. We are bound together by countless ties as one human family, and the present is closely affiliated with the past. We are very apt to forget that God cares, not for the individual only, but for the *race*, for the whole human family, and deals with Humanity as a unity. ("Christ Jesus, who gave Himself a ransom for *all*; the testimony to be borne in its own times.") The harsh and isolated individualism we are so apt to fall into has no place with Him. We are apt, too, to forget what we owe to those who have gone before us, apart from whose life and toil and suffering we could never have become what we are. In the glowing words of Professor James: "Bone of our bone, and flesh of our flesh, are these half-brutish prehistoric brothers. Girdled about with the immense darkness of this mysterious Universe even as we are, they were born and died, suffered and struggled. Given over to fearful crime and passion, plunged in the blackest ignorance, preyed upon by hideous and grotesque delusions, yet steadfastly serving the profoundest of ideals in their fixed faith that existence in any form is better than non-existence, they ever rescued triumphantly from the jaws of ever imminent destruction the torch of life, which, thanks to them, now lights the world for us" (*Human Immortality*, p. 66). We surely ought to think of those to whom we owe so much. We cannot be content just to leave them in the darkness for ever. And, in historic time, there have been myriads who had no opportunity of rising to those higher conditions which may be supposed to make continuance in life possible There are millions to-day to whom the gates of this possible Hereafter have never been opened. If we believe in God as the Infinite Reason and Love; if we remember that we and all beings in all worlds live and move in an *Infinite* which is around and before us in all its fulness; if we believe that, as Christianity teaches, our being has its source in an Infinite Love which goes forth into creation just in order to spread abroad itself in finite forms infinitely, if we take seriously the Christian conception of God as the Father of men, and believe in the reality of a perfect Love that cannot be satiated,—it will not be so hard also to believe that an existence beyond bodily death stands open to the human race, that in other environments life shall be carried forward and perfected, that what the Infinite Love desires shall be realised in the working of the perfect Reason and Might of Him " who faints not, neither is weary, neither is there any searching of His understanding."

(2) Our Theodicy has implied a universal Purpose and a Divine working which does not cease with " time " in this world, and which has regard not only to the individual but to the race. We certainly do not witness the complete working out of a worthy Divine purpose in this present

world, whether we think of individual lives or of the life of Humanity as a whole. There have been, and are, individual lives which present on the whole not unworthy representations of an Ideal life in various aspects of it. But in none, save One, do we see the very highest realised in all its completeness; and if each individual life perishes entirely in death, we cannot but ask, what ultimate value or good there is in it all? We do not seek Immortality because this life is not worth living, but because it is so well worth living. We feel that we have never yet nearly realised the possibilities that belong to the life we have been made partakers of. Our desire is not for mere happiness, but for higher, truer, better life. In our individual lives we seem only to have a beginning—a beginning with a certain measure of approach towards a goal which, although it shines upon us, is never actually reached in this world—one which is, in fact, *infinite* in its scope. Nor do we think of ourselves merely, but of the many who have had no real opportunity in this earthly life, who have yet carried its burdens and endured its sufferings.[1]

Nor can we behold the destined end in the perfecting of the human race as such *on the earth*. Even were that perfection reached in this world, the world itself, Science assures us, must, in all probability, become some time or other, be it longer or shorter, unfit for the abode of human beings—unfit to sustain life itself—so that, if this life were the only possible one, all would come to nothing in the long

[1] Renan puts it well from the personal point of view, when he says "I should like two things first, that my sacrifices to goodness and to truth should not have been offered up for nothing and to empty vacancy,—I do not want to be paid for them, but I desire that they may fulfil some purpose, and, in the second place, I should be very glad that what little I have done should meet with somebody's acknowledgment I want God's esteem, nothing more, this is not exorbitant, is it? Do we reproach the dying soldier with taking an interest in the issue of the battle, and wishing to know whether his general-in-chief is pleased with him?" (*Philos Dialogues*, p. 79).

run And even were this not the case, what of all those who have suffered and perished before the perfection of the race has been reached? Manifestly, a worthy Divine purpose in the creation cannot be worked out in this finite world, which, just because of its finiteness, must come to an end. It is true that in some way life may be started again; but this implies the possibility of existence beyond its present conditions, which is all that is required as a physical foundation for belief in Immortality.

CHAPTER II

REASONS FOR BELIEF

"*Scientific Monism*" *and Future Life*

THE "Monism" which we have criticised is in general *negative* with respect to Immortality. Spencer is practically silent on the subject, although the closing pages of his *Autobiography* show that even he could not wholly stifle a personal longing for the assurance of something beyond the Universe that we can see. His principles of the disintegration of Matter and the dissipation of Energy bring the world that has been evolved to an end again; Evolution is ever succeeded by dissolution, and, although the cycle may be recommenced, there is no suggestion of the survival of the individual. This conclusion, however,—the necessary end of all evolution in dissolution,—has an important bearing on the problem. Buchner is also silent or negative on the question. Carus write beautifully and impressively concerning the certainty and the value of " Immortality " : " Our existence after death will not merely be a dissolution into the All, where all individual features of our spiritual existence are destroyed. Our existence after death will be a continuance of our individual spirituality, a continuance of our thoughts and ideals. As sure as the law of cause and effect is true, so sure is the continuance of the soul-life even after the death of the individual, according to the law of the preservation of form" (*The Soul of Man*, pp 423, 424). But in that "death of the individual" the personal self seems to perish, and the value of our "spiritual immortality" (by no means to be made little of) is solely for the future of the race, which must itself, as we have seen, come to an end on the earth. Haeckel is even contemptuous in his denial of Immortality. "We come (there)," he says, "to that highest point of superstition, which is regarded as the impregnable citadel of all mystical and dualistic notions" (*Riddle of the Universe*, p. 67). He seems to take it for granted that Immortality is necessarily associated with "Dualism." Professor Lloyd Morgan, however, in his *Introduction to Comparative Psychology*, affirms "the conservation of consciousness" to be real, and in his article in the *Contemporary Review* before referred to, he says that, while we cannot at present solve the problem of Immortality, "Science gives no grounds for denying it," and, that it is in every way well to live so that "if in some way that we do not understand, that which with our limitations of conception we speak of as the future life should be realised, you will have no cause to regret your action" (*Contemporary Review*, June 1904).

Within the last quarter of a century or so there has been a great change in the attitude of men of Science, and of Evolutionists in particular, towards this subject. In the days when Spencer, Tyndall, and Huxley seemed to sweep the field, it looked as if the cessation of being at death was about to become a settled article of the scientific creed. But in recent times we have Physicists like Crookes and Lodge, Evolutionists like Wallace, Fiske, and Le Conte, not to speak of many Psychologists and Metaphysicians, earnestly affirming either the reality or the possibility of a life beyond. In his Ingersoll Lecture, Dr. Osler, with the physical facts full in view, and with a most critical attitude towards all supposed "proofs," still assumes a hope. To one who has lived in the period referred to, the change seems a very great and suggestive one. While it witnesses to an ineradicable instinct in man, the difference of tone is owing perhaps as much to our better knowledge (or sense of our want of knowledge) of the inner constitution of "matter" as to the undoubtedly valuable work of the Society for Psychical Research. A general sobering down of Science, a growing consciousness of her limitations, and an increasing development of human sympathy, have also had much to do with it.

The main Difficulty

The main difficulty and the real ground of objections, whether these are urged by Haeckel or by any one else, is the relation that certainly holds good during mundane life, from the humblest creature up to man, between the bodily organism and the conscious mental life. It *seems* to follow that when that relation is annulled, as it appears to be in death, all manifestation of the mental life that has in some way, to all appearance, depended on it, or been in inseparable connection with it, must come to an end, just as truly as the lower functions of our bodily life are then ended. And this seems to be the case even although we do not suppose that the brain *produces* thought: whatever the relationship between Mind and Body may be, it *seems* to be one that is essential for the existence of each.

Spiritualism

Now, it must be frankly admitted that we have as yet no complete scientific evidence of the survival of the soul after bodily dissolution. In only one case can it be positively affirmed that a spiritual Being has manifested Himself from the other side. In that case only is the affirmation open to universal verification. There are many alleged instances of such reappearances, or communications, adduced by modern Spiritualism ; not a few have been collected by the Society for Psychical Research, and by others ; numerous examples are set forth by Mr. Myers in his valuable and suggestive work on *Human Personality and the Survival of Bodily Death*; but with respect to most of these cases there is always a doubt left, either as to the sufficiency of the evidence, or as to how the appearances, etc., are to be accounted for. Since the human Personality has been more closely studied, in its more hidden powers, and in its exceptional and abnormal conditions, the possibilities attaching to such states are seen to be very great, and may go a long way towards explaining many of the facts that Spiritualism relies on. For his own part, the present writer must honestly say that, although his attempts to get some satisfaction from Spiritualism proved abortive, he cannot but feel that there are cases (in Mr. Myers' book and elsewhere) which, *as far as one can see*, cannot be explained (if the evidence be sufficient, as in the cases referred to it *seems* to be) otherwise than as visitations or communications from a spiritual world ; yet he cannot feel such confidence in them as to build upon them as evidence,—the appeal is too much to what is individual, to be effective in a general argument,—and in certain more definite alleged instances of spirit-communication—through Mediums especially—the evidence seems to come *far short* of being convincing. The triviality and positive contradictions in what purport to be communications from a spiritual world are in themselves strong reasons for suspicion.

Reasons why no Demonstration should be given

There are, however, important *reasons* why, if there be a life beyond, it should not be manifest to us in this present life. If it be indeed a life *beyond sense,* how can it be manifested to us while we are in a world where our senses (or sense in some form) are the sole means, we do not say of communication, but of observation of that which is beyond us? We know for certain that even in this world there is all around us a vast region of possible sights and sounds and other experiences which may be, in some measure, open to other creatures, but which is closed to us. So may there not be a real spiritual world all around us, of which we are normally unconscious—a world which can only, under certain abnormal conditions of our organism, not at our command, be in any striking manner made manifest?

And we can see good and wise reasons why this should be so. It is in relation to this present world we have to live our life; not in relation to that other world as a manifested sphere. Would our ordinary life in this world be possible, if " the other world " were as manifest and real to us as this one is? One can easily see points at which its realised presence would operate so as to make our life here, in the various relationships which we hold, very uncomfortable, if not impossible. Our organs of discernment have, we must believe, been developed on the lines of what would be most *useful* to us, if open communication with the unseen world would not have been useful in the furtherance of life on earth, there was in this fact a good reason why it should be closed to us. The mere belief in a life beyond is not necessarily elevating in itself. We have abundant evidence of this in our knowledge of ancient Egypt, where the other world seemed to be made almost as real as this present world (it is perhaps for this reason that there is so little reference to a future life in the Mosaic religion), and from observation of African savages of to-day.

But still more important, if the idea of the Creator is, as Christianity teaches, to develop in man a character which reflects, or in some real measure realises and expresses, the

Divine character in finite forms, it is necessary that man should become established in goodness in its highest forms—in the love and practice of goodness *for its own sake purely*. Otherwise, man can never stand forth in the moral image of God. But if another world, in which the rewards and penalties incurred in this present life were made manifest as our inevitable experience, if that other world were as naked and open to our vision as is this present world, such a development of the highest character would seem to be impossible. In spite of ourselves, we should have an eye to the consequences. If we were as sure that it ultimately paid to be good as is the boy to whom his father has promised some coveted treasure if he obeys, we should be strongly tempted to be good just because it paid, which would be the negation of the highest form of goodness; "other-wordliness" would be just as fatal to the highest life as "this-worldliness" is to it now. There is thus a *rational necessity* that the life beyond should be veiled from our eyes, an *ethical* reason why we should have to "walk by faith and not by sight."[1] If man ever reaches a condition in which the open vision of the other world will not be injurious but helpful to him, then, we may believe, that vision will not be withheld. It is possible that we are moving on towards such a stage of our earthly life.

In what follows, therefore, we shall (1) state what seem to be the chief grounds of our *faith* in a life beyond; (2) try to show the reasons we have, in the light of Science, for regarding such a life as *possible*, and (3) state the specifically Christian doctrines of Continued Being, "Resurrection" and "Eternal Life."

---

[1] Professor Upton, in his Hibbert Lecture on *Theism*, maintains the same view "If earth is to be really a place for the growth of disinterested virtue and goodness, then *scientifically demonstrated knowledge as to the eternal consequences of moral conduct must be withheld*" (italics his). He quotes from Browning's "La Saisaz" in illustration (p 342)

Grounds of Belief

It is unnecessary to state a variety of reasons for believing in Immortality if the reality of God is held to have been established. If God is a Reality, Immortality for beings formed in His image is a certainty. It follows of necessity. A God who was only God to man in this present fleeting life would not be *God* at all. He would belong to Time merely, not to that Eternal sphere above Time which is that of the life of God, and to which, if He is what Christian Theism holds Him to be, He must intend to raise us. This was Christ's argument for Immortality. " God," He said, " is the God not of dead but of living persons "—referring to those who had departed *this* life (strictly, however, to those who were God's people); in the words of an apostolic writer, " He is not ashamed to be called their God, for He hath prepared for them a city "—that " city which has the foundations, whose architect and builder is God." If *God* is a Reality, Immortality is sure.

But, without assuming that Theism has been proved, we shall seek to show that the same facts of the Universe that lead to belief in God lead also to belief in Immortality.

1. There is the argument from *Reason as manifested in the evolution of the World.*

(1) If the world be that rational world which all Science assumes it to be, it must have a rational meaning as a whole, and it must have an ultimate rational consummation. These are simply necessities of Reason. If, not only for the individual, but also for the race, it all ends in nothing, what rational meaning, or end, can be ascribed to it? Such an anticlimax would be the very negation of Reason. What we witness is an *evolution*, but if nothing permanent comes out of the process, what sense has there

been in it ? An eternal beginning and an eternal passing away of all that has been produced, a perpetually recurring cycle of evolutions and dissolutions, with no abiding results, seems so utterly opposed to all that is rational as to be quite incredible. If Evolution has done such great things for us in the past, may we not hope for still greater things in the future, not merely in a world where everything is transient, but in an enduring sphere ? A non-Theistic writer says, " Meanwhile we, who weep at the self-inflicted miseries of man, rest in sure and certain hope that no force and no combination of forces can stop that process of Evolution which from a speck of jelly has developed such living forms as Charles Darwin and Herbert Spencer, and which has produced the beauty of the earth and the heavens from formless ether " (Hird, *Evolution*, p 230) This is but poor consolation, and it does not bring us within sight of any rational meaning in the process. What avails this grand prospect to the thousands for whose miseries we now "weep", what good shall this future perfection of Humanity bring to *them*; what avails the work Evolution accomplishes for our great men, if, after it all, it but pulls them to pieces again; and what signifies their work ultimately for the race, when the last favoured members of it shall have perished ? We are rationally compelled to believe that this "evolution" which has done such great things for us in the past, *proceeds* in ways unseen by us now, and that it brings a real and permanent good to the beings to whom it has made such an expectation possible.

Reason, if it is present in the process, must be vindicated in the outcome. Individual forms have been for ever passing away; the process has been moving on ever towards the higher development of species, and this again with a view to the introduction of still higher species; but if, when the goal has been reached in man, the human species and each individual member of it, ultimately fall back again into nothingness, this would indeed seem to be the *reductio ad absurdum* of the process itself. It may be said that there is possibly some ultimate result beyond anything that we can see or imagine; but what we have to seek is something that will commend itself to that reason in us which is acknowledged on all hands to be the crown of the whole world-process.

(2) This terrene evolution has issued in the production of *spiritual beings* who live their life in a spiritual world which is far more real to them than the world of "matter and force" that issues in it. It is in that spiritual life—intellectual, emotional, free, effective—that all our real life is centred. It is to this entirely invisible sphere of mind, feeling, sentiment, moral conduct, religious aspiration and life, that all our interests belong, and it is in relation to that *spiritual world* that each man's character is formed and his destiny worked out. Surely, then, if the whole preceding working in the material sphere has issued in this spiritual world of human life and activity, we are bound to believe that in that world there are permanent results to ourselves as individuals of the life we have lived therein.

We must therefore believe that, as the process proceeds, and individual forms appear and disappear, there are lasting *results* gathered up in a world that is unseen—in that spiritual sphere in which our higher human life is actually lived—however little able we may be to trace the working; and that the highest results of Evolution, reached in human personalities, do not become at length the same as if they had never been gained at all. If in human personalities the goal of a rational process is reached, the simple fact that it has been reached by rational working forbids the thought that these personalities are simply dissolved again into nothingness.

Death

(3) Here also, under this argument from Reason, we have to take account of the origin and real meaning of *Death*. We shrink from the "King of Terrors," but really he has been a very good friend to man. We have already seen that death came in to serve the development of higher life. Unicellular organisms may, in a sense, live for ever, but they can never develop into anything higher. Apart from death there would have been no progress, and man would never have been reached at all. And after he was reached, had not death continued operative, not one of us now living would have had the chance of participating in life; there would have been no room for us; not only no "platter at Nature's board," but no place for us in the world. Moreover, apart from death, the tenderest feelings and highest aims of Humanity would not have been awakened. Death is here as the servant of life. What a contradiction it would be, therefore, if that same ordinance of death should become the final destruction of the very life to produce and to serve which it came into play—when that life had reached its highest form! Death, therefore, which has as its function *the promotion of Life*, cannot be that final destroyer of life which we have been too ready to imagine it might be. May it not rather still be, as it has been in the past, a means to a higher stage of being; may it not very well be true that death is

"but a covered way which opens into light"?[1]

---

[1] G F. Fechner says, "Man lives on earth, not once but three times: the first stage of his life is continual sleep (in the womb); the second, sleeping and waking by turns; the third waking for ever. . . . The act of leaving the first stage for the second we call Birth, that of leaving the second for the third, Death Our way from the second to the third is not darker than our way from the first to the second one way leads us forth to see the world outwardly, the other to see it inwardly" (*Life after Death*, pp 14, 15)

2. There is the argument from *Love*. The Reason that is manifested in the Universe shows itself to be one with Love. This is its highest manifestation in man, and its highest law *for* man. The supremacy of Love over the life may be said to be universally acknowledged. But this Love is only another name for the Power which shows itself as formative in our Humanity. In other words, the Power that forms us men shows itself as a loving Power, with a good will toward us all. Whether we personalise that Power or not, we cannot doubt its good intention in giving us being, and in making itself felt as the highest Reality and the supreme Law of life, after it had wrought so long and patiently to reach us. Surely we must think of it as a " Love that will not let us go." If the supreme law of our life is Love, then the Power that gives us to discern this— imposes it on us, works it in us as the result of our experience —must itself be in such unison with that law that we can confidently say, " All's Law and all's Love." It has made *us* so that we cannot bear to part for ever with those whom it has made us love; and can that same formative and all-working Power permit us to be torn from itself by that which we have seen was employed as a means of reaching us ? In this present life there is much that inevitably works against the Love that is deepest in the creation , there is much suffering entailed on individuals ; some are snatched away before they have had full opportunity of living , hearts are ruthlessly severed in ways which our relation to our bodies alone can account for. Do all these experiences not only disappoint ourselves, but defeat the Love that gives us life, that rises in us as that which is highest and best, and that, in its finite form, binds hearts to hearts and to the great central Heart itself? Is all the suffering in human life endured in vain ? The past history of the evolution forbids the thought. Throughout its course there has been much suffering, but none of it has been in vain. *Man* is its final

product; and so we must believe that the sufferings of our human life, under the dominance of the Cosmical Reason and Love, are working out lasting good "to them that are exercised thereby." Moreover, the Love that lives in us is in itself something of God in us. It belongs in its essence to a higher realm than the physical. With nothing is the personality so completely identified as it is with the Love that inspires and dominates the life—it is its very essence, indeed. In the very existence of that Love in us we have something within us that is deathless. Surely we must say with Emerson,

> "Hearts are dust, hearts' loves remain;
> Heart's love will meet thee again."

3. There is the argument from *Spirit*. The all-formative Power is revealed as spirit within ourselves. We are self-conscious spirits in our inmost being. The result of the process of Evolution, so far, has been the impartation to us of this spiritual nature Now, man as spirit, however closely he may be related to his body, stands out of the world of Time and Sense—of Time and Space. We live also in that world, and receive impressions from it, but there is "an inmost centre in us all," that unifies and interprets sensations in a spiritual manner, which thus shows itself to be *above* their succession in time, and even, in its lowest form, to rise *out of* the world of Time and Sense We are made *Persons*, free, self-originating centres of Power. But we shall have to return to this subject of our spiritual being (which is quite in keeping with "Monism") in another connection Meanwhile we remark that it is one of the greatest of mistakes to speak of the deathless life as "future" merely, and of Eternity as something distant from us into which we enter only when we die. As spiritual beings we already live in Eternity, we are not to *be* immortal merely, we

already partake of a deathless life. In the words of Professor Lloyd Morgan, " We *are*—not shall be—immortal. This body, this series of mental processes, those temporal and spatial manifestations, may pass away. But that eternal essence which is of the spiritual order dwells securely in the now which is for ever" (see also H Munsterberg in *Atlantic Monthly* for April 1905 ; Royce's Ingersoll Lecture ; Haldane's *Pathway to Reality*)

4. We need only refer briefly to the *moral order*, which manifests itself as superior to the physical; to the need for events in that order working themselves out to a rational conclusion, and of character finding its fruition and that complete realisation which it does not find in this life. Justice, as well as Love, demands a continuity of Life beyond the present If that were lacking, the very highest conceptions and Ideals that have been caused to arise within us would be put to "permanent confusion." Justice to the individual self, with its often baffling experiences, crowned by death at the last, demands it, and we may well be sure that this feeling for justice will not be disappointed

> "Thou wilt not leave us in the dust ·
> Thou madest man, he knows not why;
> He thinks he was not made to die ;
> And Thou hast made him , Thou art just."

5. We need also only mention the *instinctive craving* for Immortality It is almost universal, although it can be quenched, like all the higher feelings of our nature. It is decried by anti-Theistic writers as selfish and unreasonable. It is, we think, quite the reverse of that. Men do not seek it for themselves merely, but for man as man, and especially in view of the many who suffer in this life. We cannot understand the superior sympathy of those who can look upon their suffering fellow-mortals and be content to see them bereft of all future hope. But,

whatever its character, it is *there*, and it has not been given to mock or deceive us. Nay, there is more; there has been, as Mr. Fiske has so well shown, wrought in man by the very process of Evolution, not only a craving for Immortality, but *a belief in a world unseen* to which we stand in an ethical relation. Now, as all our inner experience has been wrought in us by something really existing outside of us, if here "only the subjective term is real, and the objective term is non-existent, it is something utterly without precedent in the whole history of creation" (*Through Nature to God*, p. 189).

6. There is the influence which the belief has exerted on man.

We know well that there are two sides to this, and, as we have seen, there are good reasons why the other world, or belief in it, should not so obtrude itself on us as to interfere with our present life. We know also the possibilities of superstition. Yet although belief in another world has not been an unmixed good, it has been under the influence of the conviction that this present world is not all, but that there are enduring results beyond death and the grave, and spiritual influences coming to us from that source, that the highest elements in our personal life have been developed Take away this belief from man; confine his outlook to this world only; then the descent into what would be but a higher animalism would be only too probable. Let us make Society ever so good on earth, if we rob man of Immortality his good becomes little else than animal felicity, and his being is unspeakably lowered and lessened. Indeed, the higher progress aimed at would be simply impossible under those conditions; man would inevitably become more earthly and worldly than ever For then there would be *nothing else to look to*.

7. Once more, we need to remember that the question does not affect ourselves only, but also the

Power that gives us our being, it affects its character for Reason, for Goodness, for Justice, for competence to carry onward what it has begun. Nay more, that Power has in some real measure identified itself with us. There is not merely *man* as a wholly separate being, there is something of the Divine Power itself at the foundation of our being. We cannot draw the line which separates our free personality therefrom. Even Haeckel describes that which he terms " phronetic energy " as the highest form of the Energy that has been working from the beginning. That Energy has so conditioned itself as to give rise to our personality. According to Haeckel and others, it would seem to be glad to get rid of us again But it has made itself in some degree one with us; should we not also say, up to a certain point, responsible for us ? There is therefore not only man to be considered here, but also the all-working Power in the highest form of its Self-conditioned working.

8. Lastly, we are entitled to adduce—simply as facts in history—the witness of the Consciousness of Christ and of His " Resurrection." Just as we have in Him the complete manifestation of God and of man, so we have in Him who is the Crown and Head of our Humanity—in Whom its life in the fulness of its truth was realised—the one clear revelation of the life of man beyond Death. It is true that the appeal is still to *faith*; but faith itself, real faith as distinguished from mere credulity, is always grounded in Reason, is in fact the highest exercise of Reason itself in us. And this evidence appeals to a rational faith at many points. Of course it is assumed that, as is almost universally acknowledged in some form, Christ occupied a *unique* position in relation both to man and to the Power that gives us being—which found in Him the highest earthly expression—such as makes His equally unique " Resurrection " and the manifestation in Him of a life beyond not wholly incredible.

While He was as truly *human* as Divine, yet if He was altogether just such a man as others, we should find it extremely difficult to believe in the exceptional experience that is thus claimed for Him.

(1) Not only did Jesus Christ affirm with an assured confidence that there was a life which death could not harm; not only did His conception of the meaning of the "world-process" and of its goal in "the Kingdom of God" essentially imply an Eternal Life above Time and Sense; not only did "recompense" and the moral issues of life demand it, and man's sonship to God make it certain, but it was *one of the very deepest assurances of His soul* that, whatever might befall Him as the Christ, He should rise triumphantly above it, and "come again," even from beyond death, "in power and glory." The place that this conviction held in the soul of Christ, and the strength that it gave Him to pursue His course even up to "the gates of Hades," is not always adequately realised. But it ran through His whole experience, and it was really, in one aspect, the demonstration of the soundness of this conviction that was given in that consummation which we familiarly term His "Resurrection." Apart from this consummation, His life would have been an enigma and His death a complete contradiction of all that man has been led to regard as highest and most sacred in the Universe. Had those bigoted and cruel Jews triumphed so as to bring to an end the *personal* life of Christ, then the darkness that fell at the ninth hour might well have continued for ever. But it was not so; and in the fact of the triumph of the personal Christ over death, and so over the human enemies of God (although they did not believe themselves to be such), God Himself was revealed in what is perhaps His clearest manifestation as supreme over all things and powers, and at the same time a life beyond death was made evident.

(2) So much that is material has gathered around our thoughts of "Resurrection," that its reality, even in the case of Christ, seems to many open to question. The emergence of "a dead man" from the tomb seems so contrary to all experience and to all Scientific teaching, that it is deemed "an incredible thing that God should raise the dead." To suppose that *the person* was ever in the tomb would indeed be "sheer Materialism." But it must be said that those who believe that Christ emerged from the tomb in a bodily form do not suppose that *He Himself* was ever laid in that tomb, any more than they think that their loved ones are really laid in the grave; the resurrection of the body was intended to be *evidential* of the conquest of the Spirit over death—a manifestation of the fact for the sake of the disciples. They believe that the body underwent a change, a gradual spiritualisation, such as was witnessed in a temporary form in the Transfiguration—a witness to the supremacy of spirit over matter. They hold that the new revelations of Science concerning matter make credible all that is related of the appearances and actions of the risen Christ in His spiritual body, save perhaps His eating and drinking, which must be put down to later accretions to the record or be in other ways accounted for. Even though we may not ourselves see grounds for belief in this form of "the Resurrection," yet, knowing so little as we do of the ultimate constitution of things, we are not in a position such as warrants us to say that it may not be the true account of it.

(3) But, of course, this is not the only possible way of viewing the matter. All Christians do not believe that the *bodily* resurrection of their Master was necessary for His real resurrection out of death. They think rather of the up-rising of His spirit in the completeness of its union with God, when the body of flesh had been put off; and they regard such appearances of Christ as are historically

well-evidenced as being of the nature of "manifestations" for the sake of the faith of His disciples. If this meant merely that Christ survived death as others are believed to survive it, we have already seen that it would be inadequate. Why should this one man *only* be able to do what no one else can be proved to have done? The Resurrection of Christ must be founded on the uniqueness of His Being or Person, and must be taken in such a sense as will correspond with the uniqueness of His relation to both God and man. This, as already said, does not make Him the less genuinely human and representative of Humanity.

(4) There are still others who, while they believe earnestly in a unique resurrection of Christ, see no need for contending even for such appearances as are recorded in the Gospels. They may not dispute them, but they feel the difficulty of harmonising the different narratives, and also of keeping the idea of a revivification or resurrection of the *body* clear from that of a resuscitation of the person. Even the latter, if it could be proved, would not stagger their faith in the least degree. They regard the union of Christ with God as something pertaining to *the spiritual person*, not to the bodily form. They know that Christ lives now, for He lives in them. They are not greatly concerned with the question of *how* Christ rose into a glorified life in the spiritual and eternal sphere—in other words, *in God*, they regard it as one which, with our present knowledge of the records, is extremely difficult to solve. They hold that the real proof of the personal resurrection of Christ is given in that spiritual presence and working of Christ with and through His disciples to which the early history of Christianity bears witness, the reality of which it is open to men to-day to verify by their entering into such a personal union with Christ as He seeks for from them. The abiding Christian ground of certainty is not merely

the historical fact of the resurrection of Christ, but the experience of life *now* in union with Christ and with God. That the first disciples *believed* that Christ was risen is admitted on all hands; that He *is* actually alive in God and spiritually efficient—a Divine-human spiritual Presence and Power in which we ever live and move—is something we can verify in our own spiritual experience, if we come into the requisite conditions for its verification. Of course, it cannot be verified as an *external* fact apart from spiritual experience; but it is possible for us to-day to come into such a relationship to Christ as to have a deep conviction created of His real, abiding, personal Presence.

CHAPTER III

THE *POSSIBILITY* OF SURVIVAL

IN seeking now to show, in the light of our knowledge of Nature and of Man, that the survival of the spiritual self is possible, we repeat that the chief objections to it arise from the assumption that it implies an unwarranted kind of *Dualism* of soul and body, and that it is inconsistent with the relation of soul and body as we actually behold it.

Such Dualism, however, is by no means implied; the survival of the soul can be quite consistently maintained on genuinely Monistic principles. We do not believe that the soul is specially created, or that it "comes in" at any stage of the development of the organism, as if from without. The self is a unity, one aspect of which is physical and the other spiritual; but it may be found that the spiritual is, both logically and chronologically, first and deepest—*that* to the expression and temporal life of which the bodily side only ministers. It by no means follows that the spiritual being perishes when the bodily organism is dissolved.

The Sub-conscious

1. In seeking to expiscate the relation of soul and body, in view of the possible survival of bodily death, great stress has been laid by Mr. Myers and others on the *sub-conscious or subliminal self*. The reality of the sub-conscious element is acknowledged on every hand: the questions are

as to its origin and functions, actual and possible. That it plays a great part in our mental history no one can doubt. Much of our mental life goes on beneath consciousness, and only rises at a certain stage above the threshold of the normally conscious self. There is doubtless also much that never appears at all in our ordinary consciousness, but makes its presence manifest in sleep—in hypnotic and other abnormal conditions. It may have much to do also with intuition and with genius, and may account for many of the exceptional manifestations which Mr. Myers adduces. But whether we are to regard it as essentially *higher* than our normal consciousness (not to say as the representative of a prior metetherial existence and of a more permanent self, as Mr. Myers contends) may well be doubted. It would rather seem that, while the normal conscious self is a consciousness *adapted* to the needs of this present earthly life in the environment amid which we presently find ourselves, and concerned with that only, in our sub-consciousness are retained elements belonging to previous stages of our gradually developed terrene existence, and that it still receives and retains everything in our experience, although only those elements which are of use *now* come into our normal consciousness. There may certainly be contained in it elements which have an important function in relation to a life beyond the present bodily form of existence, and which *may* be adapted, or, for aught we know, may *now* be becoming adapted, to life in other than an earthly environment. In one respect, indeed, it may be rightly spoken of as *higher* than the ordinary consciousness—in the sense in which "instinct" is more unerring than reason in creatures; there may therefore be retained in it more of that *formative* power which is deeper than the free reason in man, and which, although *conditioned* in a lower form, is in itself Divine. What possibilities may be hidden in those mysterious depths of our being, no one can say.

The importance of this subliminal self and of the various facts relating to it lie in this they show us that there is much more within ourselves than we have ordinarily imagined—an active mental life, indeed, in operation beyond our ordinarily *conscious* selves; and that even now processes may be going on which have a relation to the continuance of our existence. Even now the *Self* may be, all unconsciously to our normal selves, building up an organism in which our life shall proceed, in a higher environment, after death has divested us of the grosser body. There are many familiar facts that show that the normal "consciousness" is not essential to the permanence of the mental life. It may come and go while the self endures. Our present bodies were formed for us without our consciousness. What may now be going on beneath consciousness, or rather, perhaps, *beyond* consciousness, who can say?

The Spiritual Self

2. It is of the greatest importance to realise the essentially *spiritual* nature of that *self* which each man knows himself to be, *however it may have arisen.* This seems the securest ground for our argument. The self, although it has always a physical side, knows itself as a spiritual being as distinguished from all that is material, even from its own material organism, no one particle of which is the same in the adult as it was in the child, or, to put it otherwise, from its own material *side.* Its real life is *subjective*, not objective, the objective only ministers to it. The soul, or spiritual self, is not merely, as we are so often told, "the sum total of our cerebral functions," but a *unity* in the midst of these which apprehends and unifies their results, and, in a large measure, directs and controls their operation. It is not only conscious, but *self-conscious.* Apart from this self-conscious unity there would

be no *soul* in the proper sense of the word, any more than there is in the animals that are beneath this self-conscious, unifying power.

What our argument in the first Part has gone to show is, that the all-formative Power in Nature is revealed as *Spirit* within ourselves : we are free, self-conscious spirits in our inmost being That all-forming Power, in itself spiritual, realises itself creatively in us as spirits in finite form. The Intelligence which is the real formative Cause of the world, which shows itself in the ideal or principle of organisms, manifests itself in man as a self-conscious principle. It has been all along the universal formative principle, and it continues to manifest itself as such in our whole inner life, while making us personally free—sharers in that which is the essential life of Spirit. Man, on the spiritual side, is not merely a conscious being, but a self-conscious, self-originating, self-acting spirit. This gives a *real substantial existence* to spirit in man. As a real self-conscious self each man stands above all that is of the outer world merely.

No one has stated more strongly the impossibility of not believing in the reality of the *self* than Mr. Spencer has done. " If we say," he remarks, " that the successive impressions and ideas which constitute consciousness are affections of the Mind, which as being the subject of them is the real *Ego*, we imply that the *Ego* is an entity. If we say that these impressions and ideas are themselves the very body of this substance—the modified forms which it from time to time assumes—this still asserts that the conscious self exists as a permanent continuous being, since modifications necessarily involve something modified. If we take the sceptic's position, and argue that our impressions and ideas themselves are to us the only existences, and that the personality said to underlie them is a fiction, we still make the very assumption which we repudiate.

For an impression necessarily implies something impressed; even the sceptic must consider these as *his* impressions and ideas. And if he admits, as he must, that he has an impression of his personal existence, what warrant can he show for rejecting this impression as unreal while he accepts all his other impressions as real?" (*First Principles*, p. 47, abridged).

Yet he argues that, "unavoidable as is this belief," it admits of "no justification by reason." It would be strange indeed if this were so, and we ask anxiously for the proof of the assertion. When it comes, it amounts simply to the statement, after Mansel, that because a true cognition of self "implies a state in which the knowing and the known are one—in which subject and object are identified," it is one "which is the annihilation of both." Surely we have here a strange mistake. What is *self*-consciousness, but just a knowledge of the subject and object as one? We cannot even have simple "consciousness" without it When Mr Spencer asks, "If the object perceived is self, what is the subject that perceives? or, if it is the true self that thinks, what other self can it be that is thought of?" the simple answer to both questions is that it is just the one only, self-same self that knows *itself*; no other self is necessary or conceivable.

Man as a self-conscious, spiritual self, however closely related to his body he may be, stands also *above* the body (though not *separate* from it)—*out* of the world of Time and Sense. We also indeed live in that world and receive impressions from it,—the raw material, so to speak, of our mental life,—but these are received, unified, and interpreted in a spiritual manner—transformed into spirit (just as, at a lower stage, ordinary substances are transformed into protoplasm) in what Kant has named "the unity of apperception." Sensations do not merely "come" to the self: it is active in regard to them. Even in its first and lowest act, the self shows itself to be (as the late T. H. Green rightly affirmed) *above* succession in time, above the series of its impressions. In even the humblest form of "sense-perception" it proves itself to belong to another order than the physical and to a higher world than that which is ruled by Time. The spirit in man is also above *Space*. Although our bodies are ever in space, yet except as we are related to our bodies, and, through them, to the external world, *Spirit* has in itself no relation to Space whatever. Although so often forgotten, it is simply a truism to say that you cannot speak of "the dimensions" of a thought, a feeling, a volition, or figure a spirit as extended. As Sir Oliver Lodge remarks, "We are never confined to our bodies." Instead, therefore, of "leaving our bodies" when we die, our bodies leave us, instead of the soul or spirit "going" somewhere, we only find ourselves where we have always been—in a spiritual world, and *as* we have formed ourselves in it. As already said, we do not need to wait to "enter Eternity," we are in Eternity here and now, only when the "here" and "now" of limited place and temporal succession are for us no more, we shall *realise* what has been truth for us all along. There is nothing in a true "Monism" opposed to this.

We know by experience and observation what wonderful powers belong to the human spirit; its capacity to feel, to perceive, and to know, to render all that comes to it from the physical world into spiritual terms; not only to *receive* impressions and have perceptions, but to go out into the world for them; to take into itself the *meaning* of things; to map out for itself and follow definite trains of thought, it may be concerning its own self, or on the most abstruse subjects, to gather knowledge in almost unlimited measure—in actual, unlimited measure, we may truly say; to, in some real measure, control the body and the passing

THE *POSSIBILITY* OF SURVIVAL 417

thoughts and feelings, emotions and desires; to carry the memory of long-past events, losing *nothing*, in fact; to voluntarily recollect, calling up, it may be in a moment, the "forms and scenes of long ago"; to picture for itself far distant scenes, or realms of pure imagination, and to project itself into them; to soar beyond the stars, to take the whole world into itself; to rise in aspiration even to *God*, and to enter into free personal union with the Eternal Source of being. Is it credible that it is "organised matter" merely that can do all this? Then we have its powers of Will and Action, from the lower or the higher motives, with all the results that flow from human action in the world, into which human Wills enter as new personal Powers. And if we dive down into the realm of the subconscious, or observe what happens in dreams, under opiates and stimulants, in hypnotic and other abnormal states (not to bring in telepathy, clairvoyance, and the like), we shall see that there is really no end to the possibilities that are open to this marvellous *self* of ours. To attribute all this to a material organism, a network of cells and nerves merely, seems to be the climax of the impossible. To say that a material *thing* that we can see and touch, that might be held in one's grasp, that only endures as long as it is fed and supplied with physical energy, that, as respects its material, has been formed over and over again, can possess all these powers, seems utterly incredible. Of course, if there were scientific grounds for the assertion we should be compelled to believe it, but Science affords no grounds for any such assertion.

The opposing Arguments

Let us look now at *the opposing arguments*.

1. According to Haeckel and his followers, the soul is simply "the sum total of the physiological functions" of

the material, psychic, and phronetic organs; it is, he says, "merely a collective title for the sum total of man's cerebral functions; and these are just as much determined by physical and chemical processes as any of the other vital functions, and just as amenable to the law of substance." When these functions cease to be performed, the soul ceases to be. What is here said of the Brain as a *physical* organ may be perfectly true, but it does not affect the question. The soul must not be confounded with its physical organs or with the functions they perform merely.

These organs are there, and these functions are performed *to serve the soul*, which is in itself deeper and different from them all. Haeckel's statement is only nominally saved from sheer Materialism by his affirmation of a spiritual side to matter from the first. But he seems to leave this out of account as being anything effective, and has only physical agencies in operation. Strictly speaking, Haeckel can only say that the soul is the outcome of all the working of his *two-sided* Substance, reaching its culmination in man. But even supposing the soul to have been actually *produced* in this way, there was, by his own assertion, a *spiritual* side to its origin; and, moreover, whether that spiritual side be acknowledged as anything effective or not, it by no means follows that the soul, *once produced*, simply passes out of existence again, when the forces that have brought it into being cease to operate. Supposing the soul to be (as we believe) the very end of the working of all the forces that operate in Nature, their ultimate function would be to give rise to this very soul, and it would be absurd to suppose that it just passed again out of existence. The soul may thus have come to have *a real existence in itself* independent of those forces that have brought it into being, like anything else that has been produced.

The Brain itself, we have already seen (Part I. chap. iii.) is the result of spiritual influences affecting "matter."

That wondrous *phronema* of which Haeckel speaks so interestingly, with its millions of "sensory" and "reasoning" cells, in which the whole working of Power in Nature culminates, has been slowly built up—as he indeed says—partly by the experiences of our ancestors, and partly by our own experiences. There is not a single cell or fibre in it that has not been so built up. But these experiences are essentially *spiritual* in their nature (as all "experience" is), the result of feelings, sensations, perceptions, concepts, associations, reasonings, desires, volitions, actings, innumerable. They represent the spiritual experiences of the race, as well as those of its ancestors. These were by no means material or physical only; matter is only that which conveys, preserves, and expresses them, and makes them instrumental to the mind that at length rises out of the primitive vague sentiency in protoplasm to self-conscious spirit and fully formed personality in man. The matter itself is spiritual through and through; in its very essence it is spiritual. The consciousness that arises is the manifestation of a working which has been throughout of a spiritual character. When Haeckel declares consciousness to be only a special form of nervous energy, he forgets that he has affirmed a spiritual aspect to energy, that all energy is spiritual, and that it is only what we should look for to find that spiritual energy manifesting itself in this special form. He himself describes mental forces in order to distinguish them from other forms of nervous energy as "phronetic energy." It is not anything material, after all, that we have essentially to do with—cells and fibres—but *energy*, it is energy in its highest form—energy which is from the first the manifestation of a spiritual Power.

To say that the Brain *produces* thought, feeling, etc., is but a crude statement of what *seems* to be the case on a merely surface view of things. No doubt there is a real dependence of the entire spiritual being on his organism for manifestation, expression, sane and wholesome action, in this present embodiment. "Mental disease" (although often mentally and morally induced) depends essentially on disease in some part of the Brain As the Brain is, even the character will tend to become, and it is one of the surest things that when the Brain ceases to act, all thought, consciousness, etc., *through this material organism*, come to an end. These and similar facts cannot be disputed; they follow necessarily from the fact of our physical embodiment, and they seem to shut up many to a practical Materialism. But the "matter" of our organism is only the medium of a Power that is in itself rational and spiritual, and our cerebral organs are from first to last formed to serve a *spiritual self* which does not necessarily perish with these organs in their material form.

2. To say that "*Thought is a function of the Brain*" is supposed to settle the whole matter. When the Brain ceases to function, the soul is supposed of necessity to perish

As respects "function," Professor James has pointed out, in his Ingersoll Lecture on *Immortality*, that there are other kinds of "function" than that of production. There are "releasing functions," like those of the cross-bow trigger, and "transmissive functions," as in the case of light passing through a coloured glass or prism. Consciousness, he says, may be an eternal Reality, and the Brain merely transmissive of it in our experience. Still, this does not help us much. For the thought thus transmitted does not seem to be our own, and for its transmission and existence *in our consciousness* we are, to all appearance, dependent on the action of the Brain. But there is another way of viewing the matter.

The great truth which throws light on this whole question of *function*, and which so greatly helps us to realise the possibility of a continuance of life after the present bodily organism has been dissolved, is that which we have already (in the first Part) made large use of, viz., that *function precedes organisation*. The *function* is, primarily, that of the being which becomes organised, not of the organ which fulfils it. It is a great mistake, as Mr. T. H. Green remarks, to "confuse a function with the organ through which that function realises itself." Function is ever before organisation; it expresses a *want* of the creature, and the entire organisation is developed to meet and minister to its wants. Even in the lowliest conscious being, a sense of want—a *spiritual* feeling—something *subjective*—is at the centre of its life; and as the evolution proceeds on its upward way, these wants increase and ascend, the subjective element develops, till, to minister to that self-conscious being that man is, as he stands in his entire environment, the marvellous cerebral organism, which Haeckel rightly calls "the most wonderful piece of mechanism in the Universe," has been gradually developed. When it is said that the Brain is "the organ of thought," or that thought is "a function of the Brain," that can only mean *that the Brain performs that function as part of the organism and for the sake of the organism as a whole*. Thought is a necessity for the being that has become thus embodied in organic form, but the *entire organism* has been formed to meet the wants or fulfil the functions necessary for that being. Deeper than the Brain, deeper than any portion of the organisation, is the *spiritual self* That self *feels*—which nothing material can do, it represents in itself an ultimate Reality which cannot be resolved into, or derived from, anything else; and it is to answer to the needs of this *sentient* being in its environment, however humble, that each organ is developed and the entire form put on.

The fact just stated seems to be far too little realised, especially in its bearing on the possibility of the survival of the soul; but a reference to any good text-book of

Biology or of Zoology will verify what we have said. We have given some quotations bearing on the subject in Part I. chap iii., but the importance of the fact that function precedes organisation is so great, in the present connection, that we give here a quotation at some length from Professor Nicholson's well-known *Manual of Zoology* (fifth edition). "Among the simpler Protozoa, the general protoplasm of the body discharges indifferently the functions of nutrition, reproduction, and relation, no particular portion being set apart for the discharge of any particular function. Hence those types exhibit nothing which can be properly spoken of as 'organisation,' nor do they show anything of that phenomenon which is spoken of as 'specialisation of function.' Among the higher Protozoa there is a commencement to a differentiation of the protoplasm into organs, and there is therefore to some extent a physiological distinction between different parts of the organism.

"On the other hand, among the Metazoa, where the organism is an aggregate of cells, there is always, to a greater or less extent, what has been happily called 'a physiological division of labour,' some of the cells being concerned with the nutrition of the organism, others with its reproductive functions, and others with its relations to the world outside it.

"Hence in the Metazoa there occur in varying degrees a specialisation of function, or, in other words, a setting apart of special cells for the discharge of special functions. As the result, there is in varying degrees a metamorphosis of the cells into different tissues. Hence *pari passu* with, and in consequence of, the physiological division of labour in the cells of the organism, there is produced an ever-increasing complexity of organic form and structure.

"Moreover, as we pass upwards, from the lower to the higher Metazoa, we find that the primary physiological functions themselves become specialised, becoming broken up into numerous secondary functions, each of which requires specially modified cells for its discharge It follows from the above that the morphological character of animals is the result of the varying degrees to which their functions are specialised."

Thus, if we begin at the beginning of the formation of organs, it is clear that each organ is produced in order *to meet the wants* or *fulfil the functions* of the living creature. In the humblest creature there is a *self* which its organism is fashioned to serve. The brain is the organ of Thought; but although the brain acts so far automatically, it is the living being who *thinks*. Thought is a necessity for his life; it is a function, not of "the brain" but of the *self*, which the brain has been developed to be the organ of. And, as we have seen, the brain has been built up continually under spiritual influences proceeding from the innermost self. Therefore it by no means follows that that *self*, which the brain has been formed to serve, perishes when its organ becomes unfit to serve it. That the very *being* of the self depends on this its organ, we have no ground for affirming.

3. *A spiritual side to our being* is acknowledged on all hands. The question really is, What becomes of *this personal, spiritual side* of our being, when the chemical combinations which hold together the grosser elements of matter are broken up? It was at least *as real* as the material side; as a self-conscious, personal element, it was surely much more real, *what becomes of it at death?* It is not the spiritual being that life ceases to animate, but *the matter of the organism*. When this latter element becomes no longer fit to serve the organism, what ground have we for saying that the spiritual side, which the material side only ministered to, has disappeared? What warrant is there, in consistency with the Monistic asser-

tion of a "two-sided substance," for affirming that the spiritual side here has wholly passed away? In spite of their "two-sided substance," they speak as if "matter" were necessary for the very *existence* of spirit; but, by their own showing, is it not quite as true that spirit is necessary for the existence of "matter"? Why emphasise the lower side at the expense of the higher, or, if they will not say "lower" and "higher," the visible at the expense of the invisible, the material at the cost of the spiritual, the impersonal to the utter loss of the personal? There does not seem to be much "reason" in that! And if, as they say, the material and the spiritual always go together, must there not be still in some way a material side to the spiritual self (or a finer ethereal one), although imperceptible to our senses? "Monism" would seem to demand this.

We have already seen that the spiritual side is first and deepest, abiding essentially the same in the normal man amidst constant physical change, and that, while there is always a physical side to our spiritual experience, the spiritual side shows itself throughout to be the supreme and dominant element. We know this in our experience—in the very fact that we *have* experience. It is on that side that we have our self-consciousness and personality; it is from that side that our life is governed. There is never a purely physical course of influence or action. Even beneath consciousness, in "elementary sensation," the "mind" is active. Sensation is always, in its very lowest degree, a mental fact. Apart from the mental side, there would be *no* sensation. We have seen something of the action of the spiritual side of our being in perception, memory, imagination, emotion, reasoning, and will. However unconsciously, to our normal consciousness, it is the spiritual self that brings our sensations together and receives them in a unity, that transforms physical impressions into spiritual experiences, and incorporates them in a unified mental life.

THE *POSSIBILITY* OF SURVIVAL

We go forth to meet the world, as it were; *we* make a mental effort to know, to think, to understand, to recollect, *we* select from amongst the thoughts which are ever passing through the Brain those which we choose to hold, to follow out, to make our own; *we* voluntarily attend to them or decline to attend; *we* choose some and repress or reject others; *we* freely start and deliberately pursue, it may be with effort, trains of reasoning, etc. Equally manifest is the primacy of the mental side in *emotion* and its *control*, where we come still more distinctly on the action of the central, voluntary self or will. In the action of the will —hesitating, delaying, deliberating, deciding, acting or refraining from action, however strong the inducements from the physical side of our being may be—we see very clearly the supremacy and the dominating influence of the spiritual side of our being All which confirms the conviction that, while the two sides are always *there*, the spiritual side is first and deepest—that to which the physical only ministers.

We have a further illustration of the supremacy of the mental side in the effects which purely mental influences have upon the body. A purely spiritual idea conveyed in the faintest whisper, or read on the written page, may cause the blood to course with vehemence through the body. An item of information, conveyed by speech or writing, may cause fainting, convulsions, even death. It was not any physical force that initiated that which had such issues, but something as purely spiritual as ever the spiritual can be found in this world.

The Self and Consciousness

It is of great importance to remember that there are not only the changing experiences that come to us through the working of our central organ of Thought, but that, deeper than these, there is the self that *has* these experiences, the self that is immediately known in all experience, that has in itself the thoughts, the feelings, the emotions that arise, and that can retain or reject them, incorporate them with itself or cast them out, as it were, as it chooses, the self that knows itself as such or is self-conscious. That self also stands, no doubt, in a certain necessary relation to the flow of blood and other physical contributories to mental life, *so far as consciousness in the body is concerned*. But does this self disappear, is it wholly blotted out, when this present mode of consciousness ceases? We know that this is not the case as long as certain vital functions are maintained, even though consciousness may be lost for a lengthened period. Consciousness may come and go, and yet the self endure all the time. *This* consciousness is not identical with the spiritual self or Ego, but is a state or mode of its existence. *We* are conscious, or *we* may be unconscious.

But this, it may be said, is just what is true of the *organism*: it is *the organism* that is conscious or unconscious. We are, however, now dealing with the organism on its *spiritual* side. *That* must have existed in some form *before* any such consciousness was possible to it; there must have been somewhat that had the capacity of becoming conscious in or by means of that organism. It is the spiritual self, we have seen, that forms the entire organism to serve it; the physical side always expresses and ministers to the spiritual. And as this must have existed, in however "bare" or potential a form, before consciousness through that organism came to it, so it may exist, in its completed or filled-out form, after that organism has ceased to serve it, especially since it is, in man, a fully-formed, self-conscious, spiritual being. It is one of the contributions of the newer Psychology to our knowledge, that it makes it plain that consciousness, as we know it, is not essential to mental life. Beneath our consciousness there is a deep (to us, in ordinary), unconscious, yet truly mental order. All our conscious mental life begins in and rises up from "the unconscious." What relation does this deep mine of the unconscious hold to our cerebral organ?

The Relation of Consciousness to the Organism

The seeming entire dependence of consciousness on our material organism appears to many a clear proof that when that organism has been dissolved, consciousness must cease for ever; nothing can remain, the very Self disappears. This is one of the commonest reasons of distrust of the possibility of a life beyond. But, *What is consciousness?* Perhaps the best material illustration of it is that suggested by Huxley's reference to " a red-hot poker and its redness," which we have already seen used in another connection by Mr. Mallock. We may imagine *the glow* to represent consciousness. It is there only when the iron is in a certain condition, viz., red-hot—showing what is technically called "radiant heat." Now, what causes this glow? Wherein does it reside? The heated condition of the iron may be said to be its cause—although this is only one of many conspiring causes. But that means *movement*, the rapid movement of the particles of the iron, and movement is not a material thing. But is there nothing more? What is it that *has* the glow, or that manifests it to us? It is a scientific fact that it is *the Ether*, set into oscillation by the movements of the particles of the iron. There was *something there*, therefore, in addition to the visible iron, to take, or, if we may suppose it for a moment to be conscious, to "experience" and manifest the glow—*the invisible Ether.* So, in the case of all consciousness, there is *the invisible spiritual self* (whether expressed in Ether, as some believe, or not) in some real way present so that it is able to become conscious under certain conditions. And it does not follow that it entirely disappears and cannot come into consciousness again when the organism decays, any more than that the Ether vanishes when the iron is cold.

The same reasoning applies to the common, but often misstated analogy of the Organ and its Music. The Brain is compared to the Keyboard, and the impressions that come from without are likened to the Player. Destroy the Keyboard, or remove the Player, and the Music ceases. But again we ask, *What makes the Music?* None of these factors alone. Apart from the *invisible air* (not to mention the ideal element in the mind of the Composer) there would be no Music. The Music is "made" simply by certain vibrations of the air in relation to our sensorium; and although Organ and Player may both go, that remains, and may be made Music again.

Memory

It is often said that apart from *Memory* we cannot look for any continuation of our actual being. This certainly seems to be true. But it is just in certain aspects of our capacity of Memory that we see one of the clearest illustrations of the reality and marvellous power of the spiritual self. The phenomena of Memory cannot be wholly explained by any merely physical registrations or traces in the Brain. There are associations, but these are essentially spiritual; deepest of all, they belong to Mind. The whole, or almost the whole, occurrences of the entire life may be recalled voluntarily; and sometimes, apart from the will, they may, in what seems a moment of time, pass before the Mind's eye and be recognised as such, as in the case of almost drowned persons. We already, in a sense, *know* what we may be laboriously seeking to recall, so that we recognise its truth when it comes to us. There are *two* elements at work in voluntary recollection. The Mind has the capacity of taking in and remembering an almost infinite (perhaps we should say, an altogether infinite) number of facts, thoughts, feelings, reasonings, conclusions, and of recalling and recognising these at will more or less freely. It can take into itself and hold there the *meaning* of things. No merely physical explanation can be given of these powers. No amount of merely "physical registration" can account for our common experiences of memory. No piece of organised "matter" can take in and hold the *meaning* of things. To give an everyday illustration. The present writer was recently on his way to a library to return a book which he had been interested in reading. In the tramway car he remembered that there was a certain passage which he ought to have noted down. He read it over several times in the car, trusting to his memory to be able to recall it verbally, taking in its substance or meaning at the same time. When he returned home he was too busy to find time to note down the passage, and it was not till he went to bed that he remembered about it Should he try to recall it there and then? No; he felt too tired · "It is there all right, and I shall find it when I want it" Where was it? It was not till the following evening that he endeavoured to write it down, but although he remembered the *substance* or *meaning* perfectly, the *words* were only imperfectly recalled. Now, where was this all the time? Partly in the Brain, it may be said, and partly in the Mind. Granting to the Brain all that may be claimed for it, where, above all, was the *meaning* of the passage stored, if not in the spiritual Self? · *That* remained when the "words" that expressed it had disappeared. This illustration suggests that, while certain of the lower aspects of memory may disappear when the material organism is dissolved, memory in its higher aspects, being essentially spiritual, shall remain. The authors of the *Unseen Universe* say: "If we turn to thought, we find that, inasmuch as it affects the substance of the present visible universe, it produces a material organ of memory. But the motions which accompany thought will also affect the invisible order of things, and thus it follows that, *Thought conceived to affect the matter of another Universe simultaneously with this may explain a future state"* (p. 159). This possibility has also to be kept in view.

"Thoughts" also come to us from without, from beyond ourselves—"ready-made," as has been said: they can be received complete in a moment of time, and retained in memory; which facts can only be explained by a spiritual receptiveness beyond the immediate working of the Brain. And if we follow the working of the Mind into Dream-land and into its more abnormal manifestations in Telepathy, Clairvoyance, Exaltation, and Hypnosis, we shall find ourselves face to face with other facts which ordinary physical explanations cannot meet.

Self-formation and Character

Still further, all the while of our earthly life, and deeper than our changing experiences, the Self is more and more fully forming itself. We are constantly building up a distinctive *character*; which is our true, and the really determinative Self, in all that we do.

The physical side of our changing sensations, perceptions, thinkings, feelings, may all be traced; but in what elements is this deeper factor of *character*—or the life of our true inner self—being built up? It is not dependent on the Brain-changes which give us the material of our ordinary mental life; it is dependent on these only for the reception of such material. In itself it lies beyond these, and remains unchanged (although always developing) amidst them all. We might well ask, indeed, *What* is that "matter" with which even our *changing* mental life is immediately related? What part does the Ether play in this relation? Still more emphatically may we inquire, With what kind of "matter" are the *sub-conscious* elements in us related? Can it be to ordinary matter as we commonly see it in the physical world? We *know* that the "matter" of the Brain has a fineness beyond power of expression, or even of conception. May there not then be something *deeper* than those chemical combinations which death dissolves—something which remains?

Recent Science helps us here greatly. "Matter," we have seen, is not what we have thought it to be. The chemical "atoms" that make up our bodies and brains may all be dissolved and yet something *real* (something tangible, may we not say?)—the real essence of matter—will remain. "Matter" has been reduced to "electrons," and, as Mr. Zimmern says in his recent book, *What do we know concerning Electricity?*—Electricity *may* exist "apart from matter. This is not absolutely proved, but it is highly probable. In that case, electricity would be a sort of ethereal matter, which, besides being always intimately united with ordinary matter, is also capable of existing independently. This, however, applies only to negative electricity." And he says again, "The reality concerning what we call molecules, atoms, and electrons is, no doubt, infinitely more complicated than anything our faculties enable us to conceive" (pp. 123, 128). We have already quoted the saying of a German Scientist to the effect that our modern analysis of matter takes us to the borders of a new and as yet mysterious world. Is it not with this *deeper reality* that our whole mental life, and especially that deepest element of self and of character, is ultimately in contact? The grosser physical structure and the blood that represents the physical life may be necessary only to receive experiences from, and to convey action to, the physical world around us in which our being is meant to realise itself, and by means of which we are "educated" and made "rational" beings. Certain it is that, deeper than ordinary matter, its very basis indeed, there is the, as yet, inscrutable *Ether*, and it is not there, in our Brains, for nothing. We are nct now speaking of what Haeckel derides as an "ethereal soul," but of that Ether, the ubiquitous reality of which he maintains, as the possible material of the spiritual and surviving consciousness, if such should be required. Mr. Spencer (although he does not deem it an explanation) says that "the only supposition having consistency is that that in which consciousness inheres is the all-pervading Ether" (*First Prin.*, p 177). Is it not possible, even most probable, that there is an ethereal environment in which life may proceed beyond the present body; nay, is it not actually *in* that environment that our mental life now proceeds? And just as there is mental life *beneath* consciousness, may there not be mental or spiritual life *above* or *beyond* consciousness? If some kind of substance holds together the *sub*-conscious elements of our being, may there not be *ultra*-conscious elements held together in a similar way? May we not, in fact, be building up for ourselves, unconsciously, in a similar substance, an abiding spiritual self? Science forbids us to say that this is not possible. As we have seen, it is all along *the spiritual* that is *formative*, in this sense "the soul" (as even Haeckel seems to teach) forms the body; not as a conscious agent, but as the principle of organic unity which becomes conscious in us—our real self —and goes on building up the personality in freedom; and there is much to suggest that if some kind of "substance" is necessary for continuance of being, it is not far to seek.

Telepathy, etc.

That this is so, the facts of Telepathy, and we must add, we believe, of "phantasms of the living," prove. We have avoided *building* on such facts, for although Sir W.

THE *POSSIBILITY* OF SURVIVAL

Crookes, Sir Oliver Lodge, and not a few other eminent Scientists accept these facts—at least those of Telepathy—they are not as yet universally accepted. Sir W. Crookes and Sir Oliver Lodge are both very decided in their acceptance of Telepathy. The first-named said in his address as President of the British Association in 1898, that for the introduction of spiritualistic facts " it would be well to begin with *Telepathy*, with the fundamental law, as I believe it to be, that thoughts and images may be transferred from one mind to another without the agency of recognised organs of sense—that knowledge may enter the human mind without being communicated in any hitherto known or recognised ways. Confirmation of telepathic phenomena is afforded by many converging experiments and by many spontaneous occurrences."

More experimental evidence is demanded, but experiment can scarcely bring us to the truth on such subjects; for these experiences come, for the most part, in unsought and inexplicable ways. Many who cannot see their way to accept " Spiritualism," are constrained to admit that *Telepathy* at least is proved, and they account for " spiritualistic " experiences by means of it and similar powers (see Mr. Podmore's writings).

The evidence for phantasms of the living seems also to be good. The present writer feels bound to say that he has had (quite unsought and unthought of) *one* experience which he cannot account for save as a " phantasm of the living " at the moment of death—the person appearing being in New York, and the percipient in Scotland. But if even *Telepathy* be true, it implies that there is *some element* different from ordinary matter, to which Thought is so related that it can be conveyed to any distance There seems to be little room for doubt as to this. But if so, then surely it shows that Mind is *always* related to an element the existence of which does not depend on the laws that rule in the case of ordinary matter, and which is not affected by the dissolution of ordinary matter.

Besides Telepathy, and perhaps still more decisively, what is termed *Telekinesis* has been established—the latter experimentally. We may here refer especially to the evidence of Dr. Maxwell, Professor Richet, and others, as given in the recent work entitled *Metapsychical Phenomena.* Telekinesis means movement of material objects without any visible contact. Now, if such movements be possible, as seems to be well established, there must be some kind of material with which personal energy is associated other than that which is commonly recognised. Dr. Maxwell regards this energy as being " of nervous origin," and " of the same order as that which provokes muscular contractions." The force " becomes exteriorised if accumulated and wrought up to a sufficient tension" (pp. 384, 385). But where there is force in action there must be some *medium* by means of which it is conveyed and enabled to act. Sometimes in this relation it seems to act like " attraction and repulsion" These facts are adduced here solely as evidence of the existence of some kind of unperceived " material" which may afford that which is necessary for the existence of spiritual *form* apart from the body of flesh. Our mental life may be all along in relation to this finer material, however it be named. Indeed, we might go farther, and say that there seem to be facts fairly well established which suggest that we are, not sometimes merely, but always, beyond our bodies in that " general consciousness" which is beyond our usual or normal consciousness, and only occasionally comes into the ordinary conscious field, for the most part under abnormal conditions. For this reason we may, under certain circumstances, become aware of what is happening " outside" of ourselves as embodied, as well as (when the exteriorised force is strong enough) be able to act telekinetically—getting, it would seem, beyond ordinary

THE *POSSIBILITY* OF SURVIVAL

space limitations, and, possibly, above time limitations also. This is quite in harmony with Monism, for there is always (in the phenomenal world) some kind of material supposed as the other side of spirit.[1] These matters, however, are not at present so fully investigated as that we can build on them as assured grounds of belief in an existence beyond our present bodies. As already said, they are used here only as evidence that we stand in relation to a material other than that which we commonly think of when we speak of " matter." But, indeed, Science shows us this plainly in what it now reveals respecting the sub-atomic and ethereal constitution of matter. It has fully confirmed in this respect the contention of Professors Tait and Balfour Stewart in their *Unseen Universe*, that the visible world of matter is derived from an unseen ethereal world.

Consciousness and Stimuli

Again, consciousness as we commonly know it is dependent on some *stimulus*. Our stimuli come normally to us from the external world through the organs of sense; but they may also arise from within. It is this fact that gives us many of our strange experiences in dreaming. We see there the consciousness responding to quite other than the normal stimuli. We there note also " entirely new concepts of Time and Space . dreams that on the waking plane would require years of time for their enactment, find on the dream plane that even a moment is sufficient for the dreaming consciousness to appreciate them in their minute details. Thus De Quincey had one

[1] Mr Andrew Lang has said of the facts of "telæsthesia" (perception of events distant beyond any conceivable range of hyperæsthesia) " I am as certain of the occurrence of such facts, as I am of the presence of my writing materials I am certain of it in evidence which I can neither dispute, nor, by any effort of my poor ingenuity, explain away" (*Hibbert Journal*, April 1904)

dream which apparently extended over some sixty years, but which actually occupied scarcely as many moments. Uxhill also, on three successive nights, not only saw his whole life pass in review, but appreciated its moral bearings" (Dr. Anderson, *Reincarnation, A Study of the Human Soul*, p. 47).

Experiences of this kind are familiar to all. A full record of many such and of others of a still more wonderful character will be found in Myers' *Human Personality*, etc. They are very important as showing us the self not only responding to new stimuli, but finding itself in quite a new relation to the Universe—to Time and Space. The experiences of Swedenborg ought also to be referred to in this connection.

We trust that enough has been said not only to show that that continuation of life which we have good rational, moral, and religious grounds for expecting, is *possible*, but also to indicate to some extent *how* it is possible If it be said that since there is a spiritual side to all animals, plants, and even inanimate objects, we might as well ask what becomes of *it* on dissolution, the answer is that it is not there *in the same form*. Such an objection would have force if continuance of existence—that is, *personal* existence—were based on "Life" merely. But our basis is not merely Life or Vitality, but the actuality of the conscious *Self* as *spiritual* and as attaining in man to self-conscious form, to personality and individual character. The humblest creature has, indeed, a self, and we do not affirm that it necessarily perishes. But it is with *man* we are dealing at present, and the form in which the spiritual element is present in him makes all the difference. It is a self-conscious, personal form, such as we do not see in even the highest animal. On the principles of Monism there has been a *spiritual* evolution as truly as a material one, and in all evolution the spiritual element is first and deepest. May not the spiritual element in man have attained to a form in which it shall endure in a way impossible to such lower forms of being as have not attained to personality?[1] May it not be so related to a spiritual, and, probably, an ethereal environment, as to build up therein an abiding self? Animal consciousnesses in the past have contributed to human consciousness in the present; man has been the goal of the animal, and there is no comparison between a mere animal and a fully formed spiritual *person* such as man has become.

What is dissolved at death?

Besides, as we have already seen, there is still another question that must be asked: *How far has " the physical basis of Mind" actually been dissolved?* Into atoms, certainly. But Science is now teaching us that these atoms are not ultimate. What *is* ultimate Science is not yet able clearly to say. As far as it goes, it is *Ether* in some form. Therefore, *there may not really be* that complete dissolution even of "the physical" that has been imagined. So far as contact with the external world is concerned there is dissolution, and so far as consciousness is given by our relation to this world and the forces that normally play upon us therefrom, consciousness must cease. For such consciousness the grosser forms of matter are

[1] This has been copiously illustrated by Professor Le Conte, in his *Religion and Science* and *Evolution in relation to Religious Thought.* The process of Evolution, he says, was one of *increasing individuation*, not only of matter, but of force, and the Divine Energy became "completely individuated as a separate entity, and therefore self-conscious, capable of separate existence, and therefore immortal" in the spirit of man. There was a "development of spirit in the womb of Nature . *in man at last it came to birth.*" It is now separated from Nature, though not wholly; "capable of independent life, born into a new and higher plane of existence " This is illustrated by a drop of water gradually drawn up more and more from a level water-surface, till at length the perfect globular drop is formed, which *remains*, even though the lifting-force is removed (*Evolution*, etc, pp. 318–320)

necessary, in a vital condition, and for this again we must have the circulating blood. When these fail us, *this*-world consciousness ceases. But it by no means follows that the physical basis of the Mind is so completely dissolved that the Mind (in so far as it is related to such a basis) is destroyed, that all consciousness ceases, or that, if it does cease, it cannot be started again in relation to the stimuli of an ethereal or a spiritual world.

With the advent of conscious and of self-conscious beings a new world has appeared, a new and quite higher order of being and life has arisen out of and above the physical order. That *spiritual world* has been, manifestly, the goal of all the working in the physical sphere. We cannot suppose that it just falls back again into nothingness, or that it is merely poured once more into undifferentiated spirit with no abiding result. Must we not believe that our life is continued in that spiritual order, so that when death dissolves the *chemical* basis of our life (and death can do no more) the *ethereal* basis remains untouched, and our life goes on in a higher world, into which, by our rise above the physical, we have already entered; as members of which we already live, just as truly as we live in a physical world; and that we find ourselves there just as we have formed ourselves in relation to it. The spirit, we repeat, is always the formative principle, and we believe that wherever it is it can never cease to act. So that, if some kind of substance is necessary for our continued life, that substance will be at hand, ready to meet the requirements of the spirit That there *is* such a substance we have seen reason to believe.

Is a Material Basis necessary?

In what we have said it has been assumed that some kind of material basis is necessary for the continued life of the spirit, or of man viewed on the spiritual side of his being. But what our previous argument has sought to establish is that the all-working Power has realised in us its own spiritual being in finite form, which, becoming thus individuated in us, is at the same time our true selves, standing in personal relation to the all-transcending, all-containing Spirit. And what we have in "matter" at bottom is not any material *thing*, but *energy*—a form of power—which is also spiritual. In the last analysis, therefore, we, as spiritual beings, do not stand in relation to a hard, substantial thing, called "matter," nor to a more illusive kind of substance called "ether," but to a form of *power*, with which we in our spiritual being are continuous. It is not with matter but with movement (motion) we are in immediate relation. And although, of course, for motion there must be something that moves, it is easy to conceive that this, let us say, physical motion, has resulted in our case in a spiritual being to whom the power of originating motion belongs, although not of creating it. This is something *done*, not to *be* done, and although in our present bodily life our contact with the outer world depends on those bodies of flesh and blood, these bodies belong to spiritual beings who, as such, are not necessarily dependent on them. Through their ministrations we have been brought into a higher form of existence, and in it we may endure even though the mundane ministration of these bodies ceases. Since we are, on the one side of our being, purely spiritual, we can conceive how that spiritual side may persist, not as a form of energy merely, but as *spirit* (which is the only known source of energy), even apart from any such material, or quasi-material, substratum as we can now imagine. Monism applies only to the developing or phenomenal world of spatial existence, and a Spiritual Monism assumes the existence above and beyond this extended world of a purely spiritual world, from which this present world is derived, and into which its completed results pass. It is conceivable that when spiritual being in its highest form has been produced, the phenomenal world has been transcended and the higher realm of purely spiritual life entered on. It is further possible that the human finite spirit may rise into such indissoluble, personal union with the Eternal Spirit, and belong to it in such a way that an eternal spiritual life in God is its sure destiny. This, as we shall see, is the Christian doctrine.

Still, for spirits as yet imperfect, and capable of development, some *form* would seem to be necessary. Form may be deemed necessary also for *recognition*. Given the possibility of spiritual form, recognition presents no difficulty. The object of our love is not the body of flesh and blood, but the spiritual being that is manifested by means of that body. It is the spiritual being that we know and love, and it is not difficult to conceive that finer material may give a yet truer and fuller expression to that spirit. This may be so completely the case that at first we may not "know each other there," and one interest of the future life may be in our gradually coming to do so. On a purely spiritual theory the problem of recognition is not so easy to solve, although it is not insoluble; in all probability, the most of us will feel, with Tennyson, that such a view

"Is faith as vague as all un-sweet:
Eternal form shall still divide
The eternal soul from all beside;
And I shall know him when we meet."

Fechner, however, has much that is suggestive as to the possibilities of a purely spiritual existence. "Instead of the intercourse of *thoughts*, a higher intercourse between spirits and spirits will begin. And as the intercourse of human thoughts takes place in a human spirit, so the intercourse and communion of spirits will take place in that higher spirit whose all-connecting centre we call God. Just as one thought of ours understands and influences another without the mediation of mouth, ear, or hand; as thoughts meet and part without an outward link or separation, so secret, close, and immediate will the communion of spirits be." " Clearly, distinctly, objectively, the inhabitants of the Hereafter will see each other, in the same shape of which we in this life preserve but a faint likeness, a dim contour, in our memory. For they interpenetrate each other with their whole nature, of which a small portion only enters our minds when we remember them. In order to attract them, it will be necessary to direct one's attention towards them, in after-life as well as at present" (*Life after Death*, pp. 58, 84).

Dr. Royce also has reminded us, in his Ingersoll Lecture, that we never in this world truly and fully *know* the individual, or realise our own individuality, and that there may be—should we not rather say, there *must* be?—means, beyond Time and Space, in the completely spiritual world, of both such realisation and knowledge. That complete self-realisation is possible only in God, is certain. Mr. Haldane has also, in his Gifford Lectures, dealt with this intensely interesting subject, and finds the immortality of the soul, not by regarding it as a " substance," but as a " subject," which is related, in that consciousness of identity called love, to subject and not to substance. When we love, it is a purely spiritual affection towards one with whom, while he is outside our spiritual selves, we are one. In this love we may find the life that endures.[1]

[1] While reading one of Mr. Haldane's volumes, a flock of large birds came suddenly into view, circling through the air. What *are* these? Do they represent *Mind* come into form? They have their experience; does it in any way belong to or pass into the Absolute Mind? Individually, they are transitory,—does anything remain when their individual forms pass away? Is it not possible that all that pertains to the finite material form and function belongs to the individual consciousness, and passes away with the individual form, but that whatever rises *above* this enters also into the absolute Mind and remains part of its possession? and is it not further possible for a *personality* so to pass into and belong to that Absolute Mind as to endure therein? (If, how-

Theosophy

We have made no reference to the Theosophic belief in "Reincarnation," now held by many to whom the older views of Soul and Body and of Immortality have become impossible. There is much that is suggestive put forth by writers who adopt that theory, and Science seems to be confirming to a measurable extent some of their affirmations concerning Matter. But the facts of Heredity, and what we know concerning birth into this world, seem to be fatal to the theory. Its law of "Karma," or, in plain words, cause and consequence, is an indubitable one, but it need not be worked out by an ever-recurring round of births on earth, but rather, at least where there has been progress in the right direction, in an onward course of continuity. Where there has not been such a beginning even, it is to be hoped and expected that there will be possibilities of education in the world beyond. We repeat that the question of *room* need not concern us; Professor James has shown this in his Ingersoll Lecture. We are on every hand *in* an Infinite that can never find complete expression in any number of finite beings, and in that Infinite there is abundance of room,—still they come, but "yet there is room." We can never choke up the Infinite spatially, we can never exhaust its possibilities, we can never satiate the Perfect Love.

But there is one theory of Reincarnation closely (as we shall see) related to the Christian doctrine of a Resurrection which seems not unworthy of consideration as a *possible* theory of Immortality, and it will sometimes occur to the mind that is familiar with the conception of physical Evolution and Dissolution. The spiritual elements of our being cannot pass away, may they not remain in some way as elements given to the Universe by our life, and

ever, there is to be any hope of salvation to the sinful, or of progress to the imperfect, beyond this life, there must be some kind of *form* to clothe the spirit.)

may they not all enter into and be found again in that *new evolution* which is said to succeed every dissolution? In this way it is just *possible* that we may all be working over and over again pre-existing elements of spiritual life, that this may go down to the very basis of life, so that no conscious life has ever been lost—

> "That nothing walks with aimless feet :
> That not one life shall be destroyed,
> Or cast as rubbish to the void,
> When God hath made the pile complete",

and only when the process has been completed may we find *ourselves* in true and permanent form. Supposing that all other forms of belief in Immortality should fail us, there is this possibility still to fall back upon. The one thing concerning which we can, on purely rational grounds, be absolutely sure of is, that the individual lives that are the highest outcome of the evolutionary process, with capabilities of endless progress, already living in a spiritual and eternal world in which are the issues of life, cannot be lost; for, as already said, this would be the *reductio ad absurdum* of the creative, or evolutionary, process itself We have simply sought in this chapter to show *how*—founding mainly on the reality of the spiritual self—survival is possible. Let us turn now to the Christian doctrine of continued life and resurrection.

Note.—It is hoped that it is not out of place to state here that, shortly after the MS. of this book was sent to the publishers, the writer had the misfortune unexpectedly to lose a devoted wife. She was deeply interested in this subject, and before she passed away the writer promised to cherish her spiritual presence, and asked her (if it was right and not hurtful) to try to manifest her presence to him. He feels bound to say that he believes she has done so.

CHAPTER IV

THE CHRISTIAN DOCTRINE OF CONTINUED LIFE AND "RESURRECTION"

OUR Lord, according to the Synoptic Gospels, does not formally teach anything respecting "the Future Life" specifically different from the beliefs commonly held among the pious Jews of His time, viz., that at death the spirit passed to the invisible world, and at the Resurrection entered on "Eternal Life." He did not indeed affirm the resurrection of the body that had been laid in the tomb, nor need we take His use of the popular forms of speech as in all respects decisive respecting His own beliefs, as some unwarrantably do. His whole type of thought was spiritual. But the *expressed* difference in His teaching from that of the Scribes of His day was (as Dalman remarks) with respect to the "Righteousness" which makes men partakers in the Eternal Life of the Kingdom of God, and hence also as to the presence of the power of that Life in men here and now.

In His answer to the Sadducees, it might seem that He made future life depend on the Resurrection; but their question was not respecting the survival of the soul, with regard to which the difficulty they stated did not arise, but with respect to *bodily resurrection*,—"Whose wife shall she be in the Resurrection?" Jesus in reply affirmed the Resurrection, but declared its nature to be not carnal but spiritual. Not that there should be no more distinction

CHRISTIAN DOCTRINE OF CONTINUED LIFE 445

of sex, but no more "marrying and giving in marriage"; because, no doubt, the world should then be completed and the permanent state entered on. Quoting the words in Exodus, "I am the God of Abraham, the God of Isaac, and the God of Jacob," "God," He declared, "is not the God of dead, but of living men." This is contained in the "triple tradition." Luke adds, "For all live unto Him"; whether in actual embodied or disembodied existence, or in the Divine thought, memory, or life, may be uncertain.

But that our Lord believed in a continuity of life beyond death, there can be no doubt. "Be not afraid," He said, "of them which kill the body but are not able to kill the soul" (according to Luke, "have no more that they can do"), which clearly affirms a life that endures after the death of the body. This also follows from His frequent sayings concerning "saving the life and losing it," or "losing it and finding it." We have abundant evidence of His affirmation of a real spiritual world in which were God and the Angels—the Angels who were active Divine agents even in this world, and whom He said those who entered the Eternal Kingdom should resemble. Life here, He taught in the parables of the talents and of the pounds, was a training for higher service. The faithful servant should receive a generous welcome and an entrance into "the joy of his Lord." According to Luke, He assured the dying robber, "Verily I say unto you, To-day shalt thou be with me in Paradise." He Himself, when dying, said, "Father, into Thy hands I commend (or entrust) my spirit." The parable of the rich man and Lazarus, based on the reality of conscious life in the unseen world, and belief in the presence and operation of spirits—the "demons"—who "possessed" men living in the flesh, may also be here referred to.

In the Fourth Gospel we have a distinctly spiritual

view presented, although still, in some parts, with references to Resurrection "at the last day." But there is no real contradiction, or need of supposing that all those passages which speak of raising up at the last day are interpolations. It is "Eternal Life" that is the theme, and that life in its fulness was only to be entered by means of such a resurrection. But "the Life" is present now in Christ, and all who believe in Him are made partakers in it. They have "passed from death into life." "Your fathers did eat the manna in the wilderness, and they died. This is the bread that cometh down from heaven, that a man may eat thereof and *not die.*" "As the living Father sent me, and I live because of the Father; so he that eateth me, he also shall live because of me." The Jewish view is stated by Martha,—" I know that he (my brother) shall rise again in the Resurrection at the last day." Jesus replied, "*I* am the Resurrection and the Life: he who believes in me, even if he has died, shall live; and every one who is living and is a believer in me shall never, never die" (εἰς τὸν αἰῶνα). Christ brings in His own person the power of the Resurrection into the world, and those who believe in Him are the subjects of it. The life is thus continuous: "If a man keep my word he shall not see death for ever"—the same strong form of statement as before.

Quite in keeping with this are those other sayings: "He that loveth his life loses it, and he that hateth his life in this world shall keep it (guard it) unto life eternal If any man serve me, let him follow me; and *where I am there also shall my servant be.*" "In my Father's house are many mansions (abodes, or resting-places); if it were not so I would have told you; for I go to prepare a place for you. And if I go and prepare a place for you, I come again, and will receive you unto myself, *that where I am ye may be also.*" According to this Gospel (and in truth),

His "coming again" is in Spirit, so that this (as well as the former passages) points to a present life of the believer with Christ in the spiritual world. Again He says " Yet a little while and the world beholdeth me no more, but ye shall behold me, because I live, and ye shall live. In that day ye shall *know* that I am in my Father, and ye in me and I in you,"—which implies the sharing with Him of such higher life as shall give them a higher knowledge. Once more, He prayed: " Father, those whom Thou hast given me—I will that where I am, there they also may be with me; that they may behold my glory, which Thou hast given me: for Thou lovest me before the foundation of the world" There is no hint of a preceding resurrection in connection with these sayings. They clearly imply an abiding life-power in the spirit of the believer, conforming him to Christ, and carrying him through death to where Christ is in His glory.

In St. Paul we seem to be, to some extent, carried back again to the Jewish conceptions (of course he was earlier than the Fourth Gospel); yet with an important difference arising out of the relation of the believer to the risen and glorified Christ. Paul laid great stress on a bodily resurrection—not of the body that was laid in the grave. He did so for two reasons: (1) because he believed that Christ had risen and was exalted in a glorious body; and (2) because he looked for the complete life of the redeemed in the Kingdom of God established here, in a renewed and glorified world. Many passages prove that Paul believed in the entrance on the fulness of Eternal Life by means of a " Resurrection." He looked for this at the second coming of Christ at the end of the age. Then the dead should come with Christ in new spiritual bodies like their Lord's, and the living should experience a corresponding change. He expected at the same time a renovated and glorified world—*this world* delivered from " the bondage of corruption," made fit to be the scene of the fully emancipated life of the sons of God. The *spirit* of the Christian man was delivered now; but the body was still subject to death, and he longed for "the redemption of the body" and "manifestation of the sons of God"; "waiting for a Saviour who should change the present body of our humiliation into the likeness of the body of His glory." Therefore to the last he laboured "if by any means he might attain to the resurrection from the dead." It was certainly not the body that had been laid in the grave that St. Paul believed should be raised. It was not the resurrection of "the body," still less of "the flesh"; but "the resurrection from the dead." "That which thou thyself sowest," he says, "is not quickened except it die: and that which thou sowest, thou sowest not the body that shall be, but bare grain, it may chance of wheat or of some other kind; but God giveth it a body even as it pleased Him, and to each seed a body of its own." As from the vital principle of the seed, after its old body has "died," a new and richer body issues in the uprising and fruitful corn, so is it in the Resurrection as Paul conceived it. The body of flesh and blood had been formed by the animal soul to express and serve it; the new body should be the outcome and expression of the spirit as the life-principle of the believer in Christ: it is sown a natural (psychical) body; it is raised a spiritual (pneumatical) body. "If there is a natural body, there is also a spiritual (body)." This was necessary for entrance into the "Kingdom of God," which "flesh and blood could not inherit." As already said, Paul looked for an embodied existence in the Kingdom of God in a transformed world. The shadowy life of the Sheol of the Jews or of the Hades of the Greeks could not content him. Yet he believed in the reality of that invisible world, and he did not dread to enter it. Because *Christ was there*, and while we are here "in the body pent" we are separate from Him ("we walk by faith not by sight"). He was *willing*, therefore, to be "absent from the body and at home with the Lord." He did not wish to be "unclothed" (Christ Himself was, of course, clothed with that glorious body which is the type of ours), but "clothed upon" with that resurrection body, which was "a building from God, eternal in the heavens" Although he speaks of those who had fallen "asleep in Jesus," and of Christ Himself as "the first-fruits of them that sleep," and laid stress on the resurrection, he by no means thought of life in the invisible world as unconscious. And although a development may be traced in his thought and feeling, there is no radical change of view, when he speaks of being "present with the Lord," or when later he says to the Philippians that he longed "to depart and to be with Christ," which to him would be "very far better" and a decided "*gain*" as compared with the earthly life He could not have spoken as he did had he not believed that those who, as he says elsewhere, "die to the Lord" enter on a blessed life with Christ. Those who died to their Lord were like retainers who had been out in their lord's service in the field returning to his Mansion, and, as Christ Himself had said, being welcomed and entering into their lord's joy. It was in heaven also that the "glorious body" should be received. The life of the heavenly world was very real to Paul; for had he not been "caught up to Paradise" and heard words which he dared not utter? The Resurrection was the *revealing* of the sons of God— their *manifestation* in the full glory of their sonship. Even in 1st Thessalonians it is *from heaven* that Christ is to bring His saints.

The actuality for the believer of such a present and continuous life with Christ follows necessarily from his relation to Christ. In Christ the sin that keeps men out of "Eternal Life" is taken away, and from union with Christ the Divine Spirit which is the power of the eternal life in man comes and takes possession of the human spirit. *If Christ is alive and present everywhere*, it follows, as He himself said, that those who are united with Him—made one with Him—are in spirit and person present with Him. Again, since it is the Spirit of God and of Christ in them that is the power of the eternal life, with which Spirit as a principle their inmost self is identified, there can be no violent break in the continuity of their existence. And since it was the *Spirit* of Christ that was the power that formed His resurrection body (however that may be conceived), wherever that Spirit is the deepest life-principle of a person a similar result must inevitably ensue. As already said, it is ever the spirit or ideal life-principle—the spiritual side of the Monistic synthesis—that is first and deepest, and expressed by that which is material It has preserved the earthly form and the identity of the person through all the changes of the material atoms of the body. it is not itself material but spiritual; it does not perish at death, but works on formatively, carrying the person into a higher life and a wider consciousness, and providing the self with whatever organ of expression and action may be necessary. Just as the new-born child finds itself in a body which its life-principle had, all unconsciously to itself, formed for it, to be the organ of its conscious mundane life, so, all unconsciously to the person, the formative spirit, one with the Spirit of Christ, has been providing a spiritual body to be the organ of the person in the spiritual world; or, when the fleshly organism ceases to be serviceable the spiritual *self* goes on forming such a body as is necessary. This body will, of course, be the expression of the spirit. It may not be the ultimate form of the person—the ultimate "resurrection body" the spiritual body may be perfected only with the perfecting of the personality. The natural conclusion is,—while this does not exhaust the idea of " Resurrection,"—that, just as the Parousia or " coming " of

CHRISTIAN DOCTRINE OF CONTINUED LIFE 451

Christ in His Kingdom has proved to be spiritual and continuous, the " Resurrection " must be similarly understood.

The body that the spirit finds itself clothed with at death is not indeed such a body as can *normally* manifest the person in this material world. Even Christ is not so manifested But if we believe in Christ as He in this connection specially asked His disciples to do (John xiv. 1), we believe in One who is everywhere present,—" with us always,"—and we ought also to believe in the presence of the departed as being " where He is," according to His word. They are present with and in Him. Christ's presence is spiritual, to be apprehended only by faith and suitable receptivity, but it is none the less a most real and influential presence. So is that of the departed in Him. No longer, indeed, after the type of the soul-life, or in affinity with the things of the external world (which does not mean that they have no interest in earthly persons and their life,—who has a deeper interest in us than Christ has?), but after the type of that higher life which is presently " hid with Christ in God," and, most probably, as " ministering spirits," in a service for which there are wide fields both in that unseen world into which thousands are continually entering in all grades of ignorance, and in this present world, in which comfort, help, and guidance are so greatly needed. Our stubborn, sense-born unbelief may, quite unnecessarily, shadow our lives, and, mayhap, also grieve the departed, as well as Him in Whom they are " alive for evermore," and under Whom they would fain be helpers of us who, while we belong to earth, belong also, even now, to the spiritual world.

But, further, it ought to be said that from the Christian standpoint it is not necessary, in order to conceive of continued conscious life with Christ in God and to realise the presence of the departed with Christ, to affirm an embodiment, at least of a type similar to that which our present experience leads us to think of. The question will arise, Is Christ really now embodied in some permanent form? If so, how can He be everywhere present? Christ is now one with God, who is in Himself *Spirit*—one with the Father, yet distinct in His Divine humanity. There may be distinctions of fully formed spirits in themselves as truly as of those in bodily forms. The conscious person is a spiritual being; consciousness itself is spiritual, and is the highest revelation of the spiritual to us. Although in this life the contents of our consciousness come to us for the most part (although not wholly) by means of the bodily organism, they are themselves always spiritual, and there are distinct, well-defined relations among them. The formation of this spiritual consciousness and personality is just the great end of all the Divine working which the Monism of the phenomenal world only serves. The *person* to whom the two-sided life belongs is himself a spiritual being. If we believe in *God*, we must believe in a Divine and Eternal Consciousness, quite apart from the "matter" which He employs to work out His creative purposes. "God is Spirit," and the human spirit can have real spiritual communion with God and with Christ, and a consciousness of spiritual realities and life. The Christian believes in a spiritual world and in spiritual influences, which come to him through channels other than the ordinary individual consciousness. Although we are individually conscious through cerebral motions, consciousness cannot be *located* anywhere in space. It belongs to the spiritual world even now. There is also, we have seen, a wider consciousness of which we are only occasionally aware to some extent, never fully in this life. At death, when the material centre no longer ministers to the spirit, we may simply enter on and live in this wider consciousness, independent of Time and Space as we are now related to them. Instead of actual defined bodies, there may rather be a constant *possibility of embodiment or expression*. As the conscious self is spiritual and belongs to the spiritual world, it must endure therein with the relationships it has formed. The Christian consciousness which is formed through a relation to Christ can never cease to be, and can never be separated from Christ.

This leads us, finally, to a wider view of the "Resurrection." We *all* live to God, in spiritual reality at least, and it may be that, when this world's course is run, *all* shall again appear in such new bodily investiture as is implied in the Christian doctrines of the Resurrection and the Judgment, when "each one may receive the things done in the body." *All lives* have been lived in conscious or unconscious relation to a spiritual and eternal world; *all have sent something of themselves onward into that unseen world*, and it may all in due time be found again, each one, as Paul taught, reaping exactly *what* and *as* he had sown: "whatsoever a man sows, *that* shall he also reap." May we not say that this is the Christian form of the doctrine of *Karma*?

With the Resurrection there is associated the deliverance of the creation itself from that "bondage of corruption" (or thraldom of decay) in which it seems now to be "groaning and travailing in pain", the "regeneration" or new-creation, the "new heavens and earth" when the old shall have passed away and "all things have become new." There is also, as we shall see, a Cosmic relation attributed to Christ.

Renan, in his *Vie de Jesus*, chap. v., has a suggestive passage which may be here quoted. "Who knows if the highest term of progress after millions of ages may not evoke the absolute consciousness of the Universe, and in this consciousness the awakening of all that have lived? A sleep of a million of years is not longer than a sleep of an hour.[1]

---

[1] As we have seen, although in the spiritual world our relation to Time is other than it is here, there is no unconsciousness or literal "sleep of the Soul"

St Paul on this hypothesis was right in saying, '*In ictu oculi.*' It is certain that moral and virtuous humanity will have its reward, that one day the ideas of the poor but honest man will judge the world, and on that day the ideal figure of Jesus will be the confusion of the frivolous who have not believed in virtue, and of the selfish who have not been able to attain to it "

We do not need to be in theological agreement with M. Renan to deem this view worthy of consideration. It is certainly in keeping with those *periodic cycles of life*—of evolution and dissolution and fresh evolution—which modern knowledge suggests, as well as with the Christian conception of universal renewal; and, quite apart from Christianity, it will sometimes occur to the mind familiar with scientific conceptions as a possibility

And if we realise our relation to the *race* as Christianity shows it us, is it not *possible* that no individual will come into his *full and permanent* inheritance till it comes to all the race? St. Paul had to remind the Thessalonian believers that they who were on the earth at the coming of the Lord (as they at that time looked for it) should not "come before," or "forestall," those who had previously passed away. And the author of the Epistle to the Hebrews says of the Old Testament saints, that though they held the faith, they had not received the fulfilment of God's great promise, for He had provided something better for them and us, "so that apart from us they were not to be made perfect "—" attain to full blessedness." May there not be a deep, underlying, and universal principle here, wholly in keeping with the relation of the individual to the race? Is there not a preparation going on in the invisible world with a view to something yet to come to Humanity as such?

As we have said, M. Renan's suggestion leads us to view the subject in its *Cosmic aspects*. His fuller statement of the theory in his *Philosophical Dialogues and Fragments* (Trubner & Co.) is well worth quoting, especially as it is not widely known, for although it may seem fanciful at first sight, it is very suggestive, and has a close relation to certain Christian conceptions. "Yes," he says, "I conceive the possibility of the Resurrection. . . . If ever, in the final phase of Evolution, the Universe be resolved into a single Absolute Being, that will be the complete life of all, he will revive in himself the life of all those beings that have vanished from existence, or, if you prefer it otherwise, in his bosom all those will live again that have before-time existed." Then all apparent and real injustice will be repaired, and each one, however humble and unnoticed of men, all as they have contributed to the general result, all who have felt and desired more intensely than they have been able to act, will find their true place and recognition. " I speak of life as regards its influence, or, as the Mystics have expressed it, as a life in God . . . It is in the memory of God that men are immortal" " A Consciousness may thus be conceived which will sum up all others, even those which have preceded, which will embrace them so far as they have contributed to the good or the absolute"

This all-containing Consciousness is, in his view, "the last term of a God-developing Evolution . . . in whose infinity would be summed up myriads of lives, those that are dead and those that are living. All animate nature would produce a central life, a grand hymn issuing from thousands of millions of voices, just as the animal springs from millions of organic cells, and the tree from millions of buds. A single Consciousness would be the work of all, and all would participate in it." The inumerable sacrifices of which the world has been the scene would thus be all justified in the great result (pp. 70–78)

Now, this conception of a great Consciousness in which myriads of consciousnesses should be contained, as the final result of an evolutionary process which takes up into itself all Divine and spiritual influences, has no small affinity with certain Christian conceptions. We have seen that, while God is not in Himself *merely* Ideal, as M. Renan seems to say, and that, while He is certainly not realising Himself in the world as if for the first time, *the very idea of a Divine immanence as the power of the world's evolution* implies that He is realising, or expressing, His life in the world in countless finite forms. This is just the great world-process. It has the Divine Thought behind it—realising itself in its outcome—with, according to Christianity, nothing less than the *Divine Sonship* as the Ideal. Christianity, however, does not teach that the goal can be reached as M. Renan imagined, by the advance of Science; it is distinctly an ethical one, and the Divine Ideal is revealed as *having been realised* in Jesus Christ. But Christ stands not alone. He is the Head of a Body of which each human individual is in the ideal truth of his life a member. Those who realise this, their true relation to Christ, *already* live their life in Him. In Christ, we have already beheld, in an individual form, but inseparable from the race, *that very self-realisation of God in the world* of which M. Renan speaks. This is just the profound truth of the incarnation of God in human form as the result of the whole Divine working in the world. The Christian *now* draws his life from Christ, lives to Christ, dies to Christ, lives spiritually *in* Christ and Christ in him. As St. Paul said, "I live; and yet no longer I, but Christ liveth in me"; and it was his supreme desire to be at the last "*found in Christ.*" The "appearance" or "manifestation" of Christ (His Parousia, arrival), of which the New Testament speaks so much, with which is associated the *Palingenesia* (regeneration), the Apocalypse, or "revealing, of the sons of God," that "end of all things" which is also a new beginning—"a new heavens and earth" —for which the whole creation seemed to Paul to be so earnestly longing—may well be conditioned by such a summing up of the lives of all in Christ as *the realised Ideal of the creation.* " Then cometh the end, when God shall be all in all."

It is distinctly taught in the New Testament that "*in Him,*" *i e.* Christ (as their Ideal), " were all things created, in the heavens and upon the earth . . . all things have been created through Him and unto Him, and He is before all things, and in Him all things consist (hold together)," and that "it was the good pleasure of the Father that in Him should all the fulness dwell; and through Him *to reconcile all things to Himself"* (Col. i 16–20). And again, that it was God's purpose "*to sum up all things in Christ,* the things in the heavens, and the things upon the earth" (Eph. i. 10, 11). These greatly-overlooked sayings have surely both a deep and a wide significance They set forth that which has been rightly termed " the Cosmic relations of Christ," and they point to some great Cosmic event culminating in His Person as the realisation of the fulness of God in the completion of the world-process. When that Divine goal is reached in Him, a universal consciousness, or at least the consciousness of all who have lived to God, or have fulfilled their designed function in the world, may well be experienced.

Consciousness and the Self in relation to the Spiritual and Eternal World

As we have seen in a former chapter, man as a spiritual being really lives his life in a spiritual world. The Monism we have advocated has, we must once more repeat, reference only to the world of Science—the world as it exists in Time and Space, *with a view to a spiritual and eternal world.* In addition to what has already been said on this subject, we may here also quote what M. Renan has well expressed with respect to spiritual survival and re-living in the realised Divine Ideal of the world. "When the Brain is decomposed," he says, "no consciousness, in the ordinary sense of the word, can continue. But the life of man, in the whole of the general scheme, the place he occupies in it, his share in the general consciousness, this has no connection with an organism; this is eternal. Consciousness has a relation with space; not as residing in a certain point, but as feeling in a definite space. The *idea* has no such relation; it is purely immaterial; neither time nor death has any power over it. The ideal alone is eternal; nothing but itself and what constitutes it endures" (p. 79). Again, "The soul and its personality must be conceived of as things distinct from consciousness. Consciousness has a distinct connection with space; not that it has its habitat in a given point, but that it acts within certain defined limits. The soul, on the contrary, the personality of each individual, is nowhere [that is, spatially]; since man often acts with more effect at the distance of a thousand leagues than in the district which he inhabits. The soul is where it acts, where it loves. God being the ideal, the object of all love, is therefore essentially the *locus* of souls. The place of a man in God, the opinion that is held of him by absolute justice, the rank he holds in the only true world, which is the world according to God—in a word, his share in the general Consciousness, that is his true being." And we all instinctively know it to be so, for men will shorten their days, and, if need be, suffer death for this, their true life. Jesus is the great example of this "Is not Jesus a thousand times more really alive? Is He not a thousand times more beloved in our day than when He went up and down Galilee?" It is not a matter of reputation or of memory merely, but one of actual life *in God*. "The categories of time and space being merged in the absolute, existence in relation to it is as much what has been as what will be Thus it is in God all souls that have lived still live. Why, then, might not the supremacy of Mind, which is the end and aim of the Universe, be thus the resurrection of all consciousnesses? Mind will be all powerful, the idea will be all reality. What does such language as this signify but that in the idea everything will revive?" (pp. 105, 106).

M. Renan recognised the harmony of this (so far, at least) with Christian teaching; for into the mouth of one of the interlocutors in the Dialogue from which a considerable portion of the foregoing has been quoted, is put the saying, "It is nearly so that the priests deliver themselves, but the phraseology is different" The *sense*, no doubt, is also different in some important respects; but, at the same time, profound Christian truths are *suggested* by what he says. What M. Renan speaks of as "the Ideal" is from the Christian standpoint the "spiritual" and the Divine; and what he attributes to the supremacy of "Mind" is ascribed by Christianity to the realisation of true ethical and spiritual life as a whole—that which was realised and manifested in Christ, in Whom the Divine evolution of life culminated, and through Whom it is to be realised in the race. We may here simply quote again the grounds of the Christian hope, which hope seems to be quite in harmony with these suggestive utterances: "Because I live, ye shall live also"; "I in them and Thou in me, that they may be perfected into one"; "When Christ who is our life shall be manifested, we also shall be manifested with Him in glory." In any case, this is the distinctively Christian hope It relies on that power of God which was "manifested in Christ, when He raised Him from the dead and seated Him at His own right hand in the heavenly places," and in Whom He is "to reconcile *all things* to Himself"

In a former chapter we have seen the *possibility* of

universal survival: the rest we must leave in the hands of the Perfect Reason and Love.

The tendency at present is to seek for grounds, and even for proofs, of Immortality, or, at least, of full conscious existence hereafter, altogether apart from any reference to Christ in that relation to Humanity in which Christianity affirms Him to stand. But (1) it cannot be said that, after all our searching, we yet *know* the *mode* of entrance into the fulness of life beyond, or even that of the continuation of our being after death; and (2) if Christ is what Christianity affirms Him to be—He in Whom God has realised His life in human form—in Whom the Divine world-process has reached its culmination, and in Whom the Eternal Life comes in all the fulness of its power to men—He must hold some such special relation, not only to the highest life of mankind here, but also to the possibilities of a life hereafter. May it not be found that the speculation which leaves Christ in His relation to God on the one hand and to man on the other hand, altogether out of account, omits a vital element for the solution of the great problem? Christian faith certainly gives us *something definite* to rely on, in what has been already realised and manifested in Christ, Who is "the Head" of our Humanity—Who is "not ashamed to call us His brethren."

CHAPTER V

Eternal Life the Divine Purpose   Conclusion

To make men partakers in eternal life is the great purpose of God in the creation. The mere survival of the soul, of course, stops far short of this. Eternal life is something very much higher, and not in the future only. It is in its essence a present experience through spiritual union with God, and it is as such that it is represented as the source of a blessed "resurrection." To the pious Jew "Eternal Life" was life in the coming Kingdom of God, conceived externally—something to be "entered on" or "inherited." Christ, in whom the eternal life was manifested, showed it to be life-union with God as He comes to men *now* in His Kingdom, although its consummation is in the realm of the unseen and eternal.

The soul that has come to God, as God is revealed and comes to us in that Christ who also represents the true self of every man, has already risen into a life which is essentially, in the highest sense, the life of God within it—a life the principle of which is necessarily eternal For it is that very life of holy, universal, rational Love which is the Divine Life itself. Whatever intellectual difficulties, therefore, may confront the soul that has thus entered into union with God, and whatever may be the conditions of the experience of that life in all its fulness, that soul feels assured that nothing can dissolve the union, that "neither death, nor life, nor angels, nor principalities, nor things present, nor things to come, nor powers, nor height, nor depth, nor any other created thing, shall be able to separate us from the love of God, which is in Christ Jesus our Lord."

The type of that eternal life has been manifested in Christ, of Whom it is finely said that He, "as our forerunner," has entered into the eternal inheritance. It is a life *in* God above Time, above all that is of sense merely, a life in God in which the personality, far from being lost, finds the fulness and the fruition of its being. It is not like the colourless drop, simply returned to the ocean again, but like the drop which has attained a specific colour of its own and retains it; while yet nothing is really *added* to the Divine Life, which only in this way expresses and realises its Infinite perfection in finite forms brought into eternal union with itself. It is the Eternal Fatherhood realising itself in the creation by "bringing many sons unto glory." Whatever theory may be held of the resurrection of Christ, whether in the Body that was laid in the tomb, or with that Body etherealised or spiritualised, or without any Body at all, the Christian man knows that Christ not only survived death (as he believes other men will do), but in His Divine-human uniqueness rose into a life in which He is wholly one with the Infinite Father, and in which He is spiritually present with all His followers and operative in and through them all. His presence and operation are in " the Holy Spirit " which comes to men in Christianity as " the Spirit of Christ." And wherever that Spirit becomes the real principle of a man's life it ensures ultimate conformity to Christ in His Resurrection life and glory. To bring men into this eternal life in union with God is the final purpose of Christianity, and we have in this possible union with God a ground of confidence superior to all others. Therefore, after all our reasonings, we come back to Christ, saying with His disciple of old, " Lord, to whom shall we go? Thou hast the words of eternal life." Our reasonings

ETERNAL LIFE THE DIVINE PURPOSE

carry us so far, but Christ is the living "Word" in Whom the eternal life is revealed, and "the Way" through Whom we are brought into living, ethical union with the Father. He does not tell us how this life expresses itself beyond this world He asks us to have faith, and enables us to say with His apostle, "He Who formed us with this very end in view is God, Who has given us His Spirit as a pledge and foretaste of that bliss" As it is essentially an ethical and spiritual union, it is one that is open to every man, although its completeness is to be found through the development of our entire higher nature—a fact which many Christians are too apt to overlook.

Christianity teaches that to raise us all into this eternal life was the very object of the creation, and of that equally Divine and creative work which we call "our Redemption in Christ." In creation the Father-Spirit goes forth to impart His very life to human children conceived in His own image. But in order to effect this He must give rise to a world which shall be the scene of finite individual existence. He must so condition His own Being that this world shall in due time be the result. Life in the image of God—free, personal, spiritual life—cannot be directly created; souls cannot be thrown off from the Divine life ready formed; the Divine end can only be reached as the result of a long process of evolution. This is just *why* there is an evolution, and also *what* it is. The dawning consciousness must appear in lowliest form. Education must be given through contact with the rationally formed Universe, which becomes thus the means of mediating the Divine Reason and Spirit to man, until at length rational beings are, by their necessary relations to that Universe, formed. For this, a Body in relation to the physical world must be the organ of the developing individual spirit. Social relationships must come into being in order that ethical life may be born in man and gradually developed. Through his relation to the

Universe around him, and from the wants that arise from his deepest nature, religious or spiritual life in relation to God must be quickened. He must discover that he lives, not merely in a physical, and in a humanly social, environment, but in a spiritual environment as well; he must find out by experience how important this spiritual environment is for his life; he must realise the blessedness of life in union with God as his knowledge of God gradually increases; he must also discover the estrangement from God in His Ethical truth of the merely "natural life" with which he has been gifted,—that that life is not an end in itself,—and, rising above it,—"dying to it,"—enter into a free personal union with God in His transcendency. He must, perhaps, pass through a long and hard discipline to wean him from the world,—a discipline which is not completed in this life for many individuals and for many races,—which fact suggests an "intermediate" condition, and gives its importance to the general question of the survival of the soul. He must be led to believe that God is his supreme Good, and that in union with God alone his true life—his real self—is to be found. And just as in natural evolution the phylogenetic process is summarily repeated in the history of each individual, so is it with this religious preparation and development in general. The individual soul must be weaned from the world, must be made to feel the disharmony there is between God and a merely "natural" life—the sense of sin,—be brought into that ethical living union with God that is opened up for all in Christ; and have, through what it experiences, the spiritual life more or less developed, or at least quickened within it. Then, when all this necessary work has been done, those elements which merely ministered to the Divine final purpose, including our bodies of flesh and blood themselves, may all be left behind, and only *the result* endure.

This may be well illustrated from the opening of

ETERNAL LIFE THE DIVINE PURPOSE 465

Browning's Poem "The Ring and the Book." He has found an old book containing a story of events in Rome, and to make it a poem, he treats it after the manner in which the goldsmith treats the gold in order to fashion it into a ring.

"Do you see this Ring?
                    'Tis Rome-work, made to match
. . . .
Etrurian circlets.   .   .   .   .   .   .
                    There's one trick,
(Craftsmen instruct me) one approved device
And but one, fits such slivers of pure gold
As this was, ...

To bear the file's tooth and the hammer's tap :
Since hammer needs must widen out the round,
And file emboss it fine with lily-flowers,
Ere the stuff grow a ring-thing right to wear.
That trick is, the artificer melts up wax
With honey ; so to speak, he mingles gold
With gold's alloy, and, duly tempering both
Effects a manageable mass, then works ,
But his work ended, once the thing a ring,
Oh, there's repristination ! Just a spirt
O' the proper fiery acid o'er its face,
And forth the alloy unfastened flies in fume ;
While, self-sufficient now, the shape remains,
The rondure brave, the lilied loveliness,
Gold as it was, is, shall be evermore
Prime nature with an added artistry—
No carat lost, and you have gained a ring
What of it ? 'Tis a figure, a symbol, say ,
A thing's sign now for the thing signified "

So the bodily life was necessary for the individual existence and education of the spirit , pure spirit could not have been wrought into shape any more than the pure gold The work done, Death is the acid that removes the alloy, and, according to the Divine Thought at least, " the spirit returns to God," as He meant to fashion it. Since God is Spirit, the life of *Spirit* must be the full and perfect life."

Conclusion

Our object in writing has not been theoretical merely, but practical as well. We have sought to show the grounds of belief in Christian Theism, including Freedom and Immortality, in order that we may be inspired to a more confident faith in, and a completer practical expression of, our Christianity.

It is beyond the scope of our present effort to deal, in any detail, with the relation of Christianity to this present world in the social aspects of life. But the future can never be severed from the present, and the Christian Ideal is the Reign of God in His transcendent truth, righteousness, and love on the earth—the establishment of His Kingdom here. All human sympathy, every desire to cheer and help one another and to uplift those who seem to stand beneath us; every social movement that is grounded in Reason and inspired by Love—aiming at making this world what our best thoughts, feelings, and convictions tell us it ought to be—are, according to Christianity, the working of God in man. The Christian Spirit can never rest till the world becomes the " Kingdom of God," and God's will is done on earth as it is in heaven It ought to be plain to all who believe in God that it is only He who began the creation that can perfect it. But He has given rise to a world of free personalities, and it can only be through their obedience to the inspiration of His Spirit—the Divine Reason and Love, or " the Spirit of Christ," in man—that the Divine purpose can be accomplished. And if men realise that the " eternal life " in virtue of which they hope for the continuation of their being, is just this very life of God's Spirit in them now, they will be inspired to work with God for the realisation of His purpose in this world, they will see that they can only have the fulness of eternal life in their experience by so doing. The idea that " Eternal Life " is something to be entered on in the future, instead of something that must *enter us* here and now, has been a most disastrous one for the world. But surely we are now leaving this idea behind us, and in this very fact new hope shines forth for this present world. As it is in Christianity we have the fullest manifestation of God, in the form adapted to our deepest need, so it is through it—from Christ in His Life and Teaching, from Christ on that Cross which declares the Reason and Love that are at the foundation of the Universe, and reveals it as coming through self-sacrifice for both individual and social salvation—that the supreme Power goes forth to raise the individual into that eternal life of God. And it is just as individuals truly rise into that life, and give expression to it in their human relationships, that Society will become God's Kingdom in which His will is done as it is in heaven. Herein lies the importance of belief. Not that a man's belief can in itself, in some mysterious manner, save his soul, but because a true belief in Divine Realities, as Christianity declares them, may be the means of bringing a man into true union with God, inspiring him to seek the highest life and to endeavour to realise the Divine purpose in the world. Apart from the life and action to which it leads, the truest belief is of no value to its holder, and of course in forming our beliefs the first and last question must always be, *What is true?*

It must be acknowledged that when one looks back on the past history of mankind and thinks of the myriads who have passed away in very low stages of development, or looks out on the world of the present and contemplates the backward condition of many peoples, the different forms of religion, many of them so full of superstition and even of cruelty, the way in which human lives are sacrificed in needless warfare, the miserable struggle for life that proceeds in many places under the most trying conditions in our highest civilisation, the dominance of devotion to earthly interests merely, and all amidst what seems to be the silence, or even the apparent absence, of a living God who cares for His human children, groping in the darkness after Him and crying out for Him, our faith in a Divine meaning and purpose in human life is often sorely tried, and many find it impossible to hold it. Yet we cannot but believe that a Divine Reason and Love are deepest of all in the Universe, and we see the Divine Thought and Purpose made manifest in Christianity, the highest form of Religion. We cannot doubt, therefore, that there must be some rational explanation of what appears so strange, and some God-like outcome of the whole. That explanation is to be found, we believe in the fact that God in Himself is *Spirit*, and that what we have before us is an *Evolution* in which the Divine Life is imparting itself to us in finite form—slowly, in this sense, realising itself in us,—a process which is not yet completed— which is not completed for individual lives in this world, but which goes on towards completion, not only here, but in another environment.

The fact that we have so many and such varied forms of Religion, while Christianity is the final and perfect form, is entirely in keeping with what we behold in the general working out of Evolution as a whole. It was always along one definite line that life found the advance that culminated in man. As it moved upwards, many organic forms were left behind. But when man was reached the Divine Reason and Love that had been working all along became centred in a separate, conscious, personal form, with a power of free, rational, and loving action in the world. The very dissatisfaction that we experience with things as they are, and the sympathy we feel with those that suffer, are the evidences of the presence and working of the Divine Reason and Love *within ourselves*; and it is for us to work with and for God to make the world what Reason and Love tell us it ought to become. The responsibility is laid on us   It is possible for those who have received the true light to bear it to those who have not yet received it; it is possible for man to remove the ignorance, to rectify the evils that remain in the world, to care for the weak, to leave behind those social forms and institutions that have served their purpose for such as will serve the present well-being of men, to be in many ways a Helper of His brethren, and so, at once, a true member of the Body of Humanity, and an instrument of God in the world.   Man's highest calling is to be a free organ of the Divine Spirit, his greatest dignity is to be found in becoming a co-worker with God, and it is in this life in active union with God that *Eternal life* is realised.

The Cross of Christ declares, we believe, that the creation has its origin in the self-sacrificing Love of God, Who eternally conditions His Being so as to give rise to the worlds.   It is this that creates "the Riddle of the Universe"; but it is this also that is its solution, and that brings to us the supreme inspiration to arise and work for the realisation of the Divine Ideal in ourselves and in the world.   God is first, God is now, in some measure in everything, in this world He is most fully in ourselves, and God at last will be "all in all."   But it is through man's voluntary and earnest, self-sacrificing co-operation, and free self-identification with the Divine Purpose, that the grand result will be secured.   We have sought to vindicate human freedom, but there is a higher Freedom ever before us in the complete unity of our individual wills with the Divine Will, and we need to remember the poet's words,

"He is a slave most base
Whose love is only for himself, and not for all the race,"

and those of the Christian apostle. " He that loveth not his brother whom he hath seen, how can he love God whom he hath not seen ? "

There is a final question that may be asked, although it has already been answered by anticipation, What is the end of it all for the individual? Supposing all that has been said to be true, what has he to look forward to as *eternally* satisfying? A life of mere passiveness or inactivity would be far from satisfactory. And if we reach "perfection," does not that involve stagnation? But what Christianity sets before us is an entrance into the very life of God. The ideal is an infinite one, and can never be finally reached, but only for ever more fully entered on and realised. It is a life of Reason and Love, to the possibilities of which no bounds can be set—the very Life that gives rise to and realises itself in the self-giving and self-finding of creation. This is the Eternal Life, and, surely, to share in it is the highest thing, and the best, that can be set before a created being. It is nothing less than, in the words of a New Testament writer, " being made partakers in the Divine nature."

INDEX

ABSOLUTE, the, 196, 247; and finite forms, 441 (note)
—— consciousness and resurrection, 453-457.
Adamson, Prof, and Monism, 185; on Mind and Body, 192
Adaptations in Nature, 112, 113, 114
Agnosticism, 10 15, 23, 84, 187
Allman, Prof, on development of germs, 170
Altruism, 129, 216, 217, etc
Amœba and consciousness, 228
Anaxagoras, ref, 244.
Anderson, Dr, *Reincarnation*, 436
Animal Evolution, 99-106
—— World, Life in, 255; Will in, 362-366, Consciousness, 75, 209, 363, 437
Anthony, St, temptation and Freedom, 335, 337.
Anthropomorphism, 307.
Anti-Theism, 11, 14
Anti-Theistic argument from Transformation of Energy, 79-84
Apocrypha, doctrine of Reason in, 244
Apperception, 368, 415
Argument, the, 20-33
Arnold, M, quoted, 287.
Atomic Theory, 67, 205.
Atoms See *Matter*
Attention, faculty of, 338, 368, 369.
Augustine, on God and Evil, 260.

BACTERIA, their place in Evolution, 113.
Balfour, A J, on Will and Conservation of Energy, 236-238
Bastian, Dr C, on Brain development, 99; origin of Life, 208, the Will, 327, Free-will, 346.
Beginning, no absolute, 164, 165, 173
Belief, importance of, 5, 7; in Christianity, 5, 9, 467; in God, 5, 9, 10, 24 *seq*, simplicity of grounds, 21, 24, in Immortality, 405.

Belief, power of, 235.
Berkeley and External World, 187
Berthelot quoted, 60, 61, 62, advances in organic chemistry, 283
Bible, doctrine of Reason in, 244
Body, the need for, 463, 464, 465. See *Brain, Mind, Soul, Self, etc.*
—— the spiritual, 413, 432, 434, 435, 437, 438, 441 (note), 448, 451
Boscovich, theory of the atom, 68.
Brain, the, development, 36-40, 99, 212, 418, 419; fineness, 214; control (centres in), 232, 348, comparative size, 293
—— and Mind, 36-44, 85, 350-354, 417, 418, 419, and character, 353, and thought, 394, 417-425; and function, 420, 421.
Brotherhood, the ideal, 4; its realisation, 313
Browning quoted, 10, 218; illustration from *The Ring and the Book*, 465
Buchner, L, and Monism, 13, and God, 15, on origin of Reason in man, 38; our senses, 50, Monism and Matter, 77-78, "Love" in Evolution, 125; and Materialism, 154, Immortality, 392
Burbank, L., modifications of flowers and fruits, 96
Burke, J Butler, on Origin of Life, 209 (note)
Burns quoted, 256.

CAILLARD, Miss E. M, quoted, 51.
Caird, Dr Edward, on rationality of the World, 64, Monism, 179, Theistic argument, 195, Hegelian doctrine of Reason, 198, and Spiritual Monism, *ibid* (note)
Caird, Dr. John, on rationality of the World, 65; Theistic argument, 30, 194, and Monism, 198, the wider Design argument, 199, motives, 332.

Carlyle, T, on belief, 7
Carpenter, Dr W B, on external perception, 190; correlation, 229, 230; psychical influence, 235 (note), Free-will, 345
Carus, Dr Paul, and Monism, 14; on Causation, 32; origin of Reason in man, 39; Brain development, 99, function and organ, 99, 100, Evolution, 116; his Monism, 181; a God-man, 294 (note), the Trinity conception, 317; Immortality, 392
Causation, the argument from, 24-37; mechanical and scientific, 25, 26, Spencer on, 24; Haeckel, 25, 28, Whetham, 26; Romanes, *ibid*, Lloyd Morgan, 27; Upton, 27; Cudworth, 31; Carus, 32.
—— philosophical and Theistic, 26, 27
—— and Reason, 54, psychical, 229-231 (and note); will-power, 235 (and note)
Cause, definition, 25; of the Universe, 27, etc, causes, finite and personal, 325
—— and consequent, 260, 442, 453.
—— the Ultimate, 151, etc. See *Source*
Cell, a structure, 170, 171, soul cells, 170
Chance, 254 (note).
Chemical elements, 48, 49, 160, 161, 206, union, *ibid* (note)
Christ, and Love, 4; revelation of God, 58, 251, 263, 280, of Love, 274, 289, complete union with God, 286, culmination of both natural and spiritual Evolution, 289
—— supremacy as Teacher, 291, 292, the problem in Him, 292, Person and Work, 292, Incarnation of God, *ibid*, not the product of Nature merely, 294-296, relation to God, 299-301, 303, to Humanity, 301, 460
—— in God, 321
—— in relation to Immortality, 406, 460, His consciousness and future life, 407; His resurrection, 408-410, the Christian's relation to, 449, 456, 460, 462, the self-realisation of God in the world, 456, Cosmic relations, 457, 460
—— See *Incarnation*
Christianity, the religion of Love, 1, 2, the God of, *ibid*, a Religion, 3, practical, 5, its highest function, 315, as the highest religion, 468
—— and Freedom, 377-381
—— and Immortality, 385 *seq*, 444-460, 463 See also *God, Incarnation,* etc

Cleanthes quoted, 308
Clerke, Miss A M, on Evolution in the Heavens, 109 (note)
Clifford, Prof, "Mind-stuff," 115.
Clodd, Edward, *Pioneers of Evolution*, 141, on the Incarnation, 293
Coleridge, S, on "spirit," 86; the Will, 329, 365, 366, 371.
Collins, Wilkie, illustration from, 56.
Conclusion, 466-470, object practical, 466, the present world, *ibid*; Eternal life in relation to, 466, 467, the Social Ideal, 467; the aspect of the world, 467; the trial of faith, 468; the explanation, 468, culmination of Evolution in Christ and Christianity, 468; God within, *ibid*; man's power and responsibility, 469, the revelation of the Cross, *ibid*; the Riddle and its solution, *ibid*; man's part, *ibid*; the higher Freedom, *ibid*, the goal of the individual, 470
Conditioned and Unconditioned, 149, 203, 221, 222, 246, 277, 294, etc.
Conscience, 216, 284, 298.
Conscious, the, never from the Unconscious, 169, etc.
Consciousness, its nature, 75; evolution of, 107, 169; its rise, 189, 209, 210; cannot be created, 211; spiritual origin of, 211, 212; development of, 212; a manifestation of the one Spiritual Power, 213, 227; relation to matter, 214; as belonging to the Source of our being, 214, 215, Monistic view, 224; an Eternal, 228, 231, 241, and Self-consciousness, 231, relation to Brain-states, 231 (note), 242; and voluntary actions, 363
—— and the Self, 425-427; relation to the organism, 427, analogies, 427, 428, in relation to the Spiritual and Eternal World, 457-459
—— the wider, 434, and stimuli, 435-437
—— God-consciousness, 298, 299
—— animal and human, 437, 444
Continuity, the principle of, 293
Contradictories, impossible to believe, 16, 17
Correlation of Forces, meaning, 229, 241; Dr Carpenter on, 229, 230 See *Energy*.
Creation, 110, 111, its extent, 246, its motive, 273, 320, 321; destiny of, 320, 321, 443, 453, 457
—— and Freedom, 379, 380
Croll, Dr J, on cause of differences in Evolution, 133

INDEX 473

Crookes, Sir W., on Matter, 156; Telepathy, 433
Cross, the, of Christ, significance, 4, 274, 275, power of, 310, rationale, 313, revelation of, 469
Cudworth, on Causation, 34.

DARWIN, Dr C, on man's power of modification, 96, variations, 101, selection, 103, sociality among animals, 127 (and note), 128, 366, dawn of Freedom, 366
Darwin, Prof, on Evolution in the Heavens, 109 (note)
Darwinian Evolution, 100 seq
Dawson, Sir J W, on origin of Life, 207
Death, origin of, 121, 401; in relation to survival, 401; Fechner on, 401 (note); what is dissolved at, 437, 438 See *Survival*, *Immortality*
Democracy, the salvation of, 9.
Descartes and Dualism, 12.
Design Argument, the wider, 136, 199
Desires See *Will*, etc
Determinism, "of Psychology," 331-334; Mr Mallock on 331 *seq*; will not be smuggled into our nature, 331, motives not separate from the man, 332, Psychology and Will, *ibid*; discussion, 332 *seq*.; "bondage," 333, our desires, 334, 340, the real question, 335; Dr W Ward's statement, 335; case of St Anthony, 335, 337, 338, circumstances, 337, character, 337; spiritual influences, 339, self - government, 340; cause of volitional acts, 341, free choice, 342, 343; what makes the strongest motive, 343; Kant and Freedom, 343, 344
——— "of matter," 345-362; Scientists and Free-will, 345-347; Haeckel and the Will, 348, 349, physiological provision for volition, 348; what " the determinism of matter" implies, 349, 357; discussion, 349-362, conservation of energy, etc, 350, 359, 360, relation to the body, 350-354, character and heredity, 353-357, and Monism, 357, and a Spiritual Monism, 358-362; so-called difficulties and impossibilities, 360-362.
De Quincey, dream of, 435
De Varigny, on Evolution, 89, 91; influence of environment, 131
" Direction," immanent, 123, 124, 163, 208, 258, 259
Dolbear, Prof, on " Forces of Nature," 71, Life, 73

Drummond, Prof Henry, *The Ascent of Man*, 125
Dualism, 11, 13, 160, 177, 181, 186, 188, 228, 241; the temporary in the Creation, 177, 222, 279, transcended in Christ, 314, none in Nature, 279, etc; no ultimate, 177, 220, 286, etc
Duncan, *The New Knowledge*, 48, 69, on the chemical elements, 48, 160, 206, electric origin of matter, 69 (note), 70 (and note), energy, 72, formation of the elements, 110; origin of Life, 209

EDINBURGH REVIEW on Revelations of Radium, 156
Effort, putting forth of, 233 *seq*.
Electricity, electric origin of the atom, 68-70, 69 (and note), 157, 160, 163; electrons, 165; Zimmern on, 165, 431; in relation to survival, 431.
Elements, character of, 48; formation of, 110
Embryology, 169.
Emerson quoted, 44, 403
Energy, its nature, 71-73; Dolbear on, 71, Duncan, *ibid*; Whetham, *ibid*, Spencer, 78, 79; Haeckel, 157.
——— Transformations of, 66, 80; meaning, 81, 224, 229, 241, and mental manifestations, *ibid*, in relation to survival, 406, 439
——— "phronetic," 406
Environment, rational, as a factor in Evolution, 99, 100, 101, importance of the, 131-137; the Social, 215, Spiritual, 217, 279
Epictetus on Freedom, 379
Eternal Life, Christian conception, 368, 369, 407, 439, 444 *seq*
——— ——— the Divine Purpose, 460, how made partakers of, 461; the type shown in Christ, 462, the Spirit as the principle of, 462; Christ the Life, 462, Object of Creation and Redemption, 463, why there is an Evolution, and what it is, 463, 464, illustration from *The Ring and the Book*, 465.
Ether, the, its nature, 68, 70; illustration of Consciousness, 427; in the Brain, 432, and Consciousness, *ibid*, in relation to survival, 437, etc
Ethical Ideal, the, 8, 284, 285
——— life in God, 319
——— aspect of Evolution, 129, 130.

INDEX

Ethical inspiration and authority, 284, 288
Evil, moral, 256-257
"Evils" in Nature, 10, 166, 245-255, 257-261
Evolution, 10; Monists and, 87, 88
—— and the Rational Power, 88-137, a modal theory, 88, exaggerations, *ibid.*; what it *is*, 89; Is it proved? 91, reasons for acceptance, 91; errors respecting, 91-94; Reason in, 94, *seq*, in the present the human sphere, 94-99, mental, 98, Organic —animal life, 99-106, plant life, 106-7; Inorganic, 107-112; the environment, 100; various factors, 100, 101; in the heavens, 109 (and note); adaptations, 112, illustration, 113; Monistic view, 114-117, Reason in it all, 117
—— recently emphasised factors in, 118-137; Prof Le Conte's statement, 118, the rational factor, 119, "Projected Efficiency," 119-124, mutual aid, 124-129, reproductive factor, 129, 130, the environment and definite variation, 131; Weismann's theory; 134-137
—— ethical and spiritual, 218, 220, 288, 295
—— of morality and religion, 215-218.
—— Love in. See *Love*.
—— and Sin and Grace, 309, 311.
—— and Immortality, 386, 398-401, 455
—— a "God-developing," 455.
—— Why there is and what it is, 463-464. See *Reason*.
Expectancy, 235.
"Experience" is spiritual, 196, 212, 424.
External world, belief in, 18, 19; consciousness of, 187-192.

FAITH, importance of, 5, 8, 10; in God as Father, 308; trial of, 469.
Fatherhood of God, 1, 306-309, essential to Christianity, 306, Spiritual Monism illustrates, 307; charge of Anthropomorphism, 307, power of faith in, 308, 309.
Fechner, G. F., on man's threefold life on earth, 401 (note); purely spiritual existence, 440, 441
Feeling, rise of, etc , 209 *seq.*; ultimate, 231, and "an Eternal Consciousness," 231, a manifestation of the spiritual, *ibid*
Finot, M. Jean, on Will-power, 235 (note).

Fiske, Mr John, on origin of Reason in man, 39, 125, altruistic element, 129, evils in nature, 166, unseen world, 405
Fleming, Dr J A, on Mechanism, 54; on Monism, 183
Flint, Prof, on Reason in History, 97; Physiology and Psychology, 185, Spencer's work, 139; living matter, 264 (note).
Force, see *Energy*, Mr. Spencer's doctrine of, 138, 141, 142, 145, etc. See *Transformation*
Foreknowledge, 380, 381.
Form, laws of, 116, spiritual, 440, 441 (note)
Freedom, of Will, implied in Christianity, 6, denial of, 14, 17, 178, 248.
—— and Monistic Science, 325-381; if none, cannot infer God, 374 See *Will*.
—— the Christian doctrine of, 377-381; implied in man's nature and sin, 377; the Christian Salvation, *ibid*; bondage to the lower self, 378; the Christian deliverance, *ibid*; perfect freedom, 379, early Christian doctrine and later discussions, 379; answers to Mr. Mallock's statement of the theological questions, 379-381
Froud, J A, on belief, 7
Function and organisation, 39, 99, 100, 364, 420-423, etc.; Prof James on Function, 420; T. H Green, 421; Prof. Nicholson, 422-423

GIDDINGS, *Principles of Sociology*, 125.
God, the, of Christianity, 1, 2, need of, 5, 6, 10; present position of belief in, 9, 10, distinct from the World, 12, 13, etc.; denial of, 14; the alternative, 11, 173, 176; knowledge of, 147, etc; conception of, 151, 152, 276, 278; Being of, 175; conditioned and unconditioned, 221, etc.; idea of, 276, purpose in Creation, 461, where He is, 287; what He does, 288; distinction between, and man, 219-221, to be transcended, 177, 220, 286, etc ; as the Perfect Reason, 35, 36, 42, 44, etc. See *Reason*.
—— as Love, 267 *seq*. See *Love*
—— as Spirit, 257, 259, 280, etc.
—— the complete evidence for, 252
—— distinctions in See *Trinity*.
—— in relation to Immortality, 398, 405, 461, etc See *Source, Immanence, Transcendence, Spirit, Holy Spirit, Incarnation*.

INDEX 475

God in relation to the World, 244-266, the doctrine of a Divine Reason, 244, why not more influential, 245, what seems to oppose it, *ibid*, the Reason *in* the World not God as He is in Himself, 245-252; self-conditioned, 246, Reality, 247; the evolution of the Divine Thought—not of *God*, 247, Divine Immanence, 248-252, Spirit and Transcendence, 252; neither Pantheism nor Deism, 251, the complete manifestation only in Christ, 252; the chief points to be kept in view, 253, the wider creation, 254; the unfinished work, 254, the reign of Law that of Reason, 254, Evolution and suffering, 255, moral evil, 256, 257, the transcendent Presence spiritual, 257; the greater Personality, 258; no interference with rational laws, 258, 259, Cause and Consequent, 260; the individual and suffering, 260; Augustine and Whittier quoted, 260, 261; the nature of the rational Power *in* the World, 261-266, the Biblical Logos, 261, 262; the Principle of the World-organism, 262, 263, how possibly operative, 263-266; a continuously developing Reason, 265, 266
—— the Christian conception of, 306-321; Fatherhood, 306; illustrated by a Spiritual Monism, 307, 308, Faith in, 308, Grace, 309, sense of Sin, 309; how Grace meets, 310, Science and Sin and Grace, 311, 312; Universality, 312, 313; the Holy Spirit in Christianity, 313-315, Trinity, 313-321. See *Holy Spirit, Trinity*
Goethe, and Monism, 13, sociality in Nature, 125; carbon, 161; God, 247.
Good, the idea of the, 291
Gore, Dr. G, on Mind and Brain, 36; origin of human reason, 37, unconscious mentality, 210, consciousness, 214
Grace, in Christianity, 309; reality of, 311, 312
Green, T H, on Hegelianism, 12; rationality of the Universe, 50; an Eternal Consciousness, 228, 234, 241, consciousness and self-consciousness, 234 (note), function, 241
Griffiths, Dr, on the Bacteria, 113

HAECKEL, Prof. E, and Monism, 11, 13, etc; on Causation, 25, 28, 114, *Riddle of the Universe*, 28; on Reason, 35, Environment, 101.

Haeckel, his "Monistic Evolution" criticised, 153-178, his general position, 153-155, basis of his Monism, 155, 157, "Substance," 155, etc, inclusion of a "spiritual" side, 157 *seq*; ascription of "Sensation" to all matter, 159-162, Evolution of the Conscious from the Unconscious, 163-173, God, or an Eternal Substance, 173, misconception of what God is—not the Universe or Nature, 175, Freedom, 178, Religion and Morality, *ibid*.
—— his Monism as contrasted with a Spiritual Monism, 179
—— the Ideals of the True, the Beautiful, and the Good, 290
—— criticism of Christ, 291
—— on the Will, 348
—— and Immortality, 393
Hagenbach on the Early Christian doctrine of Freedom, 379
Haldane, R B, Theistic argument, 196; on the Trinity, 318, Spiritual Being and Immortality, 404, 441
Hamilton, Sir W, and external perception, 188
Harris, Dr S, *Philos Basis of Theism, etc*, 46 (note), on the Will, 367
Hegel, on Spirit, 86; Thought and Being, 196, 199; Reason, 198
Hegelianism, its attraction, 11; and Dualism, 197; and Spiritual Monism, 198, difficulties of, 196, 199, and the Trinity, 318 (note)
Henslow, Rev. G., on Natural Selection, 103, 131.
Heraclitus, 244
Heredity, 102, 169, and spiritual development, 298, and "Will," 355-357
Herschell, Sir J W, on Atoms, 67, 205
Hird, Principal Dennis, on the Unity of Forces, criticism of, 79, 81-83; on the future of Evolution, 399.
History, Reason in, 97
Hobhouse, L T., *Democracy and Reaction*, 7; Evolution of Mind, 63; *Mind in Evolution*, 94, 212, Freedom, 366
Hollander, Dr, *The Mental Functions of the Brain*, 353
Holy Spirit the, of Truth and Love, work of God in, 281, 286, 295, 297; Christ the Child of, 296, 300.
—— —— in Christianity, 313-315, in pre-Christian religion, 314, ethical and personal, *ibid*, one with the Presence of Christ, *ibid*; Paul's experience of, 314; to minister, the highest

function of Christianity, 315 ; through the Divine self-conditioning, *ibid*
Homogeneousness, an assumption, 164.
Humanism, 49
Humanity, unity, 312, 313 , Christ, the Ideal, 456, 457 , the Head of, 301, 460.
Hume on external world, 18
Hunt, Dr John, on Spinoza, 247 (note)
Hus, John, illustration, 53
Huxley, Prof , and Agnosticism, 23 ; on Evolution, 90 , Nature, 167 , and Grace, 311.

IDEA, the Divine, of the World, 254, etc.
—— of an organism, 106, 111, etc
Ideal, the Ethical, 216, 217, 284, 285, 302, 309 , man's ideal nature, 369
Idealism, and Reason in Nature, 64, 65
—— Subjective, 51 ; and the external world, 187-192
Idealistic Philosophy, and Theism, 30 , and Monism, 183, 184 , Theistic arguments, 192-196 ; and Spiritual Monism, 196-204
Ideas, innate, 38.
Identity, Pantheistic, Spiritual Monism does not give, 219-222
Illingworth, J. R , on "Substance," 177.
Imagination, 235
Immanence of God, true and false, 248 *seq* ; Scripture passages, 250 , and Pantheism, 249 , and Freedom, 251, 252 , in relation to Transcendency, 277, 278 , to the Incarnation of God in Christ, 294, 295, 300 , the new, in Christ, 302
Immortality, implied in Christianity, 6 , denial of, 14.
—— 385-465
—— alternative views, 385-391 ; the possibility of a limited, 385 , Christian doctrine of, 386 , Evolution and, 386 , silence of Scripture as to resurrection of the wicked, 387 , the myriads in a low condition, 387, 388 , cannot satisfy Christian or truly human feeling, 388, 389 , our ancestors, 388 , the condition of others, 389 ; possibilities of the Infinite Being, 389 , universal and eternal Divine working implied, 389 , the nature of the desire, 390 ; Renan's statement of it, 390 (note) ; an adequate goal impossible on the earth, 390, 391.
—— reasons for belief in, 392-410 ; Monism and Immortality, 392, 393 , Science and, 393 ; the main difficulty, 394 , Spiritualism, 394, 395 , reasons why no demonstration, 395-397 ; Prof. Upton on this, 397 , Grounds of Belief If God be real, 398 ; from the Reason in the world's Evolution, 398-400 , from the production of a spiritual World, 400 , from the meaning of Death in relation to Life, 401 , Fechner quoted, 401 (note) , from the Love that is Supreme, 402, 403 , from Spirit, 403, 404 , our present relation to Eternity, *ibid* ; from the moral order, 404 , from the instinctive craving and universal belief, 404, 405 , from the influence of the belief, 405 , as it affects the Divine Power, etc , 406 , from the Consciousness of Christ, 406 ; from His Resurrection, 406-410
Immortality, what we can be rationally sure of, 443
—— the Christian confidence in, 461.
Incarnation, the, of God in Christ, 291-305 ; Haeckel's criticism of Christ, 291 ; Christ as Teacher, 291, 292 , Person and Work of, 292 , objections to the Incarnation, 293 ; aid of a rational Monism to belief in, 293 , distinction between Conditioned and Unconditioned Being, 294 ; the "Logos" and immanent world-principle, *ibid* ; God in His transcendency must also be manifested, *ibid* , Christ not the product of Nature merely, but also of the Divine spiritual working, *ibid* ; so also *man* as a son of God, 295 ; failure to have regard to the transcendent Deity, 295 ; Science enables us to see in Christ the veritable Incarnation of God in human form, 296 ; the "miraculous" birth, *ibid*. , the incarnation of an Ethical Being, *ibid* ; the Divine *Kenosis* not in Time, but Eternal, *ibid* ; God so far *within* our Humanity, *ibid* , 297 , ever in His transcendency entering more fully, 297 ; the Divine Ideal of man realised in Christ, 296 ; the process, 297-300 ; the Child of the Holy Spirit, 299 ; relation to the transcendent God and Father, *ibid*., 300 ; the full Ethical union with God, 300 , manifested in the Sacrifice of the Cross, 300 , Christ as the Head of Humanity, 301 ; the temporary Dualism transcended, 301 ; Source of a new life to men, 302 ; a new immanence and transcendency, 302 , why progress slow, 302 ; a new principle which must grow, 302 ,

INDEX

real progress, *ibid*, 303; the new transcendency—Christ in God, 303; the nature of the Kingdom of God, 303; causes of delay, 304; the "coming" or "manifestation" of Christ, 304
Individualism and survival 437 (note)
Individuality, realisation and transcendence of, 217 (note), Di Royce on realisation of, 441, goal of the individual, 470
Infinite, the, 276, 277
Infinity, 17, 18
Inspiration, racial and individual, 289
Intelligence in Evolution, 94, 104 See *Reason*
Intelligibility of Nature, 45. See *Reason*
Invisible world, 165, etc
Iron, red-hot, as illustration of Consciousness, 427
Irritability in Protoplasm, 73, 209, 226
Israel, "the people of God," 289
Iverach, Dr J, on Thought in Nature, Mr McCabe's criticism of, 56, 167

JAMES, Prof W, on the Will, 240 (note); universal Immortality, 388, 389, function, 420
Janet and Séailles, on the Problem of Philosophy, 34
Jones, Prof Henry, on Reason in Nature, 64
Judgment, the final, 453
Justice and Immortality, 404.

KANT, *a priorism*, 38, on Freedom, 343, 344, unity of apperception, 415
Kelvin, Lord, Theory of the Atom, 68
Kenosis, the Divine, *Eternal*, 296
Kepler quoted, 55
Kidd, Benjamin, and "Projected Efficiency," 106, 119–124
Kingdom of God, slow progress of, 302–305
Knowledge, the question of, 23, possibility of, 50, of God, 146, 147, 151
Kropotkin, Prince, on "Mutual Aid," 106, 124–129; origin of Morality, 217 (note), "Love" in Nature, 270

LADD, Prof Trumbull, on the Brain, 214, character, 370
Laing, Samuel, on Life, 74
Lang, Andrew, on Telæsthesia, 435 (note).
Law, 109; in Nature, 44 *seq.*; laws of Nature, 163, law everywhere, 167, 254, the moral, 215–217 (and note), 284, 285, of God, 309, 311.

Le Conte, Prof, on factors in Evolution, 119, the Will, 369, individuation and survival, 437 (note)
Life, its nature, 73–75, its appearance, 107; origin, 206, 207, different views, 208, reconciled by Spiritual Monism, 208, 209 (note), Matter of, 263, and continued Being, 436
—— in the wider sense, 177
—— the Divine, 273, 278 *seq*, 315–321
—— the Christian doctrine of Continuity of, 444–460; the teaching of Christ in Synoptists, 444, 445, in Fourth Gospel, 445–447, St Paul, 447–449; actuality of life for the believer *with Christ*, 449–451; present in and with Him, 450, our want of faith, 451; the "resurrection" Body, 450, 451; how far embodiment necessary? 451–453, reality of spiritual life, 452; the Christian Consciousness, *ibid*
Lodge, Sir Oliver, on Life, 74, Electrons, 165 (note); Monism, 182, Life as an Entity, 208; Volition, 240 (note); Free-will, 347 (note), ourselves and our bodies, 416; Telepathy, 433
Logos, the, Biblical doctrine of, 244, 261, 263, 317
Love, the all-working Power as, 267–275; "Reason" in its deeper significance, 267; Feeling, *ibid*; Will, *ibid*; rational Will, 268, motived by Love, 268, 269; unity of perfect Reason and perfect Love, 269, the gradual revelation of Love in Evolution, 269, from solidarity and unity of Life, 270, rise in animal world and in man, 272, always allied to Reason, 272, the real Substance of Being, 272, the primal self-giving Love, 273; the motive of the Creation, 273, the Creation a real Gospel, 273, difficulties and their solution, 273, 274, the full revelation in Christ and His Cross, 274, significance of the Cross, 274, 275
—— source of the World, 278, the Supreme law of Life, 285; the Infinite and Perfect, 285, 319, 469
—— and Immortality, 402, 403
Lubbock, Sir John, on "the Book of Nature," 47.

McCABE, Joseph, on the rationality of the World, 56, Evolution, 87, defence of Haeckel, 163–172; Divine Immanence, 248; "Freedom," 347 (note)

McDougall, Prof., on Life, 73
McKendrick, Prof., on Monism, 183
Mallock, W. H., and Scientific Monism, 16, mode of reconciliation of Science and Religion discussed, 16-20, on Matter and Mind, criticism of, 85, 86; on Spiritual determination, 221; psychical causation and parallelism, 231 (note); Chance, 254 (note); "The Crux of Theism," 260, 273, 274
—— on Freedom and Determinism, discussion, 325-362 See *Freedom, Determinism, Will*
—— "through Matter to Mind," 373, 377
Man, the present evolution of, 96; not from a mere animal, 216, 217, the Divine Element in, 218, 220; Divine relation to, 251, development of, 255; relation to spiritual influences, 295; kinship with God, 306; Ideal nature, 369, and freedom, 378.
Manifestation after death, 443 (note)
Martineau, Dr. James, and external perception, 188
Materialism, 10, 13, 29, 158, 194, 201, 357; impossible conception, 417
Matter, its nature, 67-71, 205, 431, 437, 439, and Mind, 85, 86, etc.; Whence? 109; and Spirit, 144, 145, 146, 203, 204, etc., Elements, 205, and origin of World, 144, 263, 265, in relation to survival, 431, 432, 437; and Ether, 437, etc.
—— "determinism of," 345 *seq.*
Maurice, F. D., on belief in God, 10
Maxwell, Prof. Clerk, on the Atoms, 48, 67, 205.
—— Dr., on Telekinesis, 434
Mechanism of Nature, 54
Medium of embodiment after death, 431, 434, 448, 450
Memory, belonging to all organised matter, 225; in relation to survival, 428-430, spiritual element in, 428, its powers, 429; relation to meaning, *ibid*; what possible, *ibid*; *Unseen Universe* quoted, 430.
Mendeléef, on the Chemical Elements, 48, on the Ether, 70
Merz, J. T., on order and uniformity in Nature, 46
Metaphysics, 21, 27.
Methods of argument, 16, that of the book, 20-23
Mind, its nature, 75-77, 209 *seq.*; and Matter, 85, 144, 228; supremacy, 149, cannot be created, 211, influence on Body, 229-30 (and note),

232-236, 238, etc.; present from the first, 358, 394, and form, 441 (note)
Miraculous, the, and Revelation, 154, the Incarnation, 296
Monism, various systems of, 11, 15, "Naturalistic" or "Scientific," 11, 13, must be spiritual, 15, 21; belongs to the phenomenal world only, 13, 279, 439, 457; its attraction, 15; and Reason 34
—— criticism of "Scientific," generally, 77-79, and Evolution, 114-117, true and false, 179; of Haeckel, 178, 179, see also *Haeckel*, Spencer, 180, see also *Spencer*, Lloyd Morgan, 180, Dr. Carus, 181, Spiritual, 182, see *Spiritual*; Science and, 182, 183; Philosophy, 183 *seq.*
—— the higher, 279
—— and Free-will, 325, 359, 360.
—— and Immortality, 392, 393
—— relation to a spiritual World, 439, 457
Monist, The, 14
Moore, Dr. G., *The Power of the Soul over the Body*, 235 (note)
Morality, Haeckel on the permanence of, 178
—— evolution of, 215-217, Kropotkin on origin of, 217 (note)
Moral World, Mr. Mallock on belief in, 18, 20; necessity for belief in, 20
Morgan, Prof. Lloyd, and Monism, 14, Theism, *ibid*, 177 (note), Causation, 27, Reason in Nature, 63, 64, *Habit and Instinct*, 94, 212, Evolution, 116, 117, definite variations, 132, 133, his Monism, 180, Subject and Object, 191, 264, the Will, 238; Freedom, 346; Immortality, 393
Morley, John, on Christian Ethics and the Supernatural, 7, 8
Morris, Sir Lewis, quoted, 259
Motion, 71, 79, 439.
Motives and Will, 332, 337 *seq.*, 340, 343, etc.
Muir, Prof., on the Chemical Elements, 160, 206
Muirhead, Prof. J. H., on Mind, 76.
Munsterberg, Prof. H., on Immortality, 404
Murphy, Dr. J. J., on the rise from Unconscious to Conscious Intelligence, 210, 211 (note), Will, 363
Mutual aid in Evolution, 124-129, 270.
Myers, F. W. H., on the Subliminal Self, 411-413; *Human Personality*, etc., 436.

NAGELI, on *a priori* ideas, 38; on Evolution, 90, the Egg, 92
Natural Selection, 98, 102–105, Darwin on, 103, 120, and Reason, 103, Wallace, 104; Weismann (note), 102, 104; Henslow, 131; aspect of, 255.
Nature, Intelligibility of, 44; Uniformity and order, 45 seq; Rationality of, 46 seq; Book of, 46, 47, and scientific concepts, 49, 63, 64; as Mechanism, 54; evils in, 248; and God, 59, 248, 251, etc, as medium of spiritual influence, 287
—— man's, 215–218, 309, 368, 369, 377, 378
Neander, on Early Christian doctrine of Freedom, 379
Nerve Force and Mind Force, 229, 230
Nicholson, Prof, on organisation, 422, 423.

OMNIPOTENCE, and Reason, 258; and Freedom, 380
Order in Nature, 44, 46, 109, 258, 259, etc
Organ and Music, illustration of Consciousness, 428
Organic Evolution, 99–107
—— systems, atoms and world, 265
Organisation and function, 99, etc, in relation to Soul and Survival, 418, 420–423, 426
—— of the religious element in man, 296
Organism and Consciousness, 81, 426, 427
Organisms, analogy of, 59, 105, 111, 124, 140, 169, 262, 263, 279 (note)
Ovenden, Dean, on Thought and Force, 234 (note)

PANENTHEISM, 251, 252
Pantheism, and Monism, 12, 152, 374
—— and Spiritual Monism, 219–223
Parallelism, 228; Mr Mallock on, 231 (note), 236
Paul, St, and the Cross, 274; sin and grace, 309; spiritual experience, 314; life and resurrection, 447–449
Pearson, Prof. Karl, on Reason in Nature, 36, 40
Personality, in God, 59, 150, 258, 277, 316, 317, in Man, 219–221, 436, 437
—— and continued life, 399, 400, 426, 436, 437, 439
"Phantasms of the living," 432, 433.
Philo, 244.

Philosophy, 12, 21, 22; its problem, 21, 22, 26, 34
—— its conclusions to be reached objectively, 21, 199, etc
—— and Monism, 179; and a spiritual Monism, 183 seq
—— Idealistic, 187 seq
—— Scottish School of, 188
Phylogony, 171, etc
Physical basis of Mind, 75, 76, 209, 225, 337 See *Consciousness, Survival, etc.*
Plant life Evolution of, 106, 107
Plato, 244.
Podmore, F, and Spiritualism, 433.
Potency, the, of Evolution, 93, 166, etc
Powell-Baden, Reason in Nature, 46 (note)
Power, manifested in everything, 66 seq; Spiritual, 67, 79, 84, 85; one, 73, 76, 83, 141, 202, 206, 222, 224, 233–235; Summary, 241, 347, seq; one with Reason, 115, 117, etc See *Reason*,
—— in Will, 223–225, 371.
—— the, in Evolution, 111, 114, 117, etc.
—— Spencer on, 78.
Pragmatism, 49
Prayer, 260, 309
Pre-determinism, 375
Present position, the, 9, 10.
Principle of World's life, 59, 262, 293, etc See *Organisms*
"Projected Efficiency,' 119–124
Prothyle, the primitive, 168.
Protoplasm, 73, 75, 93, a structure, 171–173; sensitiveness in, 209, 212, 225, vegetable and animal, 225, its origin, 263 (and note)
Psychical Research, Society for, 394
Psychology, Spencer's, 37, 38, 41 See *Spencer.*
—— the newer, and "reasoning," 40; pre-conscious Intelligence, 41; the unconscious, *ibid* See *Unconscious*
—— and Physiology, 185
—— and external perception, 189, 190, 192.
—— and the Incarnation, 298, and Free-will, 340, in relation to Survival, 393, etc
—— "determinism of." See *Determinism*
Purpose, Divine, 112, 123, 130, 262, 461–464.

QUESTION, the, of Free-will, 325–330.

RACE, the, relation of the individual to, 312, 454, future for, 388–391, 454.

INDEX

Races, susceptibility to Divine influences, 289
Radium, 68, 72, 156
Rashdall, Rev Dr H, Theistic argument, 192
Reality, 5, 53, 94, 247, 272, 273 277
Reason, need for confidence in, 22, can alone give solution, 22
—— the all-working, 34–65; supremacy of, 34; Haeckel on, 35, above us all, 35; Professor Pearson's objection—none apart from Brain, 36, 40, Dr G Gore, Haeckel, *ibid*
—— mode of origin of, in man proves priority of, 36–43; Dr G Gore on the subject, 37; Spencer, *ibid*, 38, 39; Buchner, 38, Nageli, *ibid*, Haeckel, *ibid*; Carus, 39; Fiske, *ibid*; Reason in Nature before Brain in man, 40; confirmation from nature of Life, 39; of reasoning, 41; from unconscious mentality, 41, reason in man due to prior Reason in Nature, 40, 41, etc, importance of the fact, 42–43
—— only a rational answer adequate, 43; Reason alone can give, 43, 44
—— gives the Intelligibility of Nature, 44; and its uniformity, 45, rationality of Nature, 46, possibility of Truth, 51; in relation to Thought and Reality, 52, to Causation, 54, 55; Monistic Criticism, 56; Summary, 57
—— shows Mind and Purpose in Nature, 58, Self-conscious, 59, in Nature as a Principle, *ibid*, Personality, *ibid*, constantly operative, *ibid*, relation to Necessity, 60
—— in Nature in relation to Science and Religion, 60–62
—— Scientific writers and Reason in Nature, 62–63; Idealistic writers, 64–65.
—— in the wider sense, 95, 267, and Will, 267, 268; and Love, 267–269, 272, 274
—— in Evolution, 94 *seq*, work continued by man, 94–97, 98, in History, 97, in the Environment, 100, 101, 134, 137, in Natural Selection, 103, 104, 134, 137; in inorganic Evolution, 111; in Evolution as a whole, 114, 119, 123, 124, 128, 129, 136, 137, etc; inherent, 123, 124, 163, 208, 258, 259
—— how revealed in the physical world, 136
—— persistence of, 142, necessity for a physical side, 142, supremacy of, 176

Reason, Philosophical doctrine of, 244; Biblical, *ibid*; Scientific grounds, *ibid*; Why doubted? 245, the things that seem contrary to, 245, in the world as conditioned, 245, Summary statement of, in relation to the World, 253; Infinite and Eternal as the Principle of the Universe, 266 See *Principle, Organism*
—— and origin of the world, 265, etc
—— in man, 34, 35; origin of, 36 *seq*, 57, 61, 65, 84, 94 *seq*, 103, 119, 216, 218, 251, 259, 283
—— in God, 266, 319, etc; perfect Reason and perfect Love one, 269
—— all the manifestation of, 223, 241–243, 468, *passim*
—— and Will, 367, etc.
—— and Immortality, 398–400, 443
Reasoning, its nature, 40, 41
Reid, Dr Archdall, on origin of Reason in man, 63; present Evolution of man, 98
Reincarnation, 442; a possible theory of, 443.
Religion, the Christian, 1, 8, 9, 291 *seq*, 306 *seq*; 449, 460–463, 468–470
—— and Science, 60–62; permanence, 178, origin and evolution of, 215–218, its Divine Source in man, 218, in relation to God in His transcendency, 285; meaning of, 286
Renan, M, on Free-will, 327 (note), the desire for Immortality, 380 (note), absolute Consciousness and re-living, 453–459
Reproductive factor, 129–130
Resurrection of "the righteous," 385
—— of Christ as a witness to Immortality, 406–410
—— Christian doctrine of, 444–451; wider Cosmical view, 453–457.
Revelation, 154, 289–291.
—— records of, 290, superiority of the Christian, *ibid*
Riddle of the Universe, what creates and solves, 468, 469 See *Haeckel*
Ritchie, Prof, on contradictories, 17, Reason in Nature, 65, Monism, 184, the Trinity, 318
Romanes, G J., and Monism 14, on Causation, 25, 26, 31 (note), 54, uniformity of Nature, 46, Free-will, 359
Roscoe, Sir Henry, on Protoplasm, 173
Royce, Prof, on Immortality, 404; Individuality, 441

INDEX

SACRIFICE, Mr Morley on, 9 ; in Christianity, 26, 27 , of the Cross, 273-275, 300, 301, 310, 313 , in God, 273, 278, 288, 319, 321, 469
Saleeby, Dr , on Electricity, 157 , Mind and Matter, 213, 236 , the Coming of Love, 270 (note)
Salvation, the Christian, 2, 309 *seq* , 377, 378
Saunders, T. B., on Nature and Grace, 312.
Schopenhauer and Will, 268.
Science, and Religion, 9, 60-62, 151 ; and Monism, 15, 189 ; true, 19, concepts of, 49, 63, 64 , its rationality, 46, 55, etc. ; and Spiritual Monism, 182, 202 ; and the Incarnation, 292 *seq* ; and Freedom, 345-349 , and Immortality, 393 , and Matter, etc , 67 *seq* , 433, *passim*
Scripture, Prof , on Will-power, 239
Scriptures, and resurrection of the wicked, 387
Secret, the open, 34-65.
Self, the separate, 219-221, 222 , and Consciousness, 227, 425-428 ; and Will, 367, etc
—— the Spiritual, reality and importance of, in relation to Survival, 413-417 ; substantial existence of, 414 ; relation to Body, Time, Space, Eternity, 415, 416 ; and the organism, 426 ; and continued life, 436
—— formation and character in relation to Survival, 430
Self-Consciousness, and Consciousness, 149, 231 , Spencer on, 149, 414-415
Sensation, 99 ; ascription of, to all Matter, 155, 160-162 ; rise and development of, 209-210 , cannot be created, 211 , a manifestation of the one Spiritual Power, 211, 212, 424, etc.
Senses of man, 50.
Sensitiveness See *Irritability.*
Shenstone, Prof , on size of atoms, 71.
Sin, root of, 256 ; sense of, 309 , reality of, 310, 311 ; nature of, 377
Smith, Dr. W., and Survival of the fit, 387
Sociality See *Mutual Aid.*
Something from nothing, impossible, 31, 167 *seq*
Sonship to God, 306, 320, 321.
—— in God, 318
Soul and Body, 410, 417, 457-459 See *Self, Consciousness, etc.*
—— does not " come in," 411 ; as formative, 432.

Source of our Being, 24-33 , necessity of belief in, 24 *seq* , universally acknowledged, 28 ; underlies most Theistic arguments, 30 , the real question, its nature, 30 , so far known in its productions, 30-33 ; its content, 33
Species, in view in Evolution, 121, 122.
Spencer, Herbert, and Monism, 15 and Theism, 15 , on Causation, 25 , the Source of phenomena, 28 , origin of Reason in man, 37, 39, 41 ; on the atom, 68 , the one Power, 78 ; variations, 101 ; Altruism, 129 ; Transformation of Energy, 166
—— Discussion of his Evolution Doctrine, 138-152 ; value of his work, 138 ; Prof. Flint on , 139 ; Part I. of First Principles, 139 , a spiritual side, 139 , Evolution of the physical Universe, 139-142 , the Power in Evolution, 141 , the spiritual side of his theory, 142-152 ; Personality, 150 , the Unknowable and God, 159 ; Postscript to First Principles, 152
—— his Monism, 180 ; theory of origin of the world, 265 ; on transcendent Being, 277 ; and Immortality, 392 ; reality of the Self, 414, 415 ; the Ether and consciousness, 432.
Spinoza, and Monism, 12, 13 , and Reason, 37 , God as in Himself and as in the World, 247 (note)
Spirit, the revelation of, within ourselves, 66-87 , what the Universe contains and reveals, 67 ; Matter and Ether, 67-71 , Energy, 71-73 ; Life, 73-75 , Mind, 75-77 ; Monistic view, 77-79 ; anti-Theistic application, 79-80 , meaning of the unity of the Power, 80, 83 , the Power spiritual, 78, 79 ; revelation of Spirit within ourselves, 82 *seq.* ; Agnostic position, 84 , Summary, 85 , the reference to *Evolution,* 86, 87
—— essence of, 86 , one with Reason and Power, 87, 114, 115 ; Source of all, 93, 223, 241, 242.
—— ultimate, 223
—— in Monism, 113, 158 ; Source, 149, 150 ; meaning, 158, 159
—— not a force, but an influence, 221 , seen in Will, 232-240
—— and Immortality, 403, 404, 465.
—— the human and its powers, 416, 417.
Spirits, finite and separate, reality and relation to God, 219, 221.
Spiritual, nature of God, 250, 251, 257-259, 280, 452.

31

INDEX

Spiritual, power is, 65, 73, 76, 79, 83–87, etc See *Power*.
—— the, its influence in all Evolution, 99, 100, 102, 111, 128, 141
—— its self-conditioning, 221, etc ; relation to man, 218, 287 ; the spiritual side to Evolution, 142–152
—— formative, 432, 436. See *Reason, Evolution, Spencer*
—— Spiritual Evolution (see *Evolution*) and Incarnation, 294, 305
—— World and Immortality, 400, 416, 439, 465.
—— conception of future life, 438–441, 451, 465
—— the spiritual side to our being, 423, etc.
Spiritual Monism, General, and in relation to Idealism, 179–204 ; forms of Monism criticised Haeckel, 178 , Spencer, 180 , Lloyd Morgan, 180, 181 ; Carus, 181, 182 ; recognition of a Spiritual, by Scientists Lodge, McKendrick, Fleming, Weismann, 82, 83 ; by Philosophy : Ward's Spiritualistic Monism, 183, 184 ; Ritchie, 184, 185 ; Wundt, 185 , Flint, *ibid* ; Adamson, *ibid* , 191, 192 ; Religion implies, 185 ; the Unity of the World, 186 , of Mind and Body, *ibid* , desirable for Faith,*ibid*. ; Idealism and Monism, 187–192 , external world, subject and object, 187–192 , Idealistic arguments for Theism, 192–196 ; oneness of Thought and Being, 196, 197 , Hegelianism, 197–199 ; Principal Caird's suggestion, 199 , Spiritual Monism, its foundation, 200 ; defined and distinguished, 201–204 , analogy of the spoken or written word, 203 ; simplicity and universality, 204.
—— Further illustrations of, 205–223 ; World-building, 205, 206 , origin of Life, 208 ; its spiritual nature, 208 ; harmony of theories, *ibid* ; Mind and Consciousness, 209–215 ; Morality and Religion, 215–218 , not Pantheistic identity, 219–222 ; from observation of the world, 222 ; its explanation thus found as proceeding from God, 223.
—— —— Tranformations of Force, manifestations of a single Power, 224 ; further discussion of nature and rise of Consciousness, 224–227 ; relation to Dualism, 228 ; an Eternal Consciousness, *ibid* , correlation of all Forces means unity of the Power, 229 ; of mental and physical forces, 229, 230 ; psychical causation, 230 ; Feeling ultimate, 231 ; relation to an Eternal Consciousness, 231, 232 ; Will and Effort, 232–235 ; concomitancy, 236 ; objection from conservation of Energy, 236–238 , Will and Energy, 239 , shows the continuity of the Power and its spirituality, 239, 240 ; note on the Newer Psychology, 240 , Harmony with Idealism, 241 ; the Source of Unity, 242 , contrasted with Dualism, 228, 242 ; relation to Theism and Materialism, *ibid* ; the Monism of Thought and its expression, 242
Spiritual Monism and the Incarnation of God in Christ, 293 *seq.*
—— —— and Freedom, 357–360, 372.
—— —— and Immortality, 439, etc.
—— —— and a spiritual world, 439.
Spiritualism, 394, 395, 433
Stirling, Dr. Hutchison, on Idealistic Monism, 12 ; Theistic argument, 195 , Trinity, 318 (note)
Sub-conscious, the (see *Unconscious*), in relation to Survival, 410, 427, 431, 432, 434, 450
Subject, 177 ; and object, 149, 188–191, 198
Subjective order, its appearance, 75, 99, 128, 413, etc.
Subliminal Self, reality and importance of, 411, 412.
Substance, Monistic, 13, 14, 153–155, 176, etc , the term, 177.
Suffering, 255, 260, etc.
Supernatural, reality of, 8, 277
Survival of Bodily Death, *possibility* of, 411–443 ; on Monistic principles, 411 , the Soul, *ibid* , the Sub-Conscious, 411–413 ; the Spiritual Self, 413–417 ; relation to Body, Time, Space, Eternity, 415, 416 ; the powers of the human spirit, 417 ; the opposing arguments, 417 *seq.* ; Haeckel's view, 417, 418 ; the Soul as "produced,"418 , brain formation, 418, 419 ; the brain and Thought, 419–420 ; Thought as a function of the Brain, 419, 420 ; Function precedes organisation, 420–423 ; the spiritual side of our being, 423; Monism affirms a *two-sided* Substance, 423, 424, what becomes of the spiritual side? 425 ; the Self and Consciousness, 425–427 ; the relation of Consciousness to the organism, 427, 428 , the Ether, *ibid* ; analogies of heated iron and organ and music, 427, 428 ; Memory,

428-430; Self-formation and character, 430, 431; the deeper element in matter, 431, 432, the Spiritual as formative, 432; Telepathy, etc, show reality of a finer medium of Thought, etc, 433-435, Consciousness and Stimuli, Dreams, etc, 435, 436; What is dissolved at death? 437, 428, Is a material basis necessary? 438-441; note on finite mind and the Absolute, 441; Theosophy, 442; a possible theory of Reincarnation, 442, 443; personal note, 443
Sutherland, A, *Growth of the Moral Instinct*, 125.
Symonds, J. A., the lesson of Evolution, 285.

"TELÆSTHESIA," Mr. Andrew Lang on, 435 (note)
Telekinesis, 434.
Telepathy, 432, 433
Tennyson quoted, 220, 256, 404, 440, 443
Theistic argument, and Causation, 29; Idealistic, 192, 196, 199, 200, 201, 220
—— —— and Spiritual Monism, 193, 194, 242, 243, etc
Theology and Science, 151.
Theosophy, and life after death, 442, 443
Thomson, Prof. J. J., and "matter," 68.
Thomson, Prof J., *The Science of Life* on the cell, 92; Evolution, 118.
Thomson and Geddes, *Ideals of Science and Faith*, on rational order in Nature, 47, Life, 74; Ethical aspects of Evolution, 129, 130
—— —— the reproductive factor, 129.
Thought, reality of, in itself, 52-54; in Nature, 53, etc, "implicit in matter," 168 *seq*; priority of, 192, 194, etc. See *Reason*
—— and Being, oneness of, 196, 197.
—— and Force, Dean Ovenden on, 234 (note).
Thoughts, "ready made," 430
Transcendency, the Divine, 246, 249, 251; special treatment, 276-290; the Power transcending this and all universes, 276; the idea of God, *ibid*; Spencer on the transcendent Reality, 277; this the God of Religion, 277, as distinguished from Conditioned Being, 278; from the World, 279; note on a possible form of World-Evolution, 279; God as Spirit in relation to man, 280, 281; rise of a spiritual world, 281; entrance into the transcendent Reason, 283, in Imagination and Art, 283, the perfecting Reason, 283; in the Ethical life, 284; in Love, 285; in Religion, *ibid*; stated from the Divine side, 286-290, What God *is*, 287; What He does, 288; the human response, *ibid*; religious inspiration and development, 289; records of Revelation, 290; the religion first, 290; the True, the Beautiful, the Good, 290
Transcendency, the new, in Christ, 303
Transfiguration, the, 408
Transformations of Force, 80, 81, 145, etc See *Energy*
Trinity, in God, 315-321, in the Early Church, 316; not Tritheism, 317; necessary to Philosophy, 317, of Divine manifestation, 317, immanent, 318; Philosophical writers on, 318 (note), implied in the Divine Reason, 319, in the Divine Love, *ibid*; in Eternal Ethical Life in God, 319, 320, in the Ideal of the Creation, 320; wider aspects, 321; practical value, *ibid*
Truth, finding, 51, 52.
Turner, Sir W, on the cell, 170, 171.
Tyler, Prof, on development of organisms, 105; reflex action and Will, 364, 365, 366
Tyndall, Prof, on the Brain and Consciousness, 76, 242.

ULTIMATE REALITY, the, 148, 150, 151.
Unconditioned, the, 147, etc
Unconscious Intelligence or Mentality, 40, 41, 42, 190, 210 (note), 225, 240, 410 See *Sub-Conscious*.
—— Sensation, 161.
Uniformity of Nature, 45, etc.
Unity of the World, 15, 186; Source of, 242
—— of Mind and Body, 186, 188, 189, 191, 372, etc.
Universe, the, need of a rational explanation, 22, 26, 27, 34; as rational, see *Reason*; the manifestation of a Spiritual Power, 66 *seq.*, see *Power* and *Spiritual*; its contents, 67 *seq.*; origin of, 263, etc.
Universes beyond ours, 246
Universality in Christianity, 312, 313
Unseen Universe, The, quoted on Memory, 430; on Matter, 435
Upton, Prof, on Causation, 27; why no demonstration of Immortality, 397 (note)
Uxhill, Dream, 436

INDEX

VARIATIONS, 101; Spencer on, *ibid*; definite, 106, 130-137; What determines? 133-137, Weismann on, 101, 134-137
Virgin-birth, 296
Volition. See *Will*

WALLACE, Dr. Russell, on origin of Brain, 63; Darwin's work, 103 (note); Natural Selection, 104; the species in view, 121 (note)
Want and development, 99, etc.
Ward, Prof. James, "Spiritualistic Monism," 183, 184
Ward, Prof. W., on Freedom, 335.
Weismann, Prof., on Natural Selection, 102 (note); "intelligence," 104, adaptations, 112 (note), Evolution, 121-123; his Evolution theory, 134-137; Environment and Variations, 134, 135; in relation to Religion, 135-137; testimony to permanence of religion, 135; Monism, 183 (note), rise of " Spirit," 212 (note); psychical Causation, 231
Westermarck, referred to, 128
Whetham, W. C. D., on Causation, 25, 26; uniformity of Nature, 45; our model of Nature, 49, the Atom and Ether, 69, 70, Energy, 72
Whittier, J. G., quoted, 261, 401.
Wickliffe, illustration from, 53.
Will, the Divine, in relation to Evil See *Evil, Freedom*
—— and the Power in Nature, 81; Will-Power and the Spiritual, 232-240; illustrations of Will-power, 233-235; and Energy, 238, 239, 240 (note); the Newer Psychology and, 240 (note).
—— Freedom of the, the question, 325-330; importance of, 325, 326; witness of Consciousness, 326, 327 (and note); denial by "Monistic Science," 327; what the Will is, 327; meaning of Freedom, 328; Mr. Mallock on, 328, 329, Coleridge on, 329.
—— Rise and development of, 363-372, voluntary action and Consciousness, 363; Sensation, *ibid*; the Self and its organism, 364; the Will to live, *ibid*; reflex action and Will, 364, 365; in the humblest creatures, 365; development as the Self expands, 365; in animals, 366, in man, 367.; relation to Reason and Power, *ibid*, as abstract, 367; the essential element in, 368, man's nature and the Self, 368-370; character and power of choice, 370; the spiritual life, 371; Summary, 371; the physical side and the Self, 372
Will, in relation to God, the Source of the World, and of ourselves, 372-381, rejection makes it impossible to infer God, 373-375; Spirit and Will, 375, Mr. Mallock on pre-determination, 375-377, free personal Spirit leads to the Divine, 377 See *Christian Doctrine* See also *Freedom, Determinism, Spiritual, etc.*
World, Source of, 24 *seq*, 278, how it has risen, 263, 278; Evolution of; Divine relation to See *God, Source, Reason, Spiritual, Evolution, Spiritual Monism, etc.*
—— this and another, 396, 397.
—— a spiritual implied, 439, etc.
—— its aspect, 467.
World-organism, the, 111, 124, Principle of, 249, 262; its life-principle becoming manifest, 294. See *Principle, Organism*
Wundt, Prof, Monism, 185, psychical Causation, 230, voluntary action, 240, Consciousness and Will, 363; the Will, 367; nucleus of personality, 372
Wyld, Dr, dynamical conception of the world, 190; mental effort, 239 (note).

YOUMANS, Prof., statement prepared for by Spencer, quoted, 141
Young, Prof, *Evolution and Design*, referred to, 90.

ZIMMERN, A, on electric origin of matter, 165; the inner constitution of matter, 431

www.ingramcontent.com/pod-product-compliance
Lightning Source LLC
Chambersburg PA
CBHW071221290426
44108CB00013B/1246